SIMPSON

IMPRINT IN HUMANITIES

The humanities endowment
by Sharon Hanley Simpson and
Barclay Simpson honors
MURIEL CARTER HANLEY
whose intellect and sensitivity
have enriched the many lives
that she has touched.

The publisher and the University of California Press Foundation gratefully acknowledge the generous support of the Simpson Imprint in Humanities.

Incomplete

FEMINIST MEDIA HISTORIES

Shelley Stamp, Series Editor

1. *Their Own Best Creations: Women Writers in Postwar Television*, by Annie Berke
2. *Violated Frames: Armando Bó and Isabel Sarli's Sexploits*, by Victoria Ruetalo
3. *Recollecting Lotte Eisner: Cinema, Exile, and the Archive*, by Naomi DeCelles
4. *A Queer Way of Feeling: Girl Fans and Personal Archives in Early Hollywood*, by Diana W. Anselmo
5. *Incomplete: The Feminist Possibilities of the Unfinished Film*, edited by Alix Beeston and Stefan Solomon

Incomplete

The Feminist Possibilities of the Unfinished Film

EDITED BY
Alix Beeston and Stefan Solomon

UNIVERSITY OF CALIFORNIA PRESS

University of California Press
Oakland, California

© 2023 by The Regents of the University of California

Library of Congress Cataloging-in-Publication Data

Names: Beeston, Alix, editor. | Solomon, Stefan, 1986– editor.
Title: Incomplete : the feminist possibilities of the unfinished film / edited by Alix Beeston and Stefan Solomon.
Other titles: Feminist media histories (Series) ; 5.
Description: Oakland, California : University of California Press, [2023] | Series: Feminist media histories ; 5 | Includes bibliographical references and index.
Identifiers: LCCN 2022043587 (print) | LCCN 2022043588 (ebook) | ISBN 9780520381469 (hardback) | ISBN 9780520381476 (paperback) | ISBN 9780520381483 (ebook)
Subjects: LCSH: Motion pictures and women. | Unfinished films—History and criticism.
Classification: LCC PN1995.9.W6 I518 2023 (print) | LCC PN1995.9.W6 (ebook) | DDC 813/.6—dc23
LC record available at https://lccn.loc.gov/2022043587
LC ebook record available at https://lccn.loc.gov/2022043588

32 31 30 29 28 27 26 25 24 23
10 9 8 7 6 5 4 3 2 1

Contents

Editors' Acknowledgments   vii

Pathways to the Feminist Incomplete: An Introduction, a Theory, a Manifesto
Alix Beeston and Stefan Solomon   1

PART ONE. UNFOUND OBJECTS

1. Never
   Jane M. Gaines   39

2. Catastrophic Optimism in the Name of Léontine
   Maggie Hennefeld   62

3. Body Parts: Feeling Labor in Early Film Color
   Katherine Groo   85

PART TWO. REFUSALS AND INTERRUPTIONS

4. Creating the Archive for Incomplete Feminist Cinematic Narratives: The Andean-Amazonian Case
   Isabel Seguí   107

5. Women (Not) Making Movies under the Popular Unity in Chile (1970–1973)
   Elizabeth Ramírez-Soto   125

6. Writing with Jocelyne Saab: Infinite Metamorphoses and Sensitive Variations
   Mathilde Rouxel   147

PART THREE. IN PROCESS

7. Ins and Outtakes: An Interview
   Peggy Ahwesh and Leo Goldsmith   169

8. "They keep moving": Serialized Incompletion in the Work of Leslie Thornton and Lynn Hershman Leeson
   Stefan Solomon   188

9. One Long Electrical Cord: Dance, Editing, and the Creative Unfinished
   Karen Pearlman   211

10. *Shirkers* and Its Afterlives: Six Epitaphs for an Incomplete Film
    Sophia Siddique   226

PART FOUR. POSTHUMOUS RETURNS

11. Kathleen Collins . . . Posthumously
    Alix Beeston   245

12. The Fierce, Unfinishable, Feminist Legacies of Helen Hill
    Karen Redrobe   270

13. Girls Who Can't Say No: Celebrity Resurrections and the Consent of the Dead
    Katherine Fusco   300

The Ruined Map, Relinked: A Postscript
Giuliana Bruno   322

About the Contributors   349
Index   353

Editors' Acknowledgments

The beginning of this book—all three of its beginnings—centers film labor as collaborative, improvisational, open-ended, and ongoing, and such has been the labor of scholarship for us and our contributors. *Incomplete* began, more than five years ago, as a coincidence of latent research interests: for Alix, the feminist possibilities of unproduced screenplays, works made but also not made; for Stefan, the fascinating effects of durational film, works made and unmade over decades rather than months or years. One of the great joys of the intervening period has been seeing these interests, which were initially only hunches or speculations, transform into a far-ranging program for conceptualizing women's film and media history in its valences of incompletion, understood as both failure and promise, disappointment and opportunity.

This transformation occurred through shared work, a meeting of scholars and practitioners who, with their diverse forms of expertise and ways of working, can achieve more and more unexpected things together than they might do apart. Through the isolations and stresses of a deadly global pandemic—the kind of cataclysmic event that counts among the vicissitudes and contingencies we identify as structural to women's incomplete film history—we as editors have been buoyed by the brilliance and passionate engagement of the contributors to this volume. This book has taken shape over emails and Zoom calls (and sometimes even in person!) as a genuine conversation that, for us, represents the very best kind of scholarly labor: the kind that makes scholarship feel worthwhile and sustainable even in the midst of crisis and uncertainty. Long before it became a physical (or digital) object, fixed in one of its many possible forms on the page, this project—a projection and projectile, pitched forward in time and space—exceeded all our expectations. So we wish to give sincere thanks to our collaborators, now friends and compatriots, for the diligence, creativity, and enthusiasm they brought to this project, as well as for their kind support of us in bringing it to this stage of completion.

We would also like to thank the institutions where we are based for enabling our work: the School of English, Communication and Philosophy at Cardiff University and the Department of Media, Communications, Creative Arts, Language and Literature at Macquarie University. Both universities provided funds in support of this work, for which we are grateful: Cardiff University paid for the gorgeous image on this book's cover, as well as for translation work undertaken by Marine Furet, while Macquarie University contributed to the cost of indexing. We're indebted to colleagues at our institutions and elsewhere who helped us to formulate and develop the project, including by reading parts of the work in draft form; special thanks to Ailbhe Darcy, Holly Furneaux, Pardis Dabashi, and Neil Badmington for their feedback at key points in the project's development. As is appropriate for a book focused on the material conditions of creative and scholarly labor, each contributor's work emerged from particular networks of care and support, and in many cases also relied on the generosity and expert knowledge of the filmmakers and practitioners under study. These networks are made legible in the notes of acknowledgment affixed to individual chapters.

We're glad to have found such a wonderful home for this work in the Feminist Media Histories book series at the University of California Press. Thanks to editors extraordinaire Shelley Stamp and Raina Polivka, along with Madison Wetzell, Sam Warren, and the Press's editorial and production team—notably our expert copyeditor, Amy Smith Bell—for championing this project and shepherding it to publication. Thanks, too, to the anonymous reviewers of the proposal and draft manuscript, whose insightful and enthusiastic reports were a spur and an affirmation, and to Sarah Osment, whose work on the book's index was insightful, creative, and informed by her wide-ranging expertise.

Finally, Alix would like to thank her husband, Davey, for being the best person ever, and also for taking on the bulk of household labor to facilitate her scholarship and keep her alive and fed. Alix would also like to thank her academic wife, Pardis Dabashi, whose love, care, and intellectual rapport has helped to carry her through several difficult years. Stefan would like to thank Monica and Vincent, both for their unfailing support of this work and for being the reasons to forget about work altogether.

Alix Beeston and Stefan Solomon

Pathways to the Feminist Incomplete

An Introduction, a Theory, a Manifesto

ALIX BEESTON AND STEFAN SOLOMON

We could begin in the living room of *ESFIR*, a 16mm film made in 2020 by Cynthia Madansky. Within its paint-stripped walls, five young women are set in motion by minor rituals and routines (figure 0.1). One woman gets up from her chair, goes to one of the windows, and selects three roses from an assortment of plants on the sill. Gathering them together, she moves to the center of the room and lays the little bouquet on a table. At the other window, meanwhile, another woman takes up a cloth and scrubs the glass, before walking the length of the space to dust the steps of a ladder in its corner. She crosses the room again and puts down the cloth; reaching her arms above her head, she interlaces her fingers, stretching toward the ceiling.

One woman paces back and forth for a while, her heels beating time on the bare floorboards. One sits at a desk, shuffling mail, cups, other small objects. One perches on the ladder and flicks through an album of photographs. Skirting the furniture as well as one another, the women are consumed in their tasks, and they never look directly at each other. Yet their actions are no less purposeful, or coordinated, for their air of improvisation. After the woman lays the roses on the table, another woman soon picks them up, arranging them in a vase; papers get passed from one pair of hands to another; again and again, the women swap places as they track incomplete, iterated circuits of the room. The tableau keeps its equilibrium in static long shot through this incidental choreography, this choreography of incident.

FIGURE 0.1 The group of women prepare the room at the opening of Cynthia Madansky's *ESFIR* (2020). Image courtesy of the artist.

The women are preparing for something—but for what? Or for whom? A provisional space, separated from another by a gauzy white curtain and full of moveable objects—chairs to flowers, papers to dust—the room resembles what it is: a film set. Which is perhaps to call housework a kind of stagecraft, or filmmaking a kind of hospitality. Figuring the material conditions of her own work through the women's shared, quasi-domestic labor, Madansky makes arrangements for the film we're watching, the film we're about to watch. But she also makes arrangements for a film that has never been made and that isn't exactly being made now. For *ESFIR* is an interpretation of an unrealized film titled "Women," conceived between 1932 and 1934 by the Soviet filmmaker Ėsfir' Shub.

"I want to make a film about women to demonstrate that only the proletarian revolution, the new conditions of labour, the new social practice completely closes the account of the history of 'the women's question.'"[1] Shub's words, from a 1933 article describing the aims and methods of her project, interrupt *ESFIR*'s housekeeping (filmkeeping) at intervals, given in a Russian voiceover and translated to English on inter-

FIGURE 0.2 The kitchen-table reading of Ėsfir' Shub's screenplay "Women" in *ESFIR*. Image courtesy of the artist.

titles. After its opening scenes, the long middle section of Madansky's film is composed of portraits of four women in various cities in Russia and Siberia. Yet while these portraits loosely follow the model Shub devised for her film—in which particular women's lives, their struggles and their hopes, were to represent the experiences of the modern woman in the Soviet Union and her liberation from class oppression and sexual objectification under the Bolsheviks—*ESFIR* preserves "Women" as an unfinished project, poignant in its failure as well as its promise. Not realizing Shub's film, not completing it, Madansky's work enacts *and* disrupts Shub's plans. Occupying a register of feeling vastly different to the many rejections Shub's proposals received from film industry officials in Moscow in the 1930s, it entails a kind of refusal nonetheless.[2]

The script will always be unmade by Shub, an object lesson in the exigencies of all film work—and, indeed, of the gendered valences of cinematic (un)production, along with the histories we tell of the same. Is it for this reason that *ESFIR* concludes with a table reading of Shub's scenario? Four of the women who once rearranged the living room now sit, sharing a pot of tea, at a table crammed into a narrow kitchen (figure 0.2). They take turns reading excerpts from Shub's script, beginning and ending with its opening scene, a montage of female figures drawn from painting, film, and news media. The treatment of "Women" opens with a parade of "multi-colored Madonnas, Venuses, Gretchens, and Susannas," portraits framed with the question, "What is a woman, this sphinx, this riddle of a century?"[3] By contrast, ESFIR closes with this question, its answer endlessly deferred. Reading the scenario, the women make further preparations for a film that is both past and future, never quite present. We might even say that they await the arrival of Shub herself, a guest who won't show up.

Like the script's relation to the complete film it imagines—the script as itself an open question, an invitation that elicits no response—*ESFIR* is somehow precursory to the unrealized project that inspires it. Still, as the women pause from their reading, pick up their pens, and scrawl notes we can't read on the papers lying before them on the dining table, *ESFIR* evinces historical incompletion as rich potential, as raw materials for contemporary film practice—not to mention film scholarship.

. . .

Or we could make a different beginning—a beginning that is also an ending, or many endings—in a different place and time. In downtown Portland, Oregon, in the summer of 1996, Miranda July juggled a tape recorder and a camera, approaching women and girls on the street with a simple question: "If you could make a movie, what would it be about?" July typed up the answers and compiled twenty-four of them in a large black-and-white poster, four feet long, two feet wide (figure 0.3). Above the responses she pasted mug shots of the interviewees, grainy or oversaturated images that do and do not identify their subjects. Passing judgment on Hollywood fare for being sexist or racist or simply boring, the imagined movies cast women in new guises, revising the archetypes of mother or action star—or even, in one case, taking on the wider cultural logic that produces these archetypes. An anonymous woman describes a movie about "the double standard. You know how men can do whatever and women are, excuse my language, their sluts and whores." As the cars pass behind her, she smiles into the camera, an air of defiance conveyed by her up-tilted chin.

The Missing Movie Report announces that crimes have been committed and are being committed still. These movies go missing before they've been made; they go missing *because* they're not made. Often it's the simplicity and clarity of these notional productions, patterned after the lives

FIGURE 0.3 Miranda July, *The Missing Movie Report* (1996), *Joanie 4 Jackie* records. Getty Research Institute, Los Angeles (2016.M.20) © Miranda July.

of those who conceive them, which gives the strongest indictment of the commercial US film industry and its narrow range of subjects. Mauria, fifteen years old, would make a movie "about what it's like to be a young gay woman." Lisa Boyd would make one "about having a child when I was really young." Eva Marie, "about young Chicanas living in the 90s." When July's question elicits confusion, it flags the unwritten rules about who can or should make films. "I don't get to make movies," responds one elderly woman. "I'm too old for that kind of thing," says another.

So there are missing movies and there are also missing moviemakers. "I am starting a Missing Movie Search Party and Fan Club," July declared in a handmade zine sent in 1997 to the members of *Big Miss Moviola* (later *Joanie 4 Jackie*), a community of women filmmakers established by July two years earlier. "We, the Missing Movie Fan Club, pledge to build a thirst that can't be quenched by *Clueless* or *When Harry Met Sally*."[4] Recognizing every passerby as a potential filmmaker, *The Missing Movie Report* represents one of a number of inventive strategies developed by July in the late 1990s and early 2000s to, in her words, "propel the transnational seizure and employment of cinemagic to fulfill the diverse purposes of girls and women from all economic, artistic, and geographic locations."[5] The report produces a desire for what is absent, a thirst for the unmade that is also a thirst for making. It asks those who identify as women and girls to look on the world with the "reel eyes" that, July believes, they already have.[6]

The zine in which July advertised *The Missing Movie Report* accompanied one of July's Chainletter Tapes, VHS compilations of video art sent through the post to *Big Miss Moviola* subscribers. In this context, the grid of photographs in the poster visualizes the network of support, skill sharing, and encouragement facilitated by the circulating tapes. More than that: the missing movies are affiliated with the works of video art, becoming caught up in the "distributional promise" of the Chainletters, in Frances Corry's phrase: a guarantee that all movies sent to July would be seen by other women.[7] Just as July encouraged subscribers to bootleg and pass on the compilation tapes to others, so too *The Missing Movie Report* was designed to proliferate. July suggested her readers should go out and make their own reports where they lived—a practice she placed on a continuum with, even a substitute for, the creative labor of making movies. "This is an especially good thing to do," she wrote, "when you can't make your movie either. (Trade in your personal frustration for big big inspiration.)"[8]

What's the difference, then, between the video works in the Chainletter Tapes and the missing movies that ghost Portland's streets? *The Missing Movie Report* makes us miss all the movies that don't get made, but it also works to radically expand our sense of what the making of movies entails—of what counts as a movie. In the same zine that describes *The Missing Movie Report*, July writes that *Big Miss Moviola* movies "are not always made—some of them stay in ladies [sic] heads until those ladies die and if they never told anyone, then I guess those movies are gone forever. If they told even one person then that is enough."⁹ Understanding film as an essentially communicative form—an idea broached in conversation, a missive sent through the mail—July's model of production stretches it out, making it capacious enough to hold glimmers, whispers, hopes, possibilities, however faint or indistinct. As the film object dilates and diffuses, it materializes in variable, contingent forms. A Xeroxed poster, a zine, a note scrawled on the back of a napkin: the paratext might not refer to a text, but for July it's still enough.

The unmade film is in these terms *merely* an unfinished one, its measure of incompletion not diminishing its value. A beginning that is an ending is, for July, nevertheless a beginning. Such an expansive view of film admits that its histories are constituted in its exclusions, that its labor conditions are skewed along the lines of gender, race, class, age, and other forms of social difference. At once, however, it turns away from the melancholy associations of the missing or the lost, accounting for—and stimulating—the agency and activity of those whom film industries marginalize. The reel eyes of women and girls hold latent visions, if only we know how to see them.

. . .

But there are always other pathways we might take, other streets we might travel, as we feel our way haltingly into this book. Here, then, one more beginning, this time in a taxicab in Renée Green's *Some Chance Operations* (1999) as it makes a circuitous journey through Naples, Italy. The taxi plots the locations where the filmmaker and actress Elvira Notari made and screened more than sixty features and around one hundred shorts and actualities in the early decades of the twentieth century. There are two passengers in the backseat. One is the (mostly) unseen "Filmmaker," who moves through the city with a handheld camera; a proxy for Green, the Filmmaker searches for Notari, who is herself a filmmaker displaced, disappeared, from the history and life of the city she represented in her *film tratti dal vero,* a cinema based on life. The other passenger is an Italian woman named Clara, who seeks after the evidence of Notari's work. A figment of the film, Clara is nonetheless modeled on the scholar Giuliana Bruno, whose pathbreaking 1993 study of Notari, *Streetwalking on a Ruined Map,* motivates the Filmmaker to travel from New York City to Italy and teaches her to conceive of "journeys of interpretation . . . as travel stories."[10]

Notari earned the nickname "The General" for the sheer force of will she exhibited in leading Dora Film, the production company she founded with her husband, Nicola Notari.[11] And yet her prodigious work is also marked by incompletion in several senses. Curtailed in 1930 by the censorship of the Fascist regime, which objected to Dora Film's realist depiction of urban poverty, violence, and class inequality, Notari's films are now almost all lost. Apart from three features that exist in their complete form, Notari's archive represents Bruno's "ruined and fragmentary map," the uncertain coordinates of which are found in cinematic paratexts such as photographs, film stills, written synopses, newspaper articles, and reviews.[12] In Naples, traveling by car or on foot, the Filmmaker and Clara find signs not of Notari but instead of her absence. Although when Notari began making films, we hear in voiceover, "it probably seemed as if she were creating something monumental, something made to last," now virtually nobody in Naples knows of her or her work. All that remains are bare traces, tantalizing glimpses of a vanished and vanishing past—flashes, flickers, like the effect of the footage Green incorporates of Notari performing in one of her films, in which thick, horizontal black bars move swiftly across the screen, cutting up the image of Notari's face.

In the final part of *Some Chance Operations,* Green uses footage from Michelangelo Antonioni's *L'Avventura* (1960), recasting Clara— already a character, a persona—as Claudia, the central figure in Antonioni's film. Played by Monica Vitti, Claudia spends *L'Avventura* searching for her best friend Anna, who has gone missing during a vacation to the Aeolian Islands north of Sicily. Rather, Claudia spends the film searching for Anna and not searching for her: after Claudia begins an affair with Anna's fiancé, Sandro, Claudia's efforts to find her friend dwindle to nothing. Antonioni's cinema dwells in the distances between people, his characters drawn in detachment, and this theme culminates in *L'Avventura*'s unfinished—abandoned—quest. Forgotten long before the film ends, Anna never returns; it's almost as if she was never there at all.

Routing her doomed pursuit of Notari through *L'Avventura*, Green marks out the chasm left by Notari's lost and unremembered films without attempting to fill it in. She, like Bruno in *Streetwalking on a Ruined Map*, confronts the *horror vacuui*, the fear of empty spaces, by "exposing the blank, the limit, and the edge of discursive formations and creating a system of interconnections with textual remanence" out of history.[13] Their Naples is a field of voids and gaps in the aftermath of loss. Green thus enacts a mode of feminist film history as strategic incompletion, responding to the contingency and arbitrariness of historical knowledge with more contingency, more arbitrariness. Comprised of a series of relatively autonomous sequences, *Some Chance Operations* presents itself as several idiosyncratic versions of a story that may be told in a variety of ways.[14] As Notari's face appears on the screen bracketed by the repeating black bars, her mouth opens as if to speak. Seeming to freeze and stutter due to the strobe effect of the bars, her movements seem effortful, her speech somehow prohibited or resisted. Just when the words might, we think, escape her lips, the picture suddenly duplicates, and images of Notari's face are superimposed in a rapid rhythm, their divergent expressions jostling for space and attention (figure 0.4). Notari remains unheard, inhabiting her ruined and fragmentary map. But she manages to make her presence felt.

The voiceover in this moment describes Scheherazade, the Queen's consort in the Middle Eastern folktales *One Thousand and One Nights* "who thinks of a fresh story whenever her tale comes to a stop."[15] Spinning stories to the Sultan night by night, deferring their endings to preserve her life, Scheherazade is a stand-in for Notari, she who told so many tales in celluloid. She is also a stand-in for Green, and for Bruno before her: women who keep Notari alive, in a sense, by adding their own tales to hers. Indeed, like Scheherazade's unending narration, *Some Chance Encounters* is part of a larger body of work by Green that forms, as Nora Alter has argued, "a continuous structure that is not complete but integrates each video as yet another variation on a labile and changing theme."[16] This is an aspect of Green's practice emphasized in installations in which her video works are shown alongside one another, projected in different, interconnected chambers in the gallery space.

In *Some Chance Operations* and across her oeuvre, Green begins again and again, assembling incomplete and fragmentary texts that remain open to reordering and recomposition. And so too do we, the

FIGURE 0.4 Elvira Notari's face masked and multiplied in Renée Green's *Some Chance Operations* (1999). Film still courtesy of the artist and Free Agent Media.

editors of *Incomplete,* as we share Green's commitment to feminist film history as itself an unfinished project, an ongoing and active process that maps our ineluctably gap-ridden knowledge of the past in the terrain of the present.

. . .

Incomplete is the first study to establish the feminist possibilities of the unfinished film, broadly defined, across the history of the medium and in various global contexts. Whether abandoned, interrupted, or lost, unfinished films are usually dismissed as unworthy objects of study. They are seen as minor works, of marginal importance to film history: they may be only partially realized as moving images, and so be marred by gaps and flaws; or they may never materialize as images at all, and so obviate even the feeling that those gaps and flaws might have been filled or fixed in the production process. By contrast, this collection of essays enacts a feminist transvaluation of the unfinished film's signs of deficiency, recasting them as signs of possibility. Unfinished projects, we and our collaborators argue, offer ideal sites for examining the lived experiences, practical conditions, and institutional realities of film production and consumption, especially in relation to the work of women filmmakers and film practitioners.

Our focus on the unfinished allows for the recovery of projects and practitioners marginalized within film industries and scholarship alike. At the same time, we conceive of incompletion as constitutive of women's film and media history at a number of levels. We turn to the archival gaps that register, through their absent–presence, women's contributions to cinema history (part 1); the refusals and interruptions of women's creative labor, which reflect wider structural inequities within particular film industries and cultures (part 2); the cultivation of unfinishedness as an aesthetic and political strategy for feminist filmmakers (part 3); and the posthumous reworking or recuperation of women's film materials, along with the vexed ethical questions that attend such textual intercessions (part 4).

In certain respects, incompletion can be seen as a general condition of all film—indeed, of all texts. It is manifest as filmmakers and other practitioners work with and against cinema history, and as their labor is embedded in economic, cultural, and political systems. It is manifest, too, as films and their ancillary forms circulate in the world, subject to varied practices of distribution, exhibition, and curation, not to mention the involved attention and intervention of viewers and scholars—especially but not only in the digital age.[17] Conventionally, films that are branded as "unseen" or "orphaned" are said to have led only a half-life until they are projected for a waiting viewership, but even after reaching the point of exhibition, the trajectory of such films continues on in their reception.[18] As Dan North has argued, following the distinction Roland Barthes makes between "work" and "text," "no film text is truly finished: it keeps on operating in a circuit of interpretations and re-readings that are not fixed definitively to a work."[19]

Indeed, considering the unpredictable life cycle of the film object itself, replete with its restorations and director's cuts, Vinzenz Hediger has gestured to the impossibility of obtaining a "complete set of facts" about a film and suggests that in time we might even witness a "rhetoric of the open series of multiple versions" supplanting "the rhetoric of the original."[20] In the context of contemporary digital production and dissemination, this rhetoric of multiplicity is also a rhetoric of incompletion. As Nicholas Rombes has pointed out, given the "ongoing production" of films across platforms in the digital era, the moment of final "release" is "really only a technicality." "How," he asks, "can a film—

or any text—ever be considered 'complete' when it is forever being re-released in different versions?"[21]

Incompletion is thus a functional reality of film production and spectatorship, both now and in the past. The affordances of incompletion extend to our work as film scholars as well—not least because historical objects "are scattered pieces of a puzzle that we can never hope to complete." We borrow these words from Monica Dall'Asta and Jane Gaines, who offer a feminist critique of historiographical approaches that assume the neutrality, objectivity, and comprehensiveness of existing frameworks for understanding film objects and processes. Dall'Asta and Gaines caution us over an "historicist faith in filling by addition," a faith expressed in efforts to "restore totality" to narratives of film history. Gaps and silences in film history, they suggest, "might better be seen as prompting multiple narratives, none of which can ever pretend to exhaustiveness."[22] We see these gaps as corollaries to filmic incompletion in its various forms, even as unfinishedness offers a rich seam for reimagining the incomplete and incompletable puzzle of feminist film and media history. We therefore apprehend filmic incompletion as not—or not only—a phenomenon to be regretted or mourned. For feminist scholars the unfinished film encompasses more than failure or missed opportunities; it is rather a zone of potential that can transform our received understandings of cinema and media production, reception, and circulation.

In explicating the feminist possibilities of the unfinished, *Incomplete* works to uncomplete film history: to make it available to further generative, not only melancholic, acts of undoing.[23] Although our study of the unfinished film contributes to the important project of feminist recovery within film studies, which centers neglected or "forgotten" women filmmakers and their works, ours is not an attempt to simply round out existing film-historical narratives. Rather, the unfinished film is primed for denaturalizing these narratives, including as they relate to the properties of the film object, the processes and conditions of film production and circulation, and models of film authorship. Since "general history is still a masculine history," writes one of our contributors, Maggie Hennefeld, in a recent essay, "feminist histories that offer new information without conceptual invention—without breaking through the walls that sideline feminist works—will be doomed to obscurity." Hennefeld continues: "It is the project of feminist film history not just to recuperate missing or forgotten archives, but to wrest these findings from their parallel tracks."[24] As is demonstrated by the essays collected in this book, the study of the unfinished film allows us to jump the parallel tracks of general and feminist film history, finding new modes and routes of travel that circumvent or break through the masculinist norms that define the status quo of film and media studies.

Despite the denaturalizing effects and feminist potential of the unfinished film, most existing work on incomplete film projects and materials assumes that film history is essentially complete as it is and so tends to leave its terms essentially intact. In fact, it's often the case that the unfinished film is freighted with valences of disappointment and failure to the degree that it is contextualized within an auteurist frame—a view of film authorship that is highly circumscribed in gendered terms, as feminist scholars have demonstrated.[25] The unfinished film is frequently presented as a thorn in the male auteur's side, evidence of the obstacles—financial, artistic, interpersonal—preventing this romantic, solitary genius from his self-realization on screen, as well as of his dignified struggle in facing down those obstacles. Whether the object of inquiry is *Napoleon*, Stanley Kubrick's "greatest film never made," Federico Fellini's "white whale," *The Journey of G. Mastorna*, or the many incomplete works of Orson Welles, the unrealized masterpiece acquires the significance its canonical creator has already been afforded elsewhere—a point that Jane Gaines makes eloquently in the first chapter of this book.[26] It is proof of failure that returns to the auteur as more proof of his (thwarted) success; it is an addendum to an already coherent, and essentially closed, artistic career. While such studies perform worthwhile work in making present for the reader an archive of concealed film production labor, it's the sense of value or even knowledge conferred a priori by the proper name of Kubrick, Fellini, or Welles that generates this scholarly interest in the first place.

The recent essay collection *Shadow Cinema* (2021), edited by film historians James Fenwick, Kieran Foster, and David Eldridge, makes some effort to move beyond the traditional focus on the unfinished works of male auteurs. In their introduction to the volume, the editors suggest that the cultish appeal of the auteur—and the emphasis it generates on "the role of personalities in filmmaking" instead of the film projects themselves—is insufficient for the purposes of scholarly inquiry.[27] The chapter contributed to *Shadow Cinema* by Lucy Mazdon, on Henri-Georges Clouzot's unfinished *L'Enfer*, is notable for its critique of characterizations of Clouzot as "a Promethean figure, the creative genius whose overarching ambition could ultimately only lead to failure," which Mazdon makes via a discussion of the misogynist "exploitation and cruelty" that marked the director's treatment of his lead actor, Romy Schneider.[28]

Yet *Shadow Cinema*—like Dan North's earlier collection of essays on unfinished British films, *Sights Unseen* (2008)—primarily focuses on the works of male directors, producers, and other practitioners working in mostly Anglophone or western European contexts. In doing so, it largely preserves the discourse of the auteur, most overtly in a section devoted to "directors who could be considered the most important auteurs of their respective national film industries"—Jean-Luc Godard, Ken Russell, and Ritwik Ghatak.[29] This isn't to say that the essays in question are especially egregious versions of masculinist auteurism; to the contrary, the authors are careful to avoid some of its common fallacies, including by clearly locating the directors in question within their historical and industrial contexts. However, they still manage the often overwhelming volume of textual and archival materials represented by unfinished projects by subsuming them under the sign of the auteur—betraying a desire for coherence that closes off other potential lines of inquiry as well as alternative conceptions of creative labor.

What allows the auteur to inveigle himself into scholarship that seeks to draw attention away from this time-worn figure? It's not by chance but instead a function of how the unfinished film is positioned as an object supplemental to, rather than disruptive of, established film history. "This is not a history that replaces the existing knowns," write Fenwick, Foster, and Eldridge, "but rather adds shade and complexity to our established interpretations and knowledge."[30] As feminist scholars, we don't share this confidence in established versions of film history, including its models of authorship; nor do we view our task as making the finishing touches to a picture set—complete—in permanent ink. We believe that the unfinished film can be used in more radical ways to redraw and recalibrate our sense of what film is and has been, how it has been (un)made and by whom.

Bearing the signs of the networked and interdependent processes of film production in various contexts, the unfinished film promotes anti-auteurist, feminist approaches to authorship, such as those developed by Judith Mayne, Catherine Grant, Jane Gaines, Patricia White, Isabel Seguí, Karen Redrobe, and others.[31] Understanding authorship as, in Janet Staiger's terms, "a technique of the self, creating and recreating the individual as an acting subject within history," these approaches accommodate the creative agency of minoritized and marginalized subjects, including women, without falling back on a romantic view of the singular, stable author/auteur.³² The unfinished film reveals precisely that, as Gaines has written, "films do not spring fully formed from the minds of authors" but instead from the cooperative labor of agents working out of their shared "desire to make films."³³ We can see this "team arrangement" reflected in the movements of the five women around the living room at the opening of Cynthia Madansky's *ESFIR,* in Miranda July's circulation of VHS Chainletter Tapes among *Big Miss Moviola* producers and subscribers, and in the depiction of traveling companions, the Filmmaker and her friend Clara, in Renée Green's *Some Chance Operations.*³⁴

And so we, also working collectively, call for an activist, revisionist, and multivalent approach to a wide range of unfinished film projects. Some of these projects can be used to understand the labor of known filmmakers; others, as dispersed archives bearing the traces of many hands, may require us to jettison the singular filmmaker as the organizing principle for our work. In the shared efforts that shape *Incomplete,* we contribute to an emerging body of scholarship that uncovers properties by women practitioners that were left unfinished or unreleased for a range of financial, political, physical, psychological, or aesthetic reasons. Alongside previously published work by our contributors, notably Mathilde Rouxel's significant account of the unfinished films of the Lebanese filmmaker Jocelyne Saab, we learn from Samantha Sheppard's research into online crowdfunding and the problems of circulation for Black women filmmakers, Monika Kin Gagnon's writing on Joyce Wieland and "posthumous cinema," and Eugénie Zvonkine's on the films of Kira Muratova that were subjected to Soviet censorship.³⁵ Sarah Keller's *Maya Deren: Incomplete Control* (2015), meanwhile, represents a major study of the experimental filmmaker through her many unrealized and fragmentary projects. For Keller, Deren's unfinished works serve as evidence of artistic or professional disappointment and, importantly, as vital and speculative texts that gesture toward alternate horizons of possibility. "Unfinished, contingent, or liminal states appealed to Deren and her aesthetic exploited these conditions wherever possible," Keller writes. "Not benighted by failure, she in fact depended on an aesthetic of open-endedness. Even her long-unfinished projects . . . indicate an aesthetic that respects a rejection of closure and completion."³⁶

Keller's theorization of the unfinished as process, strategy, and aesthetic is foundational to this book, where we adapt her approach toward explicitly feminist purposes and a wider view of women's diverse contributions to film history.[37] Keller asks, "What does cinema studies do to account for lost work or the details of the process, as well as the runoff, the excess, the clips on the cutting-room floor, the performance of an actor or the color palate of a designer that changed a director's vision, the contributions (potential or actual) of creative personnel?" *Incomplete* offers a series of (incomplete) answers to Keller's question, which we take as a challenge not only to attend to the leftovers generated by unfinished film projects but also to elevate the processual elements of film work, even when those elements do not result in "a final product."[38] It's one thing to follow the lead of genetic criticism and read the various "avant-textes" of a finished film—storyboards, outlines, treatments, and other draft materials devised for the shooting of the film—or to try to identify the "cinematic idea" that "does (or does not) survive its multiple, material elaborations at all levels" of film production.[39] But it's quite another to pursue such documents and ideas without an end product in sight, nor even, perhaps, an authorial signature with which to validate them.

Though in some cases our contributors examine screen media in projection—including rushes, fragments, and outtakes—or keep in view "complete" and exhibited films where they usefully inform the analysis of incomplete works, the majority of unfinished film projects manifest as materials beyond or other than screen media. In engaging process over product, incompletion over completion, our investigations routinely lead us to the detritus of the archive rather than moving images (and lead us away from the comforts of film studies as a home discipline). So we draw on the tools of genetic criticism, production studies, archive studies, star studies, oral history, and other fields of inquiry—not least literary studies, a discipline with a longer history of analyzing unfinished textual materials—as we develop practices of research and analysis adequate to the occulted existence of unfinished film materials.[40]

We inhabit, in other words, a vast paracinematic archive of ideas, writing, and realia. This is an archive filled with the items of furniture, bundles of flowers, cups of tea, and loose pages of Shub's unmade screenplay in *ESFIR*; with the eidetic words of July's interviewees, leaning toward the screen but preserved in typewritten form in *The Missing Movie Report*; and with the traces of Elvira Notari and her lost films that collect in the Neapolitan cityscape in *Some Chance Operations*. Like Madansky, July, and Green, we pursue the unfinished through a variety of creative gestures that refuse to foreclose its possibilities, knowing that fragmentary and film-adjacent documents and memories—not yet, and maybe never, films—need not be forced to yield to a totalizing vision.

...

In searching out the feminist possibilities of incompletion, particularly as they recast the history of women's film practice, we participate in a well-established tradition of feminist film and media scholarship that, by necessity, engages fragmentary, lost, or vanishing artifacts and archives. Feminist film studies is an ideal location for an analysis of unfinished films, insofar as such projects raise theoretical issues and methodological challenges to which feminist scholars have long been habituated. Devalued within film and media studies, and existing as a collocation of diverse, dispersed, and often degraded textual materials, the unfinished film shares certain characteristics with the materials of women's film history more generally—as those materials, and the creative labor they register, have conventionally been coded as secondary and nonessential within masculinist understandings of film authorship and narratives of film production. Early in Renée Green's *Some Chance Operations*, we hear in voiceover the following words from Eduardo Cadava's 1997 study *Words of Light*: "The possibility of history is bound to the survival of the traces of what is past and to our ability to read these traces as traces."[41] The search Green stages is not only for the traces of Elvira Notari, then, but also for a way of reading those traces as traces. Following Giuliana Bruno's "inferential walks" through Notari's fragmentary archive in *Streetwalking on a Ruined Map*, Green's film models an important strain of feminist film scholarship that has sought over several decades to develop methods sufficiently supple, provisory, and creative to deal with texts and archives defined by contingency and equivocality.[42]

We too are inspired by Bruno's *Streetwalking on a Ruined Map*, published some thirty years ago, as we pursue, without capturing or stilling, a range of unfinished projects, fragmented works perpetually in motion; and we are delighted that Bruno has taken the opportunity to reflect on the long life of this study in the postscript to this book. In *Streetwalking on a Ruined Map*, the condition of Notari's archive—a paradoxical site of paucity and abundance, limited in terms of Notari's very few extant films and yet also sprawling, unwieldy, in the distributed paratexts of her many nonextant films—turns the scholar's work into "a game of textual pleasures."[43] This is a game played between index and inference, situating the scholar as an active and desiring subject within the space of history. Bruno argues that the case of Dora Film bears out Michel de Certeau's claim that, given the unbridgeable divides between reality and discourse, the present and the past, "historians can write only by combining within their practice the 'other' that moves and misleads them and the real that they can represent only through fiction."[44] Like Cynthia Madansky's arranged and rearranged living room at *ESFIR*'s opening, the "chance operations" of Green's film—her puzzle of (at least theoretically) moveable, autonomous sequences—extrapolate a form of feminist film history from the chancy but politicized nature of historical knowledge. Bruno's work anticipates both of these films in its affirmation of the need for feminist historiography that draws on the resources of fiction in its encounters with, or on, the ruined map of history.

Over the past two decades, scholars working across feminist, queer, and postcolonial studies, and especially in relation to Black history, have innovated methods of "critical fabulation" and informed speculation in response to archival incompletion, including as the absences of the archive register and reiterate the oppressions of a violently white supremacist world order.[45] Saidiya Hartman's influential and important work interrogates the archives of slavery and its afterlives in the United States in order to narrate the life-worlds of African American people, and particularly women and girls, as "historical agents." In her recent book *Wayward Lives, Beautiful Experiments* (2019), Hartman positions herself in "intimate proximity" to her subjects as she undertakes close and imaginative work with historical documents, writing "from inside the circle" of Black social life.[46] Her scholarly practice is, as she writes in the 2008 essay "Venus in Two Acts," "an impossible writing which attempts to say that which resists being said. . . . It is a history of an unrecoverable past; it is a history written with and against the archive."[47]

Similarly, major new work on early Black cinema by Jacqueline Najuma Stewart and Allyson Nadia Field has demonstrated how, as Stewart puts it in *Migrating to the Movies* (2005), "reconstructive work" of this period and its cultures of spectatorship "must be performed creatively."[48] Field's *Uplift Cinema* (2015) argues for a reformulation of film history via the sustained study of lost or nonextant films, which, she points out, represent more than 80 percent of films made in the silent era.[49] Analyzing films that can no longer be projected or viewed involves speculation and conjecture, as Field acknowledges, but it is a kind of speculation that is grounded in institutional, publicity, and media materials. She advocates for scholarship that—much in keeping with Bruno's method for plotting Notari's nonextant works within a larger cultural and textual field—"looks adjacently" across extant materials, "connecting the dots across disparate sources" so as to provide a "composite picture" of the experiences and effects of historical film cultures.[50]

The essays in *Incomplete* test out a range of methodologies and theoretical frameworks for analyzing filmic incompletion, which we use as an umbrella term that covers the phenomenon of nonextant films and fragmentary archives along with aborted projects, aesthetically unfinished and deliberately open-ended works, and the vital—and fraught—ongoingness of film texts and star personae in adaptation, circulation, and reception. The incomplete film is not always a lost film, and yet Field's articulation of the challenges posed by nonextant films to film history and its methods is highly relevant to our expanded field of incompletion, which we theorize primarily through the unfinished film as material, concept, and (non)event. As Field shows, the nonextant film brings into view the status of the extant film print, and usually the theatrical feature, as the privileged object in film and media studies, against which all other filmic materials are measured. "Almost as a rule," she writes, "the further from mainstream theatrically screened productions we get, the scanter the surviving evidence becomes" and the slighter the scholarly attention such evidence receives.[51]

Notions of completion play an unstated but essential function in this sliding scale. By contrast to, for instance, Miranda July's capacious view of film from idea to circulating object, the value and attention given to certain projects, texts, and archives by film and media scholars tends to track with their relative degree of finishedness—their (our) sense of closure, coherence, or comprehensiveness. If, as Field claims, it is "irrational to perpetuate extant-centric film history" given the sheer volume of nonextant films, we might also say that it is irrational to focus on finished or realized film projects, which are also vastly outnumbered by unrealized or unfinished ones. This seems especially important at a moment when film and media scholars are reappraising erstwhile "minor" works; as Elena Gorfinkel has recently written, "the field must attend to how failures, unfinished works, amateur works, and never-produced and illicit films are the majority of films that constitute the constellation we call cinema in its totality."[52]

We, like Field, want to shift away from—or at least to reflect on critically—the language of loss and destruction that dominates existing work on fragmentary films and archives and further reifies the complete, extant film. "Absence is defined by the object it regrets; it is marked by the location, position, positing, and emplacement (both in time and space) of the missing piece," Field observes. "It is just as temporally and spatially situated as is presence."[53] Field's description of the lost film's absence as a form of presence is especially germane to the essays in part 1 of this book, which approach absences as not incidental or accidental but rather as intrinsic to the film archive (and to feminist labor in and around the archive). But this description also resonates with the larger project of *Incomplete,* as we reconceive of signs of deficiency and failure as signs of possibility for feminist film scholars and, as is evident especially in part 3 of the book, feminist film practitioners.

However, whereas Field quite rightly emphasizes the study of the nonextant film as a means of understanding exhibition practices, spectatorial experience, and wider cultural life, the forms of incompletion we discuss often do not, by definition, open onto histories of exhibition and viewership. For us, the unfinished film's absence makes present its conditions of (non)production, the institutional, economic, political, and sociocultural landscape in which a given project was conceived and developed, to a greater or lesser extent. Such absences also make present the active labor of women filmmakers and practitioners—demonstrating what Monica Dall'Asta and Alessandra Chiarini have described, in their work on women's contributions to the history of found footage film, as "women's tenacious will to make cinema at all costs . . . under conditions of limitation and lack of means."[54]

In many cases, it's as if the creative and critical agency of (prospective, imagined) viewers is transferred to us as scholars as we negotiate incompletion between its archival paucity and abundance, as well as between its solid materiality—its existence in physical objects, in notebooks, screenplays, industrial documents, unfinished film fragments, photographs, magazines, and more—and its immateriality, its notionality. Occupying "an ambiguous space of imaginary plenitude" and excess, as Sean Braune has written of lost, burned, or unfinished literary texts, the unfinished film is the "remaining trace of a larger writing that exists as an imaginary supplement . . . as pure potential in a sort of libidinous energy catalyzing in the mind of the reader and critic."[55] Like the creative-industrial genre of the screenplay, which engenders in its reader, in Pier Paolo Pasolini's terms, an "intense" form of engagement that seeks "a 'visual' completeness which it does not have, but at which it hints," the incomplete projects we study grant to us an "agentic force" by their precursory or intermediary attributes.[56]

We can understand this agentic force with reference to the critical interpretative power of film spectators as demonstrated in feminist and queer reception studies, or else via "possessive" or "introspective" models of cinephilic viewership and scholarship. "As we watch a film," Maya Deren wrote in 1960, "the continuous act of recognition in which we are involved is like a strip of memory unrolling beneath the images of the film itself, to form the invisible underlayer of an implicit double exposure."[57] Deren's double exposure expands our sense of the affordances of incompletion in her work and beyond: there is the image track, and there is also the invisible track of remembrance, which continues to unspool in the viewer's mind long after the projection ends, transforming the images over time. For Catherine Fowler, Deren's observation foreshadows the work of scholars such as Stanley Cavell, Victor Burgin, and Christian Keathley to acknowledge and accommodate the role of memory in the experience of film.[58] Fowler contextualizes this scholarship alongside gallery films made in the 1990s that reenact or remake images from the history of cinema. The films she discusses—which do not include *Some Chance Operations,* although Green's film sits with them—perform a "look backward" that "goes beyond the visible image track of cinema's past because it is formed collectively from both the 'there' of cinema, or the real screened images, and what artist Pierre Huyghe ingeniously calls the 'elsewhere,' or the reactions to, feelings from, and desire for, remembered films."[59]

Fowler calls for scholarship guided by the movement of these films away from a retrospection of the *there* of cinema's past, with its negative structure of loss and mourning, to an introspection located in the *elsewhere* of the viewing process: from that which is gone, interred in the past, to that which endures in the present. We, of course, can't exactly remember many of the unfinished films we study—and many of them can only be "projected" to the degree that they are fundamentally reconstituted, as with Madansky's filmmaking with or around Shub's unmade screenplay (or equally with that of one of our contributors, the filmmaker and scholar Karen Pearlman, whose own recent work to reimagine Shub's "Women" suggests the many paths opened up by incomplete film materials).[60] Even so, we occupy this dynamic, ongoing elsewhere, the space of film as it exists beyond or outside of projection. After all, as Fowler suggests, this vantage allows us to "[remember] cinema's past as 'undead,' unfinished, and unfixed."[61]

Indeed, the incomplete objects and projects we examine are a site of projection in a different sense, since their defining measure of lack produces and reproduces our desire for them—as for those who (partially) made them. Notari's fragmented archive and nonextant films clarify for Bruno the "fantasmatic scene" of identification, (mis)recognition, and dislocation that organizes feminist scholarship, especially when it constitutes female subjects—and scholars—as creative agents or authors. "As a female voice speaking to another female voice, the authorial function is produced in a mirroring effect," Bruno writes, and so "feminist writing ingrains a (double) authorial desire and libidinal exchange."[62] More recently, Dall'Asta and Gaines have elaborated the fantasmatic scene of feminist historiography in describing the "constellations" of feminist film scholars with the subjects of their historical research. As we "find" women filmmakers and practitioners, they write, through our work with the remaining traces of their labor and lives, we "create a temporal wedge in our present that makes us momentarily coincident with the historical past."[63] We thus become imbricated with our subjects, able to locate ourselves in history and, at once, to evoke historical agents—more precisely, their images or signs—"in and for the present."[64]

Women's incomplete or unfinished films catalyze the erotic and affective impulses of feminist scholarship in a particular way. Hinting at a completion they don't have, resisting closure like Scheherazade, these projects open a space—an elsewhere—for projection and fantasy, speculation and conjecture. As filmic incompletion calls attention to our subjective, ethical, and political investments in the past, and how these investments shape our writing in the present, we partake in the processual pleasures of remembrance and transformation experienced by the spectator of complete films, extant or not. And filmic incompletion reveals to us, at once, how our objects of study have shaped us and will continue to shape us. Reflecting on the ideas she collated toward *The Missing Movie Report,* Miranda July reflected: "Some of the answers were interesting, some weren't. But was I feeling the absence now? Now that I'd called upon them, were those unmade movies changing me, like ghosts?"[65]

The cajoling ghosts of incomplete films are, in a sense, only ever elsewhere, unmoored—or suspended—in space as well as in time. This leads us to ask: *when* is the missing movie or unfinished film? Is it past, or present, or future—or somehow all of these at once? For Fowler, the gallery films that model the elsewhere of film operate in "a subjunctive mood," a grammar of doubts, wishes, and hopes that is also paramount in unfinished films, which unsettle our sense of the fixity of the past as they generate speculation about "what might have been."[66] Whereas the essays in this book aren't primarily invested in imagining unfinished projects as they might have been, the conditional tense of this question evokes the qualities of life and art that are revealed, we argue, through filmic incompletion: the contingency, unruliness, and irresolution of its unfolding. Anthropologists João Biehl and Peter Locke refer similarly to how the concept of unfinishedness unveils "worlds on edge and the open-endedness of people's becoming."[67] For our purposes, though the incomplete is suspended elsewhere and *elsewhen*—and this space is broached and to some extent structured by our work on its cast-off, incongruent materials—the incomplete nevertheless offers resources for understanding the past in its specificity and strangeness. It is a window, however smudged or cracked, onto the past in its *presentness*—the past as a series of moments whose future isn't set, when things could (still) be otherwise.

In this way, the incomplete licenses counterfactual thinking, not only in a tragic mode—as in, *we wish this film had been completed, we wish these filmmakers' efforts hadn't been interrupted or curtailed*—but also in service of interpreting the historical moment "on its own terms," from within its horizon of possibility. By refusing to "reduce all events to a single stream flowing toward some projected *telos*," as Benjamin Wurgaft has argued, counterfactual thought experiments can augment our sense of causality by allowing us to work through the alternative trajectories of a given historical moment or event.[68] By *sideshadowing* historical events as opposed to *backshadowing* them—by inhabiting a moment and proceeding outward, sideways, from its location in time and space—we can "[restore] a sense of possibility even to a story whose outcome we already know."[69] We can resist a tendency to interpret historical events in the light of their outcomes—a particular challenge when those outcomes are a source of regret or lamentation, as in the failure of a film's production or the death of a filmmaker or star. We know how the story ends, and we don't pretend that it can be changed; but we don't allow our foreknowledge of the future to overshadow the liveness of the past and of actors within its environments. The incomplete allows us to have it both ways: we encounter the past in its locatedness, its tensile now-moments; and yet we retain some measure of latitude from time's dictates and inevitabilities.

The unfinished film is a concatenation of texts that emerges from the embodied, diffuse, and networked processes of film production—and that bears the signs of these processes in its state of disruption or abortiveness. For this reason the energy of *what ifs* are valuable for feminist scholars concerned to account not only for the gendered and racialized conditions of film labor but also, importantly, for women's agency and activity in negotiation of those conditions. Though, as existing scholarship has suggested, the question of what might have been can distract us from the implications of such films for histories of production in specific cultures and contexts, it's also true that this order of question has been productive for feminist scholars and scholar–activists working toward a more just and less violent world.[70] In her telling of impossible histories, for example, Hartman adopts "the conditional temporality of 'what could have been," a temporality that allows, in Lisa Lowe's words, a "productive attention to the scene of loss, a thinking with twofold attention that seeks to encompass at once the positive objects and methods of history and social science and the matters absent, entangled, and unavailable by its methods."[71] Meanwhile, for a range of scholars, including Elizabeth Grosz, Tina Campt, and Domietta Torlasco, a feminist politic finds its temporal home in the future anterior or future perfect tense, which describes nonactual events, *what will have happened,* or even the future real conditional, *what will have had to have happened.*[72]

The future anterior is "the time in which the future can look at this present as its superseded past," as Grosz puts it.[73] It is the time of radical political change; it is the time when the past loses its hold over the present. In this vein we conceive of unfinished projects as both projections and *projectiles,* pitched forward in time and space to new worlds—even as they manifest so clearly how the old worlds could not, or would not, sustain their development. We don't seek to confer completion or wholeness to the incomplete, nor do we forget our work as also partial and unfinished—since we view our scholarly labor on a continuum with women's labor in film cultures and industries across the history of the medium. As Dall'Asta and Gaines put it, "We are constellated with women makers, then and now, in relation to the unfinished business of world feminism."[74]

Constellated with one another as collaborators on this book and with the subjects of our study, we turn—backward and forward in time, sideways and elsewhere in space—to unfinished film in its possibilities, its *prospects* for feminist film history and practice. We turn backward and forward to Èsfir' Shub, whose unrealized screenplay "Women"—and its reconstitution in Madansky's *ESFIR*—appears in a new light in the context of Shub's extraordinary efforts, across her career, to restore and archive historical footage for the sake of future filmmakers and spectators: creating a "historical document for the future," as she wrote in 1927.[75] We turn backward and forward to Miranda July, whose *Big Miss Moviola* zines were distributed to women and girls as "a challenge and a promise."⁷⁶ And we turn backward and forward to Renée Green and the continuous, incomplete structure of her film practice—wherein history remains in the present, a lost city not to be restored but explored.

. . .

Incomplete is organized in four parts: "Unfound Objects," "Refusals and Interruptions," "In Process," and "Posthumous Returns." Part 1, "Unfound Objects," accounts for the gendered politics of the film archive—its material formation, its means of conservation, its technologies of dissemination, and its uses for scholars—from the vantage point of filmic incompletion. Discussing early cinema, a period in which the archive is especially fragmentary and in which women played especially prominent roles in film production, the chapters emphasize the archive's provisionality as it interacts with the unfinished business of feminist scholarship of the silent and classical eras.

"Unfound Objects" thus responds to Paula Amad's claim, in her 2010 study *Counter-Archive,* that "the glaring gaps in cinema's historical record do not constitute a handicap for history but a challenge to produce a more sensitive historiography that moves beyond the historicist myth of the all-knowing sovereign archive." Like Amad, our contributors resist "the fantasy of awakening the sleeping documents with the (death) kiss of finite interpretation" as they devise "models of creative and critical empiricism" proper to the unsovereign, uncompletable archive.⁷⁷ Jane Gaines begins this work in chapter 1 by reflecting on the varied semantic possibilities of the term "never." For film history, as Gaines notes, this term can invoke the notion of a lost object that is to be "*never* again," or an idea that never came to fruition, and so "*never* having been." Such distinctions bear crucial implications for silent cinema, a vast archive of works that will be mostly "never again," but that also reveals a number of works conceived by female producers that were not realized on screen. Rather than bemoaning these missed opportunities, Gaines offers a speculative approach to these unfinished projects: a "never made" but also a "what if?"

In chapter 2, Maggie Hennefeld takes up the unarchival and the unwritten in relation to silent film comediennes who have yet to be identified by name. Driven to discover the identity of the enigmatic French figure Léontine, Hennefeld finds instead a model for embracing the thrill of the (unfinished) moment in Léontine's performances, which, in their impulse toward destruction, take no account of the future. Katherine Groo also seeks out the historiographical implications and artifactual expressions of archival fragmentation and anonymous women in chapter 3, where she offers a feminist interpretation of the nitrate film clippings that make up the Davide Turconi Collection Database. Groo contemplates the absent presence of thousands of unidentified women in this archive of fragments and the forms of feminist knowledge produced in and by these images—not least by the embodied traces of the labor of women who worked as colorists in early film industries.

Building on these insights about the structuring reality and historiographical opportunities of unfound objects in film history, part 2 studies "Refusals and Interruptions" of women's film labor in various national contexts. Focusing on experimental and oppositional filmmaking in Latin America and the Middle East from the 1970s on, the contributors in this section make inventive use of archival materials and oral histories in examining projects stymied by the systemic sexism of film industries and cultures, the effects of censorship, and the violent disruptions of global and local conflict. Their chapters make room for the creative affordances of refusal and interruption, along with the adaptability and resourcefulness of women filmmakers and practitioners. Given these scholars' personal encounters and close relationships with those whose work they study, these affordances are multiplied through the labor of feminist scholarship and archiving itself.

In chapter 4, Isabel Seguí attends to the work of the Peruvian filmmaker María Barea and the Bolivian filmmaker Beatriz Palacios, who in the 1990s both conceived of projects that remained unrealized despite the successes of their male contemporaries in this period. For Seguí, the study of unrealized films is essential for understanding the history of Andean women's oppositional filmmaking, given pervasive inequalities of access to resources and opportunities. Similarly, Elizabeth Ramírez-Soto finds new ways into and through the archive of women's unfinished film work in chapter 5, which explores *Tres por tres,* an omnibus film conceived by three women in Chile—Marilú Mallet, Valeria Sarmiento, and Angelina Vázquez—in the final year of the nation's Popular Unity government. Progress on the film was thwarted following the establishment of the Pinochet dictatorship in 1973, and its three filmmakers went into exile shortly afterward, continuing their careers separately. By reconstructing the film from a combination of its surviving written documents and oral histories, Ramírez-Soto reveals how this collaborative project would have explored the lives and problems of middle-class women in an otherwise masculinist film industry and political landscape.

In chapter 6, Mathilde Rouxel offers testimony of her working relationship with the Lebanese filmmaker Jocelyne Saab, focusing especially on the major projects that occupied Saab in the decade before her death in 2019. These projects were stalled or redirected due to a lack of funding, conflicts within the production teams, or the conditions and pressures of local and international politics. Yet Saab's notes, interviews, research materials, scenarios, and rushes for these projects disclose her creative process of "metamorphosis" and "variation," in Rouxel's terms, which emerged out of Saab's desire not only to tell stories that no one else wanted to tell but also to construct an unconventional mode of historical narration.

Saab's adaptive, multistage work across various projects serves as a bridge between part 2 and part 3 of *Incomplete*. Each of these parts uses the unfinished film to unveil the material, commercial, and interpersonal conditions of filmmaking for women in various times and places. However, whereas part 2's attention to refusal and interruption subtends a generally hostile and combative account of film production, part 3 shifts focus to projects by women filmmakers in which qualities of unfinishedness materialize through deliberate aesthetic strategies. Complicating narratives of artistic progress and "finished" achievements, incompletion serves feminist ends as it exceeds or reimagines its associations with loss and failure.

Part 3, "In Process," begins with chapter 7, Leo Goldsmith's interview with the experimental filmmaker Peggy Ahwesh, who has built much of her work around the use and reuse of found footage. In conversation, Ahwesh theorizes the possibilities of incompletion for the film object—through her reworking of older images, her updating of films in flux, and, recently, her curation and exhibition of alternative versions of her work alongside incomplete works by her forebears, including Maya Deren. In chapter 8, Stefan Solomon reads two film works that remained intentionally open-ended for decades: Leslie Thornton's *Peggy and Fred in Hell*, a cycle begun as an intended feature film in 1983, spanning seventeen different episodes over the following thirty years and (ostensibly) concluded in 2015; and Lynn Hershman Leeson's *Electronic Diaries*, a confessional film begun in 1984, "finished" in 1996, but then reopened in 2019. What is the significance, Solomon asks, of formally completing a project that has remained open-ended for more than three decades—or, conversely, of adding new material to a long-completed project?

Chapter 9 features filmmaker-scholar Karen Pearlman's meditation of the experiences, practices, and functions of incompletion, focusing on the role of the editor as one who in reality always works with unfinished film materials. Pearlman discusses her work-in-progress—or work-in-process—on the unbroken connections between dance and editing in the work of the US experimental filmmaker Shirley Clarke. For Pearlman, Clarke's training in dance established "one long electrical cord" that passed a current from her choreography through to her filmmaking and kinaesthetic sensibility as an editor—and remains live, ongoing, as it activates Pearlman's current creative practice.

Chapter 10 concerns "Shirkers," a film shot in 1991 that was poised to be the first independent English-language feature film in Singapore since the 1970s—before its director, Georges Cardona, absconded with the 16mm film and sound reels. Nearly three decades later, the film's writer and star, Sandi Tan, reimagined the work in a different form as the major Netflix documentary *Shirkers* (2018). In this chapter Sophia Siddique, the producer of the original "Shirkers," reflects on her overlapping roles as producer, interview subject, spectator, and scholar of the unproduced and reproduced film. Through a series of creative-critical "epitaphs" for the unfinished film of her youth, Siddique explores how this project recasts Singaporean film history and asks us to come to terms with the ghosts of the past.

Extrapolating from Siddique's sense of the haunting "afterlives" of filmic incompletion, part 4 of this book, "Posthumous Returns," analyzes the unfinished film under the sign of its posthumous completion or recovery. Earlier chapters are situated more or less expressly within a feminist recovery mode, working to restore to the historical record the authorial and creative presence of women film practitioners—albeit to restore without seeking to complete the historical record. Although the recovery framework is highly usable for the study of unfinished projects, filmic incompletion prompts us to confront the limits of recovery as a method, particularly in its positivist assumptions. As Genevieve Yue has recently argued, the "assertion of [women's] neglected or forgotten presence in various aspects of filmmaking" in feminist film studies rests on a theory of the medium's history derived from its representational functions.[78] This means, Yue notes, that feminist recovery paradigms treat film as a medium of presence rather than one formed in its absences, by all the material (bodily, technological) that remains off-screen. When it comes to incomplete or unfinished films, such material may comprise the entirety of a given project. The final part of *Incomplete* therefore accounts for posthumous returns and reworkings of film materials that counsel us against a fetishization of presence—and, differently, of absence—within film history and studies of spectatorship.

In each of the cases studied in this part of the book, which center on US cinema in the late twentieth and early twenty-first centuries, the death of a woman filmmaker or star has arrested or interposed on the course of film production, and the decisions about whether and how to complete or otherwise contribute to this unfinished work carry significant ethical and political implications. The contributors unpack these implications as they reckon with the public, textual, and technological afterlives of women filmmakers and actors, meditating on what is lost—not only found—through certain efforts to revitalize or recuperate the incomplete. Chapter 11, by Alix Beeston, concerns the posthumous dissemination and reception of the work of the Black filmmaker and writer Kathleen Collins, which was largely undistributed, unproduced, or unpublished when she died from cancer in 1988. The posthumous recovery of Collins has enabled her work to find a wide audience in recent years, but it has also, as Beeston argues, freighted that work with associations of loss and failure that obscure the dedicated, iterative, and collaborative labor that defined Collins's creative practice across her life. Drawing on archival research and oral histories, Beeston advances an alternative view of Collins's unfinished film work—specifically the unproduced screenplay "A Summer Diary"—which seeks to honor "the vital rhythms and continuities of her work-in-process."

Likewise, in chapter 12, Karen Redrobe situates the experimental animator Helen Hill within the communities and traditions in which she was working prior to her death in 2007. When Hill was murdered during a wave of post–Hurricane Katrina violence in New Orleans, she left behind an unfinished project called "The Florestine Collection." Rather than focusing on the posthumously "completed" version of the film, made in 2011 by Hill's partner, Paul Gailiunas, Redrobe examines the archive of the project to reveal Hill's place in the histories of experimental film and animation and her efforts, as a white woman in New Orleans, to grapple with racial injustice and to cultivate communities devoted to "reimagining and repairing the world in continuous, contestable, and unfolding ways." Finally, in chapter 13, Katherine Fusco explores the posthumous career of Marilyn Monroe and the issues of publicity, consent, and copyright raised by her numerous resurrections as a CGI "deepfake." Drawing on case law and feminist star studies, Fusco faces the violent side of fan and industry desires, and their gendered dimensions, in the *elsewhere* and *elsewhen* of film cultures—as stars' images such as Monroe's are put to uses to which they cannot possibly consent.

Incomplete concludes with Giuliana Bruno's postscript, which casts backward and forward, marking a pathway into and out of this book. Staging her own act of return, Bruno reflects on the journey of *Streetwalking on a Ruined Map* in the three decades since it was first published: the process of developing an innovative, subjective method for writing a history of lacunae, the subsequent reception and use of the work within feminist film studies, and the enduring (after)life of the book—and of Elvira Notari's work and memory—for Bruno personally. Like the several openings of this introduction, in which beginnings are also endings and endings are also beginnings, Bruno's postscript embeds *Incomplete* in a history of feminist scholarship that encompasses the past as well as the future: the feminist project as a continuous, incomplete structure, a challenge and a promise, an archive of possibilities for the future.

NOTES

1. Ėsfir' Shub, *Zhizn' moia—kinematograf* [*My Life—Cinema*], ed. A.I. Konopleva (Moscow: Iskusstvo, 1972), 286, cited in Graham Roberts, "Esfir Shub: A Suitable Case for Treatment," *Historical Journal of Film, Radio and Television* 11.2 (1991): 149–59, 155.

2. On the circumstances of the screenplay's incompletion, see Roberts, "Esfir Shub: A Suitable Case," 155–56; and Graham Roberts, "Esfir Shub," in *Censorship: A World Encyclopedia,* ed. Derek Jones (London: Routledge, 2001), 2235–36.

3. We cite the English translation of "Women" used in Madansky's film, which is credited to Jessica Mroz and Anastasia Karkacheva. The first of the script's seven chapters has also been translated and published by Vlada Petric as "Esther Shub's Unrealized Project," *Quarterly Review of Film Studies* 3.4 (1978): 449–56.

4. Miranda July, "U-Matic Chainletter" (July 1997): 8; digitized at www.joanie4jackie.com/chainletter/u-matic-chainletter/.

5. July, "U-Matic Chainletter," 1.

6. July, "U-Matic Chainletter," 4.

7. Frances Corry, "'LADY U SEND ME YR MOVIE': Constructing *Joanie 4 Jackie*'s Feminist Distribution Network," *Feminist Media Studies* (2020): 1–17, 2.

8. July, "U-Matic Chainletter," 8. For a useful discussion of the intersectional feminist goals of *The Missing Movie Report,* see Cara Smulevitz, "'Girl, If You Make the Movie, I Promise You Somebody Will See It': DIY, Grrrl Power, and Miranda July," PhD dissertation (University of Illinois at Chicago, 2016), 140–50.

9. July, "U-Matic Chainletter," 4.

10. Giuliana Bruno, *Streetwalking on a Ruined Map: Cultural Theory and the City Films of Elvira Notari* (Princeton, NJ: Princeton University Press, 1993), 4.

11. Stefano Masi and Mario Franco, *Il mare, la luna, i coltelli. Per una storia del cinema muto Napoletano* (Naples: Tullio Pironti, 1988), 49, cited in Kim Tomadjoglou, "Elvira Notari," in *Women Film Pioneers Project,* ed. Jane M. Gaines, Radha Vatsal, and Monica Dall'Asta (New York: Columbia University Libraries, 2013), https://doi.org/10.7916/d8-zdmp-rs37.

12. Bruno, *Streetwalking on a Ruined Map*, 3.

13. Bruno, *Streetwalking on a Ruined Map*, 150.

14. See Renée Green's remarks on this aspect of the film in "Survival: Ruminations on Archival Lacunae," in *The Archive,* ed. Charles Merewether (Cambridge, MA: MIT Press, 2006), 49–55, 52–54.

15. The voiceover is a citation of Walter Benjamin, "The Storyteller: Reflections on the Works of Nikolai Leskov," in *Illuminations,* trans. Harry Zohn and ed. Hannah Arendt (New York: Harcourt Brace Jovanovich, 1968), 83–109, 98.

16. Nora M. Alter, "Beyond the Frame: Renée Green's Video Practice," in *Shadows and Signals,* by Renée Green, Alexander Alberro, Nora M. Alter, and Nuria Enguita Mayo (Barcelona: Fundació Antoni Tàpies, 2000), 155–73, 172.

17. Digital technologies have radically expanded the senses in which we might think of the unfinished, giving rise, for example, to the idea of the "boundless media" that manifests in "new forms of durational recording, storytelling, imagemaking, and data visualization." See Erika Balsom, Mary Ann Doane, Kris Fallon, Kaitlin Clifton Forcier, and Tess Takahashi, "Boundless Media," *Afterimage* 48.2 (June 2021): 33.

18. See Dan Streible, "The Role of Orphan Films in the 21st Century Archive," *Cinema Journal* 46.3 (2007): 124–28.

19. Dan North, "Introduction: Finishing the Unfinished," in *Sights Unseen: Unfinished British Films,* ed. Dan North (Newcastle: Cambridge Scholars Publishing, 2008), 1–18, 7. See Roland Barthes, "From Work to Text," in *The Rustle of Language,* trans. Richard Howard (Berkeley: University of California Press, 1986), 56–64.

20. Vinzenz Hediger, "The Original Is Always Lost: Film History, Copyright Industries and the Problem of Reconstruction," in *Cinephilia: Movies, Love and Memory,* ed. Marijke de Valck and Malte Hagener (Amsterdam: Amsterdam University Press, 2005), 135–49, 147, 148.

21. Nicholas Rombes, *Cinema in the Digital Age* (London: Wallflower, 2009), 43.

22. Monica Dall'Asta and Jane M. Gaines, "Constellations: Past Meets Present in Feminist Film History," prologue to *Doing Women's Film History: Reframing Cinemas, Past and Future,* ed. Christine Gledhill and Julia Knight (Urbana: Illinois University Press, 2015), 13–25, 18.

23. Likewise, theories of failure in queer studies offer useful contexts for revaluing the unfinished; see especially Jack Halberstam, *The Queer Art of Failure* (Durham, NC: Duke University Press, 2011).

24. Maggie Hennefeld, "Film History," *Feminist Media Histories* 4.2 (2018): 77–83, 80.

25. See Priya Jaikumar, "Feminist and Non-Western Interrogations of Film Authorship," in *The Routledge Companion to Cinema and Gender*, ed. Kristin Lené Hole, Dijana Jelača, E. Ann Kaplan, and Patrice Petro (New York: Routledge, 2017), 205–14; and Janet Staiger, "Authorship Approaches," in *Authorship and Film*, ed. David A. Gerstner and Janet Staiger (New York: Routledge, 2003), 27–57, especially the discussion of authorship-as-personality, 33–40, and the scholarship cited at note 34.

26. The largest body of scholarship devoted to a director's unfinished works belongs to Welles, owing as much to Welles's critical reputation and the academic industry around his work as to the predominance of unfinished projects across his career. Not all scholarship is hagiographic; for example, Catherine Benamou's appraisal of the unfinished Mexican–Brazilian docufiction film *It's All True* interrogates the impression of mastery afforded to Welles. For Benamou, "the aborted text returns as a scar or 'wound' on the auteur's body: a blemish rather than a creative turning point in the director's film work as a whole." Catherine L. Benamou, *It's All True: Orson Welles's Pan-American Odyssey* (Berkeley: University of California Press, 2007), 150. On Welles, see also Marguerite H. Rippy, *Orson Welles and the Unfinished RKO Projects: A Postmodern Perspective* (Carbondale: University of Southern Illinois Press, 2009), and Josh Karp, *Orson Welles's Last Movie: The Making of* The Other Side of the Wind (New York: St. Martin's Press, 2015). Other key studies of male auteurs' unfinished works include Alison Castle, *Stanley Kubrick's "Napoleon": The Greatest Film Never Made* (Cologne: Taschen, 2017), and Federico Fellini, Dino Buzzati, Brunello Rondi, and Bernardino Zapponi, *The Journey of G. Mastorna: The Film Fellini Didn't Make*, ed. and trans. Marcus Perryman (New York: Berghan, 2013).

27. James Fenwick, Kieran Foster, and David Eldridge, introduction to *Shadow Cinema: The Historical and Production Contexts of Unmade Films*, ed. Fenwick, Foster, and Eldridge (London: Bloomsbury, 2021), 1–14, 3.

28. Lucy Mazdon, "Clouzot's *L'Enfer*," in *Shadow Cinema*, ed. Fenwick, Foster, and Eldridge, 185–98, 193, 194. The other substantive feminist contribution to *Shadow Cinema* is Hannah Hamad's analysis of how feminist activism halted the production of two films based on the Yorkshire Ripper murders in the early 1980s. In keeping with our own efforts not to fetishize presence, which we discuss later on, Hamad shows how the incompletion of a film project may well serve feminist ends. See Hamad, "The Movie Producer, the Feminists and the Serial Killer: UK Feminist Activism, Misogynist 70s Film Culture and the (Non) Filming of the Yorkshire Ripper Murders," in *Shadow Cinema*, ed. Fenwick, Foster, and Eldridge, 235–50.

29. Fenwick, Foster, and Eldridge, introduction, 8.

30. Fenwick, Foster, and Eldridge, introduction, 7.

31. See Judith Mayne, *Directed by Dorothy Arzner* (Bloomington: Indiana University Press, 1994); Catherine Grant, "Secret Agents: Feminist Theories of Women's Film Authorship," *Feminist Theory* 2.1 (2001): 113–30; Jane M. Gaines, "Of Cabbages and Authors," in *A Feminist Reader in Early Cinema*, ed. Jennifer M. Bean and Diane Negra (Durham, NC: Duke University Press,

2002), 88–118; Patricia White, *Women's Cinema, World Cinema: Projecting Contemporary Feminisms* (Durham, NC: Duke University Press, 2015); Isabel Seguí, "Auteurism, *Machismo-Leninismo* and Other Issues: Women's Labor in Andean Oppositional Film Production," *Feminist Media Histories* 4.1 (January 2018): 11–36; Seguí, "Beatriz Palacios: Ukamau's Cornerstone (1974–2003)," *Latin American Perspectives* 48.2 (March 2021): 77–92; and Karen Redrobe, "Thinking Like a Holy Girl: A Philosophy of Grandma's Bedroom," in *On Women's Films: Across Worlds and Generations*, ed. Ivone Margulies and Jeremi Szaniawski (London: Bloomsbury, 2019), 346–67.

32. Staiger, "Authorship Approaches," 50.

33. Gaines, "Of Cabbages and Authors," 108, 110.

34. Gaines, "Of Cabbages and Authors," 110.

35. Mathilde Rouxel, "A Filmmaker's Words: A Journey through the Archive of Jocelyne Saab's Unfinished Work," in *ReFocus: The Films of Jocelyne Saab: Films, Artworks and Cultural Events for the Arab World*, ed. Rouxel and Stefanie Van de Peer (Edinburgh: Edinburgh University Press, 2021), 70–84; Samantha N. Sheppard, "I Love Cinema: Black Film and Speculative Practice in the Era of Online Crowdfunding," *Film Quarterly* 71.2 (2017): 25–31, and Sheppard's forthcoming book *A Black W/hole: Phantom Cinemas and the Reimagining of Black Women's Media Histories*; Monika Kin Gagnon, "Unfinished Films and Posthumous Cinema: Charles Gagnon's *R69* and Joyce Wieland's *Wendy and Joyce*," in *Cinephemera*, ed. Zoë Druick and Gerda Cammaer (Montreal: McGill-Queens University Press, 2014), 137–58, and Gagnon's forthcoming book *Posthumous Cinema*; Eugénie Zvonkine, "'Watch Your Films Attentively': Kira Muratova's Unrealised Script as a Key to her Oeuvre," *Studies in Russian and Soviet Cinema* 8.1 (2014): 41–50, and "The Unfinished Gesture: Kira Muratova's *Long Farewells* (*Dolgie provody*, 1971)," *East European Film Bulletin* 98 (October 2019), https://eefb.org/retrospectives/kira-muratovas-long-farewells-dolgie-provody-1971/.

36. Sarah Keller, *Maya Deren: Incomplete Control* (New York: Columbia University Press, 2015), 2.

37. See also Erin Hill, *Never Done: A History of Women's Work in Media Production* (New Brunswick, NJ: Rutgers University Press, 2016).

38. Keller, *Maya Deren*, 7.

39. See Jed Deppman, Daniel Ferrer, and Michael Groden, eds., *Genetic Criticism: Texts and Avant-textes* (Philadelphia: University of Pennsylvania Press, 2004); and Adrian Martin, "Where Do Cinematic Ideas Come From?," *Journal of Screenwriting* 5.1 (2014): 9–26, 16.

40. For literary studies approaches to textual variants and unfinished works, see Jerome McGann, *The Textual Condition* (Princeton, NJ: Princeton University Press, 1991); John Bryant, *The Fluid Text: A Theory of Revision and Editing for Book and Screen* (Ann Arbor: University of Michigan Press, 2002); Sean Braune, "How to Analyze Texts That Were Burned, Lost, Fragmented, or Never Written," *symplokē* 21.1–2 (2013): 239–55; James Ramsey Wollen, "What Is an Unfinished Work?" *New Literary History* 46.1 (2015): 125–42; and Matthew Harle, *Afterlives of Abandoned Work: Creative Debris in the Archive* (New York: Bloomsbury, 2019).

41. Eduardo Cadava, *Words of Light: Theses on the Photography of History* (Princeton, NJ: Princeton University Press, 1997), 64.

42. Bruno, *Streetwalking on a Ruined Map*, 3.

43. Bruno, *Streetwalking on a Ruined Map*, 4.

44. Bruno, *Streetwalking on a Ruined Map*, 3; Michel de Certeau, *The Writing of History*, trans. Tom Conley (New York: Columbia University Press, 1988), 14.

45. Saidiya Hartman, "Venus in Two Acts," *Small Axe* 26 (June 2008): 1–14, 11.

46. Saidiya Hartman, *Wayward Lives, Beautiful Experiments: Intimate Histories of Riotous Black Girls, Troublesome Women, and Queer Radicals* (New York: W. W. Norton & Company, 2019), ix.

47. Hartman, "Venus in Two Acts," 12.

48. Jacqueline Najuma Stewart, *Migrating to the Movies: Cinema and Black Urban Modernity* (Berkeley: University of California Press, 2005), xviii.

49. Allyson Nadia Field, *Uplift Cinema: The Emergence of African American Film and the Possibility of Black Modernity* (Durham, NC: Duke University Press, 2015), 23.

50. Field, *Uplift Cinema*, 26–27. For examples of this in practice, see the essays collected in a special double issue edited by Field and released while *Incomplete* was in production, "Speculative Approaches to Media Histories," *Feminist Media Histories* 8.2 and 8.3 (2022).

51. Field, *Uplift Cinema*, 25.

52. Elena Gorfinkel, "Microhistories and Materiality in Adult Film History, or the Case of *Erotic Salad*," *JCMS: Journal of Cinema and Media Studies* 58.1 (2018): 147–52, 152.

53. Field, *Uplift Cinema*, 25.

54. Monica Dall'Asta and Alessandra Chiarini, "Editor's Introduction: Found Footage: Women Without a Movie Camera," *Feminist Media Histories* 2.3 (2016): 1–10, 4.

55. Braune, "How to Analyze Texts," 252, 248.

56. Pier Paolo Pasolini, "The Screenplay as a 'Structure That Wants to Be Another Structure,'" in *Heretical Empiricism*, ed. Louise K. Barnett, trans. Ben Lawton and Louise K. Barnett (Bloomington: Indiana University Press, 1988), 187–96, 189; "agentic force" is Braune's phrase in "How to Analyze Texts," 241.

57. Maya Deren, "Cinematography: The Creative Use of Reality," *Daedalus* 89.1 (1960): 150–67, 154–55.

58. Catherine Fowler, "Remembering Cinema 'Elsewhere': From Retrospection to Introspection in the Gallery Film," *Cinema Journal* 51.2 (2012): 26–45, 37. See Stanley Cavell, *The World Viewed: Reflections on the Ontology of Film*, 2nd ed. (Cambridge, MA: Harvard University Press, 1979); Victor Burgin, *The Remembered Film* (London: Reaktion Books, 2004); and Christian Keathley, *Cinephilia and History, or the Wind in the Trees* (Bloomington: Indiana University Press, 2006).

59. Fowler, "Remembering Cinema 'Elsewhere,'" 36; Pierre Huyghe, interviewed in Fabian Stech, *J'ai parlé avec Lavier, Annette Messager, Sylvie Fleury,*

Hirschhorn, Pierre Huyghe, Delvoye, D.G.-F., Hou Hanru, Sophie Calle, Ming, Sans et Bourriaud* (Dijon: Presses du Réel, 2007), 144. On the suspension between the past and the present in *Some Chance Operations,* see Giovanna Zapperi, "Women's Reappearance: Rethinking the Archive in Contemporary Art—Feminist Perspectives," *Feminist Review* 105 (2013): 21–47.

60. Made simultaneously, Madansky's *ESFIR* and Pearlman's *I want to make a film about women* (2019) each drew on Anastasia Kostina's English translation of Shub's script. Whereas Madansky's open, observational film takes its temporal sense from the lives of the women it documents, Pearlman borrows a rapid editing style from the Soviet women Constructivist filmmakers of the 1920s and makes more overt her attempt to discover strategies for responding to incomplete film materials.

61. Fowler, "Remembering Cinema 'Elsewhere'," 28. Fowler borrows the term "undead" from Thomas Elsaesser: "Because of its undead nature, the cinema perhaps does not have a history (of periods, styles, modes). It can only have fans, clans and believers, forever gathering to revive a fantasm or a trauma, a memory and an anticipation." Elsaesser, "Specularity and Engulfment: Francis Ford Coppola and Bram Stoker's *Dracula,*" in *Contemporary Hollywood Cinema,* ed. Steve Neale and Murray Smith (London: Routledge, 1998), 191–208, 206.

62. Bruno, *Streetwalking on a Ruined Map,* 236.

63. Dall'Asta and Gaines, "Constellations," 19.

64. Dall'Asta and Gaines, "Constellations," 21.

65. Miranda July, *It Chooses You* (San Francisco: Canongate Books, 2011), 159.

66. Fowler, "Remembering Cinema 'Elsewhere'," 36; Fenwick, Foster, and Eldridge, introduction, 2.

67. João Biehl and Peter Locke, foreword to *Unfinished: The Anthropology of Becoming,* ed. Biehl and Locke (Durham, NC: Duke University Press, 2017), ix–xiii, ix.

68. Benjamin Aldes Wurgaft, "Walter Benjamin and the Counterfactual Imagination," *History and Theory* 49.3 (2010): 361–83, 380.

69. Wurgaft, "Walter Benjamin," 370.

70. On the limits of speculation about what might have been, see Fenwick, Foster, and Eldridge, introduction, 1–4.

71. Hartman, "Venus in Two Acts," 11; Lisa Lowe, "The Intimacies of Four Continents," in *Haunted by Empire: Geographies of Intimacy in North American History,* ed. Ann Laura Stoller (Durham, NC: Duke University Press, 2006), 191–212, 208.

72. See Elizabeth Grosz, *Time Travels: Feminism, Nature, Power* (Durham, NC: Duke University Press, 2005), 71–89; Tina Campt's theorization of the tense of the Black feminist present and future in *Listening to Images* (Durham, NC: Duke University Press, 2017); and Domietta Torlasco's discussion of digital film works that "open the past of the archive to mutations that belong to the future," "dispossessing the past of its priority over the present" as it "remembers not only what happened but also what did not happen in our cinematic past (and yet might have, under different conditions), what 'will have happened' by virtue of these eccentric appropriations," in *The Heretical Archive: Digital*

Memory at the End of Film (Minneapolis: University of Minnesota Press, 2013), xiv. Torlasco's work is especially relevant to our project; similar to the works discussed in the third part of this book, Torlasco examines "fundamentally incomplete projects, without a clear beginning or a definitive end." Torlasco, *Heretical Archive,* xii.

73. Grosz, *Time Travels,* 74.

74. Dall'Asta and Gaines, "Constellations," 22.

75. Ësfir' Shub, "From My Experience," in "Esfir Shub: Selected Writings," trans. Anastasia Kostina, intro. Liubov Dyshlyuk, *Feminist Media Histories* 2.3 (2016): 11–28, 18.

76. This phrase was used in *Big Miss Moviola* zines and advertisements from 1996 on, as Smulevitz notes in "'Girl, If You Make the Movie,'" 18n8.

77. Paula Amad, *Counter-Archive: Film, the Everyday, and Albert Kahn's Archives de la Planète* (New York: Columbia University Press, 2010), 19.

78. Genevieve Yue, *Girl Head: Feminism and Film Materiality* (New York: Fordham University Press, 2021), 17.

PART ONE

Unfound Objects

CHAPTER 1

Never

JANE M. GAINES

The difference between "*never* again" and "*never* having been" is both enormous and moot. The distinction is enormous because of the chasm between existence and nonexistence, that which *was* and no longer *is* or that which *wasn't at all*. If something "had been" but cannot be "again" because now it is "not," it can at least be said that it *was,* that it *had once* existed. Then again, from the point of view of the historical present, the distinction between "*never* again," as in "*never* again to be" as opposed to "*never* having been" is moot (if "never" means "not ever" as opposed to "no longer"). For in both cases—"*never* again" and "*never* having been"—there is now nothing at all. There is nothing to point to and nothing to recover.

In philosophical terms, however, the difference is not even negligible because if the answer to the contemporary question "Does it now exist?" is "no," this implies that "what once was" might never be found to exist. Then again, the distinction between "*never* again" and "*never* having been" is important for archivists and historians of motion picture film who hold out hope of "again"—that is, of discovering the once existing but now "lost" silent-era film print, what we're calling the "Unfound Object." To be clear, then, the "Unfound Object" is in a crucial way unlike that which I'm exploring here: the "*never* having been" as the *condition of nonexistence* of the project that *never was* completed or the motion picture that *never did* exist. Or, a correction: we are concerned with motion picture film that was never completed. Here, however, we would be remiss not to parse the gradations within the category of "never made" motion picture, those ranging from having been written but *never* produced to having been publicly announced but *never* shot to having been shot but *never* released.

In motion picture archival circles, lament may be mixed with hope, expectations held out as we circulate the estimated percentages of silent-era films that survived and search holdings lists of the International Federation of Film Archives for titles we think may be extant, even if they remain unrestored and often incomplete.[1] We may have mourned this phenomenon as loss, often in the mode of what in 2007 I termed the "melodramatization of archival restoration" in reference to the decomposing image, the remains of a nitrate film print, the digital recovery of which enacted a "return from the dead," so to speak.[2] Yet sixteen years later, in chapter 2 of this volume, Maggie Hennefeld's study of French comedienne Léontine characterizes feminist archival searching as a "hopeful collective project." But still the question arises as to whether, in contrast with extant incomplete prints, we should similarly lament the titles that were dreamed about and even scripted and perhaps also cast and rehearsed, but *never,* from preproduction through release, *never* finally "made." Imagine projects that were conceptualized and even promoted as titles but that *never* finally materialized as motion picture films to be distributed and exhibited. Now think what critical interest is sparked in such films by calling them "never mades."

At the outset this research appears to be a bleak exercise—to define the *conditions of nonexistence* of the motion picture that was "never made." However, as a feminist approach, the critical possibilities are ripe for exploration especially considering that the "never made" builds on the ongoing historiographic project of numerically counting the films likely to have been produced by women in the silent era worldwide.[3] We can expect theoretical challenges ahead, such as those posed by how to study a phenomenon when no archival motion picture film object exists because it was *never* produced or how to treat the nuances in the *unfinished* "never made" in contrast with the *never-having-been-made-at-all* "never made." Then there arises the issue as to what percentage of a project constitutes an original "work," not to mention the thorny question as to whether a work portion should be considered "art."[4]

This is just to remind ourselves that a prerequisite to the consideration of aesthetic merit is usually that the work needs to take visible or audible form. But what appears here to be a drawback can be seen as an advantage. Considered as part of a new initiative in feminist film and media studies, the problematic of the "never made" is an ideal opportunity for developing a speculative history approach to research and writing.⁵ Thus my recent segue into "counterfactual speculation," the approach that in asking "What if?" encourages us to diverge from established knowledge and to wonder what it was that "could have been" if conditions had been different.⁶ We return to the archive to study the historical conditions of missed opportunity, wasted talent, and frustrated attempt, documenting the production histories of the more-or-less nearly but finally "never made." What is new here in feminist historiography? The counterfactual "thought experiment," as literary theorist Catherine Gallagher proposes, entails a shift from established fact to hypothetical "alternate" narrative.⁷ Such experiments offer opportunities for feminist scholars to imagine other scenarios for "never mades," entailing "alternate" sets of circumstances in which motion picture projects are not abandoned but are instead realized.

We're considering stories that women producers wanted to make as moving picture films for the screen but *never could,* putting emphasis on *why* these women "couldn't" as well as what challenges to empirical research methods we face in taking up the study of that which is understood as *"never* having been." We're especially interested in the *never* from the standpoint of what *might have* been "if it had not been for" historically specific barriers to entry. For women in the early motion picture industries, with many gaining experience from the 1910s in the United States as well as Europe, there might have been the expertise but not the opportunity. Women's names were often attached to motion picture film projects advertised as going into production based on nothing more than a scenario. Then, far from industry centers, countless screenplays were written, some encouraged by the correspondence courses offered by the Palmer Photoplay Corporation advertised in the pages of fan magazines.⁸ Written and rewritten but *never* produced, these "never mades" imagined outside the industry may be the most telling of all if we are studying the motion picture equivalent of what author Tillie Olsen described as "the never coming to book form at all."⁹

Perhaps these early scenarios represent stories their sometimes anonymous writers most wished to see on the screen in their local theaters—like the ideas for films solicited by Miranda July from women and girls on the streets of Portland, Oregon, in the mid-1990s, discussed in this book's introduction. But first, before we turn to two examples from the silent era, let's ask about the opposite of our category of silent-era motion picture films imagined but *"never* made" by women. For there is a long legacy of cultural investment in works that, by virtue of the *conditions of their nonexistence,* have come to have a strangely idealized status. Incomplete or unrealized or completely destroyed, some works are culturally elevated by such negative conditions. Why these works and not others?

"MISSING" WORKS AND CULTURAL VALUATION

The French theorist Henri Lefebvre's *The Missing Pieces* (2004) is a slim book comprised only of lists. Devoid of critical commentary and analysis, it is a tribute to works of culture and architecture that do not now exist. These works are "missing" either because they are thought to be "lost" or because they never materialized or were incompletely realized; in some cases they were, in our terms, "never made." Lefebvre, however, doesn't distinguish between "having once existed" and "never having existed," and all these lamented works are "missing" for him. What these works have in common is not only that they currently *do not exist* but that their cultural value is not in question despite the problem of how to apply aesthetic criteria to that which might never have existed. Lefebvre's compendium of cases is an uneven mixture of the ancient and the popular, the *never* and the *no longer*—the latter being works that were produced but have been lost or were destroyed, ranging from the works burned in the Library of Alexandria in 47 BC to the mementos of African American singer Aretha Franklin, lost in a fire at her archive in Detroit, Michigan, in 2002.[10]

Where we insist on a difference between those works that "had been" and those that "had *never*" been, Lefebvre does not. Here is a further test of the difference between the "*never* again" that *had once been*—the Alexandrian Library and Aretha Franklin's archive—and those cultural objects that *never* were but which, although "*never* having been," in Lefebvre's imagination at least *could have been*. Some of the works of culture Lefebvre lists as "missing" nearly did exist, which scholars know because of references to them, as, for example, Virginia Woolf's journal notation in 26 May 1924: "My thoughts are completely occupied by *The Hours,*" the novel that, Lefebvre laments, "would never be written," although Lefebvre is not exactly correct here because, as is well known, a version of *The Hours* became the novel *Mrs. Dalloway.* Subsequent critical attention and creative resurrection that included a 2002 motion picture turned the novel notable for its very "never having been" into a cultural milestone.[11]

But Lefebvre's *Missing Pieces* is also important for our purposes because of what emerges as a key difference but also a similarity between literary and moving picture works. The similarity is in how hopes are pinned to proven artistic talent, as we will see. The difference is that the economics of industrial production don't figure into the making of Lefebvre's sad "wish list." The usage of *"never"* encourages us to ask if there should be a special kind of disappointment reserved for motion pictures that never materialized in contrast with novels that were never written. After all, how many would-be writers have sketched out plots for novels that they would never start writing, let alone start but never finish writing? Further, in addition to the emphasis on established talent, mostly male, Lefebvre's list of the missing betrays a cultural bias in favor of completed "works" as opposed to fragments. But in the context of motion picture history, "fragment" could mean either the partially completed production or the reel of unattributed footage remaining after the physical decomposition of a multireel feature. The historian Eric DeKuyper has made an influential defense on behalf of the aesthetic value of anonymous footage, "missing pieces" in another sense of parts separated from a whole. Such footage, he says, has been "non-existent in the eyes of film history," which, as he observes, has been based on "identities" procured by the study of complete "works" and their "authors."[12]

Turning back to Lefebvre's list of motion picture projects, the irony here is that some of his examples link "authors" with stalled film projects, the consequence of which was that when no "works of authorship" were produced, their merely hypothetical existence is still guaranteed by authorship. On Lefebvre's "missing" lists are some motion picture film titles, one of which is the well-known *It's All True* (Orson Welles, 1941), which was "never completed," he says.[13] Although later a documentary on that "unfinished" project as well as significant scholarship effectively brought Welles's project "into being," the director's *auteur* status confirms a legitimacy that elevated its "never made" condition such that it achieved the dual status of "never having been made" *and* "remade." One wonders why only established *auteur* director–producers inspire the project of what we might call "critical completion" in which scholars "finish" an auteur project like *It's All True*. And let's not fail to note that even if later scholars and filmmakers effectively "finish" Welles's film for him, it still remains a Welles "work of authorship."

Or, to offer another example, Lefebvre gives German director Rainer Werner Fassbinder credit for having written a scenario for the salacious 1921 novel *Cocaine* by Pitigrilli (a pseudonym for Dino Segre) that "was never filmed," another case of artistic value attributed to a work that never existed.[14] In addition to adaptations of acclaimed novelists by auteur directors, Lefebvre is interested in collaborations that never came to fruition, such as that between French thriller director Jean-Pierre Melville and crime writer André Héléna. Betraying an impatience with the realities of motion picture production, Lefebvre remarks that "the film isn't made" because Héléna refused to shoot it in the United States.[15] *Missing Pieces* also references a never-made film adaptation of the Algerian war torture exposé *The Question* by Henri Alleg (1958). Then Lefebvre recalls that the Greek-French director Nikos Papatakis planned to engage Jean-Paul Sartre to write the screenplay and Alain Resnais to direct. But, says Lefebvre, in the present tense, "the project is abandoned."[16] Likewise, a film collaboration between the author Jean Genet and the director Bertrand Tavernier "never came about."[17] Worst of all, it seems, a sequel to *Chronicle of a Summer* (Jean Rouch and Edgar Morin, 1961) "would never be shot."[18]

So much is riding on so little. One can't help but note that Lefebvre's "missing" motion picture film list reads like another "great man" artist approach to film culture held over from literary and art historical criticism. I note Lefebvre's preferences for male "outlaws" and their works—Genet, Héléna, Alleg's *La Question* (censored in France for its depiction of French war crimes), Pitigrilli's *Cocaine* (banned by the Vatican for references to sex and drug use), and Papatakis's *Les Abysses* (refused screening at the Cannes Film Festival in 1963). This list thus replicates the deep flaw in auteur theory that has for too long set up motion pictures to be compared with other "works of art," forgetting the expense of industrial production that is the foundation of moving pictures and broadcast television, not to mention the multiplicity of creative contributions that auteurism cannot accommodate, let alone imagine. To complain that a project would "never be shot" is to mystify the economic vicissitudes of motion picture production and furthermore to evidence an elite, literary obliviousness of the range of ways in which motion picture films have historically run into difficulties—shot but never developed, shot but never edited because of an unpaid lab bill, or pitched to a producer who never raised the funds to begin shooting.

The recurrence of the term "never" in *Missing Pieces* effects a categorical lumping that consistently fails to recognize the economic exigencies of making technologically rendered works. There appears to be no cognizance of the calculation of investment and return that is historically so fundamental to the industrial commerce that includes art house cinema as well as much documentary work. Neither does the kind of technical team labor supporting the creative input of musicians and set designers, not to mention actors, figure into the calculation of the possibilities for the existence as opposed to the nonexistence of the twentieth-century culture of motion photographic works of fiction as well as nonfiction. For in the first two decades and up to the present, motion picture production companies, no matter how small, had to be capitalized. There is the companion story of silent-era independent companies, a few male-headed such as Sessue Hayakawa's Haworth Pictures, and especially those started by women in the silent era in Karen Mahar's two phases: 1911–15 and 1916–23.[19] Particularly in these two phases, the many cases of new companies named and press releases announcing motion pictures that were going into production are evidence of an understudied phenomenon—an overwhelming number of silent motion pictures planned but "never made."[20] Here is also the story of how, over the first and second decades, banks finally became involved in financing only after having been convinced of the stability of some companies that turned out to be those run by men but not women.[21]

So, not surprisingly, the question of producing motion pictures, which entails setting up companies and securing funding to rent studios and equipment and hire actors and crew, was also a matter of men enabling or thwarting efforts, even when women had the experience to plan and to carry a project to completion. She "could have" and yet she "couldn't" because male partners so often stood in the way. These partners might have been husbands or lovers as well as potential investors. Yet despite the difficulties of securing independent financing, we can't overlook the sheer number of silent-era women worldwide who at some point took up the title of "director" or "producer," which suggests a short historical period of possibility for women filmmakers and, at the same time, exemplifies the variable *conditions of nonexistence* during this period, given how many of these women's production plans "never" come to fruition.[22]

FROM "NEVER" TO "WHAT IF?"

Our topic of "never" becomes more interesting when we undertake the serious study of an entire category of works that were imagined or proposed by female producers in the silent era.[23] Representative of such a fertile imagination is Anita Stewart. In 1918 she agreed to work with

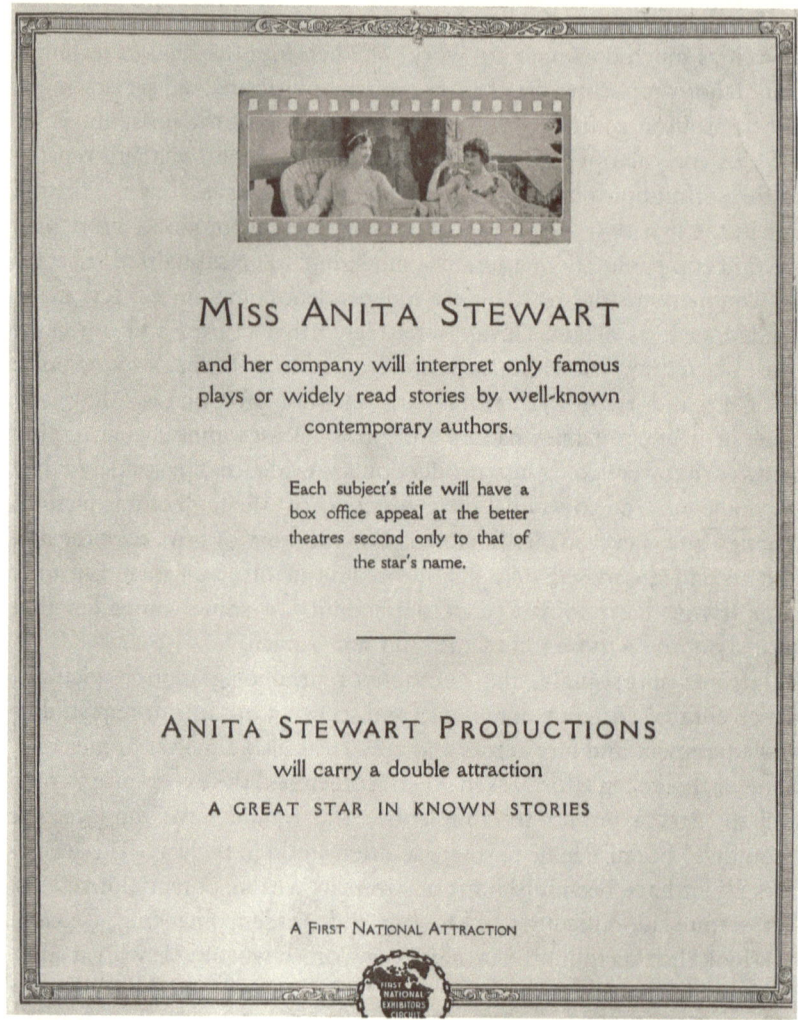

FIGURE 1.1 Anita Stewart Productions First National Exhibitors Circuit advertisement. Private collection.

the distributor Louis B. Mayer who, although he had little producing experience, wanted to finance a production company. Mayer needed a star actress, hence Anita Stewart Productions (figure 1.1).

Asked in a 1919 interview what stories she wanted to produce as films in the future, Stewart's reply provides the basis of the kind of speculation we can now start to undertake as an answer to Lefebvre's *Missing Pieces*. What came immediately to mind for Stewart were film adaptations of novels whose female heroines had been used and betrayed by men: David Graham Phillips's *Susan Lenox: Her Fall and Rise* (1917) and Theodore Dreiser's *Sister Carrie* (1900). In answer to her interviewer, Stewart affords us a theme and a narrative to complement our theorization of "never"—while also demonstrating a canny awareness of the kinds of stories that would appeal to other women, too few of which were produced in the first decade.[24] Hugh Neely, evaluating Stewart's career, thinks that within Mayer's company Stewart, who had no say in what was acquired for her, came to resent Mayer's moralistic story choices.[25] In 1922, when her contract with Mayer was up, Anita Stewart Productions came to an end as well.[26] But when we say that film adaptations of *Susan Lenox* and *Sister Carrie* would "never" be made by the actress-producer who envisioned them, we are implying what might better be spelled out. For there is a particular inflection we want to give to "never" as in "never would because never could," as in she had "no chance" under social as well as economic circumstances.[27] I emphasize the social because of the way that the contemporary #MeToo moment has led us to investigate the career setbacks as well as physical and emotional abuse suffered by women in the first decades of motion pictures.[28]

Now to recognize how many women were involved in motion picture production as directors, writers, and producers requires a more constructive critical response to "never." However, we might begin by cautioning about situations in which a motion picture production was imagined "for" a particular woman as opposed to one that a woman systematically set up over the course of a career. Let's consider the case of the actress Miriam Nesbitt (figure 1.2). Nesbitt was promoted in at least two trade press articles as the first woman in the Edison Company to direct, having been given a chance with *A Close Call*, a scenario she had ostensibly written. In his 1977 study *Early Women Directors*, Anthony Slide refers to the publicity the Edison Company circulated in the summer of 1915 around this project. However, in considering Nesbitt in the chapter titled "Other Women Directors," Slide comes to the conclusion that "there is no record that this film was ever released."[29] Another case of "never made"? We might consider Slide to be grasping at straws, given his inclusion of Nesbitt in a chapter on women directors; I find no evidence that she ever directed a film in her career at the Edison Company from 1910 to 1915.[30] However, today, in returning to the article announcing Nesbitt's directorial debut in *Moving Picture World* in the summer of 1915, we can engage in a more radical exercise

FIGURE 1.2 Miriam Nesbitt, Edison Company actress. Academy of Motion Picture Arts and Sciences.

than any scholar would have dared to propose in the 1970s, the early years of historical excavation of women's films.[31]

There is another way into the "never made" motion picture that initiates the beginning not the end of historical thinking. Instead of bemoaning the likelihood that so many proposed projects were "never made," we can turn clues left behind into the basis of a feminist historical intervention. After raising the question as to whether the motion picture was financed or whether it went into production and was or wasn't completed, we can shift to the counterfactual mode. Here is where we speculate: what if Miriam Nesbitt *had* written and directed *A Close Call?* The statements of fact in the *Moving Picture World* encourage us to think of her as the first woman to direct a production at the Edison Company—this is what is claimed. The article in question describes the plan to shoot both interior and exterior scenes in a six-week trip visiting Chicago, Illinois; Saint Paul, Minnesota; Portland, Oregon; and, in California, Los Angeles and San Diego. On a journey that is to end at the Panama Canal, Nesbitt will reportedly spend six days at Yellowstone Park and will represent the Edison Company in San Francisco at the Panama Pacific International Exposition in 1915. The plot, we are told, entails the heroine's pursuit of a missing man whom she must marry if she is to receive a fortune by a deadline.[32]

As original and intriguing as the idea may sound, this narrative is a gender inversion of the film *Personal* (Biograph, 1904), which was remade as *How the French Nobleman Found a Wife Through the New York Herald Personal Columns* (Edison Co., 1904) and *Meet Me at the Fountain* (Lubin, 1904), as well as *Matrimony's Speed Limit* (Solax, 1912), Alice Guy Blaché's version.[33] While in all four of these scenarios the male heroine must find a wife to marry by noon or lose his inheritance, Nesbitt's hypothetical *A Close Call* uses the same time deadline structure that in its very title promises to hinge the outcome on the difference of a minute. Ingeniously, however, the Nesbitt version, not a one-reel short but a four-reel feature, extends the chase across North America, first by train to the West Coast and from San Francisco by boat through the Panama Canal. The plan includes featuring the Panama Exposition and a sequence shot in San Francisco's Chinatown. A camera crew would have to have followed Nesbitt over half the continent by train and down the Pacific Coast by ocean liner.

The prohibitive expense of this multilocation shoot clues us to see the project as a complete fantasy—one likely invented for Nesbitt by an imaginative Edison publicist.[34] Yet what I propose about the case of such a motion picture "*never* having been made" is that it stimulates ideas as to what *could have been*. Answering the question "What if?," we posit Miriam Nesbitt as writing, directing, and playing an adventure heroine who actively pursues the missing man in a thrilling effort to claim her fortune against odds and obstacles. What would be required of the heroine is the ingenuity and cunning of the serial queen heroine, her heroics not, however, confined to an episode-long sequence but extended over four reels as well as across a continent.[35] At four reels this would have been an early Edison feature, albeit a short one of an estimated hour's length. Let's recall that 1915 was a key year of transition from the short to the feature fiction film, and, more important, that the Edison Company did not enter into the feature film competition with other companies as it was in decline.[36]

We can also imagine Nesbitt as part of the legacy of the action heroine, which I date from 1909 and to which the Edison Studios contributed the popular twelve-episode *What Happened to Mary?* (1912–13)—a series in which Nesbitt appeared regularly. Some such heroines moved between the roles of actress, director, and writer-producer, including Gene Gauntier, Helen Holmes, and Grace Cunard.[37] Other models include the actress Helen Gardner, who quit the Biograph Company to start her own company, which produced the feature *Cleopatra* (1912).[38] In Italy, Francesca Bertini, sharing director credit with Gustavo Serena, starred in *Assunta Spina* (Italy, 1915). In a later interview Bertini claimed responsibility for the "script, adaptation, setting and direction," and even editing—a reminder of how much work went uncredited on the early motion picture set.[39] Miriam Nesbitt, like Bertini, was a prolific actress, appearing between 1908 and 1917 in 144 short Edison Company films. Thus to imagine one woman in 1915 helps to fill out what we imagine for others—another of whom is Lule Warrenton, whose efforts to take control of production I turn to now.

THE ALL-WOMAN FILM COMPANY AND *BARTERED FLESH*

One of the most seasoned actresses of the period, Lule Warrenton had eighty-eight credits for character actor work between 1913 and 1922. Like Miriam Nesbitt, what we know today about Warrenton also comes from industry trade press articles. However, the difference between the "never made" Edison Company *A Close Call* and the All-Woman Company's *Bartered Flesh* begins with the source of the information we now have about these two titles. In the years Nesbitt worked at the Edison Company, there is no record of any woman having been given the title of director or producer, although writer is another case. In 1914, *Moving Picture World* columnist Epes Sargent reported that at the Edison Company "everyone was writing stories."[40] A story about a well-known actress directing a thrilling cross-country feature film is also just that—another story—and this leads me to think about another story: one provoked by a single reference in Anthony Slide's later work *The Silent*

Feminists to "the first all-woman film company."⁴¹ What is remarkable is that while in 1923 this company received significant industry press, by the time of Second Wave feminism in the mid-1970s, the idea of an "all-woman film company" had to be reinvented, since women's movement film collectives were unaware of any precedents.

Slide's reference to "the first all-woman film company" stands out in his 1996 study. Who, we wonder, would give this initiative such a name? Then who would announce it so prominently between July and August 1923 in all the major trade papers? That the *Exhibitor Herald* modifies "the first all-woman film company" from a statement of fact to the qualified "believed to be the only one in the world" suggests that this industry trade paper took some license with a press release.⁴² The *Exhibitors Trade Review* adds the details that the company will shoot on the Sawyer-Lubin lot in San Diego and that Lule Warrenton is both president and general director.⁴³ But because the publication *Camera!* later elevates the promotional claim that the company is the "only one" of its kind "in America, in the world, or in film history," we wonder if the original press release copy was the work of one of the four founding women who envisioned this remarkable "all-women" alternative to the "all-maleness" of the Hollywood studio and claimed it for all time—as never before.⁴⁴

The most complete picture comes from *The Story World and Photodramatist,* which describes all the key "creative positions" as filled by women. In addition to Lule Warrenton, owner and "chief producer" as well as director, women also occupy the positions of "co-director, assistant director, script clerk, screen editor, title writer, continuity writer, and publicity director," with executive positions filled by Mrs. A. (Aides) B. Shute, Mrs. Katherine Chesnaye, and Miss Edith Kendall. These women have one thing in common, the article goes on, which is *not* that they all have industry experience as one might think. What they have in common is rather that they *don't* have experience, although all have taken a photoplay writing course.⁴⁵ The Palmer Photoplay Company—the "nationally-known photoplay-writing institution of Hollywood"—is credited with having certified these women as "qualified" after their course of training.⁴⁶ But the *Exhibitors Trade Review* of 14 July 1923 takes another angle, and instead of explaining the "all-woman" initiative as connected to the Photoplay course, mentions the writing talent of all three executives: Aides Shute is a novelist, Edith Kendall a writer, and Katherine Chesnaye a short story writer as well as a world traveler.⁴⁷ And so one might surmise from the mention of "publicity director" that one of these writers, acting in this capacity, had written and circulated the press release that aimed to promote this eye-catching idea of a company run only by women.

Of course, the motion picture dream factory has been reliant historically on the practice of circulating fantasies of pictures in development to the trades. Thus the trades have been characterized by exactly the kind of promotional hype circulated in July 1923 around the "All-Woman Film Company": "Preparations are on the way for making a large regular program of feature pictures, educationals and other films."[48] But a fantasy would not become a reality merely by announcing the formation of a company. The following month, the *Exhibitors Trade Review* listed in their column "The Barometer" the title *Bartered Flesh*, directed by Lule Warrenton, described as the first picture of the All-Women Film Company produced for independent release, on which shooting in San Diego was finishing that week.[49] This news, however, is the last of the information circulated about either the company or about *Bartered Flesh*, a title for which I have found neither advertisements nor reviews.

We arrive again at the motion picture that may have been written and shot but *never* edited, halted for lack of postproduction finishing funds. The unusual *conditions of nonexistence* in this instance have to do with the configuration of experience and talent around the title *Bartered Flesh*, which promises a sensational drama perhaps involving the sex trade and the crime world. Two references in the trades are clues to the impetus behind the "All-Woman" company project. Between the lines of the phrase "women will have the say in every detail," we read the experience of frustration owing to a lack of creative control and agency for women in the film industry.[50] Strangely, a concluding sentence adds that this company is evidence that a "talented 'outsider' can enter the film industry without 'working up from the bottom,'" when the exact opposite was true in this case.[51] Lule Warrenton—president, owner, director, producer—was, as I have noted, a highly seasoned industry player who between 1913 and 1922 had worked both inside the studio system as well as outside as an independent. The "All-Woman Film Company" was her last attempt to start a company on her own terms in the twilight of her career.[52]

It is not, then, as though we have nothing to go on when we speculate about the industry conditions that brought these women together, given that the "All-Woman" initiative was associated with a veteran actress who had completed a stage career and had experience ranging from running a theatrical touring company to starting a company within Universal Pictures, as well as working as an insider in an independent company, the Frieder Film Corporation. Noticeably, after such experience the phrase "will be written by and directed by women, and women will have the say in every detail" stands as a retort to "never having been given the chance."[53] We learn more about Lule "Mother" Warrenton from her son Gilbert Warrenton, who years later was interviewed by Kevin Brownlow about his career as a cinematographer, most notably in the 1920s at Universal Pictures. He says of his "remarkable" mother that she was nearly finished with a medical course of study at University of Michigan when she quit to take over her father's touring stock company. She moved from the theater into motion pictures around 1913 and at Universal came to be respected by the producer Carl Laemmle. Gilbert got his start there as assistant cameraman, learning from Anton Nagy, one of the first émigré directors who helped to develop a studio style that had its apotheosis in Universal horror.[54]

Perhaps it was Lule Warrenton's connection to Laemmle that explains the unusual opportunity she had to set up a company within that company to specialize in one-reel films for children, with her son Gilbert serving as photographer for this "Juvenile division." The first of these films, originally titled *Calling Lindy,* was announced as featuring Ernestine Jones, a "little colored child."[55] This unusual short miraculously survives as *When Little Lindy Sang* (1916), today standing out as an early attempt to address racial prejudice.[56] After three years at Universal, having played many character roles and directing one short, Warrenton left the company but continued her commitment to directing children's films, now for the Frieder Film Corporation.[57] An advertisement of 12 April 1917 in the *Motion Picture Studio Directory and Trade Annual* announces that Lule Warrenton as Author-Producer and Gilbert Warrenton as Cinematographer were joining the Chicago-based company, named for Irene M. Frieder—herself touted as the "only woman president of an American film corporation" (figure 1.3).[58] A more interesting question than whether this claim is true is the phenomenon of so many "onlys" as well as "firsts" associated with women working in this emerging industry, such acclamation a play on novelty as much as a celebration of achievement.

Working from a studio in Lankershim in North Hollywood, west of Burbank, the independent Frieder Company announced four projects in the *Motion Picture News* of 28 April 1917. *The Birds' Christmas Carol,* adapted from a story by Kate Douglas Wiggin, was to be followed by *The Littlest Fugitive* and *Hop o' My Thumb.*[59] Of these, only *The Birds' Christmas Carol,* a five-reel feature retitled *A Bit O Heaven* (1917), was completed and released (figure 1.4). Soon after, *Moving Picture World*

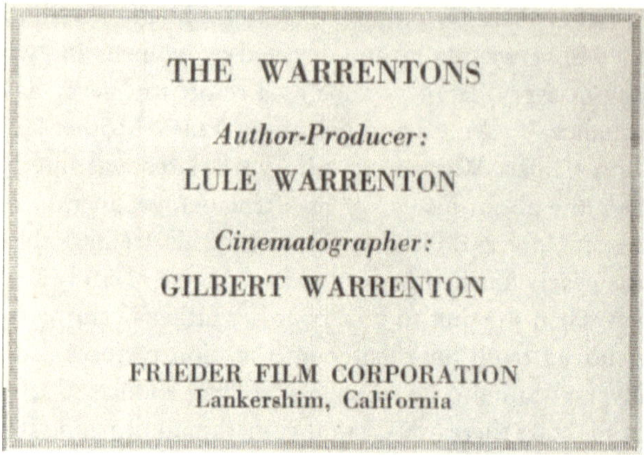

> **THE WARRENTONS**
>
> *Author-Producer:*
> LULE WARRENTON
>
> *Cinematographer:*
> GILBERT WARRENTON
>
> FRIEDER FILM CORPORATION
> Lankershim, California

FIGURE 1.3 Advertisement for the Frieder Film Corporation, *Motion Picture Studio Directory and Trade Annual* (12 April 1917).

reported on "Directress" Lule Warrenton, stating that *The Littlest Fugitive* was "finished," and that she was "beginning" *Hop o' My Thumb*.[60] The fourth and final Frieder title, *Star Dust*, was announced in June 1917.[61] We might infer from the reporting that of these films, one was distributed, another shot but not released, and two were announced as titles—if nothing else, a record of the ambition of this independent company during that short independent company phase of 1916 through 1923.

After the Frieder Film Company, it would be another six years before Lule Warrenton, then sixty-one-years-old, would start the "All-Women Film Company"—neither within the studio system nor another independent company but, finally, in a venture that would have been more "her own."[62] We can advance the hypothesis that her success at getting films shot was explained by her cinematographer son, whereas the challenge of getting them completed was the challenge of securing investment for completion. Here, then, is the point about "never" when we encounter the lament in conjunction with silent-era motion picture films by women. The economic conditions of production have historically been rigged against the industry outsider such that the question of a project's *conditions of nonexistence* needs to carry a corollary: Why weren't female-headed companies "bankable"? This question confronts the historical reality of financing that euphemistically "fell through." But rather than abandoning these embryonic projects, today we have a

FIGURE 1.4 *The Birds' Christmas Carol* (subsequently retitled *A Bit O Heaven*) advertisement, *The Moving Picture World* (10 March 1917).

chance to speculate about their completion as well as to marvel at the determination, confidence, and bravado of Lule Warrenton and her partners in founding the all-woman company and announcing *Bartered Flesh* as having been shot.[63]

That the title *Bartered Flesh* suggests the metaphor of women exchanging their bodies for what men wanted locates it in the tradition of *Susan Lennox: Her Rise and Fall,* the novel Anita Stewart wanted to adapt, or *Shoes* (1916), the Lois Weber Productions title in which a young girl "falls" because she sees no alternative to "selling" sexual favors. While the economics of women's sexual exchange for survival, the "bartering of flesh," may in the 1920s have been the basis of a social "rise and fall" narrative, the title also conjures an image of seamy sexual predation. Not surprisingly, a sleazy 1966 novel titled *Bartered Flesh* lured readers with the line "What She Was Selling Should Have Been Enough . . . "[64] Hence the title *Bartered Flesh* alone encourages our speculative inquiry—"What if" the "first all-woman company" had completed such a social issue picture? "What then?" Here I urge the beginning not the end of historical thinking, considering that in returning to these cases we participate in a work of revitalization in which the "all-women film company" becomes part of a larger story of women's work in motion pictures. This is not a story of exclusion, regret, and restitution, but one of what I call "critical completion": a story now titled "Never Again."

EPILOGUE: NEVER AGAIN

There is no more important dramatization of "Never" and the case for critical completion than Drusilla Dunjee Houston's screenplay "The Spirit of the South: The Maddened Mob" (alternately titled "The Maddened Mob: America's Shame"). Dunjee Houston, an African American historian of classics, attended a performance in her native Oklahoma of a theatrical production based on Thomas Dixon's 1905 novel *The Clansman: A Historical Romance of the Ku Klux Klan.* In answer, Dunjee Houston began to write a screenplay in verse form. As contributing editor for the *Black Dispatch,* the newspaper her brother founded, as well as a prolific journalist herself, she might have had the opportunity to publish portions of that screenplay; but although she continued to work on the project over several decades, it seems that Dunjee Houston never did. In 1933 she wrote to a friend that it was the fear of the Sedition and Espionage Act as well as the resurgence of the Ku Klux Klan that made her hesitant to publish the work.[65]

"Spirit of the South" contributes to the African American rebuke of *The Birth of a Nation* (D. W. Griffith, 1915) and, as such, places Dunjee Houston in the company of African American producer-director Oscar Micheaux and his epic *Within Our Gates* (1919). Dunjee Houston was imagining a screenplay for a motion picture that would denounce *The Clansman* a decade before D. W. Griffith produced his loose adaptation of Dixon's fiction as *The Birth of a Nation*.[66] So I close by quoting from that unpublished verse screenplay, specifically the subsection "A Place of Tragic Memories":

> In the years that followed the Civil War and Freedom;
> Here two gentle creatures toiled and saved the sum;
> To buy this vine clad home;
> then the young wife did sing;
> As from the washboard she would carefully wring;
> The rich man's clothes so oft done for meager pay;
> From early morn 'til twilight she worked away.

Is there a dramatization of race and class difference that needs to be produced more than this one written over a century ago? Here is a decided move away from the lament of "lost to history"—a mixed metaphor that never made sense—as well as from the exhaustion of complaints about exclusion. The cause of "Never Again" answers the political analysis of "never having been" as consequence of "never having had the chance"; "Never Again" answers "Never" with a commitment to produce Drusilla Dunjee Houston's screenplay "Now."

NOTES

1. David Pierce, *The Survival of American Silent Feature Films: 1912–1929* (Washington, DC: Council on Library and Information Resources and the Library of Congress, 2013), 21–25.

2. Jane M. Gaines, "Sad Songs of Nitrate," *Camera Obscura* 22.3 [66] (Fall 2007): 171–78, 174.

3. See Jane Gaines, Radha Vatsal, and Monica Dall'Asta, eds., *Women Film Pioneers Project* (New York: Columbia University Libraries, 2013), https://wfpp.columbia.edu; along with the following databases: *Women They Talk About*, American Film Institute, https://aficatalog.afi.com/women-they-talk-about/; and *The Aesthetics of Access: Visualizing Research Data on Women in Film History*, Universität Marburg, Germany, www.uni-marburg.de/en/fb09/institutes/media-studies/research/research-projects/davif.

4. See Giovanna Fossati, *From Grain to Pixel: The Archival Life of Film in Transition*, 3rd ed. (Amsterdam: Amsterdam University Press, 2018), 161–70.

5. See Allyson Nadia Field, ed., "Speculative Approaches to Media Histories," special double issue, *Feminist Media Histories* 8.2 and 8.3 (2022).

6. See Jane M. Gaines, "Counterfactual Speculation: What If Antonia Dickson Had Invented the Kinetoscope?," *Feminist Media Histories* 8.3 (2022): 8–34.

7. The concept is demonstrated in Catherine Gallagher, *Telling It Like It Wasn't: The Counterfactual Imagination in History and Fiction* (Chicago: University of Chicago Press, 2018), 1.

8. See Ann Morey, "'Have You the Power?': The Palmer Photoplay Corporation and the Film Viewer/Author in the 1920s," *Film History* 9 (1997): 300–19.

9. Tillie Olsen, "Ways of Being Silent," *Harper's Magazine* (October 1965), https://harpers.org/archive/2015/05/ways-of-being-silent/.

10. Henri Lefebvre, *The Missing Pieces,* trans. David L. Sweet (2004; Los Angeles: Semiotext[e], 2014), 43, 36.

11. Lefebvre, *Missing Pieces,* 17. See Michael Cunningham, *The Hours* (New York: Farrar, Straus and Giroux, 1998), a novel about Woolf's writing of *Mrs. Dalloway* based on the question of the relation between that novel and the novel she titled "The Hours," https://lithub.com/michael-cunningham-on-the-novel-that-would-become-mrs-dalloway-2/, accessed 15 October 2021. The motion picture *The Hours* (Stephen Daldry, 2002) is based on the Cunningham novel.

12. Eric DeKuyper, "Anyone for an Aesthetic of Film History?," *Film History* 6.1 (1994): 100–109, 104. For a challenge to the assumption that early cinema was "authored," see Jane M. Gaines, "Anonymities: Uncredited and 'Unknown' Contributors in Early Cinema," *A Companion to Early Cinema,* ed. André Gaudreault, Nicholas Dulac, and Santiago Hidalgo (Hoboken, NJ: Wiley-Blackwell, 2012).

13. Lefebvre, *Missing Pieces,* 19. But the documentary *It's All True: Based on an Unfinished Film by Orson Welles* (1993), re-released in 2020, kept alive the idea of what would have been Welles's third film. See Catherine L. Benamou, *It's All True: Orson Welles's Pan-American Odyssey* (Berkeley: University of California, 2007).

14. Lefebvre, *Missing Pieces,* 81.
15. Lefebvre, *Missing Pieces,* 41.
16. Lefebvre, *Missing Pieces,* 43.
17. Lefebvre, *Missing Pieces,* 45.
18. Lefebvre, *Missing Pieces,* 78.

19. See Karen Ward Mahar, "'A "Her-Own-Company" Epidemic': Stars as Independent Producers," in *Women Filmmakers in Early Hollywood* (Baltimore, MD: Johns Hopkins University Press, 2006), 154–78. For further illustration of Mahar's two waves, and an explanation of the kinds of companies women put their names on in the United States, see Jane M. Gaines and Radha Vatsal, "Women's Producing Companies: 'Her Own' or Not Her Own?," in "How Women Worked in the US Silent Film Industry," *Women's Film Pioneers Project,* https://wfpp.columbia.edu/essay/how-women-worked-in-the-us-silent-film-industry/#Womens_Producing_Companies_Her_Own_or_Not_Her_Own.

20. For the historical parameters that define a place from which to start, see Jane M. Gaines, *Pink-Slipped: What Happened to Women in the Silent Film Industries?* (Urbana: University of Illinois Press, 2018), 23–30.

21. On finance capital, see Gaines, *Pink-Slipped*, 28–29; and Mahar, *Women Filmmakers*, 170–71. Mark Cooper concurs with Mahar in *Universal Women: Filmmaking and Institutional Change in Early Hollywood* (Urbana: University of Illinois Press), xvii.

22. See Mark Lynn Anderson, "The Silent Screen, 1895–1927," in *Producing*, ed. Jon Lewis (New Brunswick, NJ: Rutgers University Press), 15–35; see also Gaines, *Pink-Slipped*, 25, and Gaines and Vatsal, "How Women Worked in the US Silent Film Industry."

23. The question as to the number of those who worked as or were given the symbolic title of "producer" as opposed to those who worked as "director" is still unresolved.

24. Grace Kingsley, "Anita Stewart, Producer," *Los Angeles Times*, 5 January 1919, III, 1. Graham Phillips's *Susan Lenox: Her Rise and Fall* was later adapted as a Greta Garbo vehicle, *Susan Lenox (Her Fall and Rise)* (Robert Z. Leonard, 1931). I contend that *Shoes* (Lois Weber, 1916) can be seen as a version of Theodore Dreiser's *Sister Carrie*; see Gaines, *Pink-Slipped*, 71–94.

25. Hugh Neely, "Anita Stewart," in *Women Film Pioneers Project*, https://wfpp.columbia.edu/pioneer/ccp-anita-stewart/.

26. DeWitt Bodeen, "Anita Stewart," in *From Hollywood: The Careers of 15 Great American Stars* (South Brunswick, NJ: A.S. Barnes, 1976), 125. Mahar says that Mayer was "inspired" to start Anita Stewart Productions, Inc. the year after Lewis J. Selznick started the Clara Kimball Young Company in 1916. Mayer offered the star three times what she was making at the Vitagraph Company, where she had been unhappy, and produced fifteen films with her. See Mahar, *Women Filmmakers*, 159.

27. See Gaines, *Pink-Slipped*, 193–94, for more on how women's companies were considered "unbusinesslike," and reference to some examples such as actress-director-producer Nell Shipman duped by a distributor; actress Ethel Grandin, exploited by her husband and brother-in-law in the formation of Grandin Films; and Gloria Swanson, rudely ignored by Will Hayes in negotiations around her *Sadie Thompson* (1928) project for Gloria Swanson Productions.

28. See Kerry McElroy, "Class Acts: A Sociocultural History of Women, Labour, and Migration in Hollywood," PhD dissertation (Concordia University, 2021), for the first history of sexual abuse as it relates to women's employment in the first decades of the industry.

29. Anthony Slide, *Early Women Directors* (Cranbury, NJ: A.S. Barnes, 1977), 103.

30. In *The Silent Feminists: America's First Women Directors* (Lanham, MD: Scarecrow Press, 1996), Anthony Slide describes how in 1972 he was beginning research for the *American Film Institute Catalog: Feature Films, 1911–1920* and discovered references in trade papers to films directed by women. Today we would want to call attention to the difference between the trade press article based on a press release and the production and release of the film under the title circulated. See Slide, *Silent Feminists*, v.

31. "Miriam Nesbitt Is First Woman Director for Edison," *Motion Picture News* 12.5 (1915): 44.

32. "Miriam Nesbitt, Dsrector [sic]," *Moving Picture World* (7 August 1915): 976; "Miriam Nesbitt Is First Woman Director for Edison," *Motion Picture News*.

33. Perhaps the earliest article on the feud between the Edison and Biograph companies over Edison's "remake" of the Biograph title *Personal* is David Levy, "Edison Sales Policy and the Continuous Action Film, 1904–1906," in *Film Before Griffith*, ed. John Fell (Berkeley: University of California Press), 207–18. Alice Guy-Blaché's version, however, has been overlooked in the continued discussions of early copyright that reference these films.

34. "Wright to Direct Miss Nesbitt," *Moving Picture World* (20 November 1915): 1470. Nesbitt's next project was as actress in *The Catspaw* (1916), to be directed by George Wright, and there is every evidence of this film having been completed—advertised, distributed, and reviewed.

35. See Marina Dahlquist, "Introduction: Why Pearl?" in *Exporting Pauline: Pearl White and the Serial Film Craze*, ed. Marina Dahlquist (Champaign-Urbana: University of Illinois Press, 2013), 1–23.

36. Eileen Bowser explains that there was no exactitude when it came to designating multireel films as features as opposed to "shorts," in *The Transformation of Cinema, 1907–1915: History of the American Cinema*, vol. 2 (Berkeley: University of California Press, 1994), 191.

37. See Gaines, *Pink-Slipped*, 19–24.

38. Dorin Gardner Schumacher, "Helen Gardner," in *Women Film Pioneers Project*, https://wfpp.columbia.edu/pioneer/ccp-helen-gardner/.

39. Monica Dall'Asta, "Francesca Bertini," in *Women Film Pioneers Project*, https://wfpp.columbia.edu/pioneer/francesca-bertini/.

40. Epes Winthrop Sargent, "The Literary Side of the Motion Picture World," *Moving Picture World* 21.2 (11 July 1914): 199.

41. Slide, *Silent Feminists*, 46.

42. "Company Composed of Women Organized to Make Films on Coast," *Exhibitors Herald* (14 July 1923): 25.

43. "All-Women Picture Company Enters Production Field," *Exhibitors Trade Review* (14 July 1923): 289.

44. "First All-Woman Film Company Launched," *Camera!* (April 1923): 10.

45. *The Story World and Photodramatist* (July 1923): 79.

46. *Story World and Photodramatist*, 79. Palmer Photoplay courses are referenced in "First All-Woman Film Company Launched," *Camera!*.

47. "All-Women Picture Company," *Exhibitors Trade Review*, 289.

48. "Company Composed of Women," *Exhibitors Herald*, 25

49. "All-Women Picture Company Enters Production Field." *Exhibitors Trade Review* 14.8 (June–August 1923): 334.

50. "All-Women Picture Company Enters Production Field, *Exhibitors Trade Review*, 289.

51. *Story World and Photodramatist*, 79.

52. This phase of Warrenton's career ended in 1921 as an actress in the character roles that made her famous, appearing for other companies in *The Jolt, Ladies Must Live, Blind Hearts*, and *The Dangerous Moment*.

53. "All-Women Picture Company Enters Production Field," *Exhibitors Trade Review,* 289.

54. Kevin Brownlow, "Movement in Moving Pictures: An Interview with Gilbert Warrenton, ASC," *Film History* 24 (January 2012): 324–33, 324. Gilbert Warrenton's credits include director Frank Borzage's *Humoresque* (Cosmopolitan Pictures, 1920), shot in New York for Hearst's Cosmopolitan Pictures. He was associated with the Caligari-inspired style of German émigré director Paul Leni, *The Cat and the Canary* (Universal Pictures, 1927).

55. *Motography* 16.3 (15 July 1916): 123.

56. Jane M. Gaines, "Lule Warrenton," in *Women Film Pioneers Project,* https://wfpp.columbia.edu/pioneer/ccp-lule-warrenton/.

57. *Moving Picture World* (8 September 1917): 1517.

58. *New York Dramatic Mirror* (5 August 1916): 18, 21.

59. *Motion Picture News* (28 April 1917): 2681. The American Film Institute Catalog says that *The Bird's Christmas Carol* was released as *A Bit O Heaven* on 16 June 1917, as a five-reel feature: https://catalog.afi.com/Search?searchField=MovieName&searchText=The+Bird%27s+Christmas+Carol&sortType=sortByRelevance.

60. *Motion Picture World* (28 April 1917): 625. But *Motion Picture News* (28 April 1917): 2681, says that *The Littlest Fugitive* had yet to be edited.

61. *Motion Picture News* (2 June 1917): 27.

62. See Mahar, "'A "Her-Own-Company" Epidemic.'" Mahar's reference in her title to the star company as an "epidemic" comes from "Close-ups," *Photoplay* (December 1916): 63–64. The negative associations attached to the "her own company" phenomenon included the implication that companies headed by women were standing in the way of the stabilization of a new industry that was needed to attract bank financing. See also Gaines and Vatsal, "How Women Worked in the US Silent Film Industry."

63. Monica Dall'Asta has suggested the idea that such projects might be treated as the "exceptional" or the "beautiful failure." However provocative this idea, as well as restorative a gesture, it may need to be followed by a feminist move that gives contemporary theorists more room to speculate. See Dall'Asta, "What It Means to Be a Woman: Theorizing Feminist Film History beyond the Essentialism/Constructivism Divide," in *Not So Silent: Women in Cinema before Sound,* ed. Astrid Söderberg Widding and Sofia Bull (Stockholm: Acta Universitatis Stockholmiensis, 2010), 39–47, 46–47.

64. "Helen Knew It Takes a Bad Girl to Give a Man a Good Time," declares the cover of Allan Jackson's *Bartered Flesh* (Las Vegas, NV: Neva Paperbacks, 1966); on the back cover we read: "What She Was Selling Should Have Been Enough for Any Guy—But The Stranger Wanted More."

65. Peggy Brooks-Bertram, "Drusilla Dunjee Houston," in *Women Film Pioneers Project,* https://wfpp.columbia.edu/pioneer/drusilla-dunjee-houston/.

66. See Jane M. Gaines, *Fire and Desire: Mixed Race Movies in the Silent Era* (Chicago: University of Chicago Press, 2001), 219–57.

CHAPTER 2

Catastrophic Optimism in the Name of Léontine

MAGGIE HENNEFELD

Who was Léontine? And where did she go after she vanished? I have spent the past decade playing hide-and-seek with her ghost. An internationally beloved enfant terrible, Léontine Penouillard was a tomboy, a prankster, a miscreant, and an anarchist whose insuppressible desires could never be contained by the material conditions of her social reality—so she blew it all up, episodically. From 1910 through 1912 the French film company Pathé Frères produced approximately twenty-four episodes of the *Léontine* series, fifteen of which are still extant (though several only in fragments). With titles such as *Léontine's Electric Battery* (September 1910), *Léontine Is Incorrigible* (August 1910), and *Léontine's Fireworks* (June 1910), the premise of each short film is simple: she fixates on an object to acquire or an objective to pursue and then obliviates anything that stands in her path. She was the queen of "unfound objects," attachments that unsettle the deceptive assumptions that cluster around their solidity.

But we know nothing about the actor who played Léontine. Nicknamed "Titine" in France and "Betty" in the United States and the United Kingdom, she electrified (if not electrocuted) the whole world and then vanished into thin air. Though many of her films survive, along with a chronological trail of short reviews and publicity ads, her labor conditions and life story bedevil any comprehensive attempt at recovery. This is all too appropriate, because no one took greater pleasure in the spectacle of blanket erasure than Titine. In *Léontine's Boat* (July

Catastrophic Optimism | 63

FIGURE 2.1 Léontine floods the house by sailing her toy boat indoors. *Le bateau de Léontine* (1911). Frame enlargement from 35mm print courtesy of Eye Filmmuseum.

1911), for example, she floods and destroys her entire home in a playful attempt to sail her new toy boat indoors (figure 2.1). *Léontine's Electric Battery* lives up to the incendiary promise of its title when Léontine steals an inventor's hotwired battery and then electrocutes the local police department (figure 2.2). In *Léontine Flies Away* (August 1911) she procures a bouquet of helium balloons, which swiftly launch her airborne. She flies over the village while a bewildered mob follows in frantic pursuit. Though now lost, *Léontine's Tomatoes* (November 1910) unleashed her ecstatic malfeasance in the form of projectile nightshades, which she hurls at random passersby, "leaving large red spots on their figures and clothes."[1] Léontine lives to destroy, and that is the basis of her liveliness. Her films remain instinctively hilarious to anyone who has ever dreamed of obliterating the world that fails to deliver satisfying outlets for their desires and ambitions.

Titine's apocalyptic antics, I argue, offer risky but decisive alternatives to the crisis of "cruel optimism," the late feminist theorist Lauren Berlant's affective diagnosis of neoliberal capitalism.[2] When fantasy suffuses ordinary reality, as it becomes increasingly hopeless and precarious, cruel optimism designates one's stillborn attachment to serially disappointing objects. It is like paying Amazon.com a twenty-dollar rental fee to watch a documentary about class inequality amid the collapse of financial markets and immiseration of the company's exploited workers. It is like applying to an adjunct position with a heavy teaching load while stable tenure lines and permanent faculty positions fall by the wayside of institutional austerity. It is like lobbying to levy minor carbon taxes in the swell of a looming climate apocalypse. Against the compulsive tokenism of bad faith and false hope, catastrophic optimism refuses to double down on inevitably futile attachments. Titine playfully embodies the spirit of catastrophic optimism. If her object is a toy boat and her climate is an unflooded house, she will simply plug up the drains and turn on the faucets, rather than limit her desire to the stultifying conditions at hand. She unleashes the flood on her fortified affluent home, instead of bunkering inside with a useless toy as the storm rages uncontrollably beyond her own gates.

At once, *Léontine's* unfound objecthood solicits us to extract our own aims from the endemic cruelty of toxic attachments. Why did her rampages go unseen for over a century—obscured by the limelight of male tramps and fast-talking vamps, who were repeatedly prioritized for preservation and exhibition? As Berlant argues, cruel attachments unravel when the affective pipeline between hopeful fantasy and ordinary reality frays beyond possibility of repair. Our eyeballs, assaulted 24/7 by images of senseless calamity, grow weary of all the old figures and forms. Titine wanders in through the backdoor between conventional fantasy and its plausible delivery—between expectation and hope. She was an international star, lionized as a "frolicsome lass full of mischief and the joy of life."[3] But it was not until 2010 that she made a comeback at the Cineteca di Bologna's "cento anni fa" ("a hundred years ago") series; Mariann Lewinsky included two of her films on an irresistible DVD set, *Comic Actresses and Suffragettes: 1910–1914*, which is where I first encountered them.[4]

I have since devoted my energies to spreading the gospel of Titine's revival—finding her films, ensuring their digitization, programming them far and wide, writing about them, theorizing their resonance, and revealing her specter to anyone willing to bear witness. We turn to ghosts, as feminist film scholars, when the present-facing spectrum of objects and their relation to actions seems to abandon the future to the repetition of history. That is why we take a leap of faith into incomplete archives, demanding their feminist mediation to salvage the deteriorating conditions of the apocalyptic conjuncture. This chapter is my offering against the onslaught of cruel optimism. This chapter is the story of my obsession with Léontine.

UNFINDING LÉONTINE

When I first met Léontine, I really knew her as Betty, her Anglo pseudonym for the English-speaking film market. I discovered her in the ecstatic throes of tormenting her conservative neighbors with pieces of string in *Betty Pulls the Strings* and then laughing so demonically that she's ejected from the theater in *Betty and Jane Go to the Theatre*, which costars the indomitable Sarah Duhamel. I was overwhelmed by my attraction to these films, to this undead character, and to the greater vortex of their evocative objecthood. She first accosted me (in all contexts) as I was scrambling to complete a conference paper for the Society of Cinema and Media Studies (SCMS) in 2012, a paper that ballooned into a dissertation, and then metamorphosed into a book, *Specters of Slapstick and Silent Comediennes*, in which I trace the formative influences of slapstick comediennes on the emergence of cinema.[5] These films were part and parcel of a popular wave of hysterical comedies about catastrophic kitchen maids, cross-dressing cowgirls, rebellious tomboys, and hellraising housewives that Laura Horak, Elif Rongen-Kaynakçi, and I have curated in a four-disc DVD/Blu-ray set, *Cinema's First Nasty Women* (Kino Lorber, 2022), which includes ninety-nine archival films with original scores by more than forty-five (primarily female or nonbinary) musicians.[6] Obviously, we give pride of place to the majesty of Titine.

Between 75 percent and 90 percent of all silent films are lost forever, depending on who you ask.[7] Even among the objects that survive, the vast majority wither in obscurity and inaccessibility due to the feedback loop between audience interest, institutional curation, and archival prioritization. Our big break came in 2016, when Jay Weissberg, director of the Giornate del Cinema Muto (Silent Film Festival), invited Horak and me to curate a five-screening program on "Nasty Women," which led to revival runs at the Giornate in 2019 and 2021. Working through our whiplash from the 2016 American presidential elections, which "licensed the obscenity of the unconscious," according to Jacqueline Rose, we mined the archives for instances of feminist "nastiness."[8] We focused on the intersections between our research interests in slapstick comedy and female cross-dressing. (Horak's book on gender play in silent cinema, *Girls Will Be Boys: Cross-Dressed Women, Lesbians, and American Cinema, 1908–1934*, remains essential reading for any feminist or film history enthusiast.)[9] Programming this series gave us crucial access to the archives and a platform to lobby for the prioritization of feminist prints over the predominance of Charlie Chaplin, D. W. Griffith, the Lumière Brothers, and so forth. We dedicated an entire program to Titine in 2017. Despite a few humorless holdouts, and an overdetermined conspiracy theory that the actor who played Titine was a man (she was not), the "Nasty Women" were a hit! Beyond their surface topicality, their ghosts captured the zeitgeist.

With the resurgence of popular feminism and advocacy for women's representation across the film industry, there has been a rising movement of archival activism to remake the film canon. This vital project of feminist historiography thrives in the realm of incompletion, especially given the absence of extant documentation. Passionate fellow travelers seek out alternative means of evidence—memoirs, sketchbooks, paper print fragments, urban street maps, script annotations, unpublished scenarios, even collective hallucinations—to reassert feminist film histories that have been buried in the rubble of patriarchal canonization. To destroy, as a feminist gesture, means to liberate lived experiences from the tomb of myopic empiricism. Giuliana Bruno's *Streetwalking on a Ruined Map* (1993), Miriam Hansen's *Babel and Babylon* (1991), Jennifer Bean and Diane Negra's *A Feminist Reader in Early Cinema* (2002), and Jacqueline Najuma Stewart's *Migrating to the Movies* (2005) exemplify the many formative texts that continue to inspire what now flourishes as a hopeful collective project.[10] Fostered by repertory festivals, online research forums, and curated digital databases, feminist historiography forges radical, defamiliarized objects from the ruins of the archive and against the guardrails of the canon.

Léontine's performative power easily outshone the directorial vision of whatever was happening behind the camera—especially given the fluidity between creative roles on early film sets. Her survival resonates with the field's expansive gaze at the archives of authorship and "making." Indeed, feminist historians tend to prioritize the overlooked (and uncredited) labor of female filmmakers such as Alice Guy-Blaché, Lois Weber, Germaine Dulac, Elvira Notari, and Nell Shipman, whom Alison McMahan, Shelley Stamp, Tami Williams, Giuliana Bruno, and Kay Armatage have respectively historicized.[11] Fueling these monographs about forgotten female directors, the *Women Film Pioneers*

Project popularizes the career profiles of thousands of figures who labored at every level of silent film production and craft.[12]

I see the signature of Titine all over the 1910–12 Pathé Comica/Nizza canon. In addition to her regular series, she made cameos in numerous other films (we can only guess how many total!), some of which were preserved and restored by the Eye Filmmuseum and the Gaumont-Pathé archives. For example, she plays a trombonist named Blanche Ladoré in *Love and Music* (1911), in which she hooks up with a bass drummer and then both are arrested for public noise disturbance. She also appears as an obstreperous housemaid clanging pots and pans in *Rosalie Has Sleeping Sickness* (1911), which Rongen-Kaynakçi and I uncovered on an untitled, unrestored, rare-gauged 28mm safety print at the Eye Filmmuseum in May 2019, right after the Women and the Silent Screen Conference (WSS) was held there. We couldn't even watch the film; we had to eyeball it frame-by-frame using a magnifying glass because we did not have a 28mm projector.

That lucky canister also contained *Zoé's Magic Umbrella* (1913), starring the lead actress of the Lux company's *Cunégonde* series, whom Rongen-Kaynakçi had just identified as a traveling circus performer known as Little Chrysia.[13] "For at least 10 years," confessed Rongen-Kaynakçi, "I'd thought this was a lost cause. In the end, thanks to the digitized libraries, databases and archives such as Lantern [and] Gallica ... I could gather enough leads and evidence."[14] In *Magic Umbrella,* Zoé pilfers an enchanted parasol and wields it catastrophically to multiply any object she wishes on the spot: women's hats, wooden chairs, dusty broomsticks. Zoé's conniptions embody cruel optimism in overdrive. If "all objects are rest stops amid the process of remaining unsatisfied," as Berlant claims, Zoé takes an advance on her prolongment of unfulfilled desire, flooding the present with the catastrophe of her alienated wants.[15] She also mirrors Titine, whose single-minded fixation on useless commodities—from helium balloons to overripe tomatoes to recreational fireworks to ludicrous millinery—reveals how precipitously the individual's infatuation with mediocre things becomes a collective social problem.

Is Titine my own object of cruel optimism? Absolutely not. The void of her name and excess of her malfeasance help me remain nimble and unorthodox in my own orientation to thinking and research. Whenever I begin to lose faith, she always seems to leave behind new crumbs, flashes of inspiration that radiate from the fallout of her world-shattering pranks. In

September 2019, I upped the ante on my voluble evangelism for Titine by airing my obsession in the *Los Angeles Review of Books* (*LARB*).¹⁶ One reader posted a hot tip in the comments section that she could be Leontine Sagan, the lesbian Austrian-Hungarian theater director and filmmaker whose life and directorial work have both been well-documented. How many feminist Léontines can there be in the archive? More than one? Fewer than two? Quickly, the name itself became a red herring, an unfound object—not unfounded (as in nonfactual) but with a trace of the "un-" of *unheimlich,* the German term for "uncanny," which Freud paraphrased as the feeling of being at once at home and not at home.

I do feel a bit *unheimlich* in the presence of Titine: her satanic gleam taunts me as a spectator, daring me to misrecognize her. Yet too many have fallen prey to that gamble—to assume the impulsive confidence that Titine exuberates. A French archivist suggested that she might be Léontine Massart, the Belgian silent film actress who looks nothing like our Titine! Beyond a superficial resemblance, overdetermined by period costume and grainy photo stock, Massart lacks Titine's unmistakable impish countenance. The whole world is her carnivalesque laboratory. Whether rejoicing with fireworks, jury-rigging a high-power motor fan, wielding a decapitated wolf's head, or simply tying people's precious possessions to moving vehicles, Titine never holds out for the future. That's the paradox of her charisma: if it can't be destroyed, then it wasn't worth saving. She is a creature who exists purely for the moment. "The pranks she plays are inconceivable," as *The Film Index* warned in 1910, "and what she will do or what she will not do in the future is not at all easy to say."¹⁷

Indeed not. After 1912, Titine disappeared from public view. What happened to her? Was she a casualty of war? Of influenza? Of shellshock and nervous trauma? Or yet another vibrant, talented woman consigned to domestic labor, motherhood, and the endless, invisible tedium of social reproduction? Like a flash of lightning, Titine struck again in 2019. Mariann Lewinsky, when I interviewed her for the *LARB* article, had mentioned that her friend thought she recognized the actress in a later French silent comedy. Shortly afterward, the citation crystallized: the film was *Lagourdette, gentleman-burglar,* a Gaumont two-reeler from 1916 starring the glamorous vamp, Musidora (herself a talented filmmaker and writer).¹⁸ Directed by Louis Feuillade, *Lagourdette* satirizes Feuillade's own crime serial, *Les Vampires* (1915–16), which also stars Musidora as its anagrammed eponym, Irma Vep. In this parody version of *Les Vampires,* Titine plays a character named Phémie, the cook, who abets a ruse to trick Miss Musi (Musidora) into believing that her suitor, Lagourdette, is a world-class thief. (He is not.) Musi had been pining over the novelization of *Les Vampires*, so Phémie is recruited as a plant for Lagourdette to pretend to pickpocket. Toward that end, Phémie must disguise herself as an elegant lady, bedecked in lavish fake jewels: the perfect mark.

In a meta-film allegory about the dangers of blurring fiction with reality, Titine yet again pulls the wool over everyone's eyes. She thrives in that realm of misrecognition, playing a role whose name (Phémie) is synonymous with the detachable suffix for language. Meanwhile, her character easily upstages and outperforms Musidora, which is nothing to sneeze at—Musidora was a versatile performer and held her own as a comedian. I had expected that Phémie's virtuosic performance would be credited in reviews and advertisements for the film. She commands almost half of the screen time; it is not a minor role. But her presence is ignored and her character unnoted, yielding no new knowledge as to her name, aside from the visible evidence of her persisting screen image. I've since spent countless hours scanning Gaumont films (including *Les Vampires*), hoping to catch a flicker of Titine's hellraising specter. To invoke another ghost, "Oh that this too too solid flesh would melt."[19]

BETTY IS COMING

> "Who Is Betty? Is the one unvarying question with which we have been bombarded by phone, post, and swift messenger since our announcement of Betty's approaching advent."[20]

> "What cabalistic word is this? And who is 'Betty,' and why and when?"[21]

> "Pathe Freres informed us that 'Betty Is Coming' far and wide. [But] no one appears to be in a position to inform us whether Betty is the name of a film, actress, or pet dog."[22]

It is hard to imagine a more hyperbolically anticipated and rapidly dissipated question than "Who Is Betty?" The subject of an aggressive international publicity campaign in the summer of 1910, Betty made her screen debut in the United States in July. Described as a "mischievous and willful tomboy, who shrinks at nothing so long as she can get her own way," Betty arrived already an object of misrecognition.[23] "Is Betty a favorite pug, with a face like a nightmare, or is she a petted spaniel of high degree?"[24] As it turns out, both guesses were unfounded! Betty was Titine, with a smile like the Joker, the death drive of a mutineer, the vivacity of a vaudeville fire juggler, and anarchist tunnel-vision of a Bolshevik intellectual.

Whatever happened to Betty? Of the twenty-four episodes produced in France, only ten appear to have had US releases. The latter half were reviled as "not very edifying nor funny," without "a spark of wit" or any "merit beyond a species of horseplay," a "big disappointment," and (of all things) "no place for a minister's son."[25] Her debut intersected with the escalation of xenophobic gatekeeping in the American film industry, as well as reformist hysteria about the seedy conditions in nickelodeon theaters and dubious objecthood of vulgar, lowbrow, rough-house slapstick comedies.[26] *The Acrobatic Maid* (Pathé, 1908) was revealingly panned: "This film can perhaps suit the Moulin-Rouge of Paris, but it is not a very proper film to show to an American audience. If some ignorant spectators laughed . . . many other persons, especially ladies, could hardly refrain from disdain."[27] All the same, the mystery of Betty's widely publicized anonymity overrode the American trade press's ambivalence about the mores of French slapstick comedy. "In fact," wagered *The Film Index,* "we think it is heavy odds that there will be a big Betty boom, although we understand that it is not the intention of Pathe Freres to boom Betty."[28] *The Nickelodeon* echoed that unfounded optimism: "Those persons who have had the opportunity of making her acquaintance predict that Betty will soon be all the rage."[29] Other commentators openly filled in the void of concrete information with libidinal projection: "Enraptured we gaze upon her graceful ample form as she comes to greet us in the gloaming. Long and rapturous is the kiss we press upon her pouting lips as we fold Betty to our breast."[30] To this I will add, fetishism apparently runs roughshod over the incompletion of context.

At last, Betty arrived. In the premiere episode of her US run, *Rebellious Betty* (July 1910), she bulldozes a crowd of bystanders, destroys an artist's magnum opus, steals a bicycle, and then decapitates a butler, "all simply because she has been refused the privilege of accepting an invitation to go for a motor ride."[31] But the film was maligned by *Nickelodeon* as no "funnier than the average comedy." The reviewer singled out "the decapitation and subsequent restoration of the servant" as "almost a backward step in film producing"—as if Betty was waylaying the progress of screen history.[32] *More of Betty's Pranks* followed later that month, wherein she harnesses a parked milk cart to a wild dog and sneaks into a random barn, where they share a bowl of fresh cow's milk after spilling their ill-gotten cargo. As with the butler's reversible decapitation gag, the vibrance of Titine's comedy turns on the furious tenacity of her death march, which gains joyful momentum from the episodic obliteration of its temporary props. Events proceed from the spectacle of their necessary impermanence.

Betty As Errand Girl tries to ply Léontine's restless energies with a useful trade, but she refuses to become alienated from her fledgling labor. When ordered to deliver a fancy hat to an affluent client, she impulsively steals the thing that she covets, substituting her own tiny sailor's cap for the behemoth headgear. "The situation is rapidly taken in by the milliner when she gazes with a horror-stricken face at Betty's miniature form surrounded by the enormous hat."[33] The existence of this film is a miracle in itself. It had been presumed lost and only resurfaced in 2008 on a 9.5mm Pathé Baby print that Rubén Gallo discovered in an antique shop in Nièvre, France, and then donated to Princeton University Library. (Indeed, it was still presumed lost by many, including myself, until recently when the library's Pathé Baby collection was digitized.)[34] How many other fragments lie in wait of discovery? And how many more will remain lost forever?

The survival of Titine's objecthood, coupled with its thematic of self-annihilation, converges on the larger problem at play of theorizing catastrophic optimism. The object of cruel optimism, according to Berlant, offers a landing pad to slough off the "nightmarish burden" and "psychotic loneliness" of sovereignty. These "safety-deposit objects," they write, "make it possible to bear sovereignty through its distribution, the energy of feeling relational, general, reciprocative, and accumulative."[35] In other words, sovereignty without alienating objects is a psychotically lonely proposition. Yet Titine would never shy away from the extremity of absolute sovereignty. The only relationality that accumulates in her films is the raging lynch mob behind her, whom she craftily dodges—trapping them on a balcony, leading them off course with a strawman, or assaulting them with a circus lion. As *Moving Picture World* summarized the finale of *Betty Is Still at Her Old Tricks,* "even when they [the mob] do capture the runaway horse their rage blinds them for a few minutes to the deception, and they pound away at the offending dummy, whilst Betty stands giggling at the scene a couple of fields away."[36] Anti-crowd sociologist Gustave Le Bon would have eaten his heart out.[37]

All joking aside, Titine poses a special kind of sovereign subject who takes unbridled pleasure in the immediacy of feeling "nonrelational," in foreclosing the accumulation of value on an object's forbidden uses at hand. Better that than to squirrel those objects away for an uncertain future dominated by reproductive exhaustion. She seizes the balloons and flies through the sky, snatches the roller skates and glides through the woods, and electrocutes the police force rather than risk incarcerating her desire. The world may explode in her path, but she owns the impact of her unmediated sovereignty, which we can paraphrase as the lack of distance between the acquisitive ego and the endpoint of its fixations.

I should make it explicit (if this is not already clear): Titine's destructive pranks operate purely on the level of spectatorial fantasy. In prolonged retrospect, their effect is further compounded by the happenstance of not even knowing her name. For example, there is always a gap between star image and fictional character: "the living Charlie" versus "Charlie the character," as André Bazin put it in his chapter on Charlie Chaplin. "The living Charlie remains the creator and guarantor of Charlie the character," Bazin claimed.[38] Jennifer Bean hazards a similar reading of the daredevil "serial queen" Pearl White in her evocative essay on "Technologies of Early Stardom and the Extraordinary Body," wherein the star and the woman risk becoming too much of the other, so the technological apparatus itself intervenes to manufacture a distance.[39] Whereas Bean emphasizes the revolving door between screen presence and physical absence (identification and desire), we might reframe her terms slightly to think about the problem of sovereignty and its total disinterest in the pathos of cruelty. With Titine, there is simply no virtue in absence, no time for suspense, no value remaining for the hungry spectator to accumulate.

If cruel optimism thrives in the realm of crisis—exemplified by melodrama but also, as Berlant suggests, mutations of slapstick such as "situational tragedy" and cringe comedy—catastrophic optimism collapses the extension necessary to sustain the temporality of crisis.[40] Catastrophe "happens 'all at once,'" Mary Ann Doane reminds us, whereas crisis involves the tense negotiation of time. Crisis "compresses time and makes its limitations acutely felt," but catastrophe incites "the most critical of crises for its timing is that of the instantaneous, the moment, the punctual."[41] When Titine bludgeons hotel guests with a decapitated wolf's head, and then disguises herself as an old man for the pleasure of wreaking further havoc after she is unceremoniously ejected from the hotel, there is no future stashed away in her attachment to the object. Perhaps the fake beard (as an object) bears a temporary expedience. But once she gains reentry, her appetite continues apace purely for the moment; the wolf's head is both singular/unsubstitutable and entirely instrumental; it is a detachable means to the scandalous ends of sheer immediacy. What more could you want?

Catastrophic Optimism | 73

FIGURE 2.2 Léontine mocks her victims after electrocuting them in *Le pile électrique de Léontine* (1910). Frame enlargement from 35mm print courtesy of Gaumont-Pathé Archives.

Clearly the catastrophe of Titine's objecthood missed the mark of the 1910s American film market, with its hysterical campaign to elevate motion pictures to the status of a "seventh art," or at the very least, a venue that respectable middle-class women (i.e., Titine's prime victims) would patronize with their children. "The Pathe idea of the way Betty does things may be excruciatingly funny across the pond," opined *Variety*, "but in the American houses the Betty series does not create the furore desired . . . she is more than impossible in the series that Pathe is inflicting on the American audiences."[42] This was all *Variety* had to say about the fourth release, *Betty Is Still at Her Old Tricks,* in which Betty/Titine sadistically wields her weapon of choice: a piece of string.

This was, in fact, the very first Titine film that I saw, thanks to its inclusion in Lewinsky's *Comic Actresses* DVD set. The gist is simple: Betty torments people with pieces of string by baiting them with their objects of desire. She lures a hunter with a stuffed rabbit, a shopper with a fake wallet, and so forth. But as soon as they arrive at the end of their rope—that is, at the object itself—Titine jumps out from her hiding place, laughs hysterically, and then perpetrates some absurd gesture of violence, such as smacking the hunter across the face with the dead animal. An angry lynch mob gathers behind her (they always do), but Betty eludes them by disguising herself as a scarecrow, mounting the real strawman on a galloping horse, which the raging mob instead tears to pieces. In other episodes, women's skirt hems, millinery tassels, dog leashes, jump ropes, or dangling shoelaces serve just as well as string to persecute her prey while remapping the entire world around her predilection for total chaos and demolition.

Subsequent US releases were ruthlessly lambasted. *Betty Rolls Along*, in which Betty roller skates through the forest, was condemned by the *Moving Picture World*: "One of those destructive comedies which has no real merit beyond a species of horseplay, which should be banished from motion pictures."[43] As *Nickelodeon* pithily summarized the film, "chairs are broken, tables are overthrown, and glasses are smashed." In the end, Betty's father pays damages to "the victims of his daughter's exuberance."[44] *Betty's Apprenticeship* was similarly excoriated as "simply distasteful"; "this is no finical notion," added *Nickelodeon*, "but one that a large audience seemed to share, no laughs being in evidence. Betty is funny when her tricks display wit, but not otherwise. This film was mostly otherwise."[45] The unnamed reviewer allows one exception involving Betty's substitution of a red balloon for a piece of Edam cheese.

You can see the precise distinction between "wit" and "horseplay" here, or between comedy that thrives on a deferral of difference versus gags that catastrophize the immediacy of attachment. The latter form would be exemplified by the scenes in which Betty causes a dozen hat cartons to be crushed by a steamroller, or assaults a bakery customer with gooey cake frosting, or slings a pair of naval boots at a woman with large feet. Catastrophic objects detonate on arrival; they deliberately are not worth the wait. Henceforth, Pathé attempted to present *Betty* as their own American production, even though the whole series was filmed by the Comica unit in Nice, France.[46] But viewers were wise to the deception. As one angry fan wrote to *Motion Picture News*: "In the above film, although 'made in America,' the little girl writes on French note paper!" The title in question was *The Tables Are Turned*, in which Betty's father attempts to discipline her in absentia during her piano lessons by monitoring her with a hallway mirror, which she "turns" on her watcher, catching him in the act of assaulting and molesting the kitchen maid.

By and large, Betty/Titine's episodes fared better in the UK, where virtually all of her French films enjoyed enthusiastic reception. British reviewers, those naval imperialists, seemed especially keen on *Betty's Boat*, in which Betty impulsively floods the house to sail her toy boat indoors. Interestingly, the film was included in a program alongside a drama about the Holy War crusades in October 1911. As the *Dover Express* opined, "the effects on the adjoining apartments are very far from amusing to anyone but the spectators who, however, keenly enjoy the misfortunes of other people."[47] Invoking a conservative understanding of slapstick as anathema to feeling, this reading misrecognizes Titine's sovereign jouissance as willful cruelty, whereas we know it implicitly to be a refusal of false hope. Cruelty, however, is really the only possible explanation for why the Picture Palace in Chichester, England, decided to pair *Betty's Boat* with a tinted actuality about the flooding of canals and rivers in colonial Siam.[48] "A Real Mirth-Provoker" in Johannesburg, according to the *Rand Daily Mail*, *Betty's Boat* presumably also had distribution throughout South Africa and elsewhere in the English-speaking colonized world.[49]

But no *Betty* label made wider rounds than *Betty and Jane at the Theatre*, which as far as I can tell never even played in the United States (figure 2.3). It costars Titine's pal Rosalie, played by Sarah Duhamel, who also had her own Comica series and later headlined as Pétronille for the French Éclair film company. Rosalie was known as Jane in the UK and Eva in her limited American run, which included *Eva Is Tired of Life* (1911), *Eva's Faithful Furniture* (1911), and *Eva Moves In* (1911), in which she destroys an apartment building. Why did British Jane become American Eva while Betty remained Betty? Comic series were frequently duped, adapted, translated, or pirated, making it further difficult to pin a name to a body across its transnational circulation. For example, Little Chrysia is best known as Cunégonde, but later played Zoé, who was enjoyed as Alma in Germany, and then adapted into Caroline for the UK, where Little Chrysia also starred as Arabella, in a reboot of *Cunégonde* that harkened back to her zany music hall performances on the French Riviera before beginning her career as a screen actress.

Duhamel herself was a prolific stage actress, so we have to assume that Léontine also graced the music halls of the French Riviera while making her two-year-running film series in Nice. Speaking of thespians, *Betty and Jane* takes place at a local variety theater, *Les Capucines*, where the two women indulge in their shared gusto for violent disruption. As hysterical female spectators, they emit buckets of tears, laugh uncontrollably, taunt and jeer at the players, exchange projectile perishables with other audience members, and are eventually thrown out

FIGURE 2.3 Léontine and Rosalie raise a ruckus at the local theater in *Rosalie et Léontine vont au théâtre* (1911). Frame enlargement from 35mm print courtesy of the British Film Institute.

of the house. "A screamingly funny film," raved the *Dundee Evening Telegraph,* in reference to its run at the Electric Theatre in August 1911, where it was sandwiched between a domestic drama about matrimony and an actuality about colonial exploration in the Malay Archipelago.[50]

Betty and Jane may never have made it to Malaysia (though it's entirely possible, given the colonial occupation of British Malay), but it did allegedly "cause screams of laughter" at the London Theatre in Bombay, India, and "fairly convulsed the audience" at the Posada Roller Rink in Harare, Rhodesia (now Zimbabwe).[51] Perhaps Pathé's marketing rhetoric—"Betty Is Coming," "there will be a big Betty boom," and so forth—resonated instinctively with the exporting of enjoyment and anxious paranoia about anticolonial defiance that greased the wheels of early twentieth-century European imperialism.

But to circle back to the original question: "Who *Is* Betty?" Although *The Film Index* had advertised that "anyone who wants to know can get the answer from Pathé Frères," no mention of the actor's identity was forthcoming. "Pathé Frères will not answer any questions about their leading ladies," claimed *Motion Picture Story Magazine* in 1912.[52] Her name escapes any mention in the trade press, title credits, or other archival fragments that have pricked the attention of interested parties in the twenty-first century. A black hole of self-attribution, Titine leads our gazes elsewhere.

AFFECT IN THE ARCHIVE: THEORIZING CATASTROPHIC OPTIMISM

Wouldn't you prefer a catastrophic object to a cruel one? At this point, Titine represents a lost object for me. Whenever I'm feeling aimless, I find it therapeutic to input permutations of the same keyword searches into one of five digital databases, hoping this time to yield different results. Every once in a while, I dig up little tidbits that I'd somehow missed (or episodically forgotten), but recent revelations have tended to come in the form of new celluloid restorations. Titine's films survived for so long only to collect dust in various archives. But her thundering pranks have seen the light of day thanks to the advocacy and prodigious labor of curators at the Fondation Jérôme Seydoux-Pathé, the Eye Filmmuseum, the British Film Institute, and the French Cinémathèque. Titine's unfound objecthood, for me, further epitomizes the Frankfurt School gesture to divine optimism from the spectacle of freewheeling rupture—a leap of faith into the future amid the wreckage of historical catastrophe and the irreparable loss of continuity with a godforsaken past. Léontine's very name is a life-sustaining question—a symbolic field in which the drive to know and the inability to confirm go hand in glove.

Her baffling antics partake in a vital tradition of farcical grotesquerie, exemplified, as Walter Benjamin argued, by "American slapstick comedies and Disney films," which both "indicate the dangers threatening mankind" and "trigger a therapeutic release of unconscious energies."[53] It is a pity that Benjamin was not aware of Titine. As he put it: "*the forced development of sadistic fantasies and masochistic delusions*" in certain films "*can prevent their natural and dangerous maturation in the masses.*"[54] Titine's films were produced and exhibited as tensions boiled over in Europe on the brink of World War I. Apparently they missed the mark of cathartic deterrence, so it is appropriate that they'd continue to hold Titine's biography hostage as collateral damage, given the rampant destruction that energizes all of her films.

Feminist archives, as we know from the project of this book, are pockmarked with obscene violations and erasures. Forging imaginative alternatives to those gridlocks is precisely the optimistic intervention of feminist media historiography. In contrast to catastrophic optimism, which explodes from the archives of early twentieth-century slapstick, cruel optimism has come to characterize the neoliberal addiction to placing fragile hope in ultimately disappointing or futile forms of habit. An object-attachment turns cruel, according to Berlant, when it sticks to the very thing that prevents you from flourishing. Self-help books, precarious gig-work, fad diets, television laugh tracks, multilevel marketing schemes: all these forms exemplify solicitations to cruel optimism, by which subjects of late capital hoard their shattered fantasies in airtight "safety-deposit objects."[55]

Yet the objecthood of incomplete archives defies the cruelty of manipulative investments, I argue, by virtue of its resilient commitment and intellectual plasticity. By "resilient commitment," I mean the ability to stick with an object despite its failure to fill the void—to scratch an itch, to supplement a lack, and so forth. Incomplete archives remain expansive precisely because they never deliver on the answer to a potentially solvable question. To think with unfound objects thus unites the suspicion of critical hermeneutics with the generosity posed by reparative reading, to invoke Eve Kosofsky Sedgwick's polemical opposition.[56] Ever wondrous, always paranoid: it's an affective high wire act. Unfound objects are also a far cry from "wounded attachments," Wendy Brown's incisive term for the weaponization of injury, as well as the subject positions that germinate from cruel fixations.[57] Such attachments become ossified and rigid to maintain their morbid recession of stillborn fantasy, whereas catastrophic objects stay open to playful new forms of knowledge in their gesture to blow up the canon (figure 2.4).

Titine's reckless exploits give us meta-archival alternatives to the trap of cruel optimism, or its double: the dangerous nostalgia for earlier forms that are desirable only insofar as they remain irretrievable. Her attachments are not cruel but compulsively all-consuming: her uncle's fireworks, her cousin's roller skates, her landlocked toy boat, a bouquet of helium balloons, an inventor's electric battery, a lady's ostentatious hat, and innumerable pieces of string. Hell hath no fury like the object-obsessions of Léontine! They episodically annihilate the entire world. No ordinary fantasies or defensive enactments could ever survive the apocalypse of Titine's infatuations; they steamroll what Berlant would call the *historical sensorium* with the jouissance of her insuppressible death drive. The affects Titine exhibits toward her volatile things offer vital object lessons for all feminist travelers who seek to escape the soul-sucking alienation of cruel optimism.

Catastrophic Optimism | 79

FIGURE 2.4 *Les Pétards de Léontine* (Louis Z. Rollini), collection Fondation Pathé, fonds Maurice Gianati © 1910—Pathé Frères.

Feminist historiography, like slapstick catastrophe, traverses the abyss between object-loss and present-facing possibility with playful, speculative, boundary-testing methodologies—as Jane Gaines suggests in chapter 1. "The loss of stories sharpens the hunger for them," remarks Saidiya Hartman in her essential 2008 essay "Venus in Two Acts." "So it is tempting to fill in the gaps and provide closure where there is none."[58] Hartman brings her project of "critical fabulation" to the archives of silent cinema in *Wayward Lives, Beautiful Experiments* (2019), in which she imagines a nonexistent (which is different from nonextant) silent film about the blues singer Gladys Bentley directed by the Black race filmmaker Oscar Micheaux.[59] Black feminist theory, with its driving will to imagine otherwise to disarm the traumatic inheritances of slavery and perpetual racism, fosters especially generative terrain. Jacqueline Stewart's notion of "reconstructive spectatorship," Allyson Nadia Field's book-length study of nonextant racial advocacy films, and Jayna Brown's call for Black "creative disobedience" in *Babylon Girls* each transforms the realities of the archive through hopeful methodologies that riff on its carefully researched fictionalization.[60]

In the provocative phrase of my *Incomplete* interlocutor Katherine Groo: "Let It Burn." This is the title of a sizzling 2019 article in which

Groo pursues "film historiography in flames" by elaborating the philosophical impulses of fire. She envisions the untold stories and unfound objects that might yet emerge by resisting the conservative impulse to prevent nitrate's inevitable combustion and deterioration—a project she continues in chapter 3 of this book, where she susses out the feminist affordances of film history's fragments specifically in their piecemeal, incomplete forms.[61] The labor of recovery—of finding, making visible, contextualizing, tediously restoring—is vital but can only go so far, given the hazards of how haplessly extant objects turn "unfound," just as unfounded objects often become ideologically endemic. By that I mean, just because something exists does not in itself transform the material relations of sovereignty, objecthood, and power.

Léontine knew this intuitively. That is precisely what makes her ghost feverishly unvanquishable. A new object changes nothing unless it disrupts the processes of labor production that, as Karl Marx argued (and of social reproduction, as feminist Marxist theorists argue), congeal in the form of increasingly useless commodities.[62] What would have become of a "frolicsome tomboy" like Titine if she'd simply resigned herself to that millinery apprenticeship, or to dutiful babysitting, or to more gender-appropriate toys than a landlocked naval boat? Perhaps she would have disappeared into the house like a Victorian madwoman, or slowly faded away while raising her children into the symbolic; instead, she flooded the house, while burning it all down, and now we'll never be rid of her specter. When the only alternative to incremental cruelty is spontaneous catastrophe, perhaps the question of historicizing a name is really beside the point.

LÉONTINE FOR THE CATASTROPHIC FUTURE

In October 2021, after completing a draft of this chapter, I went on yet another pilgrimage to find Titine in the Archives départementales des Alpes-Maritimes in Nice, where her Pathé Comica series was shot.[63] I felt especially hopeful searching through the Gaumont/Victorine studio collections, expecting to unearth a full cast list for *Lagourdette, gentleman cambrioleur*. I cannot tell you whether I found her there or not. If I did find her, what would that change or resolve? If I did not find her, would I even want to admit it? In the meantime, my collaborators and I will occupy ourselves by making Titine's filmography more accessible, organizing public events to view and discuss her works (along with the remains of her fellow combusting kitchen maids, unholy tomboys, and hellraising housewives), and searching, endlessly, for further glimmers of her ghost.

"Then, sometimes," as Berlant mused in 2018, "we have to face in public a crisis of the object distinct from our own ambivalence toward its transformation, when *circumstances* alter it before our eyes—whether it's the value of literary criticism, pedagogy and identity triggers, public education, or the failure of the political world to be worthy of our attachment to it."[64] Berlant called this the gesture of "genre flailing." When a necessary attachment no longer proves viable, it can be agonizing to resist repeatedly falling prey to its zombified persistence. Feminist historiography parlays that destabilizing precarity into epistemological creativity. In a similar spirit, it is my greatest hope that Titine's catastrophic archives—in addition to flooding the canon—will unleash broader forms of refusal across various cultural sectors and institutional spaces. I will tell you this much, the next time I see a firecracker in a technicality, I am going to light it.

NOTES

I would like to thank Alix Beeston, Agnès Bertola, Manon Billaut, Bryony Dixon, Mariann Lewinsky, Elif Rongen-Kaynakçi, Stéphanie Salmon, Stefan Solomon, and Jay Weissberg.

1. Henri Bousquet (1910), *Catalogue Pathé des années 1896 à 1914*, November 1910 (Bures-sur-Yvette: Édition Henri Bousquet, 1993), 353.
2. Lauren Berlant, *Cruel Optimism* (Durham, NC: Duke University Press, 2011).
3. "Who Is Betty?," *Film Index* (18 June 1910), 11.
4. Mariann Lewinsky and Eunice Martins, *Cento anni fa: Attrici comiche e suffragette 1910–1914* (Bologna, Italy: Cineteca di Bologna, 2010).
5. Maggie Hennefeld, "Léontine (or 'Betty') Series," *Specters of Slapstick and Silent Film Comediennes* (New York: Columbia University Press, 2018), 268–70.
6. See "Cinema's First Nasty Women," in *Women Film Pioneers Project*, ed. Jane Gaines, Radha Vatsal, and Monica Dall'Asta (New York: Columbia University Libraries, 2013), https://wfpp.columbia.edu/cinemas-first-nasty-women/nasty-women-bibliography/.
7. David Pierce, *The Survival of American Silent Feature Films: 1912–1929*, Library of Congress (September 2013), www.clir.org/wp-content/uploads/sites/6/pub158.pdf.
8. Jacqueline Rose, "Donald Trump's Victory Is a Disaster for Modern Masculinity," *The Guardian* (15 November 2016), www.theguardian.com/commentisfree/2016/nov/15/trump-disaster-modern-masculinity-sexual-nostalgian-oppressive-men-women.

9. Laura Horak, *Girls Will Be Boys: Cross-Dressed Women, Lesbians, and American Cinema, 1908–1934* (New Brunswick, NJ: Rutgers University Press, 2016).

10. See Giuliana Bruno, *Streetwalking on a Ruined Map: Cultural Theory and the City Films of Elvira Notari* (Princeton, NJ: Princeton University Press, 1993); Miriam Hansen, *Babel and Babylon: Spectatorship in American Silent Film* (Cambridge, MA: Harvard University Press, 1991); Jennifer Bean and Diane Negra, eds., *A Feminist Reader in Early Cinema* (Durham, NC: Duke University Press, 2002); and Jacqueline Najuma Stewart, *Migrating to the Movies: Cinema and Black Urban Modernity* (Berkeley: University of California Press, 2005).

11. See Alison McMahan, *Alice Guy-Blaché: Lost Visionary of the Cinema* (New York: Bloomsbury, 2003); Shelley Stamp, *Lois Weber in Early Hollywood* (Berkeley: University of California Press, 2013); Tami Williams, *Germaine Dulac: A Cinema of Sensations* (Urbana: University of Illinois Press, 2014); and Kay Armatage, *The Girl from God's Country: Nell Shipman and the Silent Cinema* (Toronto, ON: University of Toronto Press, 2003).

12. See *Women Film Pioneers Project,* https://wfpp.columbia.edu/; and Shelley Stamp, "Women and the Silent Screen," *Oxford Research Bibliographies Online* (December 2020), www.oxfordbibliographies.com/view/document/obo-9780199791286/obo-9780199791286-0268.xml.

13. Little Chrysia starred in the *Cunégonde* and *Zoé* series in France. Her popular characters were known as "Alma" in Germany and "Caroline/Arabella" in the UK.

14. Maggie Hennefeld, "Looking for Léontine: My Obsession with a Forgotten Screen Queen," *Los Angeles Review of Books* (24 September 2019), https://lareviewofbooks.org/article/looking-for-leontine-my-obsession-with-a-forgotten-screen-queen/.

15. Berlant, *Cruel Optimism,* 42.

16. Hennefeld, "Looking for Léontine."

17. "Who Is Betty?," *Film Index,* 11.

18. Annette Förster, "Musidora," in *Women Film Pioneers Project,* https://wfpp.columbia.edu/pioneer/ccp-musidora/.

19. William Shakespeare, *Hamlet,* Act 1, Scene 2 (1603).

20. "Who Is Betty?," *The Kinematograph & Lantern Weekly* (28 April 1910), 1429.

21. "Betty Is Coming," *Film Index* (18 June 1910), 28.

22. "Betty Is Coming," *Film Index* (11 June 1910), 4.

23. "Betty Is Coming," *Film Index* (11 June 1910), 4.

24. "Who Is Betty?," *Film Index,* 27.

25. "The Tables Turned—Pathé," *The Nickelodeon* (January 1911), 112; "Betty's Apprenticeship," *Nickelodeon*; "Betty Rolls Along (Pathe)," *Moving Picture World;* "Betty Is Punished (Pathe)," *Variety* (October 1910), 12; "The Tables Are Turned (Pathe)," *The Moving Picture World* (January 1911), 14.

26. For a detailed account of the US film industry's coordinated campaign against Pathé Frères, see Richard Abel, *The Red Rooster Scare: Making Cinema American, 1900–1910* (Berkeley: University of California Press, 1999).

27. "Comments on Film Subjects. The Acrobatic Maid," *The Moving Picture World* (December 1908), 476.
28. "Who Is Betty?," *Film Index*, 11.
29. "Shop Talk," *Nickelodeon* (June 1910), 16.
30. "Betty Is Coming," *Film Index* (18 June 1910), 28.
31. "Rebellious Betty," *Film Index* (July 1910), 13.
32. "Recent Films Reviewed," *Nickelodeon* (July 1910), 6.
33. "Betty as Errand Girl," *Nickelodeon* (August 1910), 73.
34. Gallo found this film along with approximately eight hundred other Pathé Baby 9.5mm silent films in 2008. Pathé Baby Collection, Rare Books and Special Collections, Princeton University Library, https://library.princeton.edu/pathebaby/.
35. Berlant, *Cruel Optimism*, 43.
36. "Pathe Freres. Betty Is Still at Her Old Tricks," *The Moving Picture World* (October 1910), 822.
37. Gustave Le Bon characterized modern urban crowds by their mob mentality, irrational de-individualization, and contagion of hysterical emotion. Gustave Le Bon, *The Crowd: A Study of the Popular Mind* (1895), www.gutenberg.org/ebooks/445.
38. André Bazin, "Charlie Chaplin," in *What Is Cinema?*, trans. Hugh Gray (Berkeley: University of California Press, 2004), 144–53, 144.
39. Jennifer Bean, "Technologies of Early Cinema and the Extraordinary Body," *Camera Obscura* 48 16.3 (2001): 8–57.
40. Lauren Berlant, *The Female Complaint: The Unfinished Business of Sentimentality in American Culture* (Durham, NC: Duke University Press, 2008), 176–77.
41. Mary Ann Doane, "Information, Crisis, Catastrophe," in *Logics of Television: Essays in Cultural Criticism*, ed. Patricia Mellencamp (Bloomington: Indiana University Press, 1990), 222–39, 223.
42. "Betty Is Still at Her Old Tricks (Pathe)," *Variety* (October 1910), 12.
43. "Betty Rolls Along (Pathe)," *Moving Picture World* (January 1911), 315.
44. "Betty Rolls Along," *Nickelodeon* (January 1911), 116.
45. "Betty's Apprenticeship—Pathé," *Nickelodeon* (February 1911), 223.
46. Centered in Nice and created by Roméo Bosetti, Comica was formed in 1910 but disbanded in 1914 due to the war. See Thierry Lefebvre, "Comica," in *Encyclopedia of Early Cinema*, ed. Richard Abel (London: Routledge, 2004), 150.
47. "The Queen's Hall," *Dover Express* (South-East Kent, England) (27 October 1911), 5.
48. "The Picture Palace," *Chichester Observer* (Chichester, England) (20 September 1911), 5.
49. "The Bijou," *Rand Daily Mail* (Johannesburg, South Africa) (18 August 1911), 8.
50. "The Electric Theatre," *Dundee Evening Telegraph* (Dundee, Scotland) (1 August 1911), 4.
51. "Excelsior Cinematograph," *Times of India* (Bombay, India) (17 June 1911), 12; "Posada Roller Rink," *Rhodesia Herald* (Harare, Zimbabwe) (11 August 1911), 11.

52. "Answers to Inquiries," *Motion Picture Story Magazine* (December 1912), 150.

53. Walter Benjamin (1936), "The Work of Art in the Age of Its Technical Reproducibility: Second Version," in *The Work of Art in the Age of Its Technical Reproducibility, and Other Writings on Media,* trans. Edmund Jephcott et al., ed. Michael W. Jennings, Brigid Doherty, and Thomas Y. Levin (Cambridge, MA: Harvard University Press, 2008), 19–55, 38.

54. Benjamin, "Work of Art," 38. Italics in original.

55. Berlant, *Cruel Optimism,* 43.

56. Jennifer Bean traces evocative parallels between Sedgwick's project of reparative reading and Miriam Hansen's articulation of "vernacular modernism," the transnational horizon of early cinema's "capacity to produce 'hitherto unperceived modes of sensory perception and experience.'" Though Sedgwick and Hansen were not in direct conversation with one another, as Bean notes, their overlapping methodologies provoke new lines of thought at the crossroads of affect theory and feminist film historiography. Jennifer Bean, "Editor's Introduction: Affect: The Alchemy of the Contingent," *Feminist Media Histories* 7.2 (2021): 1–20, 12.

57. See Wendy Brown, "Wounded Attachments," in *States of Injury: Power and Freedom in Late Modernity* (Princeton, NJ: Princeton University Press, 1995), 55–77.

58. Saidiya Hartman, "Venus in Two Acts," *Small Axe* 26, 12.2 (2008): 1–14, 8.

59. Saidiya Hartman, *Wayward Lives, Beautiful Experiments: Intimate Histories of Riotous Black Girls, Troublesome Women, and Queer Radicals* (New York: W. W. Norton & Co., 2019).

60. Stewart, *Migrating to the Movies,* 93–114; Allyson Nadia Field, *Uplift Cinema: The Emergence of African American Film and the Possibility of Black Modernity* (Durham, NC: Duke University Press, 2015); and Jayna Brown, *Babylon Girls: Black Women Performers and the Shaping of the Modern* (Durham, NC: Duke University Press, 2008), 7.

61. Katherine Groo, "Let It Burn: Film Historiography in Flames," *Discourse* 41.1 (2019): 3–36.

62. See Silvia Federicia (1998), *Caliban and the Witch: Women, the Body and Primitive Accumulation* (New York: Autonomedia, 2014); and Nancy Fraser, "Contradictions of Capital and Care," *New Left Review 100* (July–August 2016), https://newleftreview.org/issues/ii100/articles/nancy-fraser-contradictions-of-capital-and-care.

63. Thanks to Aurore Spiers and Colin Baldet for alerting me to the existence and location of these crucial collections.

64. Lauren Berlant, "Genre Flailing," *Capacious: Journal for Emerging Affect Inquiry* 1.2 (2018): 156–62, 156–57.

CHAPTER 3

Body Parts

Feeling Labor in Early Film Color

KATHERINE GROO

In 2011 the Cineteca del Friuli, the Giornate del Cinema Muto, the George Eastman Museum, and the L. Jeffrey Selznick School of Film Preservation publicly introduced the Davide Turconi Project, an unusual collection of film images and an enormous, decade-long undertaking of analog-digital preservation.[1] The collection consists of 23,491 nitrate film clippings, each just two to three frames in length. Most of the clippings represent the first two decades of film practice; they are fragments culled largely from French, German, Italian, British, and American films produced between 1897 and 1915. Among the fragments are numerous and extraordinary examples of early color processes. A team of archivists and researchers, directed by Paolo Cherchi Usai and Joshua Yumibe, made high resolution scans of the clippings and gathered pertinent metadata (for example, edge marks and codes, state of deterioration and fading, color details, original sources of the fragments). The original nitrate clippings were then placed in cold storage at Eastman's Louis B. Mayer Conservation Center so as to extend their shelf lives. Lower-resolution images of the complete collection are publicly available and searchable online via the Turconi Collection Database. One can sift through the clippings by title, director, and release date, as well as less common identificatory marks like intertitles, splices, and decomposition.

The story of how a collection of films came to be clippings and how those clippings came to be digitized and preserved is a winding one.

Films were passed from one set of hands to many others. The collection was named for a Jesuit priest and then a film historian. While this meandering chain of possession and fragmentation demonstrates the global excursivities and contingencies of film artifacts, nothing immediately recommends the Turconi Collection as a site of feminist practice or thought. Indeed, the site is overdetermined by male agents and authorship. As I argue in this chapter, however, the project contains numerous traces of female labor in early film history, both represented in its interrupted images and upon the surfaces of its decaying celluloid. The Turconi clipping that adorns the cover of this book, extracted from *Barbe bleue* (Pathé Frères, 1907), demonstrates this interplay between the historical production of the image and its material afterlives (in the film factory, amateur collection, professional archive, and digital database). Moreover, the material emphases and fragmentary design of the contemporary Turconi database usefully disrupt the narrative forms—lines, continuities, wholes—that tend to structure recuperative approaches to film history and exclude the unassimilable remains of women. In retaining these indices of past lives and labor, the Davide Turconi Project models and makes possible a materialist-feminist alternative. It is at once a site of memorialization and historical imagination.

First, the story. Then, its undoing. Before they were clippings, the images were films. They came from the collection of Josef-Alexis Joye, a Jesuit priest who served as vicar of St. Clara Church in Basel, Switzerland. As Alicia Fletcher and Joshua Yumibe detail in their history of the digital project and its analog artifacts, Joye collected 1,540 films between 1900 and 1911 to support a community education center known as the Borromäum.[2] More than half of the titles that Joye eventually accumulated were nonfiction films, including actualities, travelogues, ethnographic films, and industrial films. Joye died in 1919, and the films remained at the Borromäum until 1958, when another priest and caretaker of the collection, Stefan Bamberger, arranged to transfer the films to the state archive in Zurich.

Bamberger introduced Italian silent film historian Davide Turconi to the Joye collection in the early 1960s. By that point, however, numerous films showed signs of nitrate decay. Turconi tried to save the entire collection by transferring it to other institutions but managed only to secure the removal and preservation of two hundred or so films. He then made the decision to start cutting—literally, with scissors—many of the remaining films into pieces. Fletcher and Yumibe describe the process:

Armed with a pair of shears, [Turconi] began cutting clippings from the Joye prints.... He would string up the reels of nitrate film along makeshift clotheslines, some one thousand feet in length and both sticky and wet as a result of advanced nitrate decomposition, allowing the prints to dry. When the films had dried, Turconi made his clippings with the help of a rewind bench, usually two to three frames in length at a time.[3]

Joye's films thus became Turconi's clippings.

Turconi made his mark in more subtle ways as well. His cuts emphasized fiction films over nonfiction, Italian productions over other national sites.[4] Fletcher describes him as a kind of auteurist with scissors, whose "eye for dynamic, interesting images" ultimately accounts for the intrinsic value of the collection.[5] In the end, Turconi created clippings from 799 of Joye's films. He deposited the remains into envelopes marked with whatever details were known about their source. Many clippings remain unidentified. In 1976, David Francis received the surviving (unsevered) prints at the National Film Archive (now the British Film Institute [BFI]), where they were repaired and duplicated. Today they are in the process of being restored. The clippings, remarkably, were scattered like cinephilic calling cards. Turconi gave them to archives, cinematheques, and film historians. Paolo Cherchi Usai received the greatest share—more than ten thousand—and donated his portion to the George Eastman House in 2004, thus initiating the process of reassembling the fragments.

The Turconi Project has been framed—through a handful of publications, press releases, and an exhibition in 2018—as a significant resource of early color film and a lasting testament to the life and film-historical commitments of Davide Turconi.[6] For Fletcher and Yumibe, however, the collection more specifically foregrounds the materiality of the still image and demands that we reckon with the shifting role that digital technology plays in preserving analog artifacts. This guidance is well taken, and I intend to move in the directions they suggest. However, I depart from their view that the project encompasses "the broader total history of the films it documents," that the enlarged still images, the metadata attributed to those images, and the sheer quantity of clippings preserved in the collection ought to encourage us to pursue a larger whole or that totality ought to be our historiographic horizon. Instead, I would like to insist on the anonymity of historical agents and origins that persists—the losses that must necessarily remain—and the structures of the database that make us aware of that persistence. In this way I also consider the digital database of Turconi fragments as a separate archival structure, one that stands on its own and in separation from the Joye Collection and the restoration of the moving images under way at the BFI. While the aim for some may be to reunite the fragments with the films from which they were extracted, I consider here what we gain in retaining the part against the whole, the motionless fragment against the moving image. In other words, I would like to insist on the material state of things and the autonomy of the incomplete film fragment.

In this chapter I pursue a few questions that aim at the historiographic and artifactual expressions of the Turconi fragments: What remains in the aftermath of Turconi's unfinishing, his radical *undoing* of the moving images in the Joye Collection? Or what does this undoing perhaps *undo*? What is preserved in the preservation and re-presentation of thousands upon thousands of disjunctive clippings in the contemporary Turconi database? What histories—of women and their labor—do these fragments in turn encourage us to see or imagine? In short, what kind of feminist historical knowledge is constituted in this incomplete and fragmented archive? I examine the materiality of the Turconi fragments but also the *fragments of bodies* that this material makes visible. The collection indexes the past-presences of literally hundreds of women, in stuttering still-frame immobility, all of whom remain unidentified in the project's metadata (if not unidentified altogether). Their bodies, their physical there-nesses, are unrecognized and disavowed but nevertheless "there," as I argue, tangled up in the sensational colors of the frames. I consider three overlapping sites of feminist-materialist concern: the color surfaces of the clippings, the still image, and the structure of the database. I begin by briefly describing early applied color processes and the discursive field of color theories and phobias into which these images intervene before turning to examples from the collection.

A materialist-feminist framework urges us to consider how women—their bodies, lives, and labor—are depended upon, determined by, and frequently obscured by film's material processes and infrastructures. As Genevieve Yue argues, gender constitutes film material and its production processes, but this "gendered material dimension . . . disappears into the projected, immaterial one."[7] Indeed, women always have a way of vanishing from film history and rematerializing in the margins of, say, an eccentric digital collection of nitrate film frames. I am also guided here by Hannah Frank's revelatory "frame by frame" approach to animated cinema, which attunes us to an otherwise invisible world of "stray brushstrokes or strands of hair, . . . oily smudges, the literal fingerprints of the workers who handled the image."⁸ As Frank notes, while there are limits to what we can learn from a bit of ink, encountering those limits is itself a crucial aesthetic and political experience of the film image. The task then—my task—is not to restore women to view and historical mythology but to interrogate the conditions of their disappearance and the material traces of their lives that remain in small, stray drops of color.

DIFFERENCE ITSELF

Though color processes were long neglected in film studies—with color often considered a secondary or supplementary aspect of the moving image—this field of technical, historical, and theoretical inquiry has been invigorated over the past decade through a series of color-centric monographs, edited collections, conferences, and large-scale digital projects like Barbara Flueckiger's *Timeline of Historical Film Colors* and *Color Mania* initiatives.⁹ Taken together, this scholarship maps a set of loosely overlapping historical and theoretical divisions between the earliest color processes and the techniques that followed.¹⁰

There are two major categories of color technology in film. From the early 1900s through the 1920s, color was added to the image surface through "applied" or "autonomous" techniques. These techniques include handcoloring, stenciling, tinting, and toning. More than half of the clippings in the Turconi Collection contain these early applied color techniques. (This is due to the era in which Joye collected but also Turconi's interest in Pathé films.)¹¹ In the 1920s and 1930s a range of "subtractive" color systems emerged. Rather than merely *adding* color onto the surface of the film print, these techniques *generate* color (through light filters, beam splitters, special cameras, and color-forming chemical compounds) in the very processes of recording and developing the image. Subtractive systems are often interchangeably described as "mimetic," "naturalistic," and "photographic"—language that suggests something of the conceptual rift that accompanies discussions of color film processes.¹²

The color film image splits in two, signifying at once the promise of cinematic realism—that is, a mimetic re-presentation of colors in the world—and an excessive or unnecessary supplement to that world. For Tom Gunning the split marks the difference between what he describes as the "indexical" colors of subtractive systems and the "metaphorical" formations of applied coloring, between colors that are "in" the image and those that are "outside" or "upon" its surface. In his view the era of exhibitionist attractions coincides with spectatorial experiences of color's autonomous powers. This experience of color owes to the rise of aggressive, attention-seeking nonrealist techniques and the particular material appearance of applied colors. Gunning writes: "Even the slightly uneven fit between color and object in hand painting and stencil coloring, so that the colors seem to lift themselves off the surface of reality and quiver in a scintillating dance, has the effect of underscoring the independent power of color."[13] In this view, the subtractive process subordinates color to the indexical operation. In the applied image, by contrast, color stands apart from the index of the image. It hovers over the image, vibrates upon the surface of the film, and opens onto phenomenological experiences of texture, light, temperature, movement, and the materiality of the image itself, *for itself*.

The earliest formations of color are threatening to aesthetic sensibilities in the first decades of the twentieth century as well as regimes of narrative and realist sense-making. Indeed, the "color mania" of Flueckiger's project names not only a consumer desire *for* color but an experience of being overwhelmed *by* color. Artist Jonathon Rosen's contribution to *Fantasia of Color in Early Cinema*, a collection of essays and full-color image reproductions from the Eye Filmmuseum, describes his contemporary experience of early color as one that brings him into contact with the particulate and physical processes of vision: "The excitement of the new process is *palpable,* the delirious color saturation hyperreal and hallucinatory—not to mention the haptic pressure inside the eye as multi-frequency light waves of photons pour into the cornea and lens and start pushing on the rods and cones of the retina . . . making the optic nerve go berserk."[14] The language of ecstasis, mania, and fantasia—scattered across so much writing on early film color—are all imprecise placeholders of a kind. They are efforts to name a boundless and unstructured experience that takes place at the limits of language and visuality. We do not see color, but feel it with our bodies and eyes.

The split between the sensory excesses attributed to early color processes and the seeming realism of what followed does not always map neatly onto the historical shift from applied to subtractive techniques. In his history of Pathé color films, for example, Charles O'Brien argues that the company's industrial stenciling was celebrated for its realism as early as 1909 (though it was often counterpoised against the seeming restraint of early American studios and their preference for black-and-white images).[15] In his writing on early color film, Joshua Yumibe argues in a slightly different direction. For him, terms like "realism," "spectacle," and "verisimilitude" are fluid and imprecise. One can detect traces of a realist aesthetic in the earliest applied color images, but the sensorial effects of the early era also bleed across the applied-subtractive divide. "Even so-called natural color cannot be looked at only within the parameters of realism," Yumibe observes, "for even the technological reproduction of the colors of the world can be thought of as a dazzling form of attraction, particularly given the exotic and/or picturesque subject material often shot in these various processes."[16] He reminds us here that claims about the realism of color in cinema are just as phenomenological as claims about its spectacularity or sensory excesses. They are claims about our *experience* of the image (as real or not real at all). He suggests that the dividing line between spectacular/real color might track an ideological response to a specific kind of *content*—namely images of racial, ethnic, and sexual difference.[17] Gunning, too, makes a similar point, arguing that color is a sign of "difference itself."[18]

The association of color with sensuous excess and bodily difference governs Western aesthetics and art history. A few coordinates will help to situate the Turconi Collection against this horizon, though others have mapped this expansive field more carefully.[19] In his *Poetics,* for example, Aristotle privileges the clarity of the line over the potential confusions of color.[20] Similarly, in Kant's aesthetics, color is the superficial and unserious counterpart to structure and form. Colors can be pleasing, decorative, and stimulating to the senses, but they are also inessential and threatening externalities, distractions from pure judgments of beauty.[21] Those who hold a subjectivist view—that is, the view that color is mind-dependent and determined by our sense experience of the world—frequently define color as a secondary quality and a source of superficial, often feminine or exotic pleasure.[22] Galileo, Newton, Descartes, Locke, and Hume all held variations of this view. Goethe famously gets caught in a color bind of his own making. He describes his own attraction to the vibrant colors of a "well-favoured girl, with a brilliantly fair complexion, black hair, and a scarlet bodice" but also insists that the pleasures of vivid color are for "savage nations, uneducated people, and children."[23]

In his well-known writing on chromophobia, David Batchelor succinctly defines the twin ideological impulses that underpin the rejection of color: "[The] purging of colour is usually accomplished in one of two ways. In the first, colour is made out to be the property of some 'foreign' body—usually the feminine, the oriental, the primitive, the infantile, the vulgar, the queer or the pathological. In the second, colour is relegated to the realm of the superficial, the supplementary, the inessential or the cosmetic."[24] On the chromophobic view, as Batchelor describes it, color cannot express the higher or elevated concerns of the mind because it remains tied (often invisibly, indirectly) to the lowliness of certain kinds of bodies. For Rosalind Galt, chromophobia motivates the rejection of color in early film theory—including the work of Hugo Münsterberg, Béla Balázs, and Rudolf Arnheim—as inessential or secondary to other cinematic forms. Chromophobia also underpins the decorative film image and what she calls "pretty," a denigrated aesthetic category, wherein a "pernicious patriarchal and racist logic ... continues unmarked even in the absence of any thematics of race or gender."[25] The pretty image always overwhelms us. It is too colorful, too feminine, too superficial, too much.

The production and reception of early color images often model chromophobia's subtle and injurious codes. But these images are also bound up with the lives and bodies of women in profoundly literal and material ways. In early film studios and color firms across the United States and Europe, color application was done almost exclusively by women.[26] Some began the craft as colorists in lantern slide studios (or as the wives of lantern showmen).[27] In the film industry, women painted images frame-by-frame and then joined the stencil assembly line, meticulously cutting the stencils, applying the dyes, and operating the machines. It was monotonous, painstaking, and difficult detail-oriented work. When Pathé enlarged its Vincennes facilities to meet increased demand for color film in 1906, it employed over one hundred colorists (with room for many more).[28] We know the names of a few of these women—Gladys R. Scott, Élisabeth and Berthe Thuillier, Lucie and Germaine Berger, and a Mme. Florimond—but most remain anonymous figures in the early film factory.[29] Some advertised their names and skills in local trade papers.[30] Women were hired for this work because they were thought to have nimble fingers but also, as many have argued, because color *was* women's work: feminine, ornamental, superficial.[31] Crucially, women were also the most common site of applied color techniques in the film image itself.[32] That is to say, in the era of early color, women applied color to the images of other women: to their bodies and dances, their dresses and elaborate costumes.

Setting aside the enormous size of the Turconi Collection, nothing overwhelms the senses in the contemporary encounter with its images. The clippings are small and motionless. They can no longer be projected, and they are presented as if one were inspecting them on a light table. Colors here do not dance upon the photomechanical image. They are cut off from the kind of overwhelming sensory experiences—the fantasias and manias and attractions—that so frequently get ascribed to early film colors. In contemporary writing about early color, the language of sensation and sensory excess foregrounds the bodily experiences of the contemporary observer and, in my view, often enacts the patriarchal and racist logics of chromophobia. The women who made these images and appear in them seem to vanish. They return as symptom of a bodily pleasure that seemingly cannot be named or known. The Turconi fragments, *as* fragments, disrupt these unnamed pleasures, reorient the senses, and return the material traces of women and their labor to view. In what follows, I pursue those traces.

I SAW THEM WITH MY HANDS

I have taken my own cuts from Turconi, just a few clippings out of more than twenty thousand. It is worth noting, before I turn to these images, that color reproductions are not included in this chapter. I have instead included inventory numbers for all of the clippings to which I refer so that readers can easily locate them in the Turconi database.[33]

In the first set of frames, inventory number 10251, four women stand on stage, side-by-side, their arms frozen in midswing, all in different positions. Behind them (above them, alongside them), one sees a display of scattered dice, a paradigmatic sign of cinematic time, the contingencies of modernity, and the haphazard coming-into-being of these two frames, salvaged from thousands of possibilities. The frames were cut from Segundo de Chomón's *Les Dés magiques* (*The Magic Dice*) (1908).[34] The dice are stenciled yellow; the women's dresses are smudged with pink. One of the dresses, on the woman standing furthest to the left, is a deeper, richer color than all the others. It draws our eye, carries it down the line of women. Dye also gathers along the sides of the film, encircling the sprocket holes.

The second clipping, inventory number 405, contains three frames. It comes from a Pathé film, *Moïse sauvé des eaux* (Henri Andréani, 1911), a retelling of Moses's discovery among the bullrushes from the second chapter of the Book of Exodus. In the biblical story the baby is discovered by the Pharoah's daughter. The daughter has no name there, nor do any of the actresses here. (This lack of identification echoes that of Léontine, the unnamed comic actress who appears in a Pathé Frères series from the same period, and who Maggie Hennefeld seeks in chapter 2.) In the clipping, four women stand outdoors, against a backdrop of trees. Here, as in the previous image, they stand side-by-side and look outward, at us. Three of them wear cloth headdresses, flowing gowns, and dangling fringe tied around their waists. Their costumes are stenciled in pale orange and pink. The women hold their hands in the same strange gesture, under their chins, fingertips touching. No doubt they were meant to be hieroglyphic carvings come to life; here, they return to stasis. A fourth woman stands with arms at her sides. Her head and torso are covered with a gauze-like veil that drifts skyward. It cocoons and conceals her. She is not stenciled like the others. In the first frame a light circle of pink draws attention to her breast. The circle darkens, deepens in the second frame, and almost disappears in the third. The edges of the film stock are stenciled with the name "Pathé Frères," but they are also splattered with pink dye.

The third clipping, inventory number 11322, consists of two frames. The perforations along the edges of the film stock are missing and torn, leaving behind jagged little nitrate teeth. In the first frame, women stand in long gowns, each one a different color: blue, yellow, green, pink. Two arched doorways draped with dark red curtains, one on either end of the proscenium, bookend their formation. At first glance, you might count six women. On closer inspection, you will notice a seventh, one out front, concealing a body behind her. This coincidence of overlapping bodies ensures a striking line of shape and color. Together, the women become the very string of ornate gems that each one seems to wear around her neck. The second frame, taken just a fraction of a second after the first, is almost entirely the same. But here, the collar of a turquoise dress peeks further out from behind a pink one, disturbing the geometry of the first frame. In this way the concealed woman comes into better view, but so too does something of the colorist(s) who worked on these frames. A stray mark, a drip of magenta, perhaps a bit of the red curtain, also appears at the bottom of a bright yellow dress. Unidentified until 2015, these frames belong to Georges Méliès's *L'Homme mouche* (*The Human Fly*) (1902).[35]

A final two frames, inventory number 6512. The clipping was extracted from a 1906 Lubin Manufacturing Company film called *The Wreckers of the Limited Express*. Both frames are dark, overwhelmed with layered shapes and shades of gray. One can see a patch of sky, a tree line, a hillside, and a train track that disappears into the distance. In the foreground a white dress is carved out of the negative space. The woman, arms aloft, holds a bit of cloth. In the first frame the thinnest line of red ink colors the cloth. It is a crescent, a red moon. In the second frame the line changes shape. Ever so slightly, it flattens out. The red curls upward.

These clippings force an unusual encounter with the chronophotographic substrate of cinema. They reveal something of the discrete instants that make cinema's illusion of continuity possible. Here, though, the disruption is irreversible. We see a few fractions of a second, the "before" and "after" of which we can only imagine. Performances stutter and stop. Images escape their titles. We find neither *homme* nor *mouche* here, no signs of Moses or Méliès. (Indeed, Méliès's absence from the frame likely contributed to the clipping remaining unidentified for so long.) Turconi no doubt chose these images for their colors, but as a consequence of this preference, so many women are centered in these frames: facing the camera, midgesture, cut off from whatever narrative structures might explain the mise-en-scène, or distract us from their startling appearance.

In this underbelly of the moving image, one is reminded of André Bazin's ontological thinking on the photograph—"the disturbing presence of lives halted"—as well as the split between reality and imaginary that he grounds in its mechanical processes. The photographic image has long been understood as a work of mourning and spectral charm; it encourages us to linger on what we have lost—time, memory, history—and the peculiar surpluses of those objects and lives extracted from the flow. For Bazin, as many will recall, the photographic image is neither real nor unreal but both at once, "an hallucination that is also a fact."[36] That is, the photograph is not *commensurate* with nature, not merely visual evidence of the world; it is an image of nature that draws us away from it. The photomechanical index doubles, stills, and, in so doing, makes the world strange.

Roland Barthes similarly destabilizes the evidentiary value of the photograph, splitting the image between the shared codes of the "studium" and the private wounds of the "punctum."[37] More pertinent to our understanding of the Turconi Collection is his writing on the "third meaning" of the cinematic still. For Barthes the still always exceeds the denotative details in the frame (for example, settings, costumes) and the secondary or symbolic intentions of the author (what he calls the "obvious" meaning). The third meaning is "obtuse," erratic, and subversive. It is grounded in the physical and material details of the artifactual film still and yet counters whatever the moving image contains. In echoes of Barthes's definition of the "punctum," the term names our vague and imprecise attachments to an image that arrive in this most unusual site of spectatorship: at the point of cinema's breakdown, in its becoming still. Barthes describes the third meaning as "a signifier without a precise signified," because the expressions of the image do not refer us to a concept we know or a world we recognize. Counterintuitively, these photomechanical images "do not copy anything," including, most important, the film from which they were extracted.[38] They are something else altogether. Barthes writes: "[The still] is not a specimen chemically extracted from the substance of the film, but rather the trace of a superior *distribution* of traits of which the film as experienced in its animated flow would give no more than one text among others. The still, then, is the fragment of a second text *whose existence never exceeds the fragment.*"[39]

The Turconi clippings are fragments of another possible text. In their stillness one finds a detailed distribution of traits, unavailable in the flow of moving images, inaccessible to its spectators. The clippings carry with them the disturbing quality of lives (and films) come to a standstill as well as the melancholy feelings that can emerge in encounters with the photographic image. Crucially, however, the Turconi images exceed the affective regimes of the photomechanical index, those images impressed upon the surface of the film through the interaction of light and an emulsified base. Here, as I have described them, the images of the women on stage, under trees, along the railroad tracks, carry *another* kind of index—namely, the stains of color and ink.

Elsewhere I have written about the "un-iconic" indices that necessarily accumulate on the delicate surfaces of celluloid, the scratches and tears, mold spores and swirls of decomposing nitrate.[40] Following Charles Sanders Peirce, Mary Ann Doane describes these foundational expressions of the index as "hollowed out" signs, artifacts whose expressions are "limited to the assurance of an existence."[41] Like any other index, the lines and drips of color in these images are physically and causally joined to a historical source, but that source never appears within the frame. They are signs of women having worked with brushes and stencils, of women having been "there" in the studio, in contact with the film stock. In the clippings, we can see the accidents of a misplaced brush or gesture, the extraordinarily subtle changes in a simple line of color, the deep and detailed human labor brought to bear on one frame after another. But we never know with any precision who made these signs, exactly when and how they came to be as they are, what the women who made them were feeling or thinking as they worked.

The second text or counterimage of the clippings emerges in this indexical encounter between the visible and invisible women, the iconic and un-iconic signs. Indeed, what matters here, in my view, is the coincidence between the photomechanical indices of women's bodies and the partial or hollowed-out signs of other women's anonymous labor. These conjoined and simultaneous indices—their palimpsestic layering—generates a mimetic interaction between them. The contingent and material traces of the colorists' work encourage us to read the women in the images as sites of physical labor—that is, as agents equally engaged in a work of gesture, performance, and material. Likewise, the women we see in the images, stenciled and hand-colored, become proxies for the ones we do not. Stripped of movement, extracted from their narrative structures, the clippings bear witness to the gendered labor in the image and upon its surface.

The clippings counter ordinary orders of meaning, both cinematic and historical. They are not commensurate with the films from which they were extracted nor would they be improved—that is, made more meaning-bearing—through their restoration to movement. Put simply, they are not parts of a whole that remains missing. They are instead autonomous texts whose meaning depends upon their fragmentation. Their meaning exists *only* in this liminal and contingent space of cinematic breakdown and contemporary archival spectatorship. Moreover, the meaning that one finds in this sustained and unmoving contact between body and color exceeds those familiar photomechanical feelings of mourning and melancholy. Indeed, I want to insist that these are not merely indices of loss, of the films and the women who made them, of the lives that we will never know or recuperate for the historical record. Rather, what comes into view here is a kind of visual and literal fellowship between the signs of women, an index of their coming into contact. It is a feeling, however fleeting and obtuse, of *solidarity*. It is a hallucination. But maybe also a fact.

One of the persistent critiques of phenomenological arguments about photographic and moving images—which include both vague appeals to the sensory excesses of color images as well as Barthes's writing about the obtuse feelings he finds in the materiality of the still image—is that the claims are grounded in a bodily experience that is likely not our own. Of course, phenomenological frameworks have been crucial sites of feminist film critique, countering the objectifying command of optic visuality and drawing attention to the textures and temperatures of the surface, the embodied experiences and feelings of images. Laura Marks acknowledges the implicit risks of the framework. She writes: "Many of the sources for tactile epistemology may be regarded as unrigorous, romantic, or downright spooky."[42] It is perhaps easy to dismiss the traces I have pursued here as similarly unrigorous—all hallucination and no facts—grounded in my own private experience of still images that never would have circulated or screened as I am seeing and experiencing them now.

But I am not alone here. This way of seeing the film image is not limited to the contemporary spectator and the contingent coming-into-being of the Turconi Collection. In a 1983 interview early film colorist Germaine Berger, who began working for Pathé in 1911 at the age of fourteen, notes that she had never actually *seen* a film before working at the studio and *never even went to the cinema* during her career as a colorist: "We couldn't afford it. We were paid a modest weekly salary and we had to bring the paycheck home and live within our means." And yet, when asked if she recalled her first film, Berger does not recount a theatrical experience from her life after Pathé. Instead, she says, mingling sight and touch, "I saw so many of them simultaneously because I was working on them with my hands!"[43] Indeed, however idiosyncratic the encounter with a broken-down film fragment may seem, the secondary text that emerges in the Turconi Collection better approximates the one available to film colorists—and perhaps *the only one* that they would have seen (and touched). The solidarities in the clippings—the contact between the colorist's hands and the film surface, between the labor on and in the image—extend outward, to the experience of spectatorship. We are brought into community with the anonymous makers of these images, invited to see or imagine some small fragment of their point of view.

THE FINALLY AND DEFINITIVELY UNNAMED

The Turconi clippings also bring nearly every viewer into contact with the Turconi Project itself, the publicly accessible digital database that mediates and makes our view possible. Like so many digital archives of photographic and moving images, the database is a peculiar and sprawling structure, built by a team of scholars, curators, and researchers over a decade and then some. The project is framed as a work in progress with "errors and ambiguities." Corrections are invited. A small note on the reproduction of color reminds visitors that "the frames have been scanned over several years, by different people, and with different pieces of equipment, thus making it impossible to achieve a perfect uniformity in color grading."[44]

This sense of the project as an unwieldy assemblage that has been *made,* incrementally and collectively, over time extends to the experience of searching for and studying the clippings. Visitors can examine all of the clippings available for each of the eight hundred or so distinct titles, or they can move through the Turconi inventory numbers chronologically. They can also search by a handful of terms, such as "tinted," "toned," "handcolored," "decomposed," "faded," "intertitles," and "splice." These categories suggest what others have seen in these images and the concepts that they have used to organize their understanding of them. The search returns depend on archivists and researchers having equally identified those qualities in the images. In the end, all search methods feel like a roll of the dice or a chance encounter with some small detail, a few fragments out of so many thousands. Each clipping also comes with notations (beyond those left behind by Joye and Turconi): inventory numbers for related fragments, links to other archival and journal sources, corrections and discoveries, and small messages from the archivists to each other and potential visitors: "This is very confusing," "Perhaps Turconi misfiled?," "Found wrapped in paper in a tea can." Put simply, the signs of human labor and creative intervention do not end with a pair of scissors and reels of decaying film (though the effects of those decisions are perhaps easier to see).

In her essay on the historical "conditions of anonymity" for silent-era actors and writers, Jane Gaines distinguishes between the on-screen player who was "paradoxically unknown but recognizable" and the anonymous scenario writer who was neither known nor recognized.[45] It is a distinction that echoes the difference between the iconic and uniconic photomechanical indices, between the historical sources we can see in the image (for example, people, settings, objects) and the ones that we cannot. Gaines concludes by asking whether and how we ought to seek out those missing names and restore them to the record. She writes:

> The scholarship that involves supplying missing proper names is well established. But because anonymity represents the antithesis—the unnamed—the "conditions of anonymity" to which I refer here may never receive serious consideration. Further, preserving any condition of anonymity seems the opposite of the traditional work of scholarship because understanding anonymity in early cinema might require respecting the category of nameless personnel as *finally and definitively unnamed.*[46]

Gaines argues here that the material conditions of early film labor, which ensured the anonymity not only of some early film actors but also of writers and colorists, are *themselves* historical and worth preserving. We might lose the particularities of industrial, artisanal, and collective forms of labor if we insist on recuperating them all through the rigid frameworks of authorship and naming. Moreover, as I have argued in this chapter, we might miss the material indices of labor—those hollowed-out signs—that have been there all along. These indices are tied to historical sources that we cannot see or name, but they are nevertheless there, evidence of those who worked—and saw—with their hands.

The refusal to name—the insistence that we hold onto the *finally and definitively unnamed*—is a rejection of a certain film-historical method, one that strives to bring us neat origin stories, with proper names and dates, coherent narrative structures and continuities. All facts, no hallucinations. The Turconi Project is itself a site that insists on the proper name. Indeed, the name "Turconi" in this instance exemplifies the risks and erasures of naming. I struggled in the writing of this chapter with the repetition—over and again—of that singular proper name. The incessant return of the proper name is no doubt a symptom of our appetite for historical origins and order, and maybe also a sign of the insufferable resilience of auteurism. But we can refuse the limitations of the proper name and the project of historical recuperation. In my view the refusal to name is a way of holding onto the material particularities of the film fragment and making space for what will never be retrieved. It points us to the indexical evidence of things that have come into contact with cameras and film stock, including a definitively unnamed collection of women, and leaves the unknowns available to our understanding.

But it also encourages us to consider the open and ongoing *presents* of our histories, the contemporary and contingent practices of our archives and databases, and the conditions of anonymity and invisibility that persist there too. There are palimpsestic layers of human labor at work in any and every archive, ones that exceed the explanatory power of institutional or personal names. They suggest other search terms (like, say, "paper" or "tea can"), other ways of organizing and understanding the historical artifacts and ephemeral details that accumulate there, and perhaps other ways of thinking about authorship and ownership beyond, in this case, the patrimonies of Joye and Turconi. The refusal to name welcomes the ghosts but also signs of life. After all, naming, like seeing, is just one form of knowing.

NOTES

1. Paolo Cherchi Usai and Joshua Yumibe, "Gemona/Rochester: The Davide Turconi Collection of Nitrate Film Frames," *Journal of Film Preservation* 85 (October 2011): 46–49.

2. Alicia Fletcher and Joshua Yumibe, "From Nitrate to Digital Archive: The Davide Turconi Project," *The Moving Image: The Journal of the Association of Moving Image Archivists* 13.1 (2013): 1–32.

3. Fletcher and Yumibe, "From Nitrate to Digital Archive," 10–11.

4. Fletcher and Yumibe, "From Nitrate to Digital Archive," 8, 12.

5. Alicia Marie Fletcher, "Framing Early Cinema: The Davide Turconi Nitrate Film Collection at the George Eastman House," MA dissertation (Ryerson University, 2008), 23–25.

6. In addition to works already cited, see the George Eastman House Press Release for the 2018 exhibition, "Dreaming in Color: The Davide Turconi Collection of Early Cinema," curated by Joshua Yumibe, www.eastman.org/george-eastman-museum-premiere-dreaming-color-davide-turconi-collection-early-cinema.

7. Genevieve Yue, *Girl Head: Feminism and Film Materiality* (New York: Fordham University Press, 2021), 11–12.

8. Hannah Frank, *Frame by Frame: A Materialist Aesthetics of Animated Cartoons* (Berkeley: University of California Press, 2019), 2. See also her discussion of the anonymous women in Frank, "Ink and Paint," *Frame by Frame*, 74–108.

9. Flueckiger's ongoing European Research Council–funded project launched in 2012. In the autumn of 2019, Nadine Wietlisbach and Eva Hielscher curated the "Color Mania" exhibition at the Fotomuseum Winterthur in Switzerland, in collaboration with Flueckiger. See the exhibition catalogue *Color Mania: The Material of Color in Photography and Film*, ed. Flueckiger, Hielscher, and Wietlisbach (Zurich: Lars Mürs, 2020). For recent studies of film color, see Angela Dalle Vacche and Brian Price, eds., *Color: The Film Reader* (New York: Routledge, 2006); Joshua Yumibe, *Moving Color: Early Film, Mass Culture, Modernism* (New Brunswick, NJ: Rutgers University Press, 2012); Simon Brown, Sarah Street, and Liz Watkins, eds., *Color and the Moving Image: History, Theory, Aesthetics, Archive* (New York: Routledge/AFI, 2013); Giovanna Fossati, Tom Gunning, Jonathon Rosen, and Joshua Yumibe, *Fantasia of Color in Early Cinema* (Amsterdam: Amsterdam University Press/Eye Filmmuseum, 2015); Giovanna Fossati, Victoria Jackson, Bregt Lameris, Elif Rongen-Kaynakçi, Sarah Street, and Joshua Yumibe, eds., *The Colour Fantastic: Chromatic Worlds of Silent Cinema* (Amsterdam: Amsterdam University Press, 2018); and Sarah Street and Joshua Yumibe, *Chromatic Modernity: Color, Cinema, and Media of the 1920s* (New York: Columbia University Press, 2019). See also Kim Tomadjoglou, ed., "Early Color" (special issue), *Film History* 21.1–2 (2009).

10. For a slightly earlier generation of color research, see Steve Neale, *Cinema and Technology: Image, Sound, Colour* (London: Macmillan Education Ltd., 1985); Daan Hertogs and Nico de Klerk, eds., *Disorderly Order: Colours in Silent Film. The 1995 Amsterdam Workshop* (Amsterdam: Nederlands

Filmmuseum, 1996); and Paolo Cherchi Usai, "The Way of All Flesh Tones," in *Silent Cinema: An Introduction* (London: British Film Institute, 2000), 21–43.

11. On Pathé's color processes, see Richard Abel, *The Red Rooster Scare: Making Cinema American, 1900–1910* (Berkeley: University of California Press, 1999), 40–47; Charles O'Brien, "Motion Picture Color and Pathé Frères: The Aesthetic Consequences of Industrialization," in *A Companion to Early Cinema*, ed. André Gaudreault, Nicolas Dulac, and Santiago Hidalgo (Oxford: Wiley-Blackwell, 2012), 298–314; and Yumibe, *Moving Color*, 78–97.

12. For further discussion of the distinction between applied and subtractive systems, see Bregt Lameris, "Pathécolor: Perfect in Their Rendition of the Colors of Nature," *Living Pictures* 2.2 (2003): 46–58; Paul Read, "'Unnatural Colors': An Introduction to Coloring Techniques in Silent-Era Movies," *Film History* 21.1 (2009): 9–46; and Luke McKernan, "'The Modern Elixir of Life': Kinemacolor, Royalty, and the Delhi Durbar," *Film History* 21.2 (2009): 122–36; and Yumibe, *Moving Color*, 2–11.

13. Tom Gunning, "Colorful Metaphors: The Attraction of Color in Early Silent Cinema," *Fotogenia* 1 (1996), https://archivi.dar.unibo.it/files/muspe/wwcat/period/fotogen/numo1/numero1d.html.

14. Jonathon Rosen, "Gluttonous Visual Overdose," in *Fantasia of Color in Early Cinema*, ed. Fossati et al., 55–57, 57.

15. O'Brien, "Motion Picture Color and Pathé Frères," 307–308.

16. Yumibe, *Moving Color*, 7.

17. Yumibe, *Moving Color*, 121.

18. Gunning, "Colorful Metaphors," np.

19. See David Batchelor, *Chromophobia* (London: Reaktion Books, 2000); Rosalind Galt, *Pretty: Film and the Decorative Image* (Durham, NC: Duke University Press, 2011), 38–74; and Yumibe, *Moving Color*, 17–36.

20. Aristotle, *Poetics*, 1450b.

21. Immanuel Kant, *Critique of the Power of Judgment, Vol. 5*, trans. Paul Guyer and Eric Matthews, ed. Paul Guyer (Cambridge: Cambridge University Press, 2002), 203–11, 223–26.

22. For overviews of color subjectivism, see Barry Stroud, *The Quest for Reality: Subjectivism and the Metaphysics of Colour* (New York: Oxford University Press, 2000); and Alex Byrne and David R. Hilbert, *Readings on Color, Vol. 1: The Philosophy of Color* (Cambridge, MA: MIT Press, 1997).

23. Johann Wolfgang von Goethe, *Theory of Colours*, trans. Charles Lock Eastlake (Cambridge, MA: MIT Press, 1970 [1840]), 22, 55.

24. Batchelor, *Chromophobia*, 64.

25. Galt, *Pretty*, 49.

26. Yumibe, *Moving Color*, 41–48. See also Joshua Yumibe, "French Film Colorists," in *Women Film Pioneers Project*, ed. Jane Gaines, Radha Vatsal, and Monica Dall'Asta (New York: Columbia University Libraries, 2013), https://wfpp.columbia.edu/essay/french-film-colorists/.

27. Terry Borton, "Outstanding Colorists of American Lantern Slides," *The Magic Lantern Gazette* 26.1 (2014): 3–23.

28. On Pathé's expansion, see Richard Abel, *Ciné Goes to Town: French Cinema, 1896–1914* (Berkeley: University of California Press, 1994), 19–25;

Lameris, "Pathécolor," 46–58; O'Brien, "Motion Picture Color and Pathé Frères," 299–301; and Yumibe, *Moving Color,* 78–90.

29. See Stéphanie Salmon and Jacques Malthête, "Élisabeth and Berthe Thuillier," in *Women Film Pioneers Project,* https://wfpp.columbia.edu/pioneer/elisabeth-and-berthe-thuillier/.

30. See, for example, the "Situations Wanted" column of *Moving Image World* (20 June 1908): 531.

31. Colorist Germaine Berger remarkably notes that men simply "did not touch film stock." Cited in Jorge Dana, "Colour by Stencil: Germaine Berger and Pathécolor," trans. Niki Kolaitis, *Film History* 21.2 (2009): 180–83.

32. Yumibe, *Moving Color,* 49–58. See also Eirik Frisvold Hanssen, "Symptoms of Desire: Colour, Costume, and Commodities in Fashion Newsreels of the 1910s and 1920s," *Film History* 2.2 (2009): 107–21.

33. The Turconi database can be found at: www.cinetecadelfriuli.org/progettoturconi/database.html.

34. For a discussion of Chomón's prevalence in the Turconi Collection, see Fletcher, "Framing Early Cinema," 35–48.

35. Fletcher and Yumibe also refer to this clipping, which was unidentified at the time of their publication. Remarkably, I first encountered the fragment when I searched for "Méliès" in the database. It is the first (of just five) search returns.

36. André Bazin, "The Ontology of the Photographic Image," trans. Hugh Gray, *Film Quarterly* 13.4 (1960): 4–9, 9.

37. Roland Barthes, *Camera Lucida: Reflections on Photography,* trans. Richard Howard (New York: Hill and Wang, 1981).

38. Roland Barthes, "The Third Meaning," in *Image-Music-Text,* trans. Stephen Heath (New York: Hill and Wang, 1977), 52–68, 61.

39. Barthes, "Third Meaning," 67, italics in original.

40. See my final chapter in Katherine Groo, *Bad Film Histories* (Minneapolis: University of Minnesota, 2019), 255–89.

41. Mary Ann Doane, "The Indexical and the Concept of Medium Specificity," *differences: A Journal of Feminist Cultural Studies* 18.1 (2007): 128–52, 133.

42. Laura U. Marks, *The Skin of the Film: Intercultural Cinema, Embodiment, and the Senses* (Durham, NC: Duke University Press, 2000), 138.

43. Cited in Dana, "Colour by Stencil," 182.

44. The note can be found at: www.cinetecadelfriuli.org/progettoturconi/database/nota_sul_colore.html.

45. Jane M. Gaines, "Anonymity: Uncredited and Unknown in Early Cinema," in *A Companion to Early Cinema,* ed. Gaudreault, Dulac, and Hidalgo, 443–59, 448.

46. Gaines, "Anonymity," 454, italics in original.

PART TWO

Refusals and Interruptions

CHAPTER 4

Creating the Archive for Incomplete Feminist Cinematic Narratives

The Andean-Amazonian Case

ISABEL SEGUÍ

For some years now, I have been investigating filmmakers Beatriz Palacios (Oruro, Bolivia, ca. 1945–Havana, Cuba, 2003) and María Barea (Chancay, Peru, 1943–), members of the film groups Ukamau and Warmi, respectively. Although both belong to the same Andean and Latin American oppositional cinema circles and have several acquaintances in common—such as Nora de Izcue, Jorge Sanjinés, and the cinematographer César Pérez—they never worked together.[1] However, serendipitously during the 1990s Barea and Palacios developed separate unfinished projects for feature films in which the protagonists are marginalized urban children, who use Andean-Amazonian Indigenous myths as means to sublimate the hardships of their daily existence. Palacios wrote and preproduced *La tierra sin mal (Land Without Evil)*, a road movie in which a group of homeless kids—orphans and runaways—travel from the city La Paz, in the highlands of Bolivia, to the tropical region of Chiquitanía, looking for the Loma Linda (the Beautiful Hill, another way to refer to the Land Without Evil), a place where, according to Guaraní mythology, there is no death or suffering. Barea's project, *Rocío y los pollitos (Rocío and the Chicks)*, tells the story of a slumdweller girl in Lima who, to justify her father's abandonment, makes free use of the creation myth of Pachacamac, the god of the sky.

Often, feminist historians need to create the archive. Sources are not perfectly catalogued and available in publicly or privately funded institutions that preserve them for posterity. For many years the only documents for the study of *La tierra sin mal* were a weekly shooting plan and some loose pages of a draft of the script, which I found in Palacios's files at Fundación Grupo Ukamau's uncatalogued archive, which is not open to the public. However, some months ago, Pedro Lijerón—responsible for academic relations, among other things, at Fundación Grupo Ukamau—tipped me off that the full literary script of *La tierra sin mal* had suddenly appeared on top of Jorge Sanjinés's desk. Sanjinés, widower and lifelong collaborator of Beatriz Palacios, was consulting the document in the process of writing his memoir.

I jumped for joy with news of the finding. I always supposed that the whole script, and other preparatory materials, must be somewhere in the house. Still, we are talking about an uncatalogued archive, compiled mostly by Beatriz Palacios and her assistants, where the personal and institutional boundaries are not established. The Fundación Grupo Ukamau is also Jorge Sanjinés's home (he and Palacios built an apartment on the top floor), and Ukamau's archive is scattered in filing cabinets around the building. I was generously granted access to the working spaces, but I knew that I could consult only a small part. Other useful primary sources are kept in rooms that are for private use only, emerging mysteriously from time to time at Sanjinés's will. In any case, the wealth of documents I was able to access during my field trips allowed me to write a chapter of my doctoral dissertation as well as several papers in which I foreground the contribution of Palacios to the cinematic endeavors of the Ukamau group using a feminist approach that facilitates the narration of Ukamau's history from a non-Sanjinés-centric—that is nonauteurist—perspective.

The story of Palacios's files is a common one for feminist scholars and, more generally, for historians of precarious cinemas. The endangered materials lie around in forgotten, dusty, or damp boxes. We must establish personal relations of trust with those who possess them and then ask permission to access them. The most rewarding part of the process is creating bonds with the filmmakers, their families, or the custodians of these undervalued treasures. This proactive creation of the archive is always compensated in a way or another, if not by the physical findings then by the emotional gains, and often by both. As for *Rocío y los pollitos,* it was easier to find the documentation because I share a close personal relationship with María Barea, consolidated after years of field trips and online communication. So she provided me with all that is left in her files: a dossier that includes the plot summary, a detailed description of the scenes, with some dialogue, and twelve preproduction pictures of locations and characters. And since she is alive, she contributed the oral history of the production process.[2]

When analyzing the material remains of both films, it struck me that, although the plots are very different in their particulars, their narratives are structured using a similar pattern. Both are stories of children pursuing utopian horizons based on Indigenous myths. In addition, the creation and development of the projects coincide with comparable stages in the careers of both directors. At that point, Palacios and Barea were experienced filmmakers in their forties daring to do ambitious work and, in so doing, emancipating themselves from the traditional subservient role of the producer to which they had been submitted by choice or circumstance.[3] Among other innovations in approach, the poetic use of Andean-Amazonian Indigenous mythology in these narratives shows an effort to continue with the renovation of the traditional cinematic language of the New Latin American Cinema.[4] This renewal was urged by the shattering of the revolutionary dreams caused, in the 1970s, by the wave of military dictatorships (supported by the United States) and immediately after by the economic violence inflicted by the institutions of the Washington Consensus: the World Bank and the International Monetary Fund.

However, Palacios's and Barea's films are still engaged with burning political issues, making nuanced critiques of the Bolivian and Peruvian societies of the time, brutally hit by neoliberal policies, in addition to the traditional racism and classism inherited from their colonial histories. The scripts account for multiple socioeconomic aspects and show how marginalized communities organized themselves to resist capitalism and coloniality at the turn of the century. Furthermore, both works make use of feminist perspectives to frame the storytelling. Although the filmmakers were not militants, key issues on the agenda of the Latin American feminist movement appear throughout the texts, such as forced prostitution, abortion, and family abandonment. I hypothesize that due to their feature-fiction format and focus on women's and children's rights, these films, if released, would have potentially fostered the diversification of narratives in the mainstream cinema of the region, adding counterpatriarchal approaches to a market dominated by male-centered points of view, a few local—such as Francisco Lombardi, prominent in the Peruvian case, or, with less impact, Marcos Loayza, Paolo Agazzi or Juan Carlos Valdivia in the Bolivian—but mostly foreign.

In this chapter I try to bring these two unfulfilled film projects to life to counteract the irreparable loss of their staging. To that end, I use the archival material and oral histories available, including the testimony of Jorge Sanjinés, to help me reconstruct both the narrative worlds and the production context of both films. Finally, I recount ways in which these projects may soon have another life.

LA TIERRA SIN MAL: THE UTOPIA OF AN EQUAL BOLIVIA UNITED IN PLURALITY

Elsewhere I have written about the different roles Beatriz Palacios occupied throughout her career: she was the manager of the cinematic group Ukamau, the producer of the films directed by Jorge Sanjinés, an evaluator of the impact of political cinema on subaltern audiences, and the codirector of the documentary *Las banderas del amanecer* (1983).[5] Moreover, there is evidence that she wrote four separate unfinished projects. At the end of the 1970s she conceived a documentary about the five women from the mines who, in 1978, through a hunger strike, catalyzed the end of the dictatorship of General Hugo Banzer. Afterward, on an unknown date, Palacios developed the idea for the historical film *Cuatro mujeres para la guerra* (*Four Women for War*), in which the same actress would play the role of four female liberators who fought the Wars of Independence. By the end of the 1990s she was working on the preparation of the testimonial docufiction *Amayapampa o la pampa de las almas* (*Amayapampa or the Pampa of Souls*), about the events of the so-called Christmas massacre (1996). At the same time, Palacios started developing her last and most cherished project, *La tierra sin mal*, which was also the one that came closest to completion.

The idea for *La tierra sin mal* goes back a long way. It stems from Palacios's experiences interviewing street children in the 1980s.[6] She spent several years working in preproduction. Thus the film was keenly anticipated by the members of the cultural circles of La Paz, and especially by those women colleagues who knew and appreciated Palacios and had seen her unconditionally supporting her husband's projects for decades while leaving her own work aside.[7] In 2003, she was ready to start the filming phase. The script and casting were finished, the locations scouted and the funding from the Bolivian National Film Council (CONACINE) secured. Palacios had been rehearsing regularly with the cast of nonprofessional actors and training Perico, her little dog, for the starring role she had written for him (figure 4.1).[8] Even Jorge Sanjinés was ready to act as his wife's assistant for the first time in his life. At that critical moment (circa 2002), Palacios, who suffered from advanced rheumatoid arthritis,

FIGURE 4.1 Julio García Espinosa, Beatriz Palacios, and Perico, the dog actor. Photograph taken by Jorge Sanjinés in April 2001, during a visit Espinosa made to Bolivia to teach the course "Introduction to Film Direction" at the Andean Film School. Archive of Lola Calviño.

had an intense outbreak that prevented her from carrying out the shooting plans. In July 2003 she died prematurely, and the incomplete project lives now in the imagination of her admirers, who consider it an example of poetic injustice. After having sacrificed so much for Ukamau, her body failed when she needed it most to realize the project.

I asked Jorge Sanjinés directly if he believed that Palacios gave up her film projects to support his artistic career and the political program of Ukamau. He replied:

> It's possible. But she was not ambitious. What interested her was to make the best films to serve the cause of the revolutionary struggle. And she also recognized her limits. She had confidence, admiration and understood the movies we made. She did not put herself in competition, saying: "I'm going to make a better movie than Jorge." None of that entered her head. She wanted to make the movie [*La tierra sin mal*]. She had intelligence, talent, desire, and also the means, so why wouldn't she do it? I encouraged her a lot in that sense, telling her: "you have to make your movie, don't let time beat you, take your film forward."[9]

Nevertheless, the fact remains that Palacios always prioritized her husband's projects for strategic or other reasons. However, she was no victim. She had no one above her in Ukamau's organizational chart. Putting her personal work aside was a deliberate and conscious choice, maybe tinged with her own unconscious bias regarding the validity of her creative path.

All that remains today for the study of *La tierra sin mal* are the film's *guion literario* (literary script), a weekly shooting plan, and the first visual treatment. I found the latter document when this chapter was about to go to press in the archive of Fundación Nuevo Cine Latinoamericano in Havana—a sign of how the research process, in line with the theme of this collection, is ongoing and unfinished. The document, which is dated 1996, may have arrived in Cuba for pitching purposes. It has twenty-seven pages and interestingly states "by Jorge Sanjinés and Beatriz Palacios." Since Sanjinés never appears as the coauthor in subsequent versions, in the press coverage, or in his own memories, I hypothesize that Palacios added his name for leverage at the early pitching phase.[10] The final literary script, meanwhile, consists of sixty-two pages (pages nine and forty went missing). The three-page shooting plan is an exhaustive outline of the activities and resources needed for eight filming weeks. It details the scenes, actors, locations, and other logistical issues such as travel, setting, and rest days.

The script and shooting plan present *La tierra sin mal* as an ambitious and complex project devised to the last stages. The narrative is structured around three plots. The main story is that of five street children "of indigenous and mestizo extraction" called Piolas, Tonchita, Cambita, Panchito, and Tomacito, the oldest of whom is only nine years old.[11] With the dog Perico, the group make a journey of more than a thousand kilometers that starts at the city of La Paz, the seat of government of Bolivia, located in the middle of the Andes mountain range, and goes down the valleys until reaching the jungle areas of the country's lowlands. In addition to the length of the route, it is important to note the variations in altitude, with a difference of four thousand meters between the beginning at the Aymara city, El Alto, and the end, the small Guarayo town, Urubichá. Two other parallel plots place two characters right at the beginning and at the end of the journey. Juanita, an eleven-year-old girl, who initially forms part of the group of street children, is kidnapped in a brothel in the southern area (the residential area of the wealthy classes) of La Paz. Thus, through this girl, Palacios aims to show us the harsh reality of women and girls who are victims of human trafficking for sexual exploitation. The third plot focuses on Melquiades, a wise and crazy old man who is a resident of Urubichá and whom the children search for in the hope that he can show them how to get to Loma Linda, the final destination of their trip. *Loma Linda* is how Cambita refers to the Land Without Evil in the script. Palacios learned about this legend from a homeless kid from the lowlands she met on the streets of La Paz. This boy inspired not only the character but the entire story.

La tierra sin mal corresponds to the ancient Guaraní legend of Yvy Maraey, which was transcribed in written form for the first time by the German-Brazilian ethnologist Curt Unckel Nimuendajú. The concept refers to the unearthly paradise and, at the same time, to a heavenly place found somewhere on the earth and accessible in this life.[12] To save themselves from the apocalypse, the Guaraní, as Diego Villar and Isabelle Combès explain, "trust in the possibility of embarking on a journey to the Land Without Evil, where crops grow on their own, the party is eternal, and there is no death. It must be said that the guides themselves do not always agree on the coordinates . . . in the most widespread opinion, we must go 'to the east, beyond the sea.'"[13] A range of anthropologists have discussed the origin and symbolic and historical functions of this myth in the Tupí-Guaraní culture, such as Alfred Métraux, León Cadogan, Egon Schaden, and Pierre and Hélène Clastres.[14]

Here, however, I refer only to the use that Beatriz Palacios, a mestizo woman who does not belong to that culture, makes of the myth for the construction of a non-Indigenous literary and filmic story. Years later, in a very different take, filmmaker Juan Carlos Valdivia would also use the legend in the film *Yvy Maraey* (2013), which focuses on otherness. The lack of intercultural communication is an ever-present issue in Bolivian politics. After the election of Evo Morales, the first Indigenous president, in 2005, profound symbolic transformations started at the state level. Reforms included the move from the country being named a Republic to being named a plurinational state, and the promulgation of a new political constitution. This legal text, approved in 2009, incorporates the Guaraní expression *ivi maraei* (land without evil), along with other terms of Quechua and Aymara origin: "The State assumes and promotes as ethical-moral principles of the plural society: ama qhilla, ama llulla, ama suwa (do not be lazy, do not be a liar or be a thief), suma qamaña (live well), ñandereko (harmonious life), teko kavi (good life), *ivi maraei* (land without evil) and qhapaj ñan (noble way or life)."[15]

Palacios prefigures this will of uniting the country in its diversity in the plot. The highland children come to know about the Land Without Evil thanks to this boy from the lowlands nicknamed Cambita. *Camba* is the demonym used in Bolivia to refer to the inhabitants of the eastern tropical regions of the country, the land of the Guaraní and other Amazonian ethnic groups. In contrast, *Colla* is the name given to the dwellers of the western highlands. The Aymaras are *Collas,* descendants of the original peoples of the Collasuyo, the southernmost part of the Inca empire. The divide between the western and eastern parts of Bolivia is a symbolic and practical fracture that affects every aspect of national politics. In the script the character of Cambita (Little Camba) is responsible for teasing the children to pursue the utopian dream. So, in a way the trip toward the East that these vulnerable *Colla* children undertake represents the dream of a Bolivia that, overcoming its regional differences, is united by innocence and hope.

Later I will argue that this film also puts forward a feminist sensibility absent from most Bolivian films in the 1990s and early 2000s. But first I present in more detail María Barea's unfinished project so as to compare them afterward.

ROCÍO Y LOS POLLITOS: NAVIGATING EXCLUSION USING INDIGENOUS CHILDREN'S FANTASTIC WORLDS

María Barea was a seasoned filmmaker when she founded the first Peruvian women-led film collective, Warmi (Quechua for "woman"), in 1989. Her career had started at the beginning of the 1970s with her participation as an assistant producer in the only film that the Bolivian collective Ukamau produced in Peru, *The Principal Enemy,* which was shot in 1972 and released in 1974.[16] During the rest of the 1970s, Barea and her partner at the time, Luis Figueroa, a pioneer of Indigenist cinema, produced a series of movies with their small company Pukara, such as these features inspired by literary works: *Los perros hambrientos* (*The Starving Dogs,* 1977) and *Yawar Fiesta* (*Bloody Feast,* 1979). After the couple's separation in 1980, Barea directed *Mujeres de El Planeta* (1981), a documentary commissioned by the German producer Pierre Hoffmann about a collective of women organized in a settlers' neighborhood in the outskirts of Lima. This work marked Barea's cinematic and political goals for the rest of her career.[17]

In 1982, Barea founded the cinematic group Chaski and, as often happens, what started as an emancipatory project—aiming at a collaborative workflow, horizontal decision-making processes, and so on—turned into a traditionally *machista* and hierarchical structure in which Barea had little voice.[18] After fulfilling her commitments as the producer and distributor of *Gregorio* (1984), the first feature film by Chaski, she left the group. In 1989 she founded Warmi, with Amelia (Micha) Torres and María Luz Pérez Goicoechea, who had also left Chaski. As opposed to that previous group, Warmi, in its statute of constitution, had as its fundamental goal to work toward the accomplishment of the rights of women and children through film.[19]

The Warmi Film and Video Collective was active during the 1990s. Its first finished production was the documentary *Porque quería estudiar* (*Because I wanted to go to school*, 1990). The last, *Hijas de la Violencia* (*Daughters of War*, 1998). Barea directed both. *Rocío y los pollitos* was the first of Warmi's projects. Barea wrote a short version of the script and sent it to a contest organized by the Cuban film school of San Antonio de los Baños. The project did not win the funding, but Barea kept trying to raise money for the production through European development NGOs. In 1992 a group of German volunteers helped her strengthen the film dossier. Among other additions, they took a series of preproduction pictures in Villa El Salvador, which helped visualize the filmmakers' intentions. At the same time, the Warmi team were working on another project with the Institute for the Promotion and Training of Domestic Workers (IPROFOTH) and the Italian social worker Vitoria Savio. Thanks to Savio, some money arrived to fund this project, resulting in the documentary *Porqué quería estudiar* (1990) and the feature docufiction *Antuca* (1992).

Barea aimed to finance the production of *Rocío y los pollitos* with the money recovered through the commercial distribution of *Antuca*. But in December 1992 the government of Alberto Fujimori repealed the advantageous film law that, since 1972, had guaranteed the exhibition of Peruvian films in local theaters—that is, the 19.327 decree law also known as General Velasco's film law. The derogation of this law was disastrous for the precarious Peruvian film industry and effectively shut down Barea's project. Today, all that remains of the film are the materials included in the dossier: a two-page plot synthesis; a twelve-page project with a detailed description of the scenes and some dialogue, but not fully developed; and twelve preproduction still pictures that show characters and locations (figure 4.2).

The narrative has different layers. There is an overall framework of advocacy for the rights of vulnerable women and children, the inhabitants of the *pueblos jóvenes* (new villages), the name given in Lima to the settlements of rural immigrants that proliferated in the outskirts of the capital city since the 1950s. The background of the film is the struggle

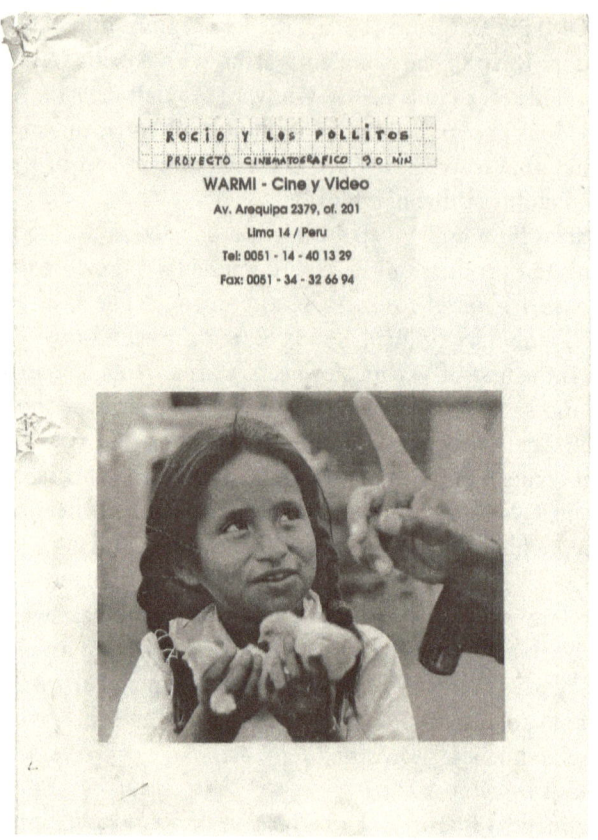

FIGURE 4.2 Front cover of the film project *Rocío y los pollitos*. Archive of María Barea.

of the women in these neighborhoods to provide for their families, and the psychological consequences of poverty and deprivation for the children. As in all of Barea's projects, the narrative revolves around the resilience of the dwellers of the slums. It highlights those skills and values that allow the women to confront the structural injustice and thrive, thanks to practices of group solidarity.

The plot focuses on an imaginative little girl, Rocío, and her mother, Panchita, a young Indigenous woman who arrived years ago at the city from the countryside, accompanied by her husband. Like most immigrants, the family lives in a straw shack in La Alborada (a fictitious name for Villa El Salvador). Panchita works as a street vendor of *emolientes*, a traditional hot beverage made from medicinal herbs, and her husband is a bricklayer. He abandons the family for another woman, which causes both economic and emotional distress for his wife and children. Panchita's son, Juanito, must leave school to help her in her informal business. The little girl Rocío, left alone all day, starts inventing stories to calm herself. She interprets the events in her life in the light of one of the Indigenous creation myths that her mother tells her at night as a bedtime story. Pachacamac and Pachamama fall in love and have two children, a boy and a girl. Pachacamac's evil brother, Wakon, also in love with Pachamama, kills his brother and tries to seduce his sister-in-law. She rejects him, and Wakon kills her too. After their assassination Pachacamac becomes God of the Sky and Pachamama, Goddess of the Earth. Their children remain in the hands of Wakon, feeling lost and alone. A series of mythical animals—the condor, the jaguar, the serpent, and the fox—help the children escape Wakon, who also dies. Finally the children are brought up to the sky by Pachacamac, who turns them into the Sun (Inti) and the Moon (Killa). From that moment on, our world stabilizes into a cycle of day and night. Perfect equilibrium is established with the children eternally circling their parents.

The little girl visualizes the legend her mother tells "like a theatrical representation" in which the actors are members of her family and acquaintances. She is the Moon, her brother is the Sun, and her mother and father are Earth and Sky. In her imagination Wakon is a neighbor who is trying to seduce her mother in real life.[20] The happy end of the tale soothes Rocío's anxiety, but she still spends a lot of time by herself while her mother and brother work in the city center, far away from the neighborhood. Yet she is not entirely alone. Panchita is involved with the women's organization of La Alborada, and Rocío's best friend, Pepita, is the daughter of the community leader, Malena. The character of Malena is based on the legendary Black activist María Elena Moyano, leader of the Popular Federation of Women of Villa El Salvador, who achieved national and international prestige for her social and political work.[21]

Given Moyano's public persona, a character such as Malena, inspired by her, introduces an explicitly political dimension to the story. The organizations of women settlers provide a series of services (food, education, and health) to help one another in the difficult conciliation of their working and domestic lives. In the absence of public services, women's organizations play a pivotal role in the community. Moreover, they foster a type of collective motherhood that is more than just a survival strategy. Lima's organizations of women settlers enable an alternative model to neoliberalism that stems from unionist traditions and the Indigenous communal ethos still in place in the Andean and Amazonian regions of the country where these migrants come from.

However, the film only uses this fascinating political reality as a background. The storytelling focuses on Rocío's audacity and the complicity of her friend, Pepita, two rebellious little girls, who hide a bunch of little chicks that Rocío gets from a rag-and-bone man in exchange for empty bottles that she steals from her mother. María Barea told me that although this idea of exchanging bottles for chicks may seem a magical-realist—or directly surrealist—invention, it was based on actual events. This was a common bartering practice, which she witnessed during the filming of *Mujeres de El Planeta* for the first time.[22] This powerfully poetic image stayed with Barea and led her to write the story that gives the name to the film. The story of the insubordination of the girls in front of their mothers mimics the insubordination of their mothers—Indigenous and Afro-descendant subaltern women—in front of the patriarchal and colonial structures that oppress them.

INTERSECTIONAL FEMINIST NARRATIVES

The list of social issues reflected in the scripts of *La tierra sin mal* and *Rocío y los pollitos* is extensive: poverty and social exclusion suffered by women and children, gender inequality, and all types of exploitation, abuse, and violence (economic, physical, sexual, and environmental). At the same time, the gender-sensitive counternarratives highlight the resourcefulness and wit of their protagonists, with an emphasis on autonomy. Perhaps the filmmakers are mirroring their struggles to live fully autonomous lives. In any case, their character construction is not patronizingly charitable. Although within the limits of rigid societal stratification, the protagonists are neither portrayed as victims nor stripped of their agency.

The children in *La tierra sin mal* use their imagination to provide for themselves while creating continuously. They perform, play music, and sing on the street. They also beg, pick up rubbish, and shine shoes. Some of their survival and leisure activities are illegal, like stealing food or consuming drugs. In several instances the storytelling aligns thematically with the Hispanic picaresque genre, a satirical subgenre of the Spanish golden age literature in which an itinerant homeless character, often a child, strives to survive thanks to his wit, committing petty crimes. Picaresque novels always make a poignant analysis of the society in which the character is immersed, showcasing structural injustices and moral hypocrisy in a raw and humorous way. Palacios's narrative includes passing references to different human and economic landscapes that help paint the country's bigger picture. On their trip the children encounter organ traffickers, corrupt senators, illegal dumpsters full of radioactive waste, clandestine graveyards, blocked roads, and military repression of peasant protests, among other intrinsically contrasting spaces and happenings.

There is less variety in the script of *Rocío y los pollitos*, first, because the story develops only in two spaces, the slum and the city center, but also because the existing script is relatively brief. For *La tierra sin mal*, the script includes sixty-five pages of dialogue, but the project of *Rocío y los pollitos* consists of only a twelve-page summary of the scenes. In any case, both stories present a chain of causes and consequences to explain the current situation of the children's vulnerability. In *La tierra sin mal* the origin stories are told through flashbacks that signal different injustices committed against the orphans' parents, all subaltern subjects from various working-class and Indigenous peasant backgrounds. In *Rocío y los pollitos* the protagonist belongs to an Indigenous peasant family, forced to migrate to the city searching for a better future to find a reality even more exploitative than the one they left. However, both films convey hope in the abilities of women and children to open avenues for individual and collective betterment. Paradoxically, these unfinished film projects focus on the potential of women and children to overcome subordination, but their incompletion proves that the counteraction they propose is often unsuccessful. Having (in Sanjinés's words) intelligence, talent, and desire does not guarantee that you will fulfill your potential or bring a project to completion, when other key elements, such as health in Palacios's case or money in Barea's, are lacking.

Regarding the most explicitly feminist elements of the narratives, one of the subplots of *La tierra sin mal* is the story of Juanita, an eleven-year-old girl deceived and held by a prostitution ring. Through her eyes Palacios allows the viewer to witness the modus operandi of human traffickers and the structural inequality that underpins sexual exploitation. The brothel is placed in the city's wealthiest neighborhood. Interestingly enough, when Juanita escapes her captors, she takes shelter in a Catholic church, where a socially committed priest helps her rebuild her life. At some point a statue of the Virgin Mary cries actual tears as a reaction to Juanita's suffering. This image of Our Lady weeping is an odd narrative device coming from a Marxist such as Palacios. Still, it produces a compelling sensation of relief to the distress that Juanita's story provokes in the reader and surely would have caused in the intended audience. The detail is probably a wink at Liberation Theology and those committed Catholic priests such as the Jesuit Catalans, nationalized Bolivians such as Luis Espinal and Xavier Albó, who, risking their lives, remained at the service of the downtrodden during successive dictatorships (Espinal—journalist, cinephile, and film critic—was assassinated in 1980).

In *Rocío y los pollitos* the gender-sensitive narrative tropes proliferate, starting with the father's abandonment of the family and the struggle of the single mother to raise her children with dignity. Moreover, small details point out ever-present problems. For instance, the girls pass by a so-called "cemetery of little angels" where the fetuses from illegal abortions are buried. No further comment is made. However, this reference makes visible a pervasive but unattended public health problem that affects mostly vulnerable women.

The explicit themes—in primary, secondary, or background narrative lines—that appear in these unfinished movies respond to a feminist agenda and would have contributed significantly to the renovation of cinematic storytelling in Bolivia and Peru. We hardly find any fiction film titles released at the end of the twentieth century that incorporate feminist approaches to the living reality of the subaltern subjects in these countries. However, we can study these incomplete processes as antecedents of some fiction films led by Peruvian middle-class women in the twenty-first century: features focused on giving voice to subaltern Indigenous women, such as the works of Claudia Llosa, *Madeinusa* (2006) and *The Milk of Sorrow* (2009), and more recently, Melina León's *Song Without a Name* (2019).

In any case, we should note that the stylized use of Indigenous myths to convey non-Indigenous narratives is problematic. Palacios and Barea were what Antonio Gramsci would call "organic intellectuals," aligned with the cause of liberation of the Andean-Amazonian Indigenous peasant populations. However, Palacios was a mestiza and Barea of Italian descent. Both of them belong to the urban lower-middle-class. Their political and social commitment and lower social origins played a part in the lack of matronizing attitudes observed in their work and daily behavior. However, since these feature films were conceived principally to be screened in commercial theaters, it is feasible to venture that the target audiences were not the Indigenous majorities but the urban middle-classes. In that sense the Indigenous myths were utilized to convey a poetic form appealing to the petty-bourgeois taste. This is a crucial point to interrogate because the intended audience affects the final form of any cinematic product. However, I do not venture to go further in my analysis because the filmic texts are not available in these cases. Based on the available evidence, it can be argued that the principal contribution of *La tierra sin mal* and *Rocio y los pollitos* would have introduced overtly feminist perspectives to urban middle-class cinemagoers, favoring a democratization and diversification of the cinematic narratives in Bolivia and Peru.

POSSIBLE FUTURE LIVES

I want to end this chapter with hope. In the previous pages we have been confronted with a frustrating analysis of what could have been and never will be. As a researcher who uses emotions as a methodology, I somatize the powerlessness in my body. If only Beatriz Palacios had prioritized her own work years before. Suppose she would have put her health and well-being before Ukamau's success. If only the Cuban jury of the contest at the Film School of San Antonio de los Baños or the European NGOs would have understood the importance of Barea's proposal, an ambitious feature about the women organized en masse in Lima. Or even if Alberto Fujimori had never come to abolish a protectionist law that allowed to fund the production of a small cinema in Peru. If only . . .

However, not everything is lost. First, thanks to the current members of Ukamau, we have recovered the entire script of *La tierra sin mal*. This finding will help scholars to characterize better the importance of Beatriz Palacios's contribution to Bolivian and Latin American cinema. I hope that Fundación Grupo Ukamau, the rights holder, publishes this invaluable source as soon as possible. Other materials related to the film—such as preproduction pictures—are probably hidden in a box somewhere, as often happens. Historians interested in artisanal modes of production must always be alert and proactively ask filmmakers and their families for their files to obtain primary sources, especially feminist historians. The archive is something that does not exist. We make it happen.

Even more hopeful is the initiative of the Peruvian filmmakers and researchers Lorena Best and Sara Guerrero, who are now conducting the investigation for the documentary *¿Usted de nuevo, señorita?* (*Is it you again, young lady?*). This archival film project aims to recover forgotten stories of Peruvian women filmmakers, emphasizing the figure of María Barea. One of the planned activities of this processual project includes an on-camera reading of the script of *Rocío y los pollitos* by Graciela Huaywa Collanqui, the domestic worker protagonist of the film *Antuca*. Huaywa would be playing the role of Panchita, the mother of Rocío, in Best and Guerrero's film.

I conclude with these two vanishing points, examples that signal possible ways of activating the latent qualities of the unfinished. It is instrumental to create the archive for unfulfilled feminist cinematic narratives in Latin America. They contain the seeds of innovations, in form and content, that will only come to fruition years, or even decades, into the future. Constructing historical genealogies that incorporate the unfinished represents a paradigmatic change that could bring bountiful harvests to our discipline. The collective work of Latin American feminist film historians toward this end is just beginning. Let us dig.

ARCHIVAL SOURCES

La tierra sin mal. Guion literario (literary script). 62 pages. Fundación Grupo Ukamau Archive (La Paz, Bolivia).

La tierra sin mal. Plan de rodaje (shooting plan). 3 pages. Fundación Grupo Ukamau Archive.

La tierra sin mal. Primer tratamiento de imagen (first visual treatment). 27 pages. Fundación Nuevo Cine Latinoamericano Archive (Havana, Cuba).

Rocío y los pollitos. Proyecto cinematográfico (film project). 12 pages. Personal files of María Barea (Lima, Peru).

Rocío y los pollitos. Sinopsis argumental (plot sinopsis). 2 pages. Personal files of María Barea.

Rocío y los pollitos. 12 preproduction pictures with captions in German and Spanish. Personal files of María Barea.

NOTES

1. When I asked María Barea about the reasons for this lack of nearness when they had so much in common, she explained that she was closer to Sanjinés's first wife, the Chilean Consuelo Saavedra, with whom she had worked in Ukamau's only Peruvian production *The Principal Enemy* (1974). When the couple split, in part because Sanjinés fell in love with Palacios, some friends and collaborators stayed loyal to Saavedra (informal conversation with María Barea in London, September 2017). As I state elsewhere, it is crucial to incorporate this type of information—considered for some too personal or gossipy—into the academic literature to correctly historicize the mode of production of nonindustrial and precarious cinemas, because the entire viability of the production depended on personal relationships of friendship and kinship. Isabel Seguí, "Auteurism, *Machismo-Leninismo* and Other Issues: Women's Labor in Andean Oppositional Film Production," *Feminist Media Histories* 4.1 (2018): 11–36, 18.

2. I want to thank María Barea and Jorge Sanjinés for granting me access over the years to their files. Special thanks go to Pedro Lijerón, Mónica Bustillos, and Luis Tapia, from Fundación Grupo Ukamau, who kindly located, scanned, and forwarded the most complete copy found, to date, of the literary script of *La tierra sin mal*.

3. Seguí, "Auteurism, *Machismo-Leninismo* and Other Issues," 21.

4. Although these two films were conceived in the 1990s, they are direct descendants of the New Latin American Cinema tradition. Both Palacios and Barea were contributors to this continental scene. When B. Ruby Rich analyzes production in the region until the 1980s, she refers to the constant actualization of the cinematic language in the New Latin American Cinema in these terms: "*La lucha continúa,* the struggle continues, but the site of the battle and the choice of the weapons changes by the decade." B. Ruby Rich, "An/Other View of New Latin American Cinema," in *New Latin American Cinema*, vol. 1, ed. Michael T. Martin (Detroit, MI: Wayne State University Press, 1997), 273–97, 294.

5. The Ukamau group is a Bolivian cinematic collective founded in the 1960s. Their feature films of the 1960s and 1970s—such as *Ukamau* (1966), *Blood of the Condor* (1969), and *The Courage of the People* (1971)—are part of the canon of Latin American Third Cinema. The group has had different phases and several members; the only remaining member from the 1960s is Jorge Sanjinés. Currently the group are in postproduction on their last film, *Los viejos soldados (The old soldiers)*, an account of the Chaco War based on a novel written by Sanjinés. On Palacios, see Seguí, "Auteurism, *Machismo-Leninismo* and Other Issues," and Seguí, "Beatriz Palacios: Ukamau's Cornerstone (1974–2003)," *Latin American Perspectives* 48.2 (2021): 77–92.

6. In a note published in the cultural supplement of La Paz's newspaper *La Prensa*, Palacios explains that she had the idea for the film when she was chronicling the life experiences of the ordinary people of La Paz. I venture she was referring to her periodic collaboration in the weekly *Aquí* in the 1980s. "Beatriz Palacios busca *La tierra sin mal* con los niños de la calle," *La Prensa*, La Paz, 12 January 2003, 6b–7b.

7. This impression was communicated to me in personal conversations by women belonging to La Paz's cultural scene, such as the artist and activist María Galindo, the videomaker Liliana de la Quintana, and the cultural manager and journalist Patricia Flores.

8. "Beatriz Palacios," *La Prensa*.

9. Isabel Seguí, interview with Jorge Sanjinés, La Paz, 12 August 2015.

10. Despite the general similarity in the scenes, characters, locations, and other key features, there are also significant differences between the earlier visual treatment of *La tierra sin mal* and the final one. In the former, the violence exerted towards or by the children is more explicit. Palacios decided to tone down the graphic harshness in later versions. The comparison between the two texts would be fascinating, but I do not have time to undertake it here at this editing stage.

11. Beatriz Palacios, *La tierra sin mal: Guion literario*, Fundación Grupo Ukamau Archive, 3. All translations are mine unless stated otherwise.

12. Diego Villar and Isabelle Combès, "La Tierra sin Mal: Leyenda de la creación y destrucción de un mito," *Tellus* 13.24 (2013): 201–25, 204.

13. Villar and Combès, "La Tierra sin Mal," 203–04.

14. Pablo Antunha Barbosa, "La Tierra sin Mal: Historia de un mito," *Suplemento Antropológico* L.2 (2015): 7–236, 12.

15. Constitución política del Estado Plurinacional de Bolivia (2009), Primera parte, Título I, Capítulo 2, Artículo 8; emphasis added.

16. At the time of the production of this film, Beatriz Palacios was not yet part of Ukamau. She would meet Sanjinés in Havana in 1973, during the postproduction of *The Principal Enemy* at the Instituto Cubano del Arte e Industria Cinematográficos (ICAIC).

17. This film was part of a series of five episodes titled *As Women See It*, which includes *Selbe et tant d'autres* by Safi Faye; *Sudesha* by Deepa Dhanraj, *Bread and Dignity: Open Letter from Nicaragua* by María José Álvarez; and *Permissible Dreams* by Atiat El-Abnoudi.

18. See Seguí, "Auteurism, *Machismo-Leninismo* and Other Issues," 26–30. For general accounts of the history of Chaski, see Sophia A. McClennen, "The Theory and Practice of the Peruvian Grupo Chaski," *Jump Cut: A Review of Contemporary Media* 50 (Spring 2008), www.ejumpcut.org/archive/jc50.2008/Chaski/; and Gabriela Martínez, "Independent Filmmaking in the Peruvian Context: Seeking Meaning," in *Independent Filmmaking around the Globe*, ed. Doris Baltruschat and Mary P. Erickson (Toronto: University of Toronto Press, 2015), 90–109.

19. Statute of Constitution of the Civil Association Warmi Collective Film and Video, Notarial Archive of Dr. Ramón A. Espinosa-Garreta, 24 July 1989.

20. María Barea, *Rocío y los pollitos: Guion literario*, personal files of María Barea, 6.

21. In 1987, Moyano was awarded the Prince of Asturias Award for Concord. In February 1992 she was assassinated in a cowardly manner by the Shining Path, a Maoist guerrilla group. When the initial story of *Rocío y los pollitos* was written, nobody could have anticipated this appalling event. The crew of Warmi were working in preproduction in Villa El Salvador when it happened. They attended and recorded Moyano's funeral, one of the most well-attended of the decade, but unfortunately the videotape is lost.

22. Isabel Seguí, interview with María Barea, WhatsApp, 16 August 2021.

CHAPTER 5

Women (Not) Making Movies under the Popular Unity in Chile (1970–1973)

ELIZABETH RAMÍREZ-SOTO

Feminist scholar Kemy Oyarzún recently wrote about the pain caused by the absence of both a history and an archive of the women who participated in the Popular Unity government in Chile (1970–73), the leftwing coalition led by Socialist president Salvador Allende. "Enormous gaps surround the women of the Popular Unity," she writes. "The epistemological and political vacuum of feminism aches. It is an emptiness of sex and gender: emptiness in and by language, a discourse that still does not assume itself to be not sexist."[1] Although Oyarzún's remarks are directed toward the need to recover the role of women politicians who were part of Allende's administration, this lament can certainly be expanded to include the women filmmakers who were part of the vibrant cultural scene that developed around it.

This chapter examines the role women filmmakers played during the period of the Popular Unity, contributing to the rewriting of a Latin American feminist film history that has been eclipsed by what B. Ruby Rich described as the "all-male pantheon" that emerged from the region since the New Latin American Cinema movement (NLAC).[2] It focuses on *Tres por tres* (*Three by Three*), a feature-length fiction film project developed in 1972–73, the last year of the Popular Unity, by pioneer Chilean directors Marilú Mallet (credited in her early work as María Luisa Mallet), Valeria Sarmiento, and Angelina Vázquez (also credited as Angelina Vásquez) but which never materialized, remaining in its scriptwriting stage. *Tres por tres* was to be a ninety-minute black-and-white

FIGURE 5.1 Angelina Vázquez (standing) with Valeria Sarmiento (sitting, middle) and other students at the Film School in Viña del Mar circa 1968. Courtesy of Angelina Vázquez.

fiction film shot in 16mm, consisting of three independent pieces, one directed by each filmmaker—an omnibus film. What linked these films together was that they would examine what the directors called in the general synopsis of their feature "the problem of women," particularly from the middle classes or the "petite bourgeoisie" in the Marxist lexicon used at the time.

Mallet, Sarmiento, and Vázquez belonged to a new generation of filmmakers that contributed to the effervescent and politically committed film culture that developed during Allende's government and that was violently crushed after the September 11 military coup in 1973; all three women fled into exile afterward, where they continued making films (figure 5.1).[3] Examining the unfinished project they planned together before the coup challenges the largely masculinist project of the Popular Unity and complicates dominant accounts of the role of women both within and outside cinema structures during Allende's government. At the same time, studying this unfinished film means to engage in the creation of what I have called elsewhere a "transnational imaginary archive" of exile cinema, an archive shaped by political violence that is dispersed throughout different corners of the world.[4]

The notion of the unfinished is not foreign to the oeuvre of these three directors. It can be found at the core of two of the most important films of Chilean exile cinema: *Journal inachevé* (*Unfinished Diary*, 1982) by Mallet and *Fragmentos de un diario inacabado* (*Fragments of an Unfinished Diary*, 1983) by Vázquez. These major works not only inscribe in their titles their status as filmic diaries but also the figure of incompletion.[5] Whereas Mallet's filmed diary offers a slice of life of the director as an exile in Montreal, Vázquez's title foregrounds the interruption of her own frustrated homecoming to Chile, a journey she registered in a written diary. The director entered semi-clandestinely in 1983 to make a film about the state of the country but was forced to leave by agents of Pinochet's dictatorship (1973–90). Vázquez's crew ended up making the film while she directed from Helsinki, where she was exiled.

In Sarmiento's case, she has been actively working to finish her husband Raúl Ruiz's incomplete films since his death in 2011, such as *La telenovela errante* (*The Wandering Soap Opera*, 1990–2017) and *El tango del viudo y su espejo deformante* (*The Tango of the Widower and Its Distorting Mirror*, 1967–2020), sharing codirecting credits with him. Unlike these productions that do exist, *Tres por tres* was never made—not a single frame of this film was ever shot. The complexities of the historical and political junction, the spiraling economic crisis, and the patriarchal culture of the Chilean left worked against the realization of this omnibus film. Nonetheless, this film project stands as a crucial reflection on the problematic status of middle-class women during the Popular Unity, political actors seldom acknowledged by the committed cinema produced at the time.

Despite the sweeping economic, cultural, and political reforms brought about by the election of Allende, women's demands were not prioritized in these radical transformations. As Soledad Novoa Donoso argues, the discourse of the "New Man" at the center of the Popular Unity addressed a masculine revolutionary subject and did not feature a corresponding narrative of liberation for women. Though commonly recognized in their status as members of the working class, notably as mothers to be incorporated in the workforce, women had problems that were supposed to be solved with the success of the revolution.[6] In her influential collection of essays *Ser política en Chile: Las feministas y los partidos*, published posthumously in 1986, feminist scholar and activist Julieta Kirkwood writes that throughout this period left-wing parties concentrated on class struggle barely addressed women's issues, preferring to ignore them instead. Even left-wing women tended to yield to the struggles that demanded changes for society as a whole, no longer speaking of "feminine problems."[7] Feminism was largely seen as a bourgeois and imported concern from white Western women.[8] In this context, "being a feminist and a revolutionary did not seem to have a possible articulation," writes Oyarzún.[9]

Andrea Giunta provides a more nuanced account of what was happening in the Latin American cultural sphere. In her view, although women artists' "identification with the political scene was overwhelmingly shaped by a commitment to revolutionary struggle," they were still concerned about the larger issues affecting women. Their demands may not have been articulated in the exact same ways as Second Wave feminisms did in Europe or in the United States, yet "in their works they explored the repertoire of issues that feminism address" and engaged in rigorous investigations to reflect on women's subjectivity and their status in society.[10] Such interest in exploring women's experiences in a critical moment of Chilean history is at the basis of this collaborative filmic endeavor developed by Mallet, Sarmiento, and Vázquez. Indeed, their film project provides an entry point to reflect on the potential articulations between revolution and feminism. For what would a film made by left-wing women directors striving to make sense of the daily struggles of middle-class women during the Popular Unity look like?

To reconstruct this film means to re-member it, to bring together its different archival traces scattered throughout different corners of the world, as this unfinished project has been shaped by the experience of political violence and displacement. Andrew Prescott has described the figure of the exile as an "anomaly" in the traditional archive, always a passing or fleeting presence. Therefore, in order "to follow the exile we must go outside the Record Office doors."[11] Leaving the conventional archive means to turn to oral history but also, whenever possible, to track down personal collections, as important documents (such as letters, film treatments and scripts, photographs, promotional and other ephemeral materials) are kept by the filmmakers (or their families), sometimes in their basements, sometimes in their cabinets, waiting to be read, scanned, classified, and potentially safeguarded by a proper institution. Since exile is a permanent condition—with many filmmakers remaining in their host countries or living in between countries for the rest of their lives—these crucial archives also remain in exile. In practical terms this means that filmmakers themselves are the ones who provide access to their materials, often allowing a generous though necessarily selective and partial access to their files.

For this chapter I have had to reconstruct, through surviving documents and oral history, the treatment for *Tres por tres*, since none of the three directors preserve a copy of the full film project. Mallet and Sarmiento keep different drafts of it in their own records, both incomplete. Mallet, based in Montreal, keeps a copy of her story titled "La mujer del block" ("The Woman of the Tower Block"); Sarmiento holds in her Parisian apartment a copy of hers, simply titled "Cuento uno" ("Story One"). These typewritten pages do not seem like the definitive version of the project, but rather drafts with crossed-out words and handwritten marks. Mallet's file consists of four loose pages. The first, titled "Largometraje sobre LA MUJER" ("Feature film about THE

WOMAN"), features a half-written short paragraph with the incomplete plot of her story. The rest of the document appears to represent more definite plans: the second page titled "La mujer del block" provides a general idea of Mallet's piece as it clearly describes the female protagonist; the third page briefly portrays all the characters involved; and the last sheet details the film's working method. Sarmiento's file comprises two pages only: the first one introduces both the film as a whole and each of the filmmakers' pieces succinctly, and it also lists the technical crew, already decided. The second page is her individual project, which describes the five scenes of her film plus its nightmarish ending. The current fragmented status of the *Tres por tres* script also suggests that this omnibus film, though planned collaboratively, had a strong individual component as Mallet and Sarmiento only preserved copies of their own parts of the project.

If I am painstakingly describing these documents, it is so that the reader can fathom the sheer dispersion and incompletion of the materials assembled here, which Giuliana Bruno has eloquently described as the "ruined and fragmentary map" of women filmmakers' lacunar archive.[12] Not residing in any physical archive, and also not published anywhere, this project is now located in my laptop. For this reason, too, this chapter includes lengthy translated transcriptions from Spanish into English of each of these surviving projects.[13] In other words, to make this transnational imaginary archive speak, I have to engage with the materiality as well as the content of these fragmented documents. "Documents can be very talkative," Arlette Farge reminds us.[14]

I refer to "surviving projects" because Vázquez's story is missing, a fact that attests to the different experiences these directors faced after the coup. Associated with the Socialist Party, though not actively involved with it, both Sarmiento and Mallet left the country only a few months after Allende's overthrow in September 1973. Sarmiento spent a brief time in Berlin, where she joined her husband before the couple relocated to Paris, whereas Mallet left for Montreal after finding refuge in the Canadian embassy. As a militant in the radical left-wing party Movimiento de Izquierda Revolucionaria (MIR, Revolutionary Left Movement), Vázquez decided to stay in Chile, even before the organization proclaimed their well-known political strategy: "El MIR no se asila" ("The MIR does not seek asylum"). She went into hiding to perform tasks for the resistance and, after two years, left Chile for Helsinki. Her mother, a Spanish exile from the Civil War, destroyed the documents that could compromise her daughter in case the secret police went looking for her, preserving only some books that she could conceal.[15]

During my research for this chapter, Vázquez generously reconstructed by heart the treatment of her segment, which she titled "Tercer cuento: Tus hambres serán las mías" ("Third story: Your hungers will also be mine"). In her seven-page reconstruction—made carefully but necessarily shaped by the passage of time—she provides a detailed description of the characters, as well as of the four scenes that constituted her piece and their corresponding visual treatment. As suggested by the title of Vázquez's segment, the order of each work did not seem set in stone, since the document that contains the general synopsis of *Tres por tres* considers Vázquez's piece as the second part of the film.

A group interview seemed the most appropriate for bringing back the memories of an unfinished film developed in a collaborative way almost fifty years ago. Thus I interviewed Sarmiento and Vázquez together via video call in August 2021; they joined from Paris and Helsinki, respectively. Although a long-standing story of common acquaintances and friendship binds these filmmakers together, this was to be the first time that the directors gathered to speak about their earliest collaborative endeavor.[16] Unfortunately, Mallet could not be present for this conversation, so I interviewed her separately a couple of weeks later. She joined me from Montreal.[17]

BECOMING FEMINIST DURING THE 1970S

Each of these filmmakers had completed at least one short documentary before deciding to embark on this feature-length project. Vázquez had made *Crónica del salitre* (*Nitrate Chronicle*, 1971) on the nitrate mine workers; Mallet had directed *Amuhuelai-mi* (1972) about the migration of Mapuche people; and Sarmiento had filmed *Un sueño como de colores* (*Color-Tainted Dreams*, 1972), about the everyday life of female strippers. This last film was considered lost for almost fifty years until it was recently found by Sarmiento.[18] The only two films these directors managed to shoot that placed women at the center were Sarmiento's *Un sueño como de colores* and Mallet's 1973 film *¿Dónde voy a encontrar otra Violeta?* (*Where Will I Find Another Violeta?*), a homage to the major composer and folk artist Violeta Parra that was almost finished when it was confiscated by the military after the coup. Since Sarmiento's short film had its first public screening in 2022 while Mallet's remains lost, they have been absent from most histories of the cinema under

FIGURE 5.2 Marilú Mallet in 1966, photographed by Gerda Sommerhoff. Mallet does not have any other picture of herself from her time working as a filmmaker in Chile. The coup and the displacement that followed resulted in the loss of most of her personal archive. The poor quality of this image speaks to the vicissitudes of an archive shaped by exile. Courtesy of Marilú Mallet.

Allende's government. This absence has served to perpetuate the masculine canon of the NLAC, preventing a thoroughgoing assessment of the role and aims of women filmmakers during the revolutionary struggle. For Vázquez, Mallet, and Sarmiento, exploring the complexities of being a woman during the Popular Unity was just as important as taking part in the political process.

Their relations to feminism were different in each case. Vázquez was marked by the strength of her mother, a widow and a Spanish exile, and by what the director describes as a clear "libertarian formation." Equally relevant was Vázquez's decade-long friendship with Claudia Lanzarotti, the daughter of experimental theater actress Eva Melnick. Vázquez and Lanzarotti (who also collaborated in her documentary about nitrate workers) read Simone de Beauvoir in their early teens, and Vázquez recalls how they would discuss the French author in the park. The influence of female relatives is also foregrounded by Mallet, who comes from a family of artists; her mother, María Luisa Señoret, was an accomplished painter, and Mallet's first husband's mother, Gerda Sommerhoff, was a German artist who introduced her to photography (figure 5.2).

Looking back, none of these filmmakers seem too eager to embrace the "feminist" label. The exception is Sarmiento, who describes her fascination with the feminist movement at the time yet also claims that the issue goes beyond the adoption of this political category: "it is not about defining oneself as a feminist or not. . . . We have always been feminists." According to Vázquez, espousing such a concept was not the most important thing then, but undoubtedly "women's everyday struggles" were "a central preoccupation for us." For Mallet, feminism was a concept she associated with the legacy of the activist women involved in the Movimiento Pro-Emancipación de las Mujeres de Chile (Pro-Emancipation of Women of Chile Movement, MEMCH, 1935–53), who pushed for women's equality, including their right to vote. Instead of this desire to gain access to the public sphere, Mallet explains, she has always been more interested in examining what she calls a "feminine sensibility." In my view these women's different approaches to feminisms reflect the ongoing discomfort of leftist women from developing countries who do not feel represented by white or "civilizational feminism."[19]

Although the filmmakers did not participate in the few existing women's groups within left-wing parties, they channeled their need to work through gender issues through an informal discussion group hosted by Sarmiento at some point between 1971 and 1972. Six to eight women would meet in her apartment in Santiago, including Vázquez. They would gather to discuss topics around the condition of women, but mostly, according to Sarmiento, to vent: "I think we were just a group of women who tried to give each other the courage to go on in real life. We were way too marginalized, so this helped us to gain some strength." Vázquez remembers they had enriching, theoretically informed conversations in which she saw a strong connection "between politics and especially the investigation of women's position in different social strata."

Interestingly, Sarmiento's first encounter with militant feminism was through a group of hippies and feminists from the United States who arrived in Chile in 1970 to make ¿Qué hacer? (*What Is to Be Done?*, 1972), a film about Allende's presidential election, codirected by Latina activist, poet, and filmmaker Nina Serrano and her then-husband, Saul Landau, who were joined by Raúl Ruiz as the Chilean counterpart in the codirection.[20] Working as an assistant producer, Sarmiento was impressed by the feminists she met during the shooting, including Serrano, the filmmaker Barbara Margolis, and the actress Sandy Archer. She spoke a lot about feminism with them and recalls with amusement that, as a form of rebelliousness, these women left their bras everywhere. Sarmiento was clear, however, that their demands were important; as she stated, "I felt very close to [their goal of] reclaiming the role of women." Reclaiming and understanding the crucial role that women were to play in the revolutionary period appears as a common goal for Mallet, Vázquez, and Sarmiento. Despite these three directors' differing approaches to women's issues, their incipient artistic concerns and shared interest in depicting the lives of ordinary women under the Popular Unity brought them together to plan a feature film.

TRES POR TRES: A SPOTLIGHT ON WOMEN OF THE "PETITE BOURGEOISIE"

Once each had completed a short film, Mallet, Sarmiento, and Vázquez felt ready to take the next step and direct a fiction feature film. According to Vázquez, they believed their previous experiences making documentaries would help them "negotiate better." So "we decided to take a leap by embarking on one project each of us," recalls Sarmiento. Mallet was struck by the fact that men were making feature films while they were not: "Patricio Guzmán had a feature film project, [Miguel] Littin also had his project, whereas we didn't." Why couldn't they also have their own feature film, she wondered. Vázquez believed, too, that a feature would help them have a theatrical release, whereas the distribution of short films was normally restricted to the alternative circuit. In retrospect, Vázquez sees their coming together as a highly strategic move: "I think that we knew—at least I knew—that it was going to be impossible for me to get the support to make a feature film." Coming together, they believed, would give them more chances to succeed in securing funding. As I have written elsewhere, their particular mode of collaboration offered them mutual support "grounded in gender solidarity, political affinities, and above all, a strong desire to make films," while respecting their individual creative quests as directors with authorial impulses.[21]

In 1973, a few months before the military coup, they decided to present their omnibus project to the state film agency Chile Films, the country's main funding body at the time. Founded in 1941, this agency lacked a clearly established mission or regulatory framework, but it nevertheless functioned during Allende's government as a sort of film institute and became one of the nation's most important production centers, principally of short documentary films.[22] Director Miguel Littin was the first president of the agency under the Popular Unity, leading the center in a short yet euphoric period in which he tried to execute what he had previously penned in the Manifesto of the Popular Unity Filmmakers,

FIGURE 5.3 Valeria Sarmiento with Diego Bonacina in Valparaíso circa 1970. Courtesy of Angelina Vázquez.

despite facing increasing setbacks in terms of distribution as well as of internal political feuds.[23] Vázquez remembers the institution in these years as a utopian space for collective creativity: "when Miguel enters Chile Films—and this is what literally happened—all of us entered too." Indeed, the workshops carried out there became an informal film school in which most of the young filmmakers took their first steps (figure 5.3).[24]

By the time they pitched their project to Chile Films, however, the leadership of the agency had changed hands. When he took over the agency in March 1973, Eduardo Paredes, a doctor who had previously been director of police investigations, had no experience in film.[25] By then, Chile Films and the film sector at large were experiencing the impacts of the worsening economic conditions of the country. Faced with a shortage of film stock and money, Paredes cancelled virtually all film production and, to keep the company afloat, prioritized distribution and service provision.[26] "In Chile the economic problem was enormous," remembered Sarmiento in an interview with Jacqueline Mouesca in 1985, "and the little money available went to the director, a man in every case."[27] "The raw material would be for the glorious films they [the men] were going to make, period," Sarmiento adds during our conversation. She is referring to the two major feature films that were to be released by Chile Films during the Popular Unity, devoted to the patriotic heroes Manuel Rodríguez and José Manuel Balmaceda, and directed by Patricio Guzmán and Fernando Balmaceda, respectively. Eventually, however, even these projects were cancelled by the new administration.[28]

As Vázquez has recalled on several occasions, she was particularly upset about the way in which she and her collaborators were received in the offices of the state film agency. She recalls that Paredes asked them, "'What do you *señoras* want?'" "He forgot," Vázquez says ironically, "to add 'who are you the wives of.'"[29] She does not remember many of the details afterward, as she was disarmed by this unwelcoming reception. But an obstacle that proved impossible to overcome was that they did not have a representative from the Communist Party in their team. Demands for artistic and other groups to represent a spectrum of left-wing political parties and views were the norm within state institutions during the Popular Unity, and Chile Films was no exception. In practice, this quota system meant continuous tensions within the agency and between its leadership and employees, and furthermore, it was one of the reasons for the blockage of different filmic endeavors such as the production of shorts and film screenings.[30] Despite the fact that, according to film critic Hans Erhmann, Paredes "put an end to the quota system," this was not what these three women filmmakers experienced in Chile Films.[31]

As previously mentioned, Vázquez belonged to the MIR, whereas both Sarmiento and Mallet were close to the Socialist Party. But this was not enough for the film agency, which demanded the inclusion of a fourth filmmaker from the Communist Party. According to Sarmiento and Vázquez, it is possible that Douglas Hübner, one of Paredes's assistants, was pushing for that fourth filmmaker to be a woman, probably Beatriz González, who was married to the filmmaker Álvaro Ramírez, with whom she often worked. In the end, the three-woman team did not manage to gain the support of Chile Films. Vázquez, disappointed, never returned to the institution.

Tres por tres was to be a fiction feature film consisting of three independent pieces of thirty minutes, each to be directed by one of these filmmakers. The common thread was their focus on "the problem of women" from the "petite bourgeoisie." Having middle-class women as protagonists on screen was a rarity at the time. The few films that dedicated attention to women would feature working-class women and their contributions to the revolutionary process from below. The three segments would also share the same crew: the cinematographer Jorge Müller, the editor Carlos Piaggio, and the sound recorder José de la Vega. Both Müller and Piaggio had worked with these three filmmakers in some capacity before, which gave them a sense of continuity and collaboration. Piaggio was the foremost editor at the time and Sarmiento, today an accomplished editor herself, learned the trade assisting him for hours in the cold rooms of Chile Films. Since they had all worked with the Argentine editor in their first documentaries, he became an important ally. Müller, meanwhile, was the gifted cinematographer of the most influential documentary of the period, *La batalla de Chile* (*The Battle of Chile*, 1973–78), a collective endeavor led by Patricio Guzmán in which both Vázquez and Mallet participated though they are seldom credited.[32] According to Vázquez, both Piaggio and Müller—the latter also a MIR militant and her close friend—"treated them as equal," something that was deeply valued within a prevailing context of what she has ironically described as *machismo-socialista*.[33]

One of the documents preserved by Sarmiento provides a synopsis of the overall film project, which I translate here:

> This feature film is based on three stories of thirty minutes. The topic is inscribed within the petite bourgeoisie in the current political moment. The three stories focus on and analyze the problem of the woman in Chilean society. The first, by Valeria Sarmiento, narrates the story of a sixteen-year-old girl, a student in an English school where she has received her whole education and where she has been culturally alienated—the film is set in her last year of high school. She tries to rebel, but rebellion within the boundaries of the petite bourgeoisie does not have a way out, nor does it make sense. The second story, by Angelina Vázquez, is about a woman from the petite bourgeoisie: the married woman, with two kids, who stands for her family, illustrating the problems of this divided class. The third story by María Luisa Mallet shows a progressive middle-class woman, who lives in a tower block. All her aspirations and values start to be in contradiction with the political process, and she turns into a reactionary person. She isolates from her old friends, and her husband ends up abandoning her.

The different approaches to the middle-class women envisaged by each individual piece respond to these directors' "common yet diverse concerns," which Vázquez emphasized in our conversation. Indeed, these three segments already carry the seeds of the distinctive bodies of work developed in the future by these filmmakers, as I expand on below. Yet whatever their differing cinematic and political stances toward their female protagonists, the three stories are placed closely in dialogue with the contemporary political landscape.

What, then, was "the problem of women" within "the current political moment" from which this project emerged? From the start, the Popular Unity had been met by stark opposition from conservative sectors of society, such as the Chilean elite and the right-wing media. A growing economic crisis that translated into a generalized shortage of goods (from food to supplies) led to a group of right-wing women mostly from the upper classes demonstrating en masse against the government in what is now remembered as "La marcha de las cacerolas vacías"

("The March of the Empty Pots") on 1 December 1971. As the historian Margaret Power has shown, the success of this large-scale mobilization emboldened anti-Allende women, who intensified their oppositional activities. Placing their roles as mothers and housewives at the center of their discourse, these women, backed by right-wing parties, managed to build a unified front of female supporters across social classes, including middle-class and working-class women that contributed to the overthrow of Allende.[34] Meanwhile, as Kirkwood argues in *Ser política en Chile,* the left-wing parties were unable to address women's particular needs and demands and therefore failed to tackle what she eloquently describes as their "political orphanhood": the lack of a horizon outside the domestic sphere.[35] For Kirkwood, the left-wing parties' inability to acknowledge and understand women's issues was a real "tragedy" which proved that "women's oppression becomes reactionary," as the movement led by the anti-Allende women clearly demonstrated.[36]

My excursion into the Chilean women's conservative movement is meant not only to provide some necessary historical context but also to argue that the accent placed on middle-class women by the stories in *Tres por tres* can be seen as a critical reflection on these women's "political orphanhood." Focusing on their protagonists' intimate universes, these narratives, more or less explicitly, depict women who are confined to the household with no alternative beyond marriage and a conventional family structure, while a shadow of a menacing future threatens their increasingly unsteady personal worlds. Indeed, as Sarmiento recalled in the conversation with Mouesca, in exile she became so "obsessed" with the anti-Allende women of the so-called "pots and pans movement" that this would be the topic of the first film she managed to direct in France: *La femme au foyer* (*The Housewife,* 1976).[37] Set in Chile, the film revolves around a conservative middle-class woman who, alienated by domestic life, does not really understand what is going on during the last months of Allende's government.

Yet, in truth, when I asked Mallet, Sarmiento, and Vázquez about the motivations behind their projects, they do not recall having in mind the political behavior of these reactionary women. They all raise different sources of inspiration. Sarmiento was interested in talking about women's education, more precisely about the education of girls from a milieu she knew well (she considers herself from the "petite bourgeoisie"). Vázquez describes herself as a "historical optimist" and as such was not concerned with these reactionary women who were going against class and gender solidarity, which she aimed to explore in her film. For her part, Mallet wanted to document the increasing polarization she witnessed in the iconic building in which she lived, a recently inaugurated tower block in the well-off neighborhood of Providencia. This housing complex was commonly associated with government sympathizers until, as Mallet recalls, things began to deteriorate and former supporters began to turn against the government.[38] Despite their diverse motivations behind these pieces, I do think that their unfinished project as a whole can be read as an early and pivotal reflection about the "political orphanhood" experienced by middle-class women, as demonstrated by the analysis of each of the three pieces below.

Sarmiento's section of the project is set in the last high school days of a young student in a traditional British all-girls school (British schools are not unusual in Chile). The plot was based on stories told to her by her sister, who studied in the Saint Margaret's British School for girls located near Viña del Mar (where Sarmiento also grew up): "I was somehow inspired by the stories she had told me about their trips to celebrate the end of their academic year," she explained to me. "Visually I thought that the idea was very interesting: the girls wore a red uniform in the English fashion, with a red tie and jacket, etc. And also the idea of the trip to the countryside: I thought that all that was very beautiful visually." The emphasis on the visual qualities of these rituals hints at Sarmiento's highly stylized cinematic universe, often constructed around the expressive use of color, as in her melodramas, or embarking on a revelation of the uncanniness of everyday life, as in her early documentaries.[39]

Sarmiento's contribution to *Tres por tres* can be seen as an early attempt to depict the influence of British culture in the country, as she would go on to do in her later adaptation of British travel writer Maria Graham's 1822 diary in *María Graham: Diario de mi residencia en Chile* (*Maria Graham: Diary of a Residence in Chile*, 2014). The draft treatment shifts between different tones and genres. It begins with a kidnapping scene: a group of students have abducted their teachers on a bus going into the woods. This is soon revealed to be a last prank from the students before they leave school forever. After the principal's admonition to the students, the usual farewell ceremony is celebrated with the British ambassador in attendance, followed by a graduation party. The protagonist has been introduced in the previous sequence while getting ready for the party at a girlfriend's place: "she flirts with her friend's brother, enticing him, but not accepting the advances of the young man." At the party, teenagers wear evening gowns as Straussian waltzes play in the background. The nameless protagonist is accompanied by her boyfriend, who acts "in the ways the petite bourgeoisie understands a young man should behave: he takes care of her and protects her." But at the end of the party the young woman loses her grip: she is drunk and begins to throw glasses and food trays over the attendants' heads. To her outrage, the boyfriend tries to make her behave properly.

The next and final scene occurs on the morning after the party:

> We see [the protagonist] waking up surrounded by dolls that she begins to manipulate. The dolls are of various types: some speak, some sing while they pierce little discs on the girl's back, others are wind-up dolls. The film finishes with the terrifying image of the main character surrounded by these semianimated beings that like robots have created a world around her in which the young woman is already part.

Cultural alienation has taken a toll on the young woman who, raised under the shadow of a foreign culture, is forced to control her urges and behave in prudish ways to comply with the expectations of her social class. The final scene encompasses Sarmiento's feminist critique of the reigning status quo in Chile at the time: there is no escape for this young woman. Coming-of-age means refusing her desires and abiding by the rules of the society around her—hence becoming part of an army of dolls, another robotlike woman living in conformity with other women. Her piece does not explicitly engage with the political moment, unlike the two other films by her fellow filmmakers. Instead, as in most of Sarmiento's oeuvre, she proposes a tangential approach to deal with the topic of women during the Popular Unity.[40] Here she chooses to create a nightmarish portrait of women's oppression that seems more attuned to the perverse fables she would later direct in Europe such as *Notre mariage* (*Our Wedding*, 1985), *Amelia Lopes O'Neil* (1990), and *Elle* (1996).

Like Sarmiento's female protagonist, Mallet's central figure in her own piece also seems trapped. Neither are liberated by the ongoing revolutionary process in the country. This is more explicitly developed in Mallet's treatment, which provides a vivid description of the main female character. This nameless protagonist represents a middle-class "type," known simply as "the woman." In her notes Mallet describes her film as

> presenting the reality of the petite bourgeoise woman who has been willingly relegated to domestic life, and who inhabits this little world of the meals, the house, the material desires, without realizing the sociopolitical reality. She is not interested in participating in political changes. She is interested in her

own values and in defending their permanence. She is progressive insofar as she can have more amenities, but if she must sacrifice a desire, she quickly turns into a reactionary.... Therefore, a conflict arises between husband and wife, a conflict that leads to the breakup of the relationship.

Though grounded in women's oppression by gender norms and conventions—her protagonist has remained inside the household—of the three sections, Mallet's is the most clearly concerned with examining the shifting political behavior of Chilean women during the Popular Unity. As mentioned earlier, the lack of goods caused by the US blockage in concomitance with the economic boycott orchestrated by the Chilean elite deeply disrupted daily routines. Mallet's protagonist finds her everyday life radically transformed by the political crisis. Described as a fashionable woman of around thirty years old who reads the popular women's magazine *Paula* (targeted to the upper and middle classes), the protagonist is initially sympathetic to the revolution, but she increasingly begins to feel that "the political and economic crisis frustrates her way of living.... Isolated and alone she turns into a reactionary."

Mallet's description of this rather frivolous woman, as she experiences the demise of her marital relationship and the loss of her friends who have distanced from the couple due to their closeness to the Popular Unity, is presented as a microcosm of the polarization of Chilean society. The husband is portrayed as a quiet and simple man from a small leftist party who works as a public servant in the agricultural field. There are several other characters delineated in the one-page document: the couple's children; the woman's relatives, all of whom frown upon her husband whom they consider *roto* (of a lower class); and two women from the neighborhood who are active supporters of Allende's government.

Although there is no detailed description of each scene, it is clear that the film was to be largely set within the domestic sphere and the *barrio*, as suggested by the film's title and the characters' layout. Further insights into Mallet's approach can be gleaned, moreover, from Mallet's visual treatment of the project, included in her documents. A page titled "Modo de trabajo" ("Working Method") succinctly lists the main points that would be considered when shooting. For instance, the film was to have little dialogue; the characters would have improvised lines; and the fictional sequences would be paired with documentary scenes. Mallet was enthralled by the use of nonactors in the films of European "new wave" directors like Roberto Rossellini and François Truffaut as well as that in the work of Jorge Sanjinés and Glauber Rocha in Latin America. She was not keen about using local professional actors, who seemed to her "extremely false" in their style; instead, she wanted to "take cinema out of that rigidity and endow it with a human touch," which is perhaps why there are no actors listed in her planning notes. It is therefore possible to distinguish in these documents Mallet's aesthetic approach in its embryonic stage; in later years she would go on to make films that playfully blur the boundaries between fiction and nonfiction, as in her landmark *Journal inachevé* or the witty *Chère Amérique* (*Dear America*, 1990).

Angelina Vázquez sets her story during the last year of Allende's government, when she had already discarded "a nonviolent political way out" following her own familial and political experience of the Spanish Civil War, which resulted in the drifting of her family until they landed in Chile. As mentioned earlier, she wanted to use her film to deal with female solidarity across classes during this increasingly tense politically situation, and she planned to do so by focusing on two families separated by class difference. The casting for this particular segment was mostly decided: two iconic stars of the New Chilean Cinema movement, Shenda Román and Nelson Villagra (a real-life couple at the time), would play Cloti and El Moncho, respectively, the couple living at a *campamento* or shantytown; Ely Menz, who was Littin's wife and who helped Vázquez in the development of the story, would play Eduarda, the middle-class woman who is married to Claudio, to be played by an as-yet-undecided actor. Cloti is Eduarda's maid and takes care of the middle-class woman's two children. Cloti is described as a childless and politically empowered woman actively involved in her community, participating in the Junta de Abastecimientos y Control de Precios (JAP, Price and Supply Committees), the Healthcare Committee, and other organizations. The two women met, we learn from the notes, when Eduarda was doing volunteer work on the site. Over the years their relationship has developed into a "complicity" by which Eduarda helps Cloti build her house at the *campamento* in exchange for Cloti's performance of some of Eduarda's "maternal" and domestic duties, which Eduarda has stopped performing due to her commitments with the political process. After she gave birth to her children, Eduarda put an end to her studies to become a doctor, but she resumed working in the shantytowns educating vulnerable people in family planning.

Vázquez was acquainted with life in the *campamentos* as she herself worked there on a regular basis alongside her friend Jorge Müller (with whom she also discussed the film's visual treatment). In the reconstruction of her missing project, she takes special care in emphasizing if not the horizontality of Eduarda and Cloti's relationship, at least the strong alliance that grows between them. This alliance is clearly seen in the second scene set inside Eduarda's house. Listening to the radio and drinking tea, the two women are described as laughing together about "the racist or hoarding behavior of some neighbors, and the relationship they establish with their maids and gardeners." There are some references in the notes to Cloti and Eduarda's partners: El Moncho is introduced as a neighborhood leader and a militant in a semiclandestine left-wing organization; Claudio is a Socialist Party member who becomes increasingly absorbed in trying to keep afloat one of the nationalized manufacturing enterprises he oversees. The men's busy agendas have left their partners to carry the domestic burden; at one point Cloti complains about *"machistas* that do nothing except for giving orders" and Eduarda's marriage becomes progressively more "unequal."

Yet these romantic relationships do not seem as significant to the two women as the complicity developed between them. An ominous atmosphere frames Vázquez's film as a whole. Just before the women are depicted chatting over tea, an establishing shot of Eduarda's house describes some menacing graffiti outside, including the notorious anticommunist motto of "Djakarta viene" ("Jakarta is coming"), which appeared during Allende's government.[41] The women have not seen this graffiti and are oblivious to the threat. The scene that follows is set in an emblematic restaurant (whose name Vázquez cannot remember, but which she describes as being *"siútico"* or tacky) in which Eduarda celebrates her mother's birthday alongside her large family. When a trivial discussion ends up with Claudio and one of Eduarda's brothers punching each other, Vázquez illustrates how the "familial and social bubble has burst," with the domestic and filial sphere mirroring, as in Mallet's case, the polarization of Chilean society.

Meanwhile, back in Eduarda's house, Cloti and El Moncho (who sometimes also works at the house) have stayed in to take care of the children, who have fallen asleep. In the kitchen the couple's romantic night is abruptly interrupted by the sound of broken glass as a Molotov cocktail is thrown through the window. The film was then supposed to cut to its climactic conclusion: a nighttime sequence Vázquez describes as "Dantesque," which depicts an enormous fire consuming the house. A dark solemnity engulfs the film's ending in which the spectator would see nothing more than a dance of lights emanating from the fire and from the attending emergency vehicles. The dramatic effect would be enhanced "by the total absence of sound," as well as by the fact that the onlookers would appear frozen while the protagonists would move in slow motion. Everyone survives the fire, and the final shot describes Cloti embracing Eduarda in "mutual consolation"; the final moments of the scene were to be filmed in a tracking shot that distances and elevates from the ground. A more explicitly political approach that emphasizes political activism, alliances across women of different social or cultural backgrounds, and a collaborative approach to filmmaking—all of these characteristics present in Vázquez's piece for *Tres por tres* will become hallmarks of her later fictional and documentary films. This work includes her groundbreaking homecoming documentary *Fragmentos de un diario inacabado,* mentioned at the outset of this chapter, or her sophisticated musical-documentary *Presencia lejana (Far Away and Yet So Near,* 1982), which includes Shenda Román in the cast.

None of the three films that were to comprise *Tres por tres* point to a hopeful future, given the close dialogue they establish with the increasingly suffocating political landscape appearing to impede any other reading. Their incomplete film project stands as quite prophetic in the different stances it develops toward the political crisis and in its analyses of the condition of middle-class women during the Popular Unity. These women were left adrift by the struggling forces around them and more often than not found themselves constrained within the walls of the household, tamed on the one hand by society's expectations and on the other by the complexities of the political process.

When Angelina Vázquez sent me the reconstruction of her treatment, which she lovingly rebuilt from scratch, she said that she felt the urge to make her film. It would be fun, she said, if Marilú and Valeria would also want to make theirs. Vázquez's reactivated desire for this unfinished film is so strong that the black-and-white 16mm film on which they originally envisaged making their project has turned into a film made in color in her imagination. Her enthusiasm is contagious. I too cannot help but wonder what shape these three stories would take if they finally materialized—as indeed they have done as I wrote this essay, playing in my head almost shot by shot. Yet I also hope that "listening" to these documents and their authors has managed to bring back to life, at least partly, a film that would otherwise be lost in the labyrinth of the always incomplete, ephemeral, and lacunar archive of exile.

NOTES

1. Kemy Oyarzún V., "Unidad Popular: Genealogías feministas interseccionales," in *La vía chilena al socialismo 50 años después vol. I Historia,* ed. Robert Austin Henry, Joana Salém Vasconcelos, and Viviana Canibilo Ramírez (Buenos Aires: CLACSO, 2020), 31–62, 56, http://biblioteca.clacso.edu.ar/clacso/se/20201201031842/La-via-chilena-al-socialismo-Tomo-I.pdf.

2. B. Ruby Rich, "An/Other View of New Latin American Cinema," in *New Latin American Cinema, vol. 1,* ed. Michael T. Martin (Detroit, MI: Wayne State University Press, 1997), 273–97, 278.

3. See Elizabeth Ramírez Soto and Catalina Donoso Pinto, eds., *Nomadías: El cine de Marilú Mallet, Valeria Sarmiento y Angelina Vázquez* (Santiago: Metales Pesados, 2016).

4. Elizabeth Ramírez Soto, "Habanera: De retornos y fragmentos inacabados," in *Una mirada oblicua: El cine de Valeria Sarmiento,* ed. Fernando Pérez and Bruno Cuneo (Santiago: Universidad Alberto Hurtado, 2021), 89–101, 89.

5. For a comparison of these two filmed diaries, see Iván Pinto, "Lo incompleto. Desajuste y fractura en dos diarios fílmicos del exilio chileno," in *Prismas del cine latinoamericano,* ed. Wolfgang Bongers (Santiago: Cuarto Propio and CELICH, 2012), 215–35.

6. Soledad Novoa Donoso, "Haga el amor y no la cama: Arte, feminismo y política: Chile 1970/1980," in *Compartir el mundo: La experiencia de las mujeres y el arte,* ed. María Laura Rosa and Soledad Novoa Donoso (Santiago: Metales Pesados, 2017), 145–51.

7. Julieta Kirkwood, *Ser Política en Chile: Las feministas y los partidos* (Santiago: FLACSO, 1986), 58.

8. Hilary Hiner, "'Memory Speaks from Today': Analyzing Oral Histories of Female Members of the MIR in Chile through the Work of Luisa Passerini," *Women's History Review* 25.3 (2016), 382–407, 397.

9. Oyarzún, "Unidad Popular," 39.

10. Andrea Giunta, "The Iconographic Turn: The Denormalization of Bodies and Sensibilities in the Work of Latin American Women Artists," in *Radical Women: Latin American Art, 1960–1985,* ed. Cecilia Fajardo-Hill and Andrea Giunta (Los Angeles: Hammer Museum, University of California; New York: DelMonico Books/Prestel, 2017), 29–34, 29–30.

11. Andrew Prescott, "Archives of Exiles: Exiles of Archives," in *What Are Archives? Cultural and Theoretical Perspectives: A Reader,* ed. Louise Craven (Aldershot: Ashgate, 2008), 129–42, 134, 129.

12. Giuliana Bruno, *Streetwalking on a Ruined Map: Cultural Theory and the City Films of Elvira Notari* (Princeton, NJ: Princeton University Press, 1993), 3–6.

13. Sarmiento has begun donating her papers to the Archivo Ruiz-Sarmiento at the Instituto de Arte de la Pontificia Universidad Católica de Valparaíso, inaugurated in 2013. However, she still holds many of her documents in Paris, including copies of the projects she never managed to complete.

14. Arlette Farge, *The Allure of the Archives,* trans. Thomas Scott-Railton (New Haven, CT: Yale University Press, 2007), 73.

15. Elizabeth Ramírez-Soto, personal communication with Angelina Vázquez, 7 July 2021.

16. For more on these filmmakers' history of friendship and collaboration, see Elizabeth Ramírez-Soto, "'Why didn't you write to me?': On Friendship, Exile, and Transnational Collaboration," in *No Master Territories,* ed. Erika Balsom and Hila Peleg (Berlin: Haus der Kulturen der Welt and MIT Press, 2022), 266–85.

17. Elizabeth Ramírez-Soto, interviews via Zoom with Angelina Vázquez and Valeria Sarmiento, 3 August 2021, and with Marilú Mallet, 18 August 2021. Unless otherwise indicated, all quotes from the directors come from these interviews.

18. This short film was released in Chile as I close this piece, and I have not been able to watch it yet. Sarmiento said in an interview that she found the negatives in her "magic closet" in Paris. Yenny Cáceres, "Cineasta Valeria Sarmiento sobre su película que estaba perdida: 'Las mujeres en la época de la UP ya estaban despertando,'" *The Clinic* (17 May 2022), www.theclinic.cl/2022/05/17/cineasta-valeria-sarmiento-pelicula-perdida/.

19. See Françoise Vergès, *A Decolonial Feminism* (London: Pluto Press, 2021).

20. For a reconstruction of the frantic shooting of *¿Qué hacer?* see Yenny Cáceres, *Los años chilenos de Raúl Ruiz* (Santiago: Catalonia, 2019), 117–27.

21. Ramírez-Soto, "'Why didn't you write.'"

22. Ignacio del Valle, *Cámaras en trance: El nuevo cine latinoamericano, un proyecto cinematográfico subcontinental* (Santiago: Cuarto Propio, 2014), 363.

23. John King, *Magical Reels: A History of Cinema in Latin America,* 2nd ed. (London: Verso, 2000), 174–75. Among other declarations, the manifesto "promised, in the vaguest of terms," according to King, "that Chilean cinema would become national, popular and revolutionary. It called on the cinema to bear witness to the heroes of Independence, to Labour leaders and to the anonymous workers, and in this way to wrestle popular memory from the hegemony of the right."

24. Del Valle, *Cámaras en trance,* 365.

25. Most accounts give March 1973 as the starting date of Paredes in Chile Films. However, a note assessing the first two months of the new administration suggests that he arrived in February 1973. Hans Erhmann, "Cine chileno: Esperanzas ... otra vez," *Revista La Quinta Rueda* 5 (1 April 1973), https://cinechile.cl/cine-chileno-esperanzas-otra-vez/.

26. Jacqueline Mouesca, *Plano secuencia de la memoria de Chile: Veinticinco años de cine chileno (1960–1985)* (Madrid: Ediciones del Litoral, 1988), 58.

27. Jacqueline Mouesca, "Una cineasta que no quiere ser transparente. Conversación con Valeria Sarmiento," *Araucaria de Chile* 31 (1985): 113–22, 114.

28. Mouesca, *Plano secuencia de la memoria de Chile,* 58; Del Valle, *Cámaras en trance,* 373. A brief note published in the online encyclopedia Cine Chile lists a total of nine unfinished films planned during the Popular Unity, some left incomplete due to the ambitiousness of the projects (as in the two cases mentioned above) but mostly due to the coup (some of these films were eventually completed). The list does not mention any incomplete film by women

directors. Marcelo Morales, "Las películas que no vieron la luz después del golpe de Estado," *Cine Chile* (11 September 2010), https://cinechile.cl/las-peliculas-que-no-vieron-la-luz-despues-del-golpe-de-estado/.

29. Catalina Donoso and Elizabeth Ramírez, "Encuentro en Valdivia: Conversaciones con Marilú Mallet y Angelina Vázquez," in *Nomadías: El cine de Marilú Mallet, Valeria Sarmiento y Angelina Vázquez*, ed. Elizabeth Ramírez Soto and Catalina Donoso Pinto (Santiago: Metales Pesados, 2016), 248.

30. Del Valle, *Cámaras en trance*, 368.

31. Erhmann, "Cine chileno: Esperanzas . . . otra vez."

32. Jorge Müller and his partner, the actress Carmen Bueno, disappeared in the hands of agents of the regime, leaving an enduring wound in Vázquez and in the Chilean filmmaking community.

33. Yenny Cáceres, "Vidas cruzadas," *Qué pasa* (2 October 2013), www.latercera.com/revista-que-pasa/6-12797-9-vidas-cruzadas/.

34. Margaret Power, *Right-Wing Women in Chile: Feminine Power and the Struggle Against Allende, 1964–1973* (University Park: Pennsylvania State University Press, 2002).

35. Kirkwood, *Ser política en Chile*, 50–51.

36. Kirkwood, *Ser política en Chile*, 52.

37. Mouesca, "Una cineasta que no quiere ser transparente," 115.

38. For a chronicle on the rise and decline of the iconic housing complex Mallet is referring to, see Jorge Rojas, "Torres de Carlos Antúnez: La amenaza del gueto vertical," *The Clinic* (18 February 2014), www.theclinic.cl/2014/02/18/torres-de-carlos-antunez-la-amenaza-del-gueto-vertical/.

39. Elizabeth Ramírez-Soto, "The Double Day of Valeria Sarmiento: Exile, Precariousness, and Cinema's Gendered Division of Labor," *Feminist Media Histories* 7.3 (2021): 154–77, 170.

40. On her "oblique" approach, see *Una mirada oblicua: El cine de Valeria Sarmiento*, ed. Bruno Cuneo and Fernando Pérez (Santiago: Ediciones Universidad Alberto Hurtado, 2021).

41. In the 1970s this anticommunist slogan proliferated in socialist countries to disseminate fear, following the mass murder of alleged communists in Indonesia after the 1965 US-backed coup.

CHAPTER 6

Writing with Jocelyne Saab

Infinite Metamorphoses and Sensitive Variations

MATHILDE ROUXEL

I met the Lebanese filmmaker Jocelyne Saab (1948–2019) on my first trip to Beirut in 2013, when I was twenty-one. I was interested in her because of the work she had accomplished during the Lebanese civil war (1975–90). Or, rather, I was interested in Saab because of her overt political commitment to social justice: I had not been able to see any of her work before meeting her. I wanted Saab to give me access to her films that were not available to view in 2013 and to grant me an interview. Our first meeting proved decisive for me. Saab, who was busy organizing the Cultural Resistance International Film Festival of Lebanon (CRIFFL), was quick to dismiss my request for an interview and to make me a counteroffer. Would I instead assist her in planning the event, which she and her associate Rita Bassil were getting off the ground—against all odds and by the skin of their teeth?

I embarked on this adventure with her. After the festival was over, Saab suggested that I assist her in writing the feature film she was working on at the time. She wanted to tell the story of the Egyptian cinema pioneer Assia Dagher, an important actor and producer during the national cinema's "golden age" from the 1930s through the 1950s. In the same period, Saab reluctantly procured some low-quality DVD copies of several of her films from trunks hidden under her bed. Later on, Saab would agree to write the preface to a book I ended up writing on her work, in which she reflected on her reticence to share her work with me:

Despite everything, I kept up the illusion that those metallic trunks could protect a lived experience made of authenticity, human adventures, and passion, and which were deeply constitutive of my identity. It took me months to find the courage—psychological, more than physical—to spread out on the floor in this cramped space and to steal under the bed to draw out, one by one, all the video cassettes of my films, the reels of film, the DVDs, and entrust them to Mathilde.[1]

By the time Saab passed her films on to me, between August and November 2013, I was a little better acquainted with Beirut, her city, since I had begun to follow her everywhere. Finally seeing the images of this place she had filmed during the civil war was a shock to me. By following her gaze as she moved through a ravaged Lebanon and listening to her voice, heard off-screen, condemn the disaster firmly, and yet without ever losing sight of the life that kept persisting, resisting, everywhere under the bombs, I became better able to understand Saab's vital, constant devotion to each of the projects in which she became involved.

With this new knowledge came a renewed fascination with Saab and her work, and I decided to set out on an extensive research project of her career, tracking down the first news reports she had directed between 1973 and 1975 in the French television archives and trying to find a way to think of her work—for television, cinema, and gallery—as a whole. This work resulted in my book, *Jocelyne Saab: La mémoire indomptée (Jocelyne Saab: Untamed Memory)*, which, upon its release in 2015, represented the first monograph dedicated to the filmmaker. Helping to develop trust and confidence between us, this book paved the way for Saab and me to make her films more readily and widely available. From 2016 on, we worked to digitize the analog media we had at hand in Beirut and to release it via video on demand. This was one of the first steps in a long journey of archival preservation and outreach that we undertook together until Saab's death on 7 January 2019, and that I am continuing under the auspices of the Association of Friends of Jocelyne Saab, of which I am the director.[2]

Alongside this academic research and the archival work that followed from it, I worked with Saab in organizing CRIFFL for several years in a row. And I had the opportunity to assist or collaborate with her on the writing of a number of her many ongoing projects in the final years of her life. Some of these projects were realized and disseminated—as was the case for her video and photography work *One Dollar a Day* (2016), which she exhibited in the French Institute in Beirut as well as in DEPO in Istanbul, and her video *Imaginary Postcard* (2016), which she composed during a residency at Boğaziçi University in Turkey in 2015 and which has been streamed on Vimeo and shown, alongside other artworks, in the exhibition I curated in the Modern and Contemporary Art Museum (MaCaM) of Alita, Byblos (Lebanon) in 2018, under the title "Jocelyne Saab Against the Tide."

Others remained, and remain, unfinished. The incomplete works include two documentary features, which evolved considerably over the course of their writing, and which I documented at every step. The first, titled "Faten Hamama's Honor" ("L'Honneur de Faten Hamama") in its last written versions, concerned the pioneering figures of Egyptian cinema (Dagher, Henri Barakat, Faten Hamama) and their relationship to Lebanon. The second, titled "Shigenobu: Mother and Daughter," concerned the fate of Mei Shigenobu, the daughter of Japanese activist Fusako Shigenobu, who had come to Japan from Lebanon in 1971 to create the Japanese Red Army (Nihon Sekigun) in support of the Palestinian cause. This last film, supposed to be primarily a compilation film, has never been completed, but Saab realized her last short film, *My Name Is Mei Shigenobu* (2018), out of this subject and the research she conducted for the full-length feature.

At the time of her death, I discovered the totality of Saab's paper archives, which the Friends' Association took in with a view to digitizing and distributing freely. These materials document the creative process of several completed works, including *Dunia, Kiss Me Not on the Eyes* (2005), which has a particularly voluminous archive. They also document many unrealized projects, developed to a greater or lesser degree. Exploring these projects, I often recalled anecdotes connected to them that Saab had once enjoyed telling me—personal information that, partial though it may be, could shed light into the shadows that proliferate in and around the unfinished projects of any deceased artist. Indeed, my six years working with Saab enabled me to grasp certain recurring mechanisms in her creative process, evident in the work I was present for as well as in many of her unfinished projects, which dated from the 1980s to the 2010s. Since she started working on projects she wrote before shooting—mainly after she left Lebanon to settle in Paris in the mid-1980s—Saab had been driven by specific characters and stories that resonated with her fascinations or that spoke to questions that her experience of the war raised for her, and she never hesitated to change completely the form of her films while conducting her research. In many projects we can follow her experimenting from classical documentary to fiction until reaching a hybrid cinematic form that often only she was able to visualize during the process of creation.³

This chapter is my testimony, reflecting on my working relationship with Jocelyne Saab. Emerging from my intimate involvement in her last two, incomplete feature film projects, "Faten Hamama's Honor" and "Shigenobu: Mother and Daughter," I describe Saab's working methods and creative process as I contemplate how best to preserve, archive, and disseminate works left in progress during the filmmaker's life or cut short by her death. First, I discuss some of Saab's in-progress films from across her prolific career, emphasizing the echoes among and links between the projects that are revealed through the archive. I am interested in particular moments when Saab was able to repurpose earlier creative work in later projects, whether cinematic or not. Second, I turn to the two major projects that took up her last years of research and creativity, which in fact hold together Saab's central preoccupations, even obsessions, as a filmmaker during her career: on the one hand, the pomp of classic Egypt and the importance of cinema to understanding the collective history of the Arab people, and on the other hand, the question of Palestinian resistance and the violence suffered by those who fight for revolution.

As the French film critic Serge Daney once said, the important thing in a documentary is to tell the story of the world and of life.⁴ In her last project Saab wanted to tell the story of a world, that of international struggle, and of several people's lives: Fusako, and her extraordinary fate; Mei, obstructed by political events beyond her control; and Saab herself, who identified with the revolutionary woman, Fusako, as well as with Mei, the woman whose youth was stolen from her in the course of others' struggle. Following the perpetual evolutions in the writing of these two projects helps us to understand Saab's conception of cinema after the end of the civil war, when the urgency of making images became a quest to discover the Arab identity and to describe the real power of resistance.

PRESERVING INCOMPLETE PICTURES

Unrealized film projects can reveal the conditions and working practices of an industry at a particular point in history, but they can also reveal how the creative process involves adaptation and transformation, requiring filmmakers to remain flexible and open to the evolution of the work if it is ever going to exist. This existence may come in variable forms, as Saab's career demonstrates, since the trajectories she follows with her projects do not always have a film as their endpoint. Saab also curated exhibitions and film festivals, such as the one we worked on together over several years, featuring her own works as well as the works of others. Creating CRIFFL was a way to keep resisting by showing the Lebanese people images they were not used to seeing; it was also a way to draw inspiration for future works, always operating under the philosophy that sees art as a tool for memory and political change.

By lingering over nonfilm archives, I seek to unveil aspects of creative and production processes, which carry the invisible or intangible beyond the cinematic: what lies hidden behind the projects that have come to life. By focusing on the processes through which Saab's projects are transformed, I approach the work of preparation and documentation as a mode of creative practice in its own right. To revalue process over product in this way is not only to reveal refusals and interruptions of women's creative labor within patriarchal film cultures, as Isabel Seguí and Elizabeth Ramírez-Soto do so effectively in chapters 4 and 5. What Saab's archive of incomplete projects shows us is that the work itself—the work *in process,* to use the terms of part 3 of *Incomplete*—can in fact nullify the completion of a film work altogether. As Georges Mourier suggests, the nonfilm material that emerges through the "project and work of preparation and documentation work [can serve] as a work of art, even going so far as to render null and void the making of the film itself."[5]

Porous, metamorphizing, Jocelyne Saab's processual materials transformed into an event or were dispersed into a broader artistic reflection beyond, behind, or around the moving image—and all the while, Saab's appetite for cinema was linked to her need to tell stories that involved her personally, despite their frequently political and public nature. In this section, I follow the trajectory of a range of projects, especially from the 1990s, to analyze how Saab found ways to tell the stories that mattered to her—in moving images and otherwise—by actively developing new approaches and new directions for her work. Saab's archive of incompletion reflects her continuous work against the tide, ready to resist the world's contradictions—which she denounced as inequitable and unfair—by any means necessary, from the treatment of the Kurds by the Iraqi army in 1974 to the situation of the Syrian refugees in Lebanon in 2016.

When she began to make her own films in 1975, Saab was twenty-seven years old. She threw herself into a war-torn Beirut, accompanied by her director of photography Hassan Naamani, and started filming its people, streets, and destroyed living spaces. By that time, Saab had been working for two years for the television program *Magazine 52* on the national channel France 3. But after the channel censored a news report Saab had directed about Palestinian women in Lebanon, she decided to become an independent director.[6] Her first feature-length documentary, *Le Liban dans la tourmente* (*Lebanon in a Whirlwind*, 1975), was released at L'Entrepôt cinema in Paris. Her next films were broadcast on television in prime time (in France but also in Sweden, Japan, Germany, and Italy, depending on the subjects), sometimes at great risk to the director, who received numerous death threats from the Phalangists (Christian militia) to whose violence against Palestinians and Muslim civilians she testified.[7]

Among these films, *Les Enfants de la guerre* (*Children of War*, 1976) was in demand from festival programmers, as is indicated by extant letters of request and transaction bills. We know, too, that the producers of a Japanese television channel, the NHK, were impressed by Saab's work on child soldiers in this film and originally ordered *Beyrouth, jamais plus* (*Beirut, Never Again*, 1976). Yet no trace of the preparatory documents for these projects remains. Indeed, we have hardly any written materials at all from the early years of Saab's career, apart from a few letters, contracts, and two scenarios for fiction films: one dating from 1976 and cowritten with Sélim Turquie (who later wrote under the pseudonym Sélim Nassib), titled *L'Arrière-quartier* (*The Hind-quarter*); the other a scenario for *Une vie suspendue* (*A Suspended Life*), which was reworked by Gérard Brach before becoming Saab's first fiction film, released at the Quinzaine des Réalisateurs in Cannes in 1985. These traces are the only lasting connection we have to Saab's early working practice and career.

It is likely that, as she lived and worked between Paris and Beirut as a young journalist, Saab did not manage her archive as carefully as she did after she directed her first fiction film in 1985; part of this archive may also have burned with her family home in Beirut in 1982. Saab seems to have become conscious of the importance of maintaining her archive through her involvement in the "Beirut, 1001 Images" project, which occupied her from the end of the Lebanese Civil War in 1991. This project saw Saab gather more than four hundred films about Lebanon, filmed by Arabic or international directors, to resuscitate the Lebanese Film Library that closed during the war.[8] Saab intended to publish a book about Beirut, coauthored by various friends, in the context of this work. In this project, and across her career, Saab's creative process was geared toward raising political and social issues, and finding ways to express them, by any means necessary. In this case, neither the film library nor the book came to fruition, but what did result was a film, *Il était une fois Beyrouth: Histoire d'une star* (*Once Upon a Time in Beirut: History of a Star*, 1994). This docudrama is centered around two young women who have only ever known Beirut at war. To learn about what their city used to be, they pay a visit to an old cinephile, Monsieur Farouk, who uses cinema to tell them the history of Lebanon and Beirut, their city, the titular "star." The films that Monsieur Farouk shows the two women are taken from thirty of the films Saab intended to place in the film library. She archived materials during this long and unexpected process of collecting, creating, reformulating, and eventually filmmaking.

In the light of Saab's extant filmography, the 1990s might be perceived as a period when failure outweighed effort. Her production, prolific up to that point, diminishes, and her cinema becomes less personal, more formatted to fit the demands of television: France 3 ordered from her a series of documentaries about the Egyptian contemporary cultural reality; in 1991 she directed a medical documentary about the in vitro process of fertilization that was broadcasted on France 2; she also worked in coproduction with the French private channel Canal Plus for a couple of films. Conversely, the records of Saab's unfinished projects in this decade demand that we acknowledge her desire to work on a great diversity of topics. Next to the films adapted for television, which generated masses of documentary content for its programs around that time, we find many personal projects. These projects are constructed between poetics and politics, on the border between documentary and fiction. Among these projects is "Joumana," for which we have drafts of scenario dating from 1997, an impressive scenario retracing the fate of a woman who was Saab's friend in the 1970s. The women grew apart after Joumana sided with the Christian Phalanges during the civil war. In the 1990s, Saab reunited with Joumana, who by this time was suffering traumatic amnesia provoked by an attack against her husband for political reasons; the film project was an attempt to rediscover Joumana's memory. This project, intermingling documentary and fictional modes, was meant to be a sensitive, eyewitness account of the Lebanese Civil War, but Joumana, faced with the pain that her returning memory caused her, refused to finish the film.

"Joumana," which represents significant creative and collaborative effort on the part of Saab and others, suggests the limitations of considering Saab's filmography without the unfinished projects she also developed, to a greater or lesser degree, throughout the 1990s. The reality of the archive, which includes the finished and the unfinished, the filmic and the nonfilmic, brings the apparent cohesion of Saab's known work and the reality of her artistic and personal desires into question, while giving us a fuller sense of the social and political conditions under which she worked.[9] For example, when viewed alongside her completed film works, it makes sense to understand the hourlong documentary *La Dame de Saigon* (*The Lady of Saigon*, 1996) in relation to Saab's longstanding interest in various revolutions and struggles for liberation: in the late 1970s she filmed the Polisario Front's guerrilla war in western Sahara, before she went on to give an account of the aftermath of the Iranian revolution at the beginning of the 1980s, and she never concealed her interest in Vietnamese resistance during their conflict with the United States. And yet our evaluation of *The Lady of Saigon* shifts in the context of the numerous unfinished projects now at our disposal. This was, in fact, only one project among several written, researched, and developed in some depth (but not funded or produced) by Saab in Southeast Asia during this period: one in India—"Histoire de Fatehpur Sikri" ("The History of Fatehpur Sikri")—and another about Hanoi— "Portrait d'Hanoï ou Comment inventer la modernité" ("Portrait of Hanoi or How to Invent Modernity").

Indeed, in a similar way, *The Lady of Saigon* as a project itself existed in different forms. Initially intended as a fictional feature, which would have been titled "Vietnam, notre amour" ("Vietnam, Our Love"), and which called for the reconstitution of underground resistance during the conflicts, the project was eventually produced as a television documentary, since this format was less expensive to produce. This documentary, broadcast on France 2, is classical in its treatment of the subject; put in perspective with the rest of Saab's filmography, it could be understood simply as an opportunity for her to direct a film with the support of a production company (ADR Production). This project also afforded her an opportunity to film in Asia, which she greatly desired to do. In the end, Saab was unable to shoot any other projects in Asia, and *The Lady of Saigon* would be the only finished film that testifies to her interest in this region. Yet this project offered a way for Saab to turn her sights far from Western countries, asserting her Lebanese identity as an Asian identity.

In the development of the "Joumana" project, and in the destiny of *The Lady of Saigon*, we can identify a tendency that is symptomatic of Saab's creative process, insofar as she always attempted to repurpose her experiences and research in later projects. When she launched CRIFFL in 2013 to promote Asian cinema in Lebanon (where it was not distributed), Saab had a firm position on Asia: Lebanon was an Asian country that should learn to detach itself from its fascination with the West and turn toward its origins.[10] During her prolonged stays in Asia, and in view of the success of *Kiss Me Not on the Eyes* in Southeast Asia, Saab strengthened and created solid connections with key actors in various film industries across Asia. She joined the Network for the Promotion of Asian Cinema (NETPAC) and wanted to give the organization a place in Lebanon through her festival. According to her correspondence with NETPAC founder and scholar Aruna Vasudev, former director of the Singapore International Film Festival Philip Chea, and others, it appears that the creation of CRIFFL was the direct result of Saab's desire to use the material she had gathered and the contacts she had established while constructing her film projects. This reality is also manifest in the construction of her final two fiction projects, the development of which I followed personally.

ASSIA DAGHER AND FATEN HAMAMA: A GENERATION IN SEARCH OF DIRECTION

As is the case with many Lebanese citizens, whose families often lived between their home country and Egypt, Saab maintained very strong connections with the North African nation. She went there with a camera for the first time when she was working as a war reporter for French television, covering the 1973 October War. She then returned four years later to film the aftermath of the 1977 bread riots in Cairo, condemning the extremely precarious state of President Anwar el-Sadat's liberal Infitah ("opening" to capitalism) policy, which was collapsing. Upon the release of *Egypt, City of the Dead* (*Égypte, la cité des morts*, 1977), Saab was banned from the country for seven years. However, she went back in 1986 for a series of television reports for France 2, and then again in 1989 to direct *Belly Dancers* (*Les Almées*), a film about Oriental dancers who were threatened by the relentless rise of religious fundamentalism. Finally, Saab mostly lived in Cairo over seven years of research, setup, and filming for *Kiss Me Not on the Eyes*, a 2005 homage to the musicals of Egyptian cinema's golden age.

Saab's fascination with Egyptian culture is present in her first fiction film, *A Suspended Life*, where rich references to Egyptian cinema abound.[11] Saab undertook a long process of research into the iconic actress Nour El Hoda; her archives contain hundreds of postcards of posters and frames of films in which El Hoda acted. There is no extant writing about a project Saab had in mind to develop out of these materials, but the collection of images appears to have led to another project that also never came to life: an exhibition titled "This Floating Object of Desire," meant to feature posters of great Egyptian films. Saab wrote a statement of intent for the project in 2011 and produced digitized versions of more than a thousand posters she found through private collectors in Cairo and Beirut, notably Lebanese collector Abboudi Abou Jaoude. This impressive research fostered Saab's interest in the political and militant aspects of the cinema of Henri Barakat, on which she led a research seminar at the Institute of Theatre, Audiovisual, and Cinema Studies at the Saint Joseph University of Beirut in 2013. This teaching experience was intended as preparatory for a film about Barakat, Assia Dagher, and Faten Hamama, developed in collaboration with students from the university. The film could not be finished in one semester, but all of the notes and transcripts of the interviews conducted by and with students are available in Saab's digital archives.[12]

The film planned and developed by Saab and her students centered on Assia Dagher, a young woman from the Lebanese mountains who was married against her will at a very young age, but who ran away with the help of her cousin, who was engaged in the resistance against the Ottoman Empire (figure 6.1). Dagher's cousin assisted her to travel to Egypt by boat, where, despite being illiterate, Dagher became one of the foremost actor–producers in Cairo, known as "Hollywood on the Nile," from the 1930s to the 1960s. In addition to her own extensive acting career, Dagher produced films with such directors as Barakat and Youssef Chahine and cast great actors like Mary Queeny and Faten Hamama. Saab's initial research, collected in a file titled "ASSIA RECHERCHE" and dated from 2012, includes Dagher's filmography in its entirety as well as other materials. Saab wrote the first story fragments in 2013, which indicate her intention to tell the story of a woman's fight for her emancipation. In the statement of intent written for the first version of the project, Saab insists upon the political dimension of her film:

> By developing, as an underlying theme, the idea of an illiterate woman who uses the image to emancipate herself and question the way to fight for herself and others through the image, I develop the psychology of an extraordinary character. By speaking of the courage of this woman alone against the world, who threw herself into cinema rather than remaining subjugated to a closed-

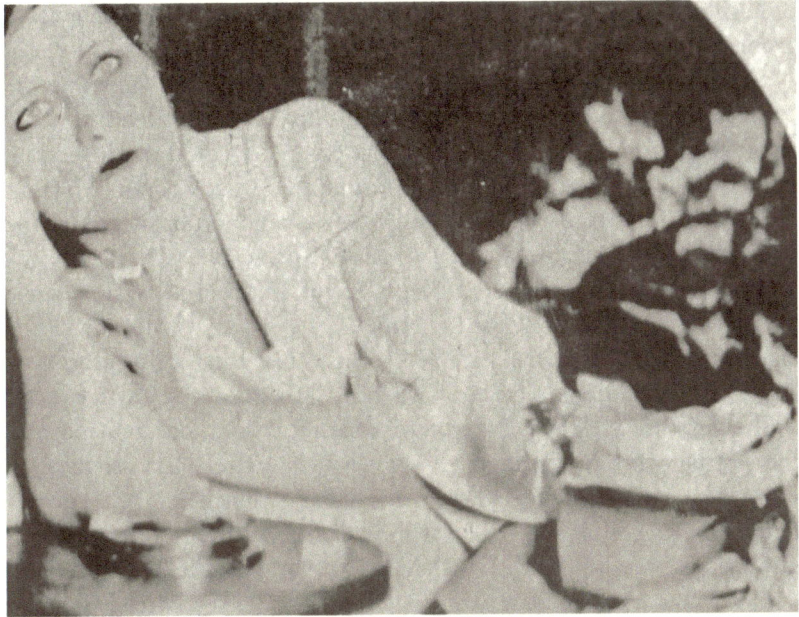

FIGURE 6.1 Portrait of Assia Dagher, pioneer of cinema in Egypt and Lebanon, one of several subjects for whom actors were scouted but not shot for "Assia Dagher," 2013. Published in Jocelyne Saab, *Zones de Guerre* (Paris: Les Éditions de l'Oeil, 2018), 141.

off and degrading regime, I create a political film. . . . By breathing life back into the golden age of cinema, with a romantic but also a political streak, I show how important it is that cinema remains independent.[13]

The following year, Saab secured a grant from the Arab Fund for Arts and Culture (AFAC) to develop this project, yet she quickly decided to reimagine the film as a docudrama with a widened focus. The film star Faten Hamama was still alive and had, on 15 June 2013, been awarded the title of Doctor Honoris Causa by the American University of Beirut; as it happened, Saab had filmed the ceremony at which this honor had been bestowed. Fascinated by this figure whose films she watched as a child, Saab had the idea to cast Hamama, who had retired from the screen many years before, in her film. The project was thus transformed, with the new synopsis, written in June 2014, beginning with the conferral of Hamama's degree in Beirut. Saab imagines the voice of an elderly Hamama telling the story of the golden age she had lived through, using images built between "fiction, documentary, and archive."[14] The university ceremony, the synopsis explains, "evokes in [Hamama] a series of flashbacks that assaults her linked to her first esthetic and cinematographic emotion when she sees in a film young Assia Dagher."[15]

Saab's film was meant to reconstitute the golden era, animating the "real facts, which belong to collective history and cinema history," as she explained in the project proposal presented to the French funding body of the Centre National du Cinéma et de l'image animée (CNC) in June 2014. The figure of Dagher undergoes a metamorphosis, too, as the focus shifts from her early years of oppression to the "extraordinary" film career that followed her arrival in Egypt. In this new version of the document, Saab shows her as the future star she became, not the victim she was as a child. In the statement of intent of the new project, now titled "Faten Hamama's Honor," Dagher's introduction notes her status as the "mother of cinema" (*"oum al-sinima"*): "From being an extra in the first film shot in Egypt, she became a silent actress and producer of more than a hundred films. She discovered and launched talents such as Faten Hamama and above all gave their chance to several directors with a thousand times recognized talent such as (Barakat, Chahine . . .)."[16]

But Faten Hamama's death on 17 January 2015 forced Saab to change her film again. Returning Dagher to the center of the film, but not returning to the classic biopic form she had initially envisaged, Saab drew on the generic and formal codes of the musicals of golden-age Egyptian cinema, as she had previously done in *Kiss Me Not on the Eyes*. The new synopsis reads:

> 1900–1960, style: Musical. Two famous figures on the beginning of the 19th century, ROSA EL YOUSSEF, actress and writer, and BADIA MASSABNI, dancer, curator of talents heading the biggest art cabaret in Cairo, tell with great panache the story of ASSIA the young pioneer of cinema actress of the silent films, and Producer, in what will become Hollywood on Nile.[17]

The film was to unfold as a musical epic, blending song and dance scenes with a melodramatic story set in an ebullient Cairo in the years prior to the Free Officers' Revolution of 1952. Encompassing an era of cultural and political upheavals, the film was to deal with Gamal Abdel Nasser's rise to power as the second president of Egypt and with the flight of film professionals after the nationalization of the film industry. Saab's vision was ambitious: she offered the part of Dagher to Salma Hayek, and intended to work with Lebanese *baladi* dancer Alexandre Paulikevitch and Badia Massabni, a performer who was then the manager of one of Cairo's greatest cabarets (figure 6.2). Unfortunately, Saab found out that she had cancer during the winter of 2015–16, which put an end to the project.

FIGURE 6.2 Portraits of Badia Massabni, owner of the most famous cabaret in Cairo, also intended as a principal role in "Assia Dagher." Published in Jocelyne Saab, *Zones de Guerre* (Paris: Les Éditions de l'Oeil, 2018), 141.

Because of Saab's adaptability, creativity, and resilience despite setbacks and changed circumstances, she was able to turn experiences of interruption or failure into opportunities for further imagining, making, and remaking. For her, developing one project was often also—or instead—developing another project later down the line; and all of her projects, as she worked across film, television, and gallery, might be realized in an unexpected form, even if only as a series of written documents now housed in her archive, which my colleagues and I seek to bring to light, to a still different kind of fruition. Not only this, but in the case of this particular project, Saab's working process is productive in another way: by sending her own students off on the research field of her own film, Saab could pass down her passion and her motivations to a group of young filmmakers, while also giving them a chance to develop research skills and to explore, as inspiration, Arabic film history.

"SHIGENOBU: MOTHER AND DAUGHTER": PERSONAL HISTORY BY ANY MEANS

Unlike the previous project, which had evolved gradually toward its hybrid musical form only to be halted, finally, by Saab's illness, Saab's portrait of Mei Shigenobu's life evolved more directly by necessity, because of the difficulties she encountered in finding funds for this film. Yet Saab's creative process led her on a similar trajectory: from a biopic driven by reconstitutions and romanticized scenes, the film became an experimental montage, enriched by archival images taken from other films, used to translate the international spirit of revolution characteristic of the times. Saab first heard the story of Mei Shigenobu at the end of 2016 from a Japanese historian and film critic, Yomota Inuhiko, who quickly became a key contributor in the project's development.[18] Mei Shigenobu is the daughter of Fusako Shigenobu, an activist in the Red Army Faction in Japan, a movement born during the student protests that erupted in 1968 against the government's decision to increase university fees. As in Germany or Italy, the Japanese youth in this period were rising against the denialism of their parents' generation, which had led them from supporting the Nazi regime to embracing consumer society under America's thumb. Their continued support of the American occupation of Vietnam was the root cause of the violence that defined the revolutionary movements that emerged in those years.[19]

Fusako came to Lebanon with a few other activists in 1971, and with Tsuyoshi Okudaira cofounded the Japanese Red Army in Beirut. The group received financial and moral support from the producer Kôji Wakamatsu, who had come to Lebanon with the filmmaker Masao Adachi to direct a propaganda film in favor of the Palestinian struggle. That film was released as *Red Army/PFLP: Declaration of World War* (1971) and included interventions from the leaders of the Popular Front for the Liberation of Palestine (PFLP) as well as Shigenobu, among others.

Mei Shigenobu was born in secret in 1973. Her mother, like most pro-Palestine leaders, was forced to leave Beirut in 1982 after the Israeli army agreed to lift the siege they had held over the city. After their departure Fusako carried on being active in other revolutionary groups, and Mei was taken in by comrades in other countries of the Arabic region, remaining hidden under various aliases during the first twenty-seven years of her life, to protect herself from the Israeli Mossad. Mei and Fusako only met a few times after that, and the moments they spent together were precious. Fusako was finally arrested by the Japanese army in Osaka in 2001, after more than two decades on the run, and was later sentenced to twenty years in jail. As a result of her mother's arrest, Mei was no longer in danger and was able to set foot in Japan for the first time in March 2001, far from Israeli security forces. Kôji

Wakamatsu went to Beirut in deepest secrecy with a television team to film Mei's testimony, which was broadcast the next day on the NHK channel of Japanese TV. Mei worked for Japanese television for a long time and advocated for her mother's release for years before returning to Lebanon.

Like Fusako, Saab also flew the flag of internationalism.[20] In Beirut she worked as a journalist with most of the revolutionary groups that had come from around the world to support the Palestinian resistance in Beirut. Saab herself had stayed in Beirut during the siege; to her, remaining in the city was an act of resistance on behalf of all Lebanese people, as she explained in her 1982 masterpiece *Beyrouth, ma ville*. And like Fusako, Saab also left after the end of the siege, once the Israeli army negotiated the departure of the Palestinian Liberation Organization (PLO) from Lebanon. Yasser Arafat had asked her to join him on the *Atlantis*, the boat that took him to Greece, before he was given shelter in Tunis, where the PLO established its headquarters until 1994; the exclusive footage that Saab obtained on board would be released as *Le bateau de l'exil* (*The Ship of Exile*, 1982).

Investigating the similarity between her experience and Fusako's, without necessarily drawing on her personal experience, seemed to Saab a means to speak one last time about those years of struggle and the siege of Beirut, a memory that haunted her. Ill, and conscious that this film would be her last, Saab was intent on paying homage to the experience that forged her by telling the story of Fusako Shigenobu's life and the fate of her daughter Mei: the devotion to a struggle against injustice, born out of the ruins of the 1948 *nakba*, and which formed the bedrock in the untamable filmmaker's identity until the end of her life. The film Saab dreamed of contended with the nostalgia for revolution, and for a relationship between a mother and a daughter broken up by the war.

When Inuhiko told Saab her story, Fusako was still in prison.[21] Inuhiko convinced Fusako to open up her archives to Saab, in particular a series of illustrated plates she drew when she arrived in prison to tell the story of Mei's childhood in Lebanon, in the midst of the civil war, and to record her memories with her daughter. Increasingly tired by her illness, Saab imagined another film from those illustrated plates; instead of a documentary or a reenactment, which required shooting, she came up with the idea to bring the drawings to life in the style of Japanese anime. The naivety of the pictures—connected to Mei's youthful innocence, which larger political events would force her to overcome—

inspired Saab to visualize the stark discrepancy between the life of a child lived in communal harmony and the violence of the armed revolution.

Moved by the story of this mother-daughter relationship, with which Saab identified in spite of herself, she decided to write a letter to Fusako, which Inuhiko translated into Japanese.[22] "Since I have approached this subject through Yomota to make a film," she wrote,

> I felt emotionally very attached to you and to May and I understand your desire of seeing May liberating herself. I realized how it was difficult for May, and how sensible she was. . . . That is why I had the idea of animation scenes for some parts of the film. Yomota really initiated me and we went to see the film on Hiroshima that is terribly moving. Since I saw this film and the more I think about it, I am convinced animation will draw better than anything else the childhood period and the nostalgia recovering it.[23]

The Japanese anime film referenced here is Katabuchi Sunao's *In This Corner of the World* (*Kono Sekai no Katasumi ni*, 2016). The film tells the story of a young girl, Suzu, who, having grown up in 1930s Hiroshima, must leave her family in 1944 to go to the nearby city of Kure, a military port bombed by American air forces. In this story of the curse of war, Saab also saw Beirut, the civil war and the siege; as she told Fusako, from this point on, she saw animation as the best way to talk about Mei's childhood in the midst of the chaos of war. It was also a way for her to tell Mei's story differently from how it had been told by Shane O'Sullivan in *Children of the Revolution* (2010), then by Eric Baudelaire in *L'Anabase de May et Fusako Shigenobu, Masao Adachi et 27 années sans images* (*The Anabasis of Mei and Fusako Shigenobu, Masao Adachi and 27 Years Without Images*, 2011). To Saab, telling this story meant speaking about the loss of innocence that she experienced herself with the war. She didn't want Mei Shigenobu herself to appear physically in her film: she knew from Baudelaire's film and rushes that Mei had a well-honed discourse while talking about her experience as a child in the revolution, and Saab was looking for a more unrehearsed expression of this curious destiny.

In keeping with her practice of repurposing existing materials and ideas, Saab planned to use sequences taken from her own films shot during the civil war between 1974 and 1982 as a counterpoint to the animated sequences. As early as the 1990s, Saab returned to and reworked materials from her own film archive of the Lebanese Civil War. *Once Upon a Time in Beirut* reuses a sequence from *A Suspended Life*; in *Strange Games and Bridges* (2007), meanwhile, Saab undertakes entirely new edits of older sequences in criticizing war's violence. In the "Shigenobu" project, Saab wanted to juxtapose her own footage with excerpts from the pink films (*pinku eiga*) produced by Kôji Wakamatsu in the 1960s and 1970s, such as *Violated Angels* (1967), *Violent Virgin* (1969), or *Ecstasy of the Angels* (1972). By tinting these images with colors associated with the radical movement—red, blue, yellow— and linking them with the visual archives of the Lebanese Civil War and the actions led of the Japanese Red Army in the region, Saab's appropriation of these images would, she hoped, give a sense of the violence of the time and enable a reflection on the violence and extreme necessity of the revolution.

Drawing to the end of her life, and at the mercy of institutional timeframes for the award of grants toward production costs, Saab was not able to bring this last film project to completion. However, she still wanted to retain something of the protracted research and working process she had undertaken. We were both in Beirut when Saab decided to adapt her project to something smaller, a trace of all the reflections that moved her during the process of writing Mei's story. Saab was physically weak but full of energy, and she decided to shoot something, which meant to rewrite something that was the opposite of what we were writing until then: a film in which Saab appears next to Mei, as if she was passing the torch from one generation to another. I participated in the research and the writing of the feature-length project, so I was well placed to help her. We wrote a synopsis in a few days and managed to gather a small team for the shooting.

In 2016, when Saab was directing *Imaginary Postcard* in Istanbul, she had imagined a series of videos directed in various countries, in the form of a letter addressed to an intellectual figure from each nation. Saab wanted to send Yomota Inuhiko a video postcard from Beirut, to pay homage to the film critic who had opened the doors of this strange and original project. Saab thought to send him a film reusing the opening tracking shot from her 1978 film *Lettre de Beyrouth* (*Letter from Beirut*) and filming Mei in the same cafés she had once filmed during the civil war. In the end, Saab decided instead to give voice to Mei. The general synopsis changed; the letter disappeared and Mei became the main character of this short video. From interviews directed by Eric Baudelaire for his film about Mei, which he gave Saab for her work, Saab compiled a six-minute film that reflects Mei's mysterious reality and her personal need to share another story of resistance. *My Name Is*

Mei Shigenobu was completed during the last week of December 2018. It was Jocelyne Saab's last film.

CONCLUSION

In Saab's body of work, incompletion generates creative energy: never exactly finished, even when they are ostensibly complete, the projects shift, metamorphose, and reappear in new guises—much as in the work of the feminist filmmakers discussed in later chapters of *Incomplete*. The reconfiguration and rewriting of various projects—by choice as much as by circumstance—led Saab to redirect and recalibrate their themes as well as their forms, as in the production of *The Lady of Saigon* for France 2, or in her final, experimental project "Shigenobu." The question that remains is how we should present this archive of incompletion alongside that of her extant and completed works?

The research we are currently undertaking as the Association of Friends of Jocelyne Saab on Saab's unfinished projects, and more widely on her paper and digital archives as whole, was born out of the urgency of gathering and restoring her (completed) films to give them visibility in the Middle East and worldwide in these times of violence, since a very few people know about them. In-depth research on an artist's work is infinite. The question of the preservation and dissemination of Saab's nonfilm (or parafilm) archive must therefore be geared not only toward making these resources accessible, as Geneviève Sellier explains writing on the classification of Jean Grémillon's archive.[24] The archive must also show the importance of these projects, which, as they were abandoned, transformed, or repurposed over her career, offer insights into the artist's methods, aims, and processes.

Saab herself wondered about the future of her unfinished works. In her photography book *Zones de Guerre* (2018), which Saab compiled and published as she was suffering from cancer, she isolates a few photograms from the documentary films she directed during and after the civil war. But she also highlights some of the projects she had not finished and that were most important to her, in addition to some location-scouting pictures and a photographic series she had made between 2007 and 2016. Next to her own images appear some Egyptian film posters featuring Nour El-Hoda as well as studio portraits of Assia Dagher and images of Faten Hamama. Jocelyne Saab found a means to incorporate something of the projects that occupied her at the end of her life, and which she could not direct, into her complete works.

NOTES

1. Jocelyne Saab, preface to Mathilde Rouxel, *Jocelyne Saab: La mémoire indomptée (1970–2019)* (Beirut, Lebanon: Dar An-Nahar Editions, 2015), 8–9, 8.
2. The Association of Friends of Jocelyne Saab is scanning and sorting all the archives (films, written, and digital) to make them available online in open source to allow any researcher or artist to access them throughout the world; we are aiming to do this by 2023. The original material will be kept by the Cinémathèque Française.
3. Saab was always proud to recall how skeptical the cinematographer Jacques Bouquin was during the shooting of her film *What's Going On?*, and how impressed he was when he watched the film before its official release. According to Saab, he said: "I never understood what you wanted to do, but apparently you knew perfectly what you were doing!" Barbara Doussot, who was supposed to edit Saab's last film, "Shigenobu: Mother and Daughter," refused to work on it without Saab because she could not understand what she was trying to do through her experimental approach.
4. See Serge Daney, *Ciné-Journal* (Paris: Cahiers du cinéma, 1986), 323.
5. Georges Mourier, "Editorial," in *La Mort des films* (Paris: Kinetraces éditions, 2017), 8–10, 8.
6. Nicole Brenez, "Each Dawn a Censor Dies," trans. Brad Stevens, *Le Magazine* (15 March 2016), http://lemagazine.jeudepaume.org/blogs/each-dawn-a-censor-dies-by-nicole-brenez/2016/03/15/jocelyne-saab-les-voies-multiples-de-la-censure/.
7. Saab was born Christian but stood with the Arab nationalists, the group that gathered all the Leftist parties, the Palestinian resistance, and the Muslim militia.
8. Mathilde Rouxel, "Jocelyne Saab, cinéaste témoin de la cinéphilie libanaise," in *Les Représentations de la cinéphilie*, Cycnos 34.1, ed. Jean-Paul Aubert, Cyril Laverger, and Christel Taillibert (Paris: L'Harmattan, 2018), 111–27, 112.
9. Elsewhere I have presented all of Saab's unfinished projects I have been able to identify so far: see Mathilde Rouxel, "A Filmmaker's Words: A Journey through the Archive of Jocelyne Saab's Unfinished Work," in *ReFocus: The Films of Jocelyne Saab: Films, Artworks and Cultural Events for the Arab World*, ed. Rouxel and Stefanie Van de Peer (Edinburgh: Edinburgh University Press, 2021), 70–83.
10. Némésis Srour, "Jocelyne Saab and CRIFFL: Dismantling Boundaries and Making New Routes for Asian Cinema in Lebanon," in *ReFocus*, ed. Rouxel and Van de Peer, 126–41, 128.
11. Rouxel, "Jocelyne Saab," 114–15.
12. The work she conducted with those students had the parallel objective of enriching her research avenues for yet another film, one that would tie together research conducted for years after the 2009 release of her final feature film, *What's Going On?*.
13. Saab, statement of intent for "Assia," December 2013. Original quotation: "En développant dans un thème sous-jacent l'idée d'une analphabète qui

passe par l'image pour s'émanciper et s'interroger sur la façon de se battre par l'image pour soi et pour les autres, je développe la psychologie d'un personnage hors du commun. En disant le courage de cette femme contre tous, qui s'est jetée dans le cinéma plutôt que de rester soumise à un régime clos et avilissant, je réalise un film engagé. [. . .] En redonnant vie à l'âge d'or du cinéma, sur une fibre romantique mais aussi politique, je montre combien il est important que le cinéma reste indépendant."

14. Saab, "Faten Hamama's Honor," 2014. Original quotation: "fiction, documentaire et archive."

15. Saab, synopsis for "L'honneur de Faten Hamama," June 2014. Original in English.

16. Saab, statement of intent for "Faten Hamama's Honor," August 2014. Original quotation: "Assia Dagher a connu une carrière hors du commun qui lui vaudra le titre de 'mère du Cinéma,' (*Oum al-sinima*), puisque de figurante dans le premier film tourné en Egypte elle deviendra actrice du muet et productrice de plus de cent films. Elle découvrira et lancera des talents comme Faten Hamama et surtout donnera leur chance à plusieurs réalisateurs au talent mille fois reconnu comme (Barakat, Chahine . . .)."

17. Saab, synopsis for "Assia," October 2016. Original in English.

18. Yomota Inuhiko, "A Mother and Daughter Reunion: How Jocelyne Saab Shot Her Last Documentary, *My Name Is Mei Shigenobu*," in *ReFocus*, ed. Rouxel and Van de Peer, 112–24.

19. Michaël Prazan, *Les Fanatiques: Histoire de l'Armée rouge japonaise* (Paris: Éditions du Seuil, 2002), 14.

20. Stefanie Van de Peer, "Guerrillas, Border Crossings and Internationalism: The Liberation of Non-Arabs in Jocelyne Saab's Early Documentaries," in *ReFocus*, ed. Rouxel and Van de Peer, 143–58.

21. She was released on 28 May 2022.

22. Inuhiko, "Mother and Daughter Reunion," 115.

23. Saab, correspondence with Yomota Inuhiko, 9 November 2017. Original in English.

24. Geneviève Sellier, "État des archives sur Grémillon," *1895, revue d'histoire du cinéma* (1997): 101–10, www.persee.fr/doc/1895_0769-0959_1997_hos_2_1_1247.

PART THREE

In Process

CHAPTER 7

Ins and Outtakes

An Interview

PEGGY AHWESH AND LEO GOLDSMITH

Peggy Ahwesh has no unfinished films—or none that are, as it were, *officially* unfinished—but the role of the incomplete, the fragmentary, and the partial is at the core of her extensive and varied body of work. An experimental filmmaker and artist since the early 1980s, Ahwesh has worked in a wide array of mediums and styles, from film and video to installation and sound. Indeed, virtually everything that's been written about Ahwesh's work notes this heterogeneity of style and form. There is the sense across Ahwesh's oeuvre of a certain resistance to the tendencies of the twentieth-century American avant-garde: particularly to the monumental, the monolithic, and the authorial consistency and Romantic subjectivity characteristic of the poetic post–Maya Deren canon—a canon, it should be noted, whose proponents often worshipped Deren as a maternal figure, while frequently overlooking or actively marginalizing other women artists.

Instead, Ahwesh's work has wended its own way, asserting a mode of what the curator Lia Gangitano, writing about Ahwesh in 2007, has called "non-technique as technique."[1] This makes for a practice that is not *avant-garde* in the historically modernist sense, but truly "experimental." That is, Ahwesh's work is not wholly of a piece with the coherent, largely male-dominated project of the postwar period—a canon stabilized by the first edition of P. Adams Sitney's *Visionary Film*, Anthology Film Archive's Essential Cinema canon, and other works—

but one that embraces a term more evocative of the principles of play, pastiche, and exploration.[2]

In his 1988 manifesto, "Modern, All Too Modern," Ahwesh's longtime partner and collaborator Keith Sanborn historicized the death of the avant-garde in the 1970s and provocatively characterized Sitney's *Visionary Film* as "the master logocentric narrative of a closed pantheon of form," one that needs to be "resisted and overcome."[3] Ahwesh's varied oeuvre enacts its own form of resistance in subtle but distinctive ways, evidenced in part by her embrace of the film and video formats in which she's worked: Super 8, 16mm, VHS, Pixel Vision, drones, even a thermographic camera. Rejecting auteurist and formal consistency, her experimentation of practice represents the truest rejection of a simple continuation of the postwar avant-garde and a grasping search for new forms and ideas. "I'm not so much an avant-gardist of the Sitney family," Ahwesh told me, "but a hybrid running heretically parallel to the canon, a bastard child of George Romero and Tony Conrad."

The unfinished, then, has a special place in Ahwesh's work not in the form of incomplete works, but in the figure of the discarded fragment, the outtake, or the remnant—all of which have been incorporated into her films. Both Elena Gorfinkel and John David Rhodes have identified the trope of the "ruin" as central to Ahwesh's body of work.[4] Similarly, appropriation—particularly deployed as a critical aesthetic practice—has provided an extensive series of techniques in her body of work: in her use and misuse of various media technologies and platforms, and in her cross-pollination of genres, including horror, melodrama, literary adaptation, documentary, and beyond. More conspicuously, though, her continual return to fragments and discards is evident in her use of found footage in multiple forms and media in films and videos such as *The Color of Love* (1994), *Nocturne* (1998), *She Puppet* (2001), *Beirut Outtakes* and *The Third Body* (both 2007), as well as in her recent series of works, including *Lessons of War* (2015), *The Blackest Sea* (2016), and *The Falling Sky* (2017), which appropriate CGI-animated news reenactments made by the online Taiwanese outlet TomoNews and Next Media. Found footage—long one of the staple subgenres of experimental film and video practice, especially in the North American context—serves Ahwesh as a means of challenging traditions (mainstream, art cinema, and avant-garde alike) that privilege the singular vision of the individual artist/auteur and seek an essence or specificity of the moving-image medium. Ahwesh's found footage works, by contrast, celebrate the porousness, promiscuity, and malleability of a shared image culture, and take up, appropriate, and hybridize moving-image materials and technologies in resourceful ways.

This conversation sprung from a presentation that Ahwesh gave in the summer of 2018 as part of Cinema Camp, a film festival and symposium held each year in an eighteenth-century neoclassical manor house in the countryside of Lithuania, east of Vilnius.[5] That year, the theme of "imperfect cinema"—derived in part from the 1969 essay by the Cuban revolutionary filmmaker Julio García Espinosa—inspired Ahwesh's talk, which touched on the role that fragmentary elements play in her own work and those of her influences (including Deren's own semiunfinished masterpiece, *The Witch's Cradle* [1943]).[6] Here, Ahwesh extends her thoughts on notions of the incomplete and unfinished as they've inspired and taken new form in her vital and diverse moving-image practice. —Leo Goldsmith

. . .

"Why did they give me a kingdom to rule over if there is no better kingdom than this hour in which I exist between what I was not and will not be?"
—Fernando Pessoa, *The Book of Disquiet* (1982), quoted in *She Puppet*[7]

APPROPRIATION/PROPRIETARY

Leo: I think you've often used the word "pastiche" to describe your work, and I'm wondering if you have a particular definition of that word, or how it might relate to more classical approaches like collage or montage? "Pastiche" often has an association with postmodernism, thanks to Fredric Jameson's use of the term, which might imply that it's a more superficial technique than the older, modernist ones. But perhaps it also implies something more fun?

Peggy: "Pastiche" is one of those words that implies a playful mix of ingredients, like the craft of working with collage materials, a soft gesture; but I also think of what I do as being hard edged—both tactical and strategic—so with me you get both the soft and the hard. The mixing or mash-up of elements charges up new meanings in the classic way of how editing operates, and I love the surprises I get by the shifts in context: surprises that really invigorate the ideas between disparate visual elements and make for fresh associations. At its best pastiche is dialectical.

The cool thing to me is that when you work with found materials, the original context and meaning, the production values, the color and tone, etc., are still there to be read as a foundation layer and even though I build on top of it, it is still a strong element of the conversation. I like that layered and shadowy form, both distorted and revealing—the relationship of the reveal in relation to layers, to history and time and surface—as a kind of palimpsest.

Calling the procedure "found footage" at this point in time seems antiquated, don't you think? I guess it does mark where I started from but not necessarily where I am now.

Leo: Yes, Michael Zryd makes a similar point in his essay on Craig Baldwin's *Tribulation 99* (1991): "footage" is a totally archaic term to describe moving-image materials, and even the processes of finding that footage are totally different now as compared to even thirty years ago.[8]

Peggy: But yes, as I understand it, working with genre and reworking material, the shifts in context, is a gesture I perform again and again in my work—and I do see it as a postmodern gesture—in a way that opposes elevated mastery and visionary eye cinema.

I have a tricky relationship with time—there is the future and the past but the present often eludes definition. I think I live in a space of slippery becoming, a moving towards something that I never quite reach. Maybe that is the "present" for everyone, but I live with a strong awareness that I work in that elusive space with the found footage: looking forward and back with some purpose, with the present as a moving target.

I think there is a chance—a potential—for change in using the tropes of genre, a reconfiguration of self and a bringing to the fore of submerged points of view, by reworking and representing its conventions. It's a rehearsal for action. Like in therapy, one repeats the story of the trauma, replaying it over and over, until through the process one is able to let go of it and then one can forget. That process of memorizing and retelling then letting go is somehow linked to the repetition of genre tropes. Then, of course, there's the potential for reparations, in the psychological sense of repair work. My 1993 short film *The Scary Movie,* for example, has two girls acting out bits and pieces of what they have absorbed from schlocky horror films. It takes on a liberatory giddiness for them—testing limits and having fun—in an intimate and nonthreatening

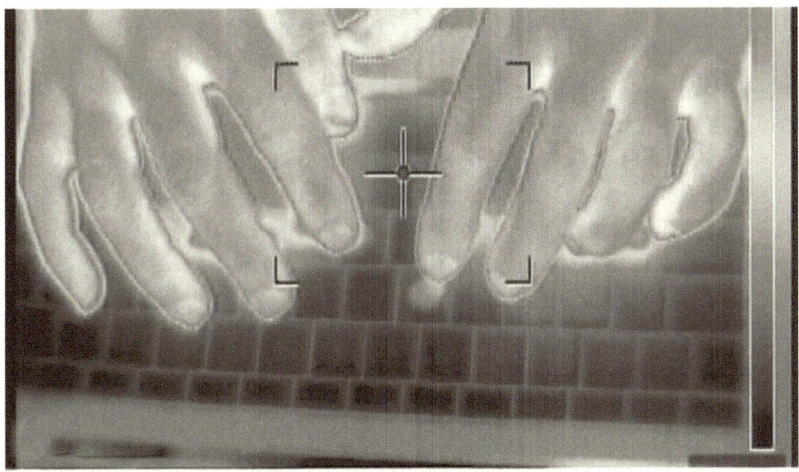

FIGURE 7.1 Still from Peggy Ahwesh, *City Thermogram* (2015). Used by permission of the artist.

theatrical situation. So it's a girl-on-girl playacting of violence in fantasy, a reworking of the tropes that is transcendent and crazy, out-of-bounds, using the safety net of genre.

Leo: What about your use of technology and nontraditional moving-image media in your work? Do you also see that as a kind of appropriation?

Peggy: I love to play around with both new and obsolete technologies and try to get them to do things against their nature. That allows me to match up the world to the non-normative way that I see it and it's the assist I need to make the visual field subjective—to bring it around to my subjectivity. I love toys and the playing field of experimentation. Walter Benjamin spoke of "refunctioning" technologies to act as instruments of progressive social change and to exploit the various malleable features of new technologies.[9] It's partly Dziga Vertov's idea of the enhancement of the senses with the aid of a machine, but also I just love gadgets.

City Thermogram, the video I made to play on the Jumbotrons in Times Square, was shot with a heat-sensitive camera that produces pseudo colors—a palette of assigned colors that correspond to temperature. I was loaned the camera and went around shooting daily, quotidian footage of life in New York City: people coming out of the subway, the heat rising out of the manholes, telephone poles, the Brooklyn Bridge, etc.—a heat tour of the city, appropriating a technology that is used for science or most likely by the military. It's a heat register about bodies, our hand-held devices, and our energy sources. I was thinking about Paul Virilio's "war model" and his book *The Vision Machine* (1994), in that the city is not merely the architecture of buildings but an interface of technology, military strategy, visual systems, and political structures that mediate our perception and define our reality. This was the foundation for *City Thermogram* and also for the single-channel version of the video called *Warm Objects*. And in another dimension, my film *the vision machine* (1997) is an essay on vision and power in relationship to women's sexuality. I have gotten a lot of mileage out of Virilio!

In my more recent work like *Border Control* (2019) and *Verily! the blackest sea, the falling sky* (2017), there is the flirtation with abstraction, which you might find contradictory to my tendency toward real-world imagery and quotation from theoretical writings. But the play of the surface and the patterns of the imagery acknowledges a digital reality. I want to retrieve a certain subjectivity from it. Of course in *City Thermogram* what we get is the machine view, but in some ways it's an odd way to trick a viewer, trick myself. Trick us all into getting past that machine view, in some way, to have a sustained experience. And the surface level of the video, with the CGI and the flat colors—it is also a critique of the surface.

> "The chief tack of warfare is accordingly not some more or less ingenious stratagem. In the first instance, it involves the elimination of the *appearance of the facts*, the continuation of what Kipling meant when he said: 'Truth is the first casualty of war.'"
> —Paul Virilio, *The Vision Machine* (1989), quoted in *Warm Objects*[10]

Of course we now are quite familiar with the way disinformation works—on a grand scale—and we see the strategy of concealing information or twisting information as the elimination of truth principles. And the military control of space ultimately succeeds by the conquest of the image. This is right out of Virilio.

But with the use of found materials one can address this—not reinvent what happened by interviews or generating original footage but by working with existing materials and pointing to the facts. I guess I'm optimistic that rather than being incorporated into the state machine, we, as illegitimate offspring, need to develop tactics to disrupt the controlling power and resist those paradigms. I'm always working on some kind of periphery with these experiences, and so it's like my little sort of sabotage, an intervention into these domains. Because I can never really fully own them. I'm always making these little attacks on the edge.

OUTTAKES/DOUBLE TAKES

Leo: I'm fascinated by the idea of the outtake in relation to your work. First, *Beirut Outtakes* isn't really made of outtakes—unless we think of an outtake as something more than its literal, technical meaning. That film seems to be made up of the outtakes of cinema history, in a way, or of the projection process more generally—the way that Bruce Conner thought of A MOVIE (1958) as being made up of those things that you weren't supposed to see in the movie theater. But this "forbidden" image is also what fascinates the viewer. Jean-François Lyotard writes about this in his essay "Acinema":

> A scene from elsewhere, representing nothing identifiable, has been added, a scene not related to the logic of your shot, an undecidable scene, worthless even as an insertion because it will not be repeated and taken up again later. So you cut it out.
> We are not demanding a raw cinema, like Dubuffet demanded an *art brut*. We are hardly about to form a club dedicated to the saving of rushes and the rehabilitation of clipped footage. And yet . . . [w]e observe that if the mistake is eliminated it is because of its incongruity, and in order to protect the order of the whole (shot and/or sequence and/or film) while banning the intensity it carries.[11]

Peggy: The footage that became *Beirut Outtakes* was given to me by the Canadian multimedia artist Jayce Salloum: he collected a jumble of decaying film scraps from an abandoned projection booth in Beirut and had them spliced together willy-nilly—upside down and backwards, perhaps never looking at it because it was in 35mm—then he had it all transferred to VHS. So films from the 1960s collected dust until about 1982 or so, when Jayce found them, and then in 2007 I made *Beirut Outtakes*. It's a time capsule of pop cultural references and an odd, condensed history of the elapsing time—and slow decay of community—in Lebanon of the civil war years (the same period documented by Jocelyne Saab, as Mathilde Rouxel discusses in chapter 6). It was all those things to me.

Outtakes of the influence of Western Orientalist values shipped for the viewing pleasure of the Lebanese audiences, embraced for their own sense of fantasy, the decay of abandonment, the sadness of the jumble of disorder in the remains.

I tried to keep a lot of the feeling of despair and desperation of that history when I edited the shots so as to not make a false organization. I also wanted, perhaps in a tribute to Bruce Conner, to leave in the absurd combination of all the bits and pieces: the fashions, the Westerns, scenes of human desire and foibles, an air-conditioner advert, the performances of belly dancers, etc. The whole spectacle of what one does see in a movie theater but here devastated by history and circumstances.

I think of my films as puzzles to be solved: if I can just figure out how all the pieces fit and get them all to talk to each other, then the whole turns out greater than the sum of the parts. And when I get stuck, I go back to the books, to get inspired and help myself grapple with the philosophical space I want the material to hold.

"I don't think about the future. I don't give myself a future and not even a present. The present keeps bending and if it becomes so heavy for me to carry it is because of this burden of lightness, this laughing load I have to hold up in the center of a dreamy day which hides me from myself."
—Maurice Blanchot, *The One Who Was Standing Apart from Me* (1995), quoted in *The Star Eaters*[12]

Leo: *Lies and Excess* is actually a film of outtakes, as I understand it.

Peggy: *Lies and Excess* has a curious history. It is a film about two women on the skids, losing at gambling in Atlantic City. The story is based on Georges Bataille's work about economic excess, and here gambling is such a potent metaphor; ranging from Native American stick games to the lottery, gambling is exciting, it's risky, a form of divination. Everyone who gambles expects to lose sooner or later. It's the opposite of our simple economic transactions and a perversion of how things function in the system of use value.

I spliced together a reel of some of the footage and then abandoned it to deep storage. A year or so later I recast and reshot the video as *The Star Eaters* (2003)—that one, may I be so bold as to say, is finished, and I have screened it many times. But recently when I found and watched the rough selects of the original *Lies and Excess*, I realized some really obvious and telling and unconscious things about what makes up a story—the minimum requirements—

FIGURE 7.2 Still from Peggy Ahwesh, *Lies and Excess* (2003–?). Used by permission of the artist.

and I had to laugh out loud. The flow was terrific, the jump cuts very lively, and the story had an open, magical quality of potential and free association. It felt unlabored and you got as much of the emotion you needed to enjoy the characters. It expressed perfectly my love of character and rejection of narrative in a running time of twenty minutes. I thought immediately of Ken Jacobs's *Perfect Film* (1986)—which is a similar reel of multiple takes, outtakes, and B-roll of a discarded news program about Malcolm X's assassination in Harlem—and also Maya Deren's *The Witch's Cradle*, her fantastic unfinished occult film—which reads now as a very contemporary storytelling strategy. I accept *The Witch's Cradle* as-is and appreciate that you can read through the gaps and sutures of the material—you can see the thought process, the working method and intention, and that is a sublime experience.

So, as it turns out, I have two films based on the same sources about women and risk taking and gambling: *Lies and Excess* and *The Star Eaters*.

AUTO-FOUND/AUTOMATION

Leo: *Bethlehem* (2009) is a curious example because it's so unmoored from the original projects (experiments? unfinished films?) from which it derives. You've said it began as a "tribute to the Bruce Conner of the period of *Valse Triste* and *Take the 5:10 to Dreamland,* with their deliberate pace and bittersweet memory of home, [and] ended as a dedication to my father, as I wound my way through personal miscellany with distance and a broader aim." But I'm wondering more specifically how you came to make it. It almost reads as a found footage film, because you seem to treat the footage as if it's alien to you, or alien to its initial purpose. You suggested something similar when you said, "Working through my archive of accumulated video footage, I pretended it was found footage from anonymous sources, editing memories like a string of pearls."[13] Can we call it a found footage film? Or an auto-found footage film? Can you make a found footage film from footage you shot yourself?

Peggy: You are right that with *Bethlehem,* which is made from my own accumulated inventory, I treat it as found footage. It is material to be sifted through and theorized and repurposed as if made by someone else. Definitely detached from the author, in this case myself.

I was charged with making a Bruce Conner tribute after he died in 2008 and it made me realize my debt to him—we were friendly, and we talked a lot in the '80s about punk music and other common interests. But I worked on it slowly, the date of the tribute show passed, and then when my father died, the project took on this new urgency. I got hooked on this idea of Conner making a found footage film with my footage and/or of me making a film from this archive which only happened to be my own.

In some ways, *Bethlehem* is a conceptual work that hints at emotional content but fundamentally does not deliver on that. It more abstractly shows the signification of shot-to-shot relations and how shots line up to suggest meaning. The video is, as I've said, like a string of pearls. Where are we going with this video? From the narrative bits to the melancholy tone and from the hard cuts to the bittersweet metaphors?

READYMADE/UNMADE

Leo: You've also talked about *Color of Love*—which uses extremely distressed and decaying footage from an amateur porno—as a film that came to you somehow just as it is (minus the music by Astor Piazzola, of course), and so this film suggests a relationship both to the Surrealists' *objet trouvé* and to Marcel Duchamp's readymade. In both cases, the question arises: what is it that artists do, exactly? On the one hand, you could say that these works undermine the very concept of an artist or author, pointing out that art is kind of where you find it. But on the other hand, especially in the case of the readymade, the point seems more that art is where *Duchamp* finds it—it requires the magical conferral of the status of art by the artist who counts (and this is related to ruminations on who counts as an artist across this book, notably by Jane Gaines in chapter 1 and Sophia Siddique in chapter 10).

Of course, with Duchamp's *Fountain*, part of the joke is that he signs it not with his own name but with a pseudonym, "R. Mutt." It's also widely believed now that he stole the idea—and maybe the original *Fountain* itself—from the artist Baroness Elsa von Freytag-Loringhoven (and again there are shades of Sophia Siddique's experience of the theft of her film work in the case of *Shirkers*). Not only this, but because the original *Fountain* was lost, Duchamp remade the work with a similar urinal in 1964. Here, the entire concept of originality and authorship breaks down: the genius and skill of the artist is constantly being deferred, and the object itself is a kind of simulacrum of art and craft.

In his book on art after Duchamp, the critic John Roberts makes the claim that the readymade stages a kind of encounter of the artistic domain of the sculpture with that of the mass-produced object-commodity as a way of making visible the chain of value production inherent in each domain. For Roberts the readymade is "a striking point of 'rendezvous' for ideas 'inside' and 'outside' of art."[14] Appropriation's unique intervention turns upon its analysis of the interaction between two systems of production and circulation: that of the artist-creator as individual and that of the worker within the industrial production model. The "inside" and "outside" of art is mapped according to delineation of different kinds of labor: the labor of the artist versus that of the artisan or manufacturer or factory worker. Roberts: "the readymade not only questions what constitutes the labour of the artist, but brings the labour of the others—ideally at least—into view."[15]

This is part of the found footage process, too: just as a urinal becomes a work of art, a newsreel image of the Hindenburg disaster—or a YouTube news cartoon, or a freaky DIY porno damaged by the rain—transforms the original object, but it also marks a gap between the original and its new form, and maybe also between one kind of artist/film-laborer and another. But it also makes me think about the relationship or difference between an artist and a thief. ("L'art c'est du vol," as François Dufrêne knew.)

READYSTROY/REDACTION

Leo: With regards to *The Color of Love*, there are of course many elements of chance that contribute to the film's form, particularly the decay which makes the film resemble *Fuses* (Carolee Schneemann, 1964), as many people have mentioned. More recently, artists like Jennifer West and Tomonari Nishikawa have explored this kind of "collaboration" with natural elements, burying film to allow it to vibe with various organic, chemical processes. There's a certain John Cage-like indeterminacy here, but also a sort of ecological cinema: "recycled images" made literal. I'm wondering if that's something you were thinking about then or think about now?

I'm also reminded of a term that Nicole Brenez coins in reference to Maurice Lemaître's Lettrist films: "readystroyed." Unlike the readymade, Brenez states, "the readystroyed compounds the found object's insolent refusal to create with the refusal even to conserve the object."[16] In *The Color of Love,* it almost seems like your intervention is one of halting this process of decay. Is that the case for you? Or is *The Color of Love* still decaying?

Peggy: I was amused by the serendipity of finding such an object in the trash. I came upon it without the artist's intervention and ego and recognized that the object had its own history—physical history—which I tried to honor in optical printing the original small-format film.

"Chance comes from night and returns to night. It is both daughter and mother of night. Night doesn't exist and neither does chance. Being, Hegel says, is the most impoverished notion. Chance, I say, is the richest. Chance. By which being is destroyed in its beyond."

—Georges Bataille, *Guilty* (1944), quoted in *The Star Eaters*[17]

MACHINATION/MACHINIMA

Leo: *She Puppet* seems to me an interesting kind of appropriation film in that you're not appropriating footage per se; you're occupying a space. You're squatting in a virtual architecture—and one that's pretty rigid. This begs the question: what kind of space is a video game? What does it mean to occupy that space?

"Although I walked among them a stranger, no one noticed. I lived among them as a spy but no one suspected. Everyone took me for a relative, no one knew that I had been switched at birth. However near my heart seemed to beat, it was always far away, the false lord of a strange exiled body. We are who we are not and life is swift and sad."

—Fernando Pessoa, *The Book of Disquiet* (1982), quoted in *She Puppet*[18]

Peggy: Your question brings to mind Harun Farocki's *Parallel I–IV* (2012–14). Farocki was the consummate generous teacher, each of his films teaching lessons by example and offering strategies for decoding how the mechanisms of vision operate. In *Parallel I–IV* he lays out the history of video games and how they differ from cinema representations. His insights into surveillance and optical technologies alert us to question them and not incorporate them without protest.

Leo: And what is perhaps most striking about Farocki's videos and yours is the extent to which they present the illusion of control over a world. In Farocki, this takes the form of, first, the possibility of creating a facsimile of the world seemingly from nothing, and to have total control over that world; and, second, the ability to navigate that world and its inhabitants and effectively do what one likes with them—usually murder them. *She Puppet* seems to explore this dynamic of control, or the illusion of it, from a distinctly feminist perspective, aligning or contrasting the rule-freedom dynamic of game-play with the circumstances of existing in the real world as a woman.

FIGURE 7.3 Still from Peggy Ahwesh, *She Puppet* (2001). Used by permission of the artist.

Peggy: She Puppet is a work about women's games and identity. It grew from an interest in trick films, early films like those by Georges Méliès, etc. I became obsessed with *Tomb Raider* and Lara Croft as a repository for our postfeminist fantasies of adventure, sex and violence without consequence. I realized that as I played it I could live-record my game-play onto mini-DV tape: an improvisation. What was evident through the violence and self-destruction was the category the female holds in our cultural imaginary. But what also interested me was the inactive, still moments, in which this mute female character explored her environment. I was self-conscious about the competitive nature of a video game and didn't want to play it too passively but having Lara Croft just stand and breathe—without any commands—became fascinating.

I structured the video around the spaces of the game. There's a constant awareness of the edges of the world, and the question of what the game designers determined to be the edges of the game world haunted me—what would happen when a player hit the boundary and could go no further, digitally speaking?

DOOMSCROLLING/DRUMROLLING

Leo: I wonder if this connects at all to the recent works you've made from the News Direct and TomoNews videos that together form the two-channel installation *Verily! the blackest sea, the falling sky.* In some ways, these are just videos you've appropriated and reedited or remixed, but it seems your take on them is more about the experience of being, living, experiencing the world (or "current events") through online spaces. "Found footage" often suggests the experience of dealing with images of the past, but these images are hardly even past—they have an instantaneous, even futuristic quality. I also wonder how that will change with time.

Peggy: It's interesting that you mention time, because I have often thought I would want to view these videos in, say, twenty years: the rush of daily news items, our collective memory of this moment, the trauma of the Trump years, the folly of these days. "Verily" is an old way to say "certainly," "yes, it's true," or "Verily I say unto thee," implying prophecy or speculation of what may come to pass. An exclamation, perhaps a warning . . .

Leo: The experience of watching these videos is something like the vertiginous spiral of "doomscrolling," being swept up in the whirlwind of often horrifying media content coming to us through our various screens. The experience is draining in a way, even as it's cute and funny. There's a sense that we don't quite know how to feel, and even the videos' initial purpose seems muddled on this point. The agencies describe themselves as follows:

> TomoNews is your best source for real news. We cover the funniest, craziest and most talked-about stories on the internet. Our tone is irreverent and unapologetic. News Direct animation fills in the gaps when video footage is missing and provides clear illustrations of news that is highly conceptual or technical in nature. With industry-leading turnaround times, News Direct's animations are available to customers within hours after a top story breaks.[19]

It's almost like they don't know why they're making the videos. To inform, to amuse, to outrage. The videos have the weird, murky goal of virtualizing real events, giving an impossibly perfect rendition of them, whereas your rendition seems to steer them in the direction of mythology, creating a violent world of bombs and children and rabid animals, where catastrophe is always unfolding and technology is always there to intervene, not always successfully. Your edit gives these videos a different arc and pace, but it seems like you also want to preserve something of the experience of glancing, swiping through these videos, as warped instant simulacra of the present.

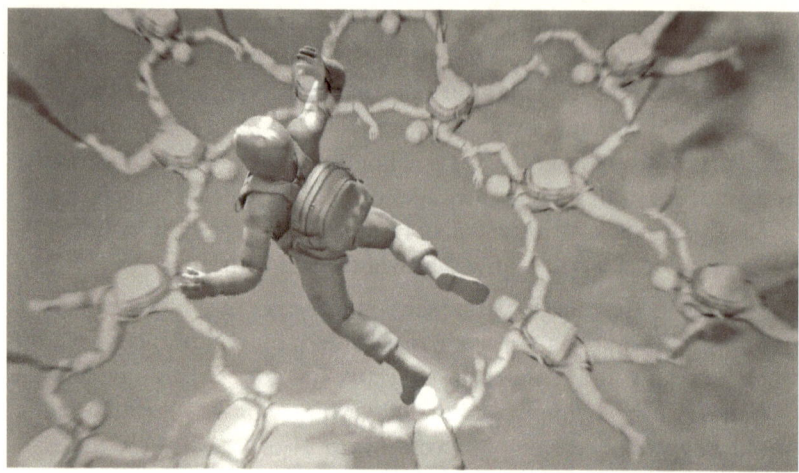

FIGURE 7.4 Still from Peggy Ahwesh, *The Blackest Sea* (2016). Used by permission of the artist.

Peggy: A number of years ago I was teaching a class in reenactment and I was poking around the Internet for examples. I found News Direct with its huge database of videos, thirty- to forty-five-second episodes from every area of reporting: trips to outer space, the release of a new iPhone, a kidnapping, etc. And it's so interesting that this disembodied and disconnected kind of fictionalized news is presented as cartoons. So, I got deeply invested in this as a philosophical puzzle, the virtual distance of the reporting and the false claims of documentary against the cute cartoon representations.

One of the first things I watched was the story about the JetBlue flight attendant, Steven Slater, who flipped out on a passenger then fled the plane via the blowup escape slide. And there were no pictures of it, so you could argue that reenactment was in order. This story showed me that we're giving up the traditional documentary reality, and the difficult task of "being there" where news is happening, in exchange for a more received kind of knowledge and a safer investment made of easy, cute-ified images.

News Direct thinks perhaps they are transcending the camera or fulfilling the fantasy of the camera in an advance from so-called traditional news, but so much has been discarded, it is problematic. This digital animation technology can significantly recast how we understand daily reality. It is an image reduced to information, and the information itself produces an aesthetic of knowledge. *Verily!* brings all of this together: the bombardment of bits of information, news, discoveries, crises, gossip, and opinion on a daily basis for all of us who are doomed to be "connected" in a technology that is a slow drain of our subjectivity. It's a cautionary tale told through a strangely hypnotic database of what propels our prurient interests, fears, and obsessions.

Leo: Part of what fascinates me about these recent videos is that your intervention occurs precisely at the level of montage and narrative—storytelling, even—as you scramble their excessively visualized and airbrushed narrativization of the real, creating disorienting, dream-like assemblages that disrupt the numb horror of the present. For example, *Verily!* assembles recreations of climate catastrophe, migrant deaths, aviation accidents, Amazon drones, and biotech implants into an overwhelming and disturbing montage of collapse and degradation. But these videos do more than wallow in despair: they utilize appropriation to generate between the videos and the viewer an active form of spectatorship that forces us into a critical relation between contemporary events and their flattened representation through contemporary online media. They index, to quote Erika Balsom, "a symptom of the perniciousness of media spectacle and an allegory of the violent techniques used to manage human and nonhuman life."[20]

This is an effect of your montage, of course, but also of recontextualization: placing them in a gallery, in multichannel installation, which opens them to something maybe more dialectical, but also makes them objects in real space, rather than fleeting impressions flashing across our tiny screens. It's also a result of the defamiliarization that happens as you—to be Benjaminian for a minute—blast them out of historical context by introducing a score from the 1940s (Ellis B. Kohs's *Passacaglia, for organ and strings*, K. 11, 1946) and epigraphs from Romantic writers such as Mary Shelley and Herman Melville. This suggests not only a scrambling of time and place, but maybe also that the effect of these images is only finalized in the strange, dislocated spatial and temporal context which you create for the viewer in the gallery space.

Peggy: A profound creative leap for me has been working with video installations set in galleries or other spaces that allow for additional layers of thought and exchange with the "viewer"—with physical bodies moving through space in addition to the meanderings of people's thoughts, the free associations and the distractions, that come with the gallery experience. It engages an expanded, decentered, unpredictable, and unfinished set of new conceptual relations. For me, it's a provocative form of intellectual montage.

NOTES

1. Lia Gangitano, "Warhol's Grave," in *LUX: A Decade of Artists Film and Video,* ed. Steve Reinke and Tom Taylor (Toronto: XYZ Books, 2000), 306–11, 307.

2. See P. Adams Sitney, *Visionary Film: The American Avant-Garde* (New York: Oxford University Press, 1974); and the overview of the Essential Cinema canon, "About: Essential Cinema," *Anthology Film Archives,* http://anthologyfilmarchives.org/about/essential-cinema. Other examples of this tendency include Sheldon Renan, *An Introduction to the American Underground Film* (New York: E. P. Dutton & Co, Inc., 1967); Parker Tyler, *Underground Film: A Critical History* (New York: Da Capo Press, 1969); and Malcolm Le Grice, *Abstract Film and Beyond* (Cambridge, MA: MIT Press, 1977).

3. Keith Sanborn (1988), "Modern, All Too Modern," in *Film Manifestos and Global Cinema Cultures: A Critical Anthology,* ed. Scott MacKenzie (Berkeley: University of California Press, 2014), 89–100, 91.

4. See Elena Gorfinkel, "Arousal in Ruins: *The Color of Love* and the Haptic Object of Film History," *World Picture* 4 (2010), http://worldpicturejournal.com/WP_4/Gorfinkel.html; and John David Rhodes, "From Ruin to Ritual," *Screen* 55.4 (2014): 494–99.

5. See Leo Goldsmith, "Exploring 'Imperfect Cinema' in a Lithuanian Idyll," *Frieze* (22 August 2018), www.frieze.com/article/exploring-imperfect-cinema-lithuanian-idyll.

6. See Julio García Espinosa, "For an Imperfect Cinema," trans. Julianne Burton, *Jump Cut* 20 (1979): 24–26.

7. Fernando Pessoa, *The Book of Disquiet,* trans. Margaret Jull Costa (London: Serpent's Tail, 2010), 162.

8. Michael Zryd, "Found Footage Film as Discursive Metahistory: Craig Baldwin's *Tribulation 99,*" *The Moving Image* 3.2 (2003): 40–61, 41.

9. For Benjamin's discussion of Bertolt Brecht's concept of "Unfunktionierung," see Walter Benjamin, "The Author as Producer," in *Understanding Brecht,* trans. Anna Bostock (London: Verso, 1998), 85–103, 93.

10. Paul Virilio, *The Vision Machine,* trans. Julie Rose (Bloomington: Indiana University Press, 1994), 66.

11. Jean-François Lyotard, "Acinema," in *Acinemas: Lyotard's Philosophy of Film,* ed. Graham Jones and Ashley Woodward (Edinburgh: Edinburgh University Press, 2017), 33–42, 33–34.

12. Maurice Blanchot, *The One Who Was Standing Apart from Me* (Barrytown, NY: Station Hill Press, 1995), 63.

13. Press release, "Peggy Ahwesh, Heart_Land," *Joan*, https://joanlosangeles.org/peggy-ahwesh/.

14. John Roberts, *The Intangibilities of Form: Skilling and Deskilling in Art after the Readymade* (London: Verso, 2007), 26.

15. Roberts, *Intangibilities of Form*, 24.

16. Nicole Brenez, *"We Support Everything Since the Dawn of Time That Has Struggled and Still Struggles": Introduction to Lettrist Cinema,* trans. Clodagh Kinsella (Berlin: Sternberg Press), 22–23.

17. Georges Bataille, *Guilty,* trans. Bruce Boone (Venice, CA: Lapis Press, 1988), 84.

18. Pessoa, *Book of Disquiet*, 131.

19. "TomoNews US—About," YouTube, www.youtube.com/user/TomoNewsUS/about, accessed 19 November 2021; "News Animation," *Next Animation Studios,* www.nextanimationstudio.com/en/newsanimation/.

20. Erika Balsom, "No Masters: The Cinema of Peggy Ahwesh," *Frieze* (November 2017), www.frieze.com/article/no-masters-cinema-peggy-ahwesh.

CHAPTER 8

"They keep moving"

Serialized Incompletion in the Work of Leslie Thornton and Lynn Hershman Leeson

STEFAN SOLOMON

Across a diverse range of media, serial forms propose, among other things, connections between intentionally discrete episodes, relations between different parts of a continuous narrative, and even a means of retroactive cohesion between heretofore unrelated objects. Seriality gestures simultaneously toward a potentially unending proliferation of links in a chain, to an indeterminate work-in-progress, and to the horizon of a bounded series whose end point has been planned in advance. Just as a series can be closed to further additions, it can also be reopened, with new elements becoming attached to a preexisting work, and so rebooting the whole enterprise.

The historical and medium specificity of the serial has to an extent dictated its possibilities, with the feuilleton of the nineteenth century designed for a devoted—and active—readership that would pursue at length a particular narrative in a newspaper or journal, usually on a weekly basis. The serials of early cinema proposed a similarly intervallic reception, albeit with the distinction that detective and Western fictions spread over a multitude of installments could not be collected by the viewer into a continuous whole; something similar would be true of long-running broadcast and cable television series prior to the advent of home entertainment. And today, while the archival possibilities afforded by the serial have proliferated, at least one by-product of digitalization has been a shift entirely away from the gaps and breaks of serialization and the time-based constraints of "appointment" media and toward binge-watching and the instantaneous "dump" of an entire series of episodes that is now commonplace across streaming platforms.[1]

In its trajectory of uneven development, the serial has been eclipsed by other release strategies while persisting in other guises. But before we arrived at seriality's shift toward simultaneity, the form possessed connotations of contingency, apprehension, and risk; the idea that the endpoint was not exactly clear, that the path to the finish had not been predetermined, meant a certain degree of uncertainty for producers and consumers alike. In contrast to the all-at-onceness of Netflix, the television series—that object that perhaps looms largest in the serial imaginary—was catalyzed by a sensitivity to its reception context amid ever faster audience feedback loops, such that a waning viewership over the course of several weeks might signal its premature end. As the platform for "undisguised commodities" propelled by market imperatives, television's example suggests that the ultimate ambition for the series is to continue without end.[2]

In this regard, the soap opera or telenovela stands as the ne plus ultra of the form, the genre driven by cliffhanger endings and complex interwoven narrative threads, which "can (theoretically, at least) go on spreading out forever in a rough approximation of the messy, dissymmetrical flux and flow of life itself, with people coming and going in and out of the endlessly elastic story-line."[3] While not always the case, closure for a television series is often consonant with failure, whether by forced cancellation at the hands of the network executives or due to the stalling of the show's internal narrative engine.[4] Notwithstanding the connections of cancellation to failure on television, as a general rule, serial works do have a "sense of an ending" and harbor an animating tension between "continuation" and "closure," driven by a desire to go on even as they must be closed off.[5]

I am fascinated by two aspects of seriality in film and video production that provide other entrées to the form: on the one hand, its continued affiliation with alternative modes that negates a loyal viewership as the cheerleaders of the work's progress and removes some serial works from the "logic" of the profit motive; and its historical feminization, on the other hand, given the discursive association of serials with female consumers and producers. Experimental film in the late twentieth and early twenty-first centuries adopts particular strategies of production, exhibition, and circulation that suggest different ways of thinking about seriality in relation to incompletion—insofar as an unfinished experimental work does not bear the same connotations of failure as it might in a commercial context, and insofar as the possibility of adding to an already "closed" work is not immediately circumscribed by traditional models of exhibition and circulation, that presuppose definitive, stable film objects. Of course, with such reworkings as the director's cut and the 4K restoration, and the option for home entertainment repackaging more broadly, this is perhaps no longer the case. However, the processual openness of the works under discussion here is not premised on the kind of value-adding or authorial control that marks the rerelease of commercial or auteurist art cinema projects.

This chapter analyzes two experimental works that were produced in serial modes. The first is Leslie Thornton's *Peggy and Fred in Hell,* a postapocalyptic episodic narrative that was released in various iterations between 1983 and 2015. Thornton's narrative is anchored by its titular protagonists and incorporates a range of found footage and makes use of 16mm, video, and digital. The second is Lynn Hershman Leeson's *Electronic Diaries,* a work whose focus is split between the intimate life of the artist and a range of social-historical concerns that emerged during its initial period of production, 1984–96. While Thornton's project would develop over three decades, she declared it finished in 2015 as *Peggy and Fred: Folding.* By contrast, Hershman Leeson had ostensibly completed her diary film in 1996, when it was released in its entirety, but she would return to the work over twenty years later, editing the earlier version and including an additional entry that served as a reappraisal of the film from the vantage point of 2019.

Viewed as inverse examples of a related phenomenon—the openended narrative work that is eventually closed; the cumulative diary work that is finished, only to be revived at a later date—each film project thus provides a different sense of the possibilities of serialized incompletion in filmmaking. As this chapter details, the relative unfinishedness of both Thornton's and Hershman Leeson's works is on the one hand completely removed from the discourse of failure that often attends incomplete works in commercial cinema, and on the other hand connected to—although not at all subservient to—dominant models of literary, cinematic, and televisual seriality. This chapter argues that in widening the scope for incompletion in serial filmmaking, *Peggy and Fred in Hell* and *Electronic Diaries* are impelled specifically by formal decisions arising from feminist commitments: respectively, as a reaction against the general antipathy to narrative espoused by the male avant-garde; and in the use of the diary form, aligning the project with other women filmmakers and writers. This chapter explores how these works provide distinct feminist perspectives on the concept of the unfinished film, and how each might render incompletion as strategy or process more than failure or lack.

PEGGY AND FRED IN HELL AND THE ARCHIVE IN MOTION

Although Leslie Thornton has produced a number of discrete, isolated film works, she is perhaps more interested in—and certainly better known for—exploring the possibilities of protracted projects. Thornton's habit of developing and returning to her own works, and recycling images so as to create new material, suggests to Mary Ann Doane that she is "continually striving to 'get it right,' the trajectory of her work nevertheless revealing an insistent distrust of the idea of the static art object or the definitive version of a film."[6] The experimental film cycle *Peggy and Fred in Hell* is indicative of the adaptive and processual aspect of the artist's practice; begun in 1983 as an intended feature film, Thornton instead chose to release the work in seventeen different two-minute to twenty-minute long episodes over the following thirty years, beginning with *The Prologue* (1985). The various episodes were arranged uniquely at different times as either longer films or installation works. They were presented under different titles before the process of accumulation ended, ostensibly, with *Peggy and Fred: Folding* (2015), which was displayed in a room devised by Thornton for the group film exhibition *The Inoperative Community* at Raven Row Gallery in London, including a window through which the film could be viewed (figure 8.1).[7] Whereas the first episodes were shot on 16mm film, Thornton made later episodes on video and digital, and recombined and reedited them constantly as part of her restless bid, in her words, to "produce work that doesn't exist yet, works that are unknown to us yet."[8]

At the level of story, Thornton's collection of films depicts the real-life siblings (and her onetime neighbors) Janis and Donald Reading (Peggy and Fred), whom she shot at different points over an eight-year period, and offers itself as an expanding archive of found footage, documentary, and experimental science fiction scenarios. The loose narrative frame sees the titular children set adrift in a postapocalyptic "Hell" shorn of the referents of the Earth we once knew. They are alone, as Thomas Beard suggests, on "an extended playdate at the end of the world," save for a being Thornton has called the "Artificial Intelligence Network," which teaches and is in turn taught by Peggy and Fred.[9] Fed images and

FIGURE 8.1 Installation view of Leslie Thornton's *Peggy and Fred in Hell: Folding* (1983–2015) as part of "The Inoperative Community" exhibition at Raven Row, London. Used by permission of the artist.

sounds by the AI from an immense audiovisual archive, these "feral children of TV" imitate and interact with the cultural debris of the twentieth century, and, as Thornton wrote in 1989, "approach this flattened spectacle like one would any desert—they keep moving."[10] Until 2015, the *Peggy and Fred* project, too, would "keep moving," an open-ended serial work that was driven by the maturation of its stars through childhood, and by its internal possibilities of reconfiguring a growing collection of new and archival footage. Although Thornton did not perhaps anticipate it, the work became a time capsule of the past, destined to be found among the wreckage by a rescue crew of the future.[11]

A work interested in—but ultimately defying—conventional narrative form, *Peggy and Fred* nevertheless surfaces in its creator's own reckoning beyond the scope of Peter Wollen's "two avant-gardes" (those filmmakers associated with the Co-op movement versus the auteurs of European art cinema), becoming what he might have nominated as one of those "films which fall somewhere in between or simply somewhere else."[12] The project as a whole emerged from a variety of directions; developing Thornton's abiding interests in language, representation, and technological mediation as explored in earlier works such as *X-Tracts* (1975), *Jennifer, Where Are You?* (1981), and *Adynata* (1983), it also aspired to a documentary approach divorced from the trappings of cinéma vérité. For my purposes, what is most interesting about the project's origins is that Thornton saw *Peggy and Fred* as a deliberate break from the modes of structural/materialist filmmaking being practiced by the "big men" of the North American avant-garde with whom she had studied at SUNY-Buffalo: Stan Brakhage, Paul Sharits, Hollis Frampton, and Peter Kubelka. In this context, narrative seemed to have been forcibly exorcized from avant-garde filmmaking. However, the prospect of its inevitable return in other guises was noted as well: Frampton's sardonic formulation of "Brakhage's Theorem" observed that for even the most abstract "finite series of shots ['film'] whatsoever there exists in real time a rational narrative."[13]

While some antinarrative positions had ossified into a type of dogma in the 1970s, it was clear that narrative forms were not wholly absent from the work of the avant-garde. This was true even in those works that were otherwise not obviously interested in the possibilities of story; there was a tendency especially in the reception of films from the Anglo-American avant-garde toward what Jonathan Rosenbaum has called "(male) autobiography via Action painting," whereby structural and even narrative conceits were imposed on otherwise abstract film materials so as to give them shape.[14] Long-form cyclical projects such as Frampton's *Hapax Legomena* and Brakhage's *Songs* (1964–69) created a model for serial experimental works that would come to guide the interpretation of those that followed.[15] For example, in the third edition of his *Visionary Film* (2000), P. Adams Sitney observed that serial works by experimental women filmmakers in the 1980s, such as Abigail Child's *Is This What You Were Born For?* (1981–87) and Thornton's *Peggy and Fred*, had trodden a path away from the earlier cycles. They may "derive from Brakhage's *Dog Star Man*," Sitney wrote, "even though the former strongly repudiates Brakhage's edenic sexuality and the latter his idealization of the child as a model of the visionary."[16] And yet at the time of their creation, some two decades earlier, such works were not necessarily understood as forming part of this lineage or even of having an obvious place within the avant-garde tradition.

By the turn of the twenty-first century, then, the prominent male filmmakers that had populated this coterie still loomed large, and their presence has had particular, gendered implications for the uneasy fit of

Thornton's work within the history of North American experimental cinema. Indeed, while the shift away from—and possible eclipse of—the "authentically modernist" avant-garde heralded in one sense an inevitable generational change, there was also a lingering sense of resistance to the unassimilable elements of "difference" that were emerging in its wake.[17] In a manifesto-eulogy to the old guard on the occasion of the 1989 International Experimental Film Congress in Toronto, Thornton, Peggy Ahwesh, and others wrote of the "60's Avant-Garde and its decaying power base," and the way that "difference" in the exhibited works was "recognized only where it can be recuperated and diluted to a tepid pluralism."[18] Around the same time, Thornton noted of this handover that

> there is also an element of sexism at work here. Experimental film of the fifties and sixties was a male-dominated practice and involved considerable grandstanding.... The development marks not only a shift in sexes, but also in the kinds of work being done. In my own case, I have been accused of working in a manner that is "feminized." Perhaps this is because the work doesn't announce its agenda, it is not confrontational in the usual sense, and it does not take an overt position in relation to power as it is currently constituted.[19]

To Thornton's mind, it was her interest in narrative that separated her from her male forebears at SUNY; but even in spite of the narrative elements of some works of the avant-garde, her approach in particular was marked as "feminized," as less overtly critical of the mystifying forms of commercial cinema.

Such was the perception of a gendered distinction between Thornton's work and that of her predecessors that it is perhaps no surprise that it seems to have worked its way into *Peggy and Fred*. The overlaps and tensions between the generational shifts and gender divisions of experimental cinema are allegorized in the opening sequences of *The Prologue*, the episode that Thornton has used to inaugurate all of the feature-length versions of the film, and one that also establishes Thornton's turn toward "the outer edge of narrative," away from the strictures of the avant-garde but clearly not rushing headlong into the arms of standard Aristotelian storytelling.[20]

Here, after seeing extreme close-up images of the yonic insides of a human throat and hearing the unmistakable seven-octave range of Yma Sumac, a sober voiceover accompanied by an image of the lower third of a General Electric television set advises us of the "preferred pitch" for both male and female voices, which we then hear in turn. The film thus begins with the viewer essentially asked to assess gendered differences as measured against culturally ingrained, normative benchmarks of auditory pleasure; and predictably, it is the lower male voice and the higher female voice that are supposed to meet with our approval. Our introductions to Fred and Peggy are likewise offered via two singing voices, one male and one female—he boldly stumbling through a medley of folk tunes and she softly reciting Michael Jackson's "Billie Jean." And the two appear at first separately as the film presents what Linda Peckham observes is a "divided focus between masculine and feminine."[21] However, the apparently "stable" gender differences of the preceding archival voiceover are substituted by two children in the process of becoming, of finding their own voices within or outside of the gender binary, and the film continues to interrogate this as it keeps moving.

In a way similar to the uncertain development of the children, according to Thornton, in the film we are not in the realms of "plot, but vertical growth, accumulation that ends up with a structure."[22] For even as we have been "introduced" to Peggy and Fred, we have begun in media res without the guiding hand of a title card, and we have very little sense of where we will be going next. Indeed, it is crucial that the experience for the viewer also mimes the experience of Thornton and the Reading children in making the film, as well as of the characters learning to adapt to their new surroundings. The child nonactors were provided, as Thornton has said, with a "fictional construct . . . having been told only their names, that they are adults, that this is their house, that they are hungry."[23] But aside from working to these rudimentary prompts, it is "as if Story is being discovered."[24] Without what Trinh T. Minh-ha has called "a meaningful narrative line to represent their experience," the two are left to their own devices, made to imagine what it is that they are doing here.[25] As Thornton notes, they are simply "acting as if they were 'actors'—what they understood their job to be because they were in a movie."[26]

As Donald and Janis Reading improvised, so would Thornton follow their lead. She had first conceived the film to be about unstoppable technological progress, particularly focusing on those technologies like the atomic bomb that were beginning to redefine the world. But Thornton's interaction with her subjects changed all of this, prompting her to shift from an interest in military weapons and technology to consider the effects of television and cinema on viewers, and especially on children. Unlike the atomic bomb, which inspired paranoia and anxiety across the globe, and promised destruction instead of creation, moving image technologies allowed for a more bidirectional flow of influences, not dissimilar to the relationship in this case between the director and her actors: viewers were not simply preyed upon by mass media but could instead interact with and learn from the images and sounds produced.

Owing both to its specific thematic interests and its refusal of closure, *Peggy and Fred* is a "prescient" work for a number of different reasons.[27] In its genesis in the early 1980s alongside software-based editing systems, as Beard notes, the project's "function as a work of art feels predictive, portending an age in which a state of unfinishedness is not only a possibility but a kind of norm."[28] Its initial mise-en-scène, featuring a television set arrayed among piles of furniture and loose wiring, appears to gesture proleptically beyond the diegesis to the various future installations of the project in gallery spaces, where it would be screened across multiple TVs and projectors, in a kind of Deleuzian "folding" of outside and inside suggested by the final surtitle of the work. This is also a claustrophobic backdrop that may be immediately and uncannily recognizable to those of us who have lived through the global COVID-19 pandemic and its protracted lockdowns or stay-at-home orders in 2020 and 2021, a period in which much of what passed for sociability—indeed for "life" itself—has been made possible only by virtue of images and sounds piped electronically into homes from often far-flung locations.[29]

And yet the film's narrative setup is more capacious in its vision; even before Zoom had entered our collective lexicon, *Peggy and Fred*'s millenarian gestures toward the cataclysmic "information explosion" foretold the rise of a cybercultural imaginary that would be properly inaugurated only in the 1990s, after the project was nearly a decade old. Whereas this futurist framework offers what Thornton has called "a richly imaginative site for speculation," she has also been hesitant to defer to the generic trappings of science fiction as "an apology" that would explain away the abiding sense of cognitive estrangement in the film.[30] And so the work is both located "there" and "here," "then" and "now," structured *between* the early warning signs portending our current reality and the fictional space of the postapocalyptic world, and also between predictions of the info-glutted world to come and its setting—precisely in "Hell"—that situates the action within an ending that has already arrived. These twinned orientations to the future and the past also resonate with the film's formal particulars, as an ongoing project that has nevertheless found its endpoint.

For viewers who had seen the work in its various iterations prior to 2015, there was no clear sense of how *Peggy and Fred* would logically complete itself, or even if its accumulation of episodes was moving the project in a direction toward a closure of sorts.[31] But for those engaging with the film in more recent years, the benefit of hindsight also entails an advanced knowledge of the work's boundaries; the awareness that the film has stopped evolving dictates its reception now in a way that its earlier openness did not. Signs of finitude were there from the beginning, of course, in the sense that any ongoing work attributed to a single individual must end. As with the diary form, discussed below with regard to Lynn Hershman Leeson's work, here the parameters of Thornton's life and career impose an obvious limit on the project's growth; but here, too, the forward movement of the film is also registered in the shift in media—from 16mm, to video, to digital—and conspicuously in the aging of the Reading children in tandem with the project.

Yet, as Catherine Russell points out, "the children grow older over the [then] thirteen years of the series, but their environment seems to regress deeper into the recesses of the archive."[32] Russell's perceptive comment points to the multiple ways of reading "movement" in the project, as it does not only suggest accretion and creation but also the editing and unmaking of earlier episodes. This has the additional effect of defamiliarizing the linearity of the film, an experience we can also gain from observing the reshuffling and reediting of the episodes with each new exhibition of the work. But even when seen in the chronological order of their production, the episodes provide a number of moments that throw time into reverse. At one point in *Peggy and Fred in Kansas* (1987), Fred hosts an interview with Amelia Earhart, as portrayed by Peggy, although it is unclear whether either of the children know the significance of Earhart's achievements. Then, in *The Problem So Far* (1996), an episode from eight years later, footage of Earhart herself appears, echoing the earlier scene, and completing a feedback loop opened by the performance of the siblings in the previous decade, but now without their involvement in the project. Elsewhere, in the episode *Introduction to the So-Called Duck Factory* (1990), Peggy recites a monologue about her and Fred attempting to catch a fish, now appearing to read from a script rather than improvising. She is noticeably older here—her voice is deeper and her face is changed—and shot in close-up, she has a commanding presence on screen, with her appearance reorienting our experience of the largely archival footage that has composed the film up until this point. In the same episode, however, we see all of a sudden a brief—and unprecedented—snapshot of Peggy when she was much younger, an image that throws the episode, and the order of the film, into disarray.

For Russell, such a moment showcases the work's "texture of discontinuity and shocking collisions," and places the body of the actor in the "machine," the "image bank of the archive."³³ While the Reading children in reality continue to grow, the archive can only look backward to the past iterations of Peggy and Fred that have already been captured by the camera. Even as they continued to live, the pair became the fossils of the archive, no longer improvising participants leading the project in different directions, but images from the past to be resurrected as objects in the film. As Thornton would reveal in 2015,

> At a number of points, over the years, I reached what I thought of as a fully rounded work. But it remained unsettled for me. It did not go far enough beyond itself, meaning, I suppose, that it did not transcend itself. In the last few episodes and finally *The Fold* the children are not the subjects. They are objects. That was the end. *Peggy and Fred* caught up with itself, with our present. Our slow-motion apocalypse, our own self-erasure.³⁴

For all its alterations in terms of sequence and composition over the years, and however infinite the possibilities of further additions, *Peggy and Fred* ultimately came to a close when Thornton felt a temporal equivalence between the world of the film and the world of the film's creation.

Given that this work was always made in a precarious way, a series *in process,* its "ending" might seem to make it a more stable object but not in fact a more secure one in its meanings. This much seems clear in another instance of the irruption of the past in the present, which lies outside the confines of the project, strictly speaking, in an epilogue to *Peggy and Fred* titled *High Heel Beloved* (2021). Made as a sort of eulogy for Donald Reading, who died in 2020, this short work—which suggests that the end is not really the end—features images of Donald and his sister at a much younger age. The film is bookended by shots recalling the 1990 episode *Introduction to the So-Called Duck Factory,* but the footage consists largely of the two children playing in a railyard, and improvising with a pair of stilettos in which they each attempt to walk around. While this fragment—which Thornton had filmed several decades earlier—had never been used as part of the project, its melancholic tone, especially when coupled with the film's haunting musical choices, seems eerily appropriate for its purpose. Just as she had from the beginning drawn on existing archives for her images and sounds, Thornton has over the past few decades created an archive of footage all her own, so that although *Peggy and Fred* is now officially closed-off as a project, Thornton continues to revisit unused materials from this work for other projects. Even in its "official" resting state as a finished object, *Peggy and Fred* is thus still in motion elsewhere.

WAITING FOR AN AUDIENCE IN
THE ELECTRONIC DIARIES

Although its generic resonances with science fiction may call to mind the black box recordings or logbook entries of an abandoned spacecraft, Thornton told me that she never thought of her work in relation to the diary form. Thornton's nonappearance in *Peggy and Fred* marks the project not as autobiographical so much as, in Thornton's terms, a "chronicle" of changing technologies and media used for lens-based capture.[35] By contrast, Lynn Hershman Leeson's *The Electronic Diaries* is grounded explicitly in the diary mode and is centered on the artist's own experiences and their mediation by world-historical events. "The planet's rage and disrepair were secondary to my own private apocalypse," she tells us as she explains the framework at the beginning of the film. "World news was background white noise to the internal flames that burned into a compulsion to tell my own story."[36] Production on that story began in 1984, with Hershman Leeson showing a trilogy of works from the project five years later and working on further installments before releasing the aggregated episodes in 1996 as *First Person Plural, The Electronic Diaries of Lynn Hershman Leeson*.[37] Following this release of the film, as she later reflected, "I stopped talking to a camera because I felt I had said everything I had to say." But she discovered that she was "wrong" about this, and twenty-two years later returned to the work, modifying the earlier entries and adding a lengthy capstone chapter that brought the diary into the present; although the work was released once more in a new version—*The Electronic Diaries* (1984–2019)—the very fact of its reopening, in a manner not dissimilar to the epilogue of *Peggy and Fred in Hell*, suggests that it too is not yet finished.

It should be said that this trajectory, from complete to incomplete, is not foreign to the diary as a form. As Philippe Lejeune describes it, the diary promises a kind of "annual life insurance," gesturing as it does toward further entries in the ledger of one's life: "The diarist is protected from death by the idea that the diary will continue," he writes. "There is always writing to be done, for all eternity."[38] While naturally bounded by the years of its creator's life, the diary—especially in its privacy and freedom from the obligation to publish—also allows for the kind of latitude seen in Hershman Leeson's project, where the apparently stable, closed object is ripe for revision and revival, encouraging additions even in the knowledge that they cannot go on forever. Most obviously associated with literary traditions, the diary privileges the author paradoxically as a performed, pluralized, accreted, and consistent identity that develops in tandem with the text and valorizes the scene of writing and the contingent process of composition. But beyond the page, the operations of the diary form always betokened the possibility of transposition to other media, from photography to film to the multimedia forms of the digital age. In the context of North American experimental and noncommercial cinema, the diary has a long history connected with the genre of home movies that emerged with small-gauge film technologies at midcentury.[39]

As David E. James has argued in relation to the long-form works of Jonas Mekas, this mode contains an animating tension, a "double gesture." On the one hand, while what James nominates as the "film diary" is a "private event" that is for its creator "a pure use value," in contrast the "diary film finds itself in an economy of films, an economy that privileges the completed artifact as a whole, the moment of projection, the spectating public, and, in some form or other, exchange value."[40] While the private/public divide that James suggests here is perhaps a little too neat, in any case it is true that Mekas's editing and mediation of a vast corpus of diary entries into the more coherent finished objects necessary for wider exhibition—what the filmmaker called diaries only "after the fact"—does reveal something of the compromise that transforms the amateur work into the industrial film fit for circulation.[41]

However, while Mekas's name may have become almost synonymous with the diary film in North American experimental cinema, James points out that the diary was taken up notably by male filmmakers "in the seventies, when the avant-garde modes developed in the sixties had generally lost their authority."[42] Indeed, the form—like its literary predecessor—has a more notably feminized history, and many of its proponents are women artists like Hershman Leeson. As Melissa Ragona points out, in James's lineage of diary filmmakers, it is Marie Menken who precedes and influences Mekas and senses the possibilities of the diary apart from its usual associations with the author; in Menken's hands the diary film is "closer to quick sketching than journal writing" and does not exhibit the "existential angst" of diary filmmakers who followed in her wake.[43] Other major practitioners exhibiting more typical modes of "introspection and self-awareness" include Anne Charlotte Robertson, whose *Five-Year Diary* was begun in 1981 and finished with her death in 2012 after she had amassed eighty-three reels of film devoted to the project; and Sadie Benning, whose Pixelvision diaries of the 1990s, begun when they were only seventeen, demonstrated the accessibility of new portable video recorders.[44] Aside from these Anglophone examples, the film as journal has been employed by women in vastly different documentary contexts; in this volume, for example, Elizabeth Ramírez-Soto mentions the two Chilean diary films *Unfinished Diary* (Marilú Mallet, 1982) and *Fragments from an Unfinished Diary* (Angelina Vázquez, 1983), made by women in exile during the Pinochet dictatorship.

Whereas the diary films that preceded Leeson's project were captured mostly on Super 8 or 16mm film, *The Electronic Diaries* foreground the video medium in their very title; the possibility in video of capturing and displaying the image simultaneously heightens the sense of the work as processual in nature and suggests a number of ways for understanding the work as both ongoing and archived, present and past. There is a gesture to the technical possibilities of video from the opening of the film, wherein Hershman Leeson shows us a production control room replete with monitor wall and mixing consoles, a high-tech version of the televisual fallout shelter at the opening of *Peggy and Fred in Hell*. At first glance the laying bare of the site of production conjures the fantasy of video's "immediate image feedback as the vehicle of a drive toward personal authenticity," in James's words, connecting the liveness of the medium with the processual work of the diarist.[45] However, as James points out, Hershman Leeson denies her audience the possibility that she as the artist is identical with her image on the screen; as her face fractures and proliferates across several screens, it soon becomes clear that everything we are seeing has been carefully edited for our viewing. "She drops us in an abyss between belief and denial, between video and life," James writes. "Her autobiographical confessions all deal in seduction."[46]

As many of the scenes involve Hershman Leeson narrating her life directly to the camera, there is both a sense that this is pure performance—especially when considered in light of her adoption of other personas throughout her career—but also that this is a true confession of everything that she has felt and experienced.[47] "It's about as real as you can get," she ensures us. "And if anybody tells me I'm making this up in my diary, they're wrong!" Throughout the work Hershman Leeson reveals to us a series of grave personal traumas, both from her childhood and from the present, and has visible difficulty in recounting some of them: the abuse she suffered both as a child and later in life; her husband leaving her; her struggles with an eating disorder. As the film proceeds chronologically, the years appear on screen, while noteworthy incidents in the filmmaker's life are situated alongside a catalogue of global media events that do not always correlate temporally, a forward and backward motion all at once: in relation to her physical abuse at a young age, she notes that Hitler himself was a "battered child," whose private suffering was "projected out on to all of Germany"; on the same day of the 1989 San Francisco earthquake, a CAT scan reveals that she has a brain tumor, and we are told that "everything else became a little unstable"; over images of the Space Shuttle *Challenger,* which broke apart soon after takeoff in 1986, is superimposed the face of her friend, the filmmaker Marlon Riggs, who died in 1994 of complications from AIDS.

This litany of death and disaster often appears to spur the film on, providing its historical waypoints and helping Hershman Leeson to order the events of her own life which—unlike the lives of many in her roster of fellow travelers—continues today. It is these specific aspects of the film that for Kristine Stiles marks it as an example of "Destruction Art," a diverse category of cultural objects that understand destruction as "a characteristic of beauty, a condition of creation, or a fundamental component of art."[48] For Stiles, destruction art incorporates that which is destructive as generative force, allowing a given work to integrate ruin into its makeup and to testify to the damage that has taken place not by itself being destroyed, but rather by continuing to exist. Hershman Leeson, Stiles writes, paradoxically "whispers as a survivor to we who bear witness to her survival: 'Don't talk about it.'"[49]

But in her continued existence, and in the appearance of the work through which she communicates both to herself and to her future viewers, Hershman Leeson carves out a space for her trauma, disclosing defiantly (and ironically) that which is taboo, secreting the secrets that the diary form often harbors. In its stubborn existence as a revelatory document, *The Electronic Diaries* joins other works in this category that express a bid for the longevity of the work in the face of the devastation the work takes as its subject, and which orbits about it. "For more than fourteen years," Hershman Leeson observes in the film, "I've been recording images of myself constantly, almost as evidence that I existed. As if I need to have this captured record in order to survive." The project thus records the artist's survival just as it makes that survival possible. Her scars, as she says at one point in the film, "are the length of this tape," and the tape continues to run. In her remarks on Hershman Leeson's work, Stiles notes that the overlaps in *The Electronic Diaries* between the work and the aging, evolving "actual body of the artist" allows them to "intervene in the imagined neutrality between subject and object where they insert the voice of survival that is the representation of the pain of destruction. Destruction art is the renegotiation of that pain."[50]

In a similar way, and thinking back to the roots of this mode of practice, *The Electronic Diaries* is also clearly interested in the connections between composition and decomposition, the recording of the work and its archival storage for posterity, but also its ephemerality and possible erasure. The precisely "electronic" nature of the diary released in 1996 thus paved the way for its later reconfiguration in the 2019 iteration of the same project, but also of the removal and reworking of those earlier, (un)finished entries. And so, while it still retains the linear composition of the original, and includes in its title the beginning and end points of the film's timeframe, the recent version also entertains the possibilities of cutting or reducing particular segments from the work. For instance, the first part of the diary, titled *Confessions of a Chameleon,* is trimmed from its former running time of twenty-two minutes, while elsewhere a long sequence linking the filmmaker's abuse as a child to a "Dracula" figure is condensed dramatically. These are decisions made perhaps both to censor or refine earlier thoughts (like the deliberate removal or destruction of bound pages); as acts of compression and deletion, they make room for the newer additions to the film, affording Hershman Leeson's most recent ideas the same screen time as her earlier moments of self-expression. Although she is by no means bound by the eighty-three minutes of the film's length, there is a sense that the removing and distilling of earlier scenes is integral to the process. After all, "life is the ultimate editing process," she reminds us at a number of points across the film.

The reediting of the project also coincided with Hershman Leeson's rising star, from a female artist who to her mind was still unjustly maligned in the artworld when she began the diaries at age forty-five, to the belated doyenne of the new media art scene today. Made to wait many decades for a proper audience, to work patiently across performance, painting, sculpture, and video until the art world was ready to catch up with her prophetic ideas about robotics, artificial intelligence, and the technological mediation of identity, the Hershman Leeson of the newer film speaks now with the assurance of critical validation. "I was seventy-two by the time that my work was all seen," Hershman Leeson says in the newer addition to the film from 2019. Her interlocutor in the scene comments: "One of the great things that you did, Lynn, was to have the wisdom to take your work seriously, store it properly, take care of it with some kind of blind faith that it would be seen eventually."

This interlocutor is none other than the director Eleanor Coppola, who was the second camera operator for Hershman Leeson's film *Teknolust* (2002), and who at the age of eighty made her debut as a feature-length fiction filmmaker with *Paris Can Wait* (2016). However, as Coppola mentions here, the majority of her work as a credited director has been on "making of" documentaries for the films made by her husband and children: for Francis Ford Coppola, *Hearts of Darkness: A Filmmaker's Apocalypse* (1991), and for her daughter, Sofia, *The Making of "Marie Antoinette"* (2007). The most famous is the first of these, which portrays the notorious difficulty involved in completing *Apocalypse Now* (1979). This film is notably about the problems faced by a male auteur, against which Eleanor Coppola understands her own long wait for an opportunity to create a feature film as part of a "process of optimism."

With a career vastly different to Eleanor Coppola's behind her now, Hershman Leeson's patient wait for recognition is inscribed in her diaries, especially since her reputation was finally consecrated in the interregnum between the first and second feature-length versions of the film. The dialogue between Hershman Leeson and Eleanor Coppola adds to the multiple valences of "survival" conjured by the project, from the survival of abuse to the survival as an artist, to the survival of archival materials. But the new millennium also introduced new meanings to the term for Hershman Leeson, connected with technological and scientific advancement. At the turn of the century, not only was "a new generation . . . being bred, one that had an almost genetic reliance on machines and technology to survive," but emerging too were the various innovations in genome programming and bioprinting that promised the survival of the human well into the future. As if to suggest an act of time travel, an LCD display in the film sends us to a time "22 years later," and Hershman Leeson relates how she felt like "that character from *Gulliver's Travels* who had woken up in a completely different world."

By 2019 everything had changed, including "the predicted evolution of our species, of our planet and of our culture," since the discovery that DNA could be used to store information even more reliably than a digital repository. This turning point signaled a major shift in the ways that we conceive of the fixity of biology and the evolution of the species, which can be brought increasingly under human control and edited in the way that one might a film. As Hershman Leeson tells us, "with DNA editing you control the narrative and the story without knowing what the ending's going to be—like making a documentary." Unlike the possibilities of DNA, Hershman Leeson realized that *The Electronic Diaries* would one day disappear because of the imperfect medium in which it was housed. While now happily reconciled with a changing body—"the white [hair] that I've earned, and the lines that I've grown"—when it comes to the artist's body of work, her desire is to forestall its decay. And so, looking beyond the diary's formal inducements to add, add, add, and instead to the afterlife of the film object itself, Hershman Leeson decided to convert her work to DNA, "the perfect archive." As she told Eileen Myles of this move in a recent interview: "I look at it as a kind of expanded cinema, because you have to put all of the information on a time line, one frame at a time, and they convert it to zeros and ones at the micromolecular level and store it as synthetic DNA, which has a life span of a million years, rather than fifty, which is what most films have."[51]

Perhaps because she was now safe in the knowledge that *The Electronic Diaries* may still exist long into the future, Hershman Leeson seems to have been able to find closure with her project once more—precisely by reopening and closing it again. This is made explicit in the closing credits sequence, a paratext that also forms part of the film proper by recapping the various phases of the director's life that we have just witnessed, this time in pictorial form. Alongside the scrolling text of the credits, we see a series of epitaphs as though engraved on an invisible tombstone, announcing Hershman Leeson's future death as a centenarian in advance of her reaching that milestone: 1941–2041 (figure 8.2). Hershman Leeson had confronted and triumphed over her own death once before in *Shadow's Song* (1990), the fourth part of *The Electronic Diaries*, when she tells—in her own explanation—that she was able to shrink her brain tumor by visualizing its disappearance.[52]

Now in this prediction of the end of her life, she appears by contrast both to accept her own finitude and to provide a date for her death that would allow her to potentially continue working for another twenty-two years. Perhaps there is more to come, the film suggests, as we are also returned once more to the past. In a postcredits sequence that reinforces this sense of formal incompletion, we flash back to an earlier point in the project, with Hershman Leeson addressing the camera directly: "Things are never over 'til they're over, right? I mean, I do these diaries and I never know how they're going to end. It's just like my life. I mean you keep searching for a good ending and hoping the same thing will happen to your life."

FIGURE 8.2 An epitaph to an unfinished life in the closing credits of Lynn Hershman Leeson's *The Electronic Diaries* (1984–2019). Used by permission of the artist.

NEVER OVER

While experimental serial forms provide a range of ways to think about incompletion, the longitudinal works of Leslie Thornton and Lynn Hershman Leeson present opportunities to think this through specifically with respect to the histories of women's filmmaking from the 1980s to the contemporary moment. In the open, ongoing nature of both *Peggy and Fred in Hell* and *The Electronic Diaries* over the course of several decades, we can witness how the perceived finality of devastation and destruction—whether predicted atomic fallout or the trauma of abuse—can be turned to generative ends, and how the unfinished nature of the two works, rather than their closure, allows us to consider other ways of valorizing incomplete work. Each work in its original moment of production may have aspired toward a particular end as a work designed to be finished for exhibition. But it is in the remaking, reworking, and reopening of each that additional possibilities arise: of new modes of circulation and reception, of new means of appraisal, and of the abiding sense that these are works that belong as much to our own time as to the decades before it.

NOTES

1. Absent the "assumed simultaneity of mass media" thanks to the "loosening of the temporal boundedness of classical broadcasting," seriality in our con-

temporary moment faces an uncertain fate. Mary Ann Doane, "Hyper-seriality: The End of the End," *Afterimage* 48.2 (2021): 49–62, 58, 59.

2. Frank Kelleter, "Five Ways of Looking at Popular Seriality," in *Media of Serial Narrative*, ed. Kelleter (Columbus: Ohio State University Press, 2017), 7–34, 10.

3. Adrian Martin, "The Nonsense of an Ending," in *Phantasms* (Melbourne: McPhee Gribble, 1994), 57–62, 59. See also Jennifer Hayward, *Consuming Pleasures: Active Audiences and Serial Fictions from Dickens to Soap Opera* (Lexington: University Press of Kentucky, 1997); and Laura Stempel Mumford, *Love and Ideology in the Afternoon: Soap Opera, Women, and Television Genre* (Bloomington: Indiana University Press, 1995).

4. For an analysis of the multiple varieties of "endings" for television series, see Jason Mittell, "Ends," in *Complex TV: The Poetics of Contemporary Television Storytelling* (New York: NYU Press, 2015), 319–54.

5. See Maria Sulimma, *Gender and Seriality: Practices and Politics of Contemporary US Television* (Edinburgh: Edinburgh University Press, 2020), 15. There are any number of exceptions to the rule of the commodity form here, especially in the realm of longitudinal documentaries, but the continuation/closure paradox still holds.

6. Mary Ann Doane, "In the Ruins of the Image: The Work of Leslie Thornton," in *Women's Experimental Cinema: Critical Frameworks*, ed. Robin Blaetz (Durham, NC: Duke University Press, 2007), 239–62, 243.

7. This exhibition borrowed its title from Jean-Luc Nancy's 1983 essay of the same name, focusing on experimental narrative film and video works that were made in, or focus on, the "long 1970s" from 1968 to 1984. In the postapocalyptic isolation of its protagonists, Thornton's work evokes the exhibition's broad concerns with the atomization of social relations in the latter half of the twentieth century, and the revival of discourses of community and "communization" in the 2000s. See Dan Kidner, *The Inoperative Community* (London: Raven Row, 2015).

8. Leslie Thornton in conversation with Dan Kidner, Raven Row Gallery, London, 14 January 2016.

9. Thomas Beard, "Scene Missing," in *Unfinished: Thoughts Left Visible*, ed. Kelly Baum, Andrea Bayer, and Sheena Wagstaff (New Haven, CT: Yale University Press, 2016), 202–5, 205; Thornton in conversation with Kidner, Raven Row.

10. Thornton in conversation with Kidner, Raven Row; Thornton, "We Ground Things, Now, on a Moving Earth," *Motion Picture* 3.1–2 (1989–90): 13–15, 13.

11. Indeed, to Thornton's mind, "P&F may be the longest standing intentionally open-ended, 'unfinished' film there is, apart from some serial works such as the doc series in GB entitled Seven Up, etc." Leslie Thornton, email communication with Stefan Solomon, 15 August 2018.

12. Peter Wollen, "The Two Avant-Gardes," in *Readings and Writings: Semiotic Counter-Strategies* (London: Verso, 1982), 92–104, 92; quoted in Thornton in conversation with Kidner, Raven Row.

13. Hollis Frampton, "A Pentagram for Conjuring the Narrative," in *Circles of Confusion: Film, Photography, Video Texts 1968–1980* (Rochester, NY: Visual Studies Workshop, 1983), 59–68, 63.

14. Jonathan Rosenbaum, "Peter Gidal," in *Film: The Front Line 1983* (Denver, CO: Arden Press, 1983), 83–92, 88. Thornton has noted that this assessment of the avant-garde made Rosenbaum unpopular in those circles at the time. See Trinh T. Minh-ha, Laleen Jayamanne, and Leslie Thornton, "'Which Way to Political Cinema?' A Conversation Piece," in *Framer Framed*, by Trinh T. Minh-ha (New York: Routledge, 1992), 243–65, 246.

15. See P. Adams Sitney, *Visionary Film: The American Avant-Garde, 1943–2000*, 3rd ed. (New York: Oxford University Press, 2002), 209.

16. Sitney, *Visionary Film*, 421.

17. James Hoberman, "After Avant-garde Film," in *Art After Modernism: Rethinking Representation*, ed. Brian Wallis (New York: New Museum of Contemporary Art, 1984), 59–73, 64.

18. Peggy Ahwesh, Caroline Avery, Craig Baldwin, Abigail Child, Su Friedrich, Barbara Hammer, Todd Haynes, Lewis Klahr, Ross McLaren, John Porter, Yvonne Rainer, Berenice Reynaud, Keith Sanborn, Sarah Schulman, Jeffrey Skoller, Phil Solomon, and Leslie Thornton, and fifty-nine other filmmakers, "Open Letter to the Experimental Film Congress: Let's Set the Record Straight (Canada, 1989)," in *Film Manifestos and Global Cinema Cultures: A Critical Anthology*, ed. Scott Mackenzie (Berkeley: University of California Press, 2014), 100–101, 101. See also Fred Camper, "The End of Avant-Garde Film," *Caesura* (4 November 2021), https://caesuramag.org/posts/fred-camper-end-of-avant-garde-film; originally published in *Millennium Film Journal* 16/17/18 (1986–87): 99–124.

19. Trinh, Jayamanne, and Thornton, "Which Way to Political Cinema?," 246.

20. Trinh, Jayamanne, and Thornton, "Which Way to Political Cinema?," 244.

21. Linda Peckham, "The Aftermath of Intelligence: *Peggy and Fred in Hell*," *Unsound* 2.1 (1983): 28–29, 29.

22. Thornton in conversation with Kidner, Raven Row.

23. Thornton, "We Ground Things," 13.

24. Trinh, Jayamanne, and Thornton, "Which Way to Political Cinema?," 258.

25. Trinh, Jayamanne, and Thornton, "Which Way to Political Cinema?," 260.

26. Leslie Thornton in conversation with Dan Kidner, Wysing Arts Centre, 5 March 2016. In terms of the overlaps of improvisation and a preconceived narrative line, Thornton also told me of her realization that Andy Warhol's *Vinyl* (1965) was a "film about narrative film" in which "the people are inventing this little world in front of the camera—partly directed, partly improvised." The narrative aspect of the work may have to do of course with its status as a pseudo-adaptation of Anthony Burgess's *A Clockwork Orange* (1962). In any case, here, in a setup not far from the locked-off cameras and claustrophobic sets of *Peggy and Fred*, are the "bare bones" of story, "the most elemental sense

of a narrative space I could think of." Leslie Thornton, interview with Stefan Solomon, 26 July 2021.

27. See Saisha Grayson, Natasha Bell, and Leslie Thornton, "Leslie Thornton: On Surviving," Smithsonian YouTube channel (16 September 2021), www.youtube.com/watch?v=lFC1ocv1ESI.

28. Beard, "Scene Missing," 205.

29. Thornton has pointed here to the influence of the futurist Faith Popcorn, who in coining the term "cocooning" in 1981 also suggested that humanity would retreat from the outside world. Thornton, interview with Solomon.

30. Trinh, Jayamanne, and Thornton, "Which Way to Political Cinema?," 261.

31. Thornton had, however, stopped filming the Reading children in 1988 and elsewhere has said that the surfeit of "possibilities and complexities" coupled with a "lack of narrative" made it difficult for her actors and led to her break from the project. Irene Borger, "Interview with Leslie Thornton," *Senses of Cinema* 22 (October 2002), www.sensesofcinema.com/2002/leslie-thornton-experimental/thornton_interview/.

32. Catherine Russell, *Experimental Ethnography: The Work of Film in the Age of Video* (Durham, NC: Duke University Press, 1999), 244.

33. Russell, *Experimental Ethnography*, 245.

34. Dan Kidner, "Leslie Thornton's 35 Years of Radical Filmmaking," *Frieze* (23 August 2018), www.frieze.com/article/leslie-thorntons-35-years-radical-filmmaking.

35. Thornton, interview with Solomon.

36. Unless otherwise noted, all quotations are taken from *The Electronic Diaries* (1984–2019).

37. Each part of the project has its own surtitle, including *Confessions of a Chameleon* (1986), *Binge* (1987), *First Person Plural* (1988), and *Shadow's Song* (1990).

38. Philippe Lejeune, "How Do Diaries End?," *Biography* 24.1 (2001): 99–112, 101.

39. There are many examples of the incorporation of the diary in experimental filmmaking in the United States, including George Kuchar's *Weather Diaries* (1986–90), but also in the United Kingdom as represented more recently by John Smith's *Hotel Diaries* (2001–2007).

40. David E. James, "Film Diary/Diary Film: Practice and Product in *Walden*," in *To Free the Cinema: Jonas Mekas and the New York Underground*, ed. David E. James (Princeton, NJ: Princeton University Press, 1992), 145–79, 147.

41. Scott MacDonald, "Andrew Noren," in *A Critical Cinema 2: Interviews with Independent Filmmakers*, ed. MacDonald (Berkeley: University of California Press, 1992), 175–205, 187.

42. James, "Film Diary/Diary Film," 151.

43. Melissa Ragona, "Swing and Sway: Marie Menken's Filmic Events," in *Women's Experimental Cinema: Critical Frameworks*, ed. Robin Blaetz (Durham, NC: Duke University Press, 2007), 20–44, 25.

44. James, "Film Diary/Diary Film," 150.

45. David E. James, "Lynn Hershman: The Subject of Autobiography," in *The Art and Films of Lynn Hershman Leeson: Secret Agents, Private I*, ed.

Meredith Tromble (Berkeley: University of California Press, 2005), 144–56, 147; originally published in Michael Renov and Erika Suderburg, eds., *Resolutions: Contemporary Video Practices* (Minneapolis: University of Minnesota Press, 1996), 124–133.

46. James, "Lynn Hershman," 147.

47. It is crucial to note that performance was a part of Hershman Leeson's life from an early age, precisely as a means of living through those traumas about which she can now speak. In this way, as Broderick Fox points out, "any fibs or exaggerations she mixes in still testify to the fact that Hershman developed an elaborate proclivity for fantasy and screen memory as survival mechanisms against incest and abuse." Broderick Fox, *Documentary Media: History, Theory, Practice,* 2nd ed. (New York: Routledge, 2018), 9.

48. Kristine Stiles, "Synopsis of the Destruction in Art Symposium (DIAS) and Its Theoretical Significance," *The Act* 1.2 (1987): 22–31, 22.

49. Kristine Stiles, "Thresholds of Control: Destruction Art and Terminal Culture," in *Ars Electronica: Facing the Future,* ed. Timothy Druckrey with Ars Electronica (Cambridge, MA: MIT Press, 1999), 123–34, 131.

50. Stiles, "Thresholds of Control," 131.

51. Eileen Myles, "Why Lynn Hershman Leeson Is Always Ahead of Her Time," *Aperture* (23 June 2021), https://aperture.org/editorial/why-lynn-hershman-leeson-is-always-ahead-of-her-time/.

52. See James, "Lynn Hershman," 156.

CHAPTER 9

One Long Electrical Cord

Dance, Editing, and the Creative Unfinished

KAREN PEARLMAN

My life is one long electrical cord (with me crawling along
the floor, trying to make a connection).
—Shirley Clarke

Almost nothing ever written about the Academy Award–winning filmmaker Shirley Clarke (1919–1997) fails to mention that she was a dancer before she was an editor and director. Also, almost nothing she ever says about her editing fails to allude in some way to her experience as a dancer. In a 1967 interview with Gretchen Berg, Clarke aligns herself with the theory that "all good film should be kinetic and choreographic," and her films embody this manifesto. She is concerned "at all times, with the choreography of what is happening on the screen."[1]

Shirley Clarke is most often remembered as the director and editor of the powerful, controversial, and formally unprecedented *Portrait of Jason* (1967), and her daring adaptation of the stage play *The Connection* (1960), with its protracted censorship battle.[2] However, this chapter focuses on the periods before and after she directed these and other long-form films in the 1960s. It looks instead at the approach she developed through making dance film in the 1950s, and the transformation of this dance-infused sensibility into the then-new medium of video in the 1970s. My aim here is to write about the choreographic sensibility of Clarke's editing as a conduit of energy through her films. I hope I can do this without killing that current off. To keep it alive, I also explore how this energy is charging my own filmmaking. This feels uncomfortable. I wish I could retreat to the safety of my academic armor, present a theory and substantiate it, rather than tell you how I feel, which, at this moment, is uneasy. But I have felt this discomfort before. Often, when starting a new film or new writing, I wish like anything it were finished. I feel myself on a precipice, the unknown yawning and fidgeting below me. The purple prose (as in the previous sentence) tumbling forth in lieu of anything useful. A structure. A starting point. Anything. But, like Clarke, I started life as a dancer and then became an editor-director, and what I propose here is that the unfinished, as uncomfortable as it may be, is our playground, our studio, our disco—it is where we dance.

It is widely reported that the revered American choreographer Martha Graham once declared "a dancer dies twice": once when she stops dancing and the other time being the usual one we all get to look forward to. I am interested in this idea, not for its Romantic celebration of dancers' intense work and short careers, but for how it suggests that stopping dancing is a kind of *finishing* that feels like a death. Maybe Shirley Clarke and I sidestepped this dancer's death by turning our "kinaesthetic imagination," in Dee Reynold's phrase, into a resource for film editing.[3]

I moped around for a while after my dance career, but I wouldn't say I felt like I died.[4] I might say I reincarnated my dance skills and sensibility into editing, but *reincarnate* isn't exactly the right word. I didn't put the skills into a new body; I put the body into a new context, finding ways for old skills to do new tricks. It seems Clarke did the same. Her interviews about filmmaking, and even more so the films themselves, suggest that you can see her dance sensibility in her editing, and that the "dance" in the editing is the source of its vibrancy, its life. Clarke says, about her first film, *A Dance in the Sun* (1953), that "all the kinds of things I discovered about the choreography of editing and the choreography of space/time came from making [it]."[5] In other words she learned to make films not by killing off her dancing, but by stretching its form first into dance films made with dancers, then into films that "dance" not with dancers but with bridges, builders, or burned-out junkies. Even through the tonal shifts these subjects necessitate, Clarke's rhythmic sensibility makes its presence felt. It is a way of seeing, shaping, and being in the world that she inherits and passes on, unfinished, alive, as long as it is in motion.

Clarke and I both got cameras for wedding presents. Hers was a 16mm film camera, mine a VHS camcorder. Neither of us was very good at shooting, though, and we both gravitated to editing instead. She told a reporter in 1975: "I developed into a good director by becoming an excellent film editor in order to camouflage the fact that I was a rotten camerawoman."⁶ When I quit dancing and gravitated toward editing, it was because I wanted to find some useful application of my accrued kinaesthetic intelligence—the knowledge I'd built from years of being soaked in movement as my primary expressive medium. Clarke doesn't call her dance-soaked skills and sensibilities "kinaesthetic intelligence"; in fact, even though she uses the words "kinetic" and "choreographic," she told Berg in 1967 that she didn't like them.⁷ Nonetheless, Clarke's interviews about filmmaking, and even more so the films themselves, suggest that you can see her dance sensibility in her editing, and that the "dance" in the editing is the source of its vibrancy, its life.

So what I'd like to write about here is the film editor's encounter of movement in raw uncut material, the ever-unfinished film, with Clarke's kinaesthetic imagination or intelligence. I'd like to propose that across her film work, from *A Dance in the Sun* in 1953 to the rooftop of the Chelsea Hotel in the 1970s, where she set up a video performance space, Shirley Clarke was cutting together one long, movement phrase from her experience of movement in the world—a movement phrase that is *unfinished* because her editing sensibility creates ideas through motion in all her films. (Unfinished too, I hope, because I intend to pick it up and keep it in motion myself, with a remix of her unfinished films I am currently hoping to make.)

THE EDITOR'S UNFINISHED

Clarke's edited movement phrases are always unfinished in part because all editors' movement phrases are always unfinished. We encounter the material in pieces and we, in the words of the Soviet director and film theorist Lev Kuleshov, "reconstruct and ultimately remake the material."⁸ The logical extension of this is that editing a film one way will necessarily leave unfinished—unpursued—many, many other ways of making and remaking it. This reality is foregrounded in the work of several of the feminist filmmakers discussed in this book, including Peggy Ahwesh, Leslie Thornton, Lynn Hershman Leeson, and Renée Green, the latter expressly generating "chance operations" across her career, as Alix Beeston and Stefan Solomon discuss in the introduction. Possibly the most often-heard film industry truism, the one that pops up near the end of every too-tight postproduction schedule (and they are all too tight), is *films are never finished, they are just abandoned*. I've heard it attributed to George Lucas and Francis Ford Coppola, and the internet credits the idea to Paul Valéry and Leonardo da Vinci too. It is irritating for an editor to hear, because *abandoned* suggests a dereliction of duty—whereas, in fact, editors don't abandon things, they rather explore possibilities and then make choices. Editors encounter footage that may have been shot with intention, conforming to an idea as written in a script, for example.[9]

But shots are malleable. They can be patterned into so many things. They have what words on the page do not have: movement. And the ways they move can be shaped into different phrases to suggest different inflections, different meanings, different stories. So, as we put them together, we take different pathways through them. We go down one road making certain kinds of connections for a while, then reverse course, keeping some connections, maybe, but also selecting other pathways through. When the film finally ends up on screen, we leave unfinished all the other possible ways we could have made it. We could try to correct the truism and say that in an editing process *one possible film is finished, the others are abandoned,* but that isn't really true either. There is another level at which editors always leave a film unfinished, which reflects an irreducible principle of editing. An edit relies on the activity of the viewer's mind to be completed. I can put two images together in the editing suite but until you see them, and mentally connect them to experience them as one thing—a moment, an idea, a relationship—the edit's work remains unfinished. So, from the editor's perspective, paths untaken are not abandoned; rather, paths through a film are forged for the maximum creative charge of unfinishedness that a particular film can bear. The work of editing, one might say, is creative unfinishing.

These things are true of all edits, but they are not the only reason I think that Clarke was working on cutting together one long unfinished movement phrase. What I'm trying to get at here is that she was conducting energy through her films via what I've theorized elsewhere as "editing thinking."[10] She cuts in a way that one of her collaborators, Andrew Gurian, describes as "Shirley-ish."[11] It is a particular way of responding to the world and the material that arises from her dance thinking, her embodied cognizing, her kinaesthetic intelligence. Her edits, like those of all editors before or since, are her thoughts.[12] Collaborators in cognitive science and film history and I have written about the ways that "professional editors . . . 'think' in dynamic, fleet, context-sensitive, ways, often so quickly that they can give the misleading impression that they weren't thinking at the time of the creative working. They generate ideas in response to material, with the material, and through their actions in relation to the material."[13] What interests me about Clarke's editing is her particular way of thinking with the material. What she sees and designs as phrases of movement that create rhythmically heightened impressions of ordinary gestures. She thinks with her hands, and tools, and the filmed material, to create a world in unique, "Shirley-ish" motion.

TIME LOOPS

My choice of a film passage to illustrate this is from *Brussels Loops,* a series of films Clarke worked on with D. A. Pennebaker, Richard Leacock, and Willard van Dyke. These filmmakers, who were each later known as groundbreaking documentary directors, shared a studio in the late 1950s. Together they blurred the credits and hierarchical filmmaking systems that were not really sacrosanct in their New York underground milieu anyway. The Academy Award–nominated *Skyscraper* (1959), for example, is a film "by" a few people, including Clarke, Pennebaker, van Dyke, and Irving Jacoby, though the Clarke editing style is certainly its defining feature. Similarly, on the *Brussels Loops,* Clarke was one of the filmmakers, directing some and editing others. She did not edit all of them, but she did edit all the ones she directed, demonstrating that, particularly in this kind of montage filmmaking, editing is really part of writing and directing—the generation of ideas, through embodied and embedded creative thinking.

The *Loops* were first screened in the American Pavilion of the Brussels World's Fair in 1958, where they were projected on walls in continuous loops that visitors experienced from a moving platform at the center of a vast hall. The impression was meant to be one of the United States in motion, and no one watching (participating?) ever had exactly the same experience as anyone else. In that sense these films remain unfinished to this day, without one single, followable trajectory. They were experienced without beginning or end, an ongoing dance of gestures and faces, roads and drivers, buildings and builders, signs and shoppers, displays, services, styles, and more.

The *Brussels Loops,* like so much of Clarke's work, were all but buried until Dennis Doros of Milestone Films, working closely with Shirley Clarke's daughter Wendy Clarke, and Mary Huelsbeck of the Wisconsin Centre for Film and Theater Research, brought them back to the world through "Project Shirley."[14] The eight years of research and recovery of Clarke's films produced a four-volume set of DVDs, culminating in the 2016 release of *The Magic Box,* which contains Clarke's dance films, performance videos, home movies, and "experimental" films, including *Brussels Loops*.

Here is a moment I encountered in the *Loops*: We see a pair of men's polished leather shoes of the lace-up '50s style. The shot tilts up to show a handshake between two white men—firm, certain, and square. The momentum of the pumping hands seems to propel the movements of another young white man who appears in the next shot. This young man lifts his hand to his hat and springs to his feet, as though the cut between the shots is the downbeat at the start of a tune. Which, of course, it is, but it's a visual tune, one played by Clarke's hands as she joins the frames and spins the moviola. The young man leans into the visual music he is there to make by reaching out to shake the hand of an acquaintance who strides into view. Sunlight warms the easygoing, well-dressed white folk and the friendly connection of white hands, dark suits, white faces, dark hats.

Now let me lay it out for you as Clarke might have felt it. She might have hummed *tilt-up stand-up,* a rhythm of rising inflections.[15] Or she might have bobbed her head ever so lightly with the *up-down up-down* of the handshakes. But my guess is that what really makes the cut "Shirley-ish" is that it is contrapuntal, composed of two rhythms. What she made—what we see—is a phrase that goes like this: *tilt-up, pump-up-down-up-down-up-down / hat-tip, stand-up, pump-up DOWN.*

The hat-tip is also the first note of the new measure—the shot that resolves the handshake rhythm with a firm *DOWN* also starts the melodic line of hat-tipping. In the shot right after the *white hands-dark suits-white faces-dark hats,* the hat motif is carried on. An older man stands up tipping his hat, this time downward and off his head, to greet a woman. He and the woman lean in to converse, and another cut brings us to a scene of two white ladies who carry on a pleasant conversation for a word or two before Clarke cuts yet again, returning to her original motion motif. As two (new) white men shake hands, the tall trees behind them underscore the vertical *up-down* of their hands, their suits and smiles, and I'm about to bounce along to describe the next shot, the one where Clarke makes clear what she wants us to understand, which is that this social world isn't only white, that this rhythm, these convocations of geniality in America, include Black people too, when I'm suddenly overwhelmed.

I stop typing. Put my head in my hands. Think about dinner, briefly, before I realize what is really giving me pause. It's like seeing a ghost, an ancestor, a spirit elder, looking at these movements, these cuts, this closely. Trying to explain them to you is like trying to explain a current: the current coming down that "one long electrical cord" to which Clarke compares her life. Through the rhythmic phrasing of her edits, the metaphorical current is live, still zapping kinaesthesia through Clarke to me. It's the same current I was zapped by, when I was about eleven, that still has me hopping around. When I edit, this is how the world becomes. These lines of movement singing out to each other to be created.

THE ELECTRICAL CORD THEORY OF THE CREATIVE UNFINISHED

There is an explanation for what I'm experiencing here; it is *entrainment* at multiple timescales. And this is key to the—my—electrical cord theory of the creative unfinished. Entrainment, in Mark Doffman's words, "describes the interaction and synchronisation between independent rhythmic processes."[16] These rhythmic processes are various, as is suggested by the range of meanings given in the *Cambridge Dictionary*: in neurology, "entrainment" refers to "any practice that aims to cause brainwave frequencies to fall into step with periodic stimulus"; in music, the "synchronisation of beats or music with natural body function or processes." Entrainment at multiple timescales, then, is synchronization occurring not just at the immediate level of a present moment—when, for example, your heart rate matches the drumbeat of a song—but also via a sense of coordination with the past, with a tradition or sensation that is inherited, passed down (or along a cross-temporal, cross-spatial current).

Writing about classical Japanese dance training processes, Tomie Hahn and J. Scott Jordan identify in dancers the "emergence of a rich phenomenal sense of belonging to something larger than the timescale of one's immediate movement planning."[17] It is this rich phenomenal sense that makes me drop my head into my hands, overwhelmed by an uncanny feeling of connectedness that I did not expect. I *feel* Clarke's editing in the same way that I feel my own. Why the "Shirley-ish" rhythms feel to me so much like my own, like what I would do with that material if it were mine to edit, I'm not sure. Maybe it's the inheritance passed on from one Jewish-New Yorker-dancer-turned-editor-turned-director to the next. Maybe it's because I trained with the dancer who appears in *A Dance in the Sun*, Daniel Nagrin, who perhaps imparted some of the same rhythms to us both. Or maybe it is because of the ways Clarke was influenced first by Maya Deren's *A Study in Choreography for Camera* (1945) and then, in film school, by Soviet montage editing. I received those influences in that order too. Whatever kinaesthetic sensibility is being transmitted, I am being schooled by her across decades, by movement phrases she designed before I was born. These activate my embodied cognition in the moments I watch them, and in the moments I emulate them, kinetically, in my own dance films—and, indeed, in my films that are not dance films but that are still always, inevitably, patterned by my deeply inscribed dance sensibility.[18]

Dance training is body to body, and in classical forms it comes through teachers to students with only slight variations over generations, referencing, as Hahn and Jordan write, "long-term historical timescales of tacit knowledge transfer."[19] The embodied transmission of editing practices is also often tacit knowledge transfer, but it comes through differently than dance does. Clarke did not teach someone to edit who taught someone to edit who taught me to edit. Her lessons to me are rather more *direct* than that, even though I never met her as far as I'm aware. (We may have crossed paths in some of the video facilities Clarke helped to establish and sustain when I was a young dancer in New York City who was interested in dance film. I like to think so, but I'll never know.) The body-to-body transfer of knowledge was from one *film's* body to the next. From her *In Paris Parks* (1954), following her then four-year-old daughter's exploration of spaces in Europe, to my *Down Time Jaz* (2002), following my then four-year-old daughter's exploration of spaces in Europe. From her hybrid documentary *Ornette* (1985) to my hybrid documentary *I want to make a film about women* (2020).

This is why I sense a ghost, I think. I feel Clarke there because as I watch her edits, I am seeing her thoughts, embodied, living, unfinished—until I put them together and move with the phrase of movement that she was making, become entrained with it, by it, through viewing. The idea of entrainment also underpins my claim that Clarke is working on one movement idea throughout her oeuvre. There is, within her, a unique rhythmic skill that arises from the confluence of her training, her cultural contexts, and her perspective on them. I use this word *skill* in the way that McArthur Henare Mingon and John Sutton do when they write about the skilled performance of the traditional Māori dance form Haka as "embodying and transmitting dynamic and culturally shared understandings of both the natural and the social world."[20] Clarke is using her skill in this sense to entrain her own cultural understanding of the natural and social world onto the phrases of movement she designs in editing.

I call this skill "trajectory phrasing," which describes "the manipulation of *energy* in the creation of rhythm."[21] When Clarke is shaping the phrasing of energy across shots, she is not just connecting the shape and direction of moving hands and bodies, she is phrasing the intention with which they are performed into a connected flow. She uses individual movements imprinted *on* shots to build phrases of expressive movement *across* shots the way a musician uses notes to build melodies or beats to build rhythms. This is an intrinsic skill developed through years of dance training.[22] When Clarke trained as a dancer by day and danced through the night in jazz clubs, she developed embodied knowledge of how the phrasing of movement and the effort or intentions behind movement works to convey a perspective or idea. Clarke's trajectory phrases change in quality and kind as her contexts, technologies, and perspectives change over time, but the skill of shaping them is indelibly informed by her own entrainment at multiple timescales into music and dance.

CLARKE'S ACTUAL ELECTRICAL CORDS

When, in the early 1970s, Clarke described her life as "one long electrical cord (with me crawling along the floor, trying to make a connection)," she was only partially making a metaphor about the energy she conducts through her work from filmmakers of the past and passes on to filmmakers of the future. She was also talking about the literal tangle of electrical cords that overtook her working space when she started using video in the 1970s. After making more dance films, and more films that she considers dance films but that don't have dancers in them (such as *In Paris Parks* and *Skyscraper*), Clarke made dramas, adaptations, documentaries, and hybrids on film in the 1960s, all of which she considers "kinetic" films.[23] Then, in the 1970s, she turned to video.

Clarke is still thinking in dance in this phase of creativity. She doesn't, for example, start a video production company but instead invents a video performance troupe. This troupe, the TP Videospace Troupe, was a very loose association of artists, including her daughter, the video artist Wendy Clarke, and other video artists such as Andrew Gurian and DeeDee Halleck.[24] Many other people, including famous ones like Yoko Ono and Nam June Paik, would have wandered through the troupe's base in Shirley Clarke's home in the Chelsea Hotel over the course of the 1970s and 1980s. It is significant to this discussion though that the video art made there was not meant to be finished and screened later. It was improvisational performance art that happened to be recorded on tape. In an interview in the early 1970s, Clarke stated that she "want[ed] to work with Video as a process art form ... Video Theatre ... live video mixes."[25]

Clarke's video performance troupe toured the college circuit (a uniquely 1970s American circuit of liberal arts colleges with dance departments and film departments and cinematheques) just as a dance company would have. In fact, had I ever seen her in when I was growing up, it would have been through my family's subscription to the Washington University in St. Louis's Modern Dance Concert Society, though I'm not sure this series was quite modern enough to take on Clarke. I certainly have no memory of being part of Clarke's project, which adopted, as she put it, "anyone who has any interest or background in electronics or film or theatre to become temporary members of our troupe."[26] By the time I was gifted a video camera in the late 1980s, the space and troupe were dispersed. But I was the beneficiary, no doubt, of Clarke's advocacy and her adventurousness and was taught to use video editing gear by people who were taught by people she taught.

The video works made and performed by Clarke's troupe were improvisational encounters of body parts with television monitors (figure 9.1). Her collaborator, Andrew Gurian, remembers one such event in this way:

> Clarke constructed a bank of four cameras in front of one person, whose head, arms, torso, and legs became the source of the four (live) images. Next, four people contributed one body part each to create a new composite, and then live body parts were combined with recorded ones. Members of the workshop played with a variety of totem images; and whatever or whosever arms, legs, heads, and torsos were on screen, this Totem could dance in ways no human being could.[27]

Clarke was deliberately, perpetually, finishing and unfinishing these videos, by creating them through live entanglement with the viewer's mind. Like all live performance, once you leave the theater where you have participated in these video dances, the experience is not finished—it lives in you and otherwise evaporates, its energy returning to the ecosystem to be recycled into fuel for the next encounter.

Although Clarke's actual electrical cords were necessary to make her totems work, I am struck by another connection of timescales being made by putting together of body parts to make a totem. Four people contributing "one body part each to create a new composite" stretches

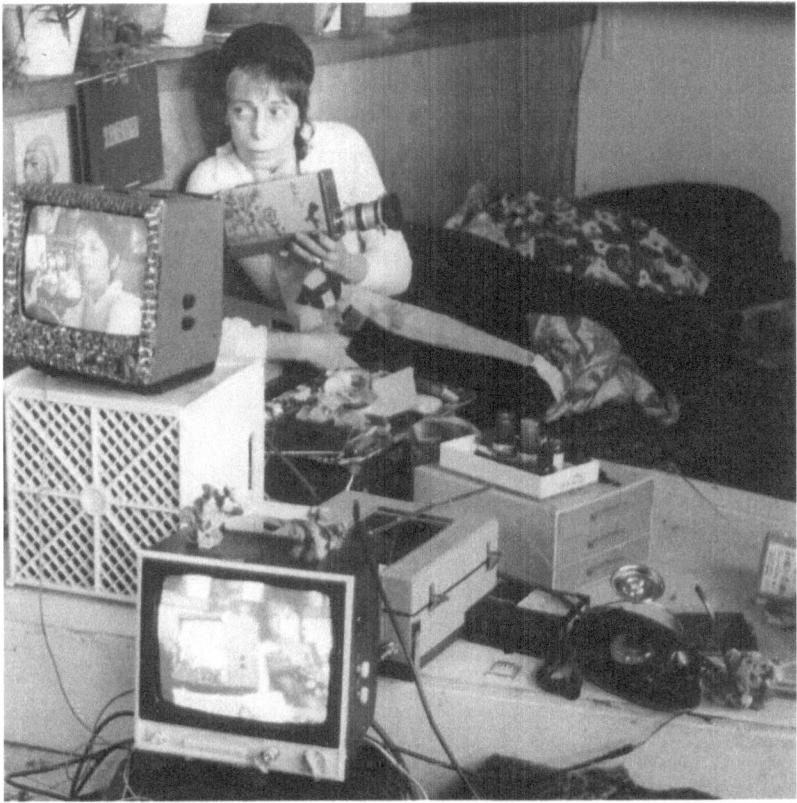

FIGURE 9.1 Shirley Clarke with Video Setup, Chelsea Hotel, 1970s. Photographer unknown. Used by permission of Wisconsin Center for Film and Theater Research.

the electrical cord backward in history to the Soviet montage filmmakers. In 1921 the filmmaker Lev Kuleshov wrote a funding request asking for stock to shoot six experiments to test "theoretical laws of cinematographic art." On his list of proposed experiments is a dance to be shot from one camera set up and then reshot, in fragments, to be "presented with the help of editing." He also requests film stock to shoot an "arbitrary combination of parts of the body of different people in order to create a desirable model actor."[28] These experiments were part of Kuleshov's efforts to demonstrate that "the basic strength of cinema lies in montage, because with montage it becomes possible both to break down and to reconstruct and ultimately remake the material."[29]

Kuleshov was interested in remaking dance for the screen for very similar reasons to Clarke. Clarke, as Bruce Bebb explains, "started directing films in 1953 because all of the dance films that she had seen struck her as needlessly bad."[30] Similarly, as Ana Olenina observes, Kuleshov was "vexed by the problem of putting dance on screen"; in 1920, Kuleshov lamented that "the dance that lasted only thirty seconds on stage seemed to drag on forever."[31] To solve this disjunct between the temporal experience of a live performance and what we call "screen time," Kuleshov and Clarke both appreciated the distinction between, in Clarke's words, "a dance film that was a record of an existing dance and one that was choreographed for the camera."[32] Given this distinction—which is now axiomatic in dance filmmaking—Kuleshov, as Olenina notes, "urg[ed] filmmakers to recognise editing as the most powerful tool they have at hand" in the cinematic presentation of dance.[33]

Clarke's totems of the 1970s are in a sense prefigured in Kuleshov's unrealized experiments with creating a human form from fragments. They are also prefigured by an unfinished experiment of her own, which can be seen in *The Magic Box* DVD. In 1953, Clarke went to Paris to film with famed mime and teacher Etienne Decroux. He wasn't there, so she made *In Paris Parks* instead. *In Paris Parks* is a complex rhythmical construction of children playing, puppet shows, vendors, toys, bicycles, some fleeting glimpses of racist old women staring cruelly at Black toddlers who stare in fascination at the camera, and more. That it is Clarke's first dance film made without dancers is ironic because she went there to make a film with a dancer who wasn't there. But she went back again later and managed to shoot with Decroux. In the uncut material for the film, you can see Clarke draping all but one part of Decroux's body in black cloth and then framing a close-up of the movement of the one white-powdered limb. One leg. The other leg. An arm. His torso. His face.

It is an odd, ghostly set of images. When I talked to Denis Doros about them, he said, "I don't know what she was thinking." So I'm wondering, maybe, if by connecting that experiment backward to the Soviets—and forward to the totems of the 1970s—we can decipher something about what was on her mind. My take on it is that if Clarke had ever edited these shots, she might have made a human at multiple timescales: a fragmented construction temporally aligned, through editing, into rhythmic specificity of some kind. I hope to get my hands on this material to test my sense of her embodied cognizing with my own dance-soaked editing thinking. Not to finish her film, exactly, but to put it into motion as one of her ever-unfinished and unfinishing trajectory phrases.

I don't know how I'll do this, but seeing *A Dance in the Sun* recently, suddenly, what felt like dozens of electrical cords winding through my life suddenly connected. I remember Nagrin teaching me, in the 1970s, the contrapuntal rhythms of Jazz dance styles from the 1940s, which, of course, he would have learned from Black artists' inventions from the 1920s. Thinking about him working with Clarke in the 1950s, I jump cut to a thought about the germinal cinematic time–space inventions Maya Deren made in *A Study in Choreography for Camera* in 1945, which build on another of Kuleshov's experiments, this one connecting disparate spaces through movement made in the 1920s but long since lost.[34] A brief notion flashes by of the uneasy ways Clarke and Deren cohabited the tiny, marginal space available for women in the avant-garde film scenes in the 1950s. I splice this thought to the cinematic time–space inventions Deren made in *A Study in Choreography for Camera* that Clarke revised and remade, but better, in *A Dance in the Sun* (there, I said it; but Clarke's version is better, and sacred sites of worship must tumble sometime). I'm humming along, internally editing thinking about these multiple timescales as though they are some kind of tessellated, episodic memories, and an idea comes to me for the film I will make. Not exactly a structure, but an image. A starting point. Something.

NOTES

Acknowledgment and thanks to Wendy Clarke, Denis Doros, Andrew Gurian, Mary Huelsbeck, Richard James Allen, Desmond Bravo, Lana Chryssavgis, and Timothy Sharp. My thanks to the editors of this volume, Alix Beeston and Stefan Solomon, for their insights, encouragement, and thoughtful edits.

Epigraph: This quotation is the title of an interview held in Shirley Clarke's archives at the Wisconsin Center for Film and Theater Research (WCFTR), Box 12, Folder 1. The interview, which is one of two in the folder, is not dated; however, it is possible to deduce from the films and technologies mentioned, and those not mentioned, that it would have occurred in the early to mid-1970s. There is no byline for the interviewer, and most of the handwritten annotations are illegible; however, one at the top can be made out, which says: "Somewhat Curated Transcript."

1. Shirley Clarke, cited in Gretchen Berg, "Interview with Shirley Clarke," *Film Culture* 42 (Spring 1967): 53–55, 53.

2. In the book I am writing about Shirley Clarke (*Shirley Clarke, Thinking Through Movement*, Edinburgh University Press, forthcoming 2024), it is my intention to unpack several aspects of the connection between Clarke's dancing, editing, and directing that have previously been unexplored. Saying "previously unexplored" isn't saying much, because Clarke is certainly one of the most egregiously undertheorized filmmakers of the twentieth century. My book will

consider the themes dance can express without words and how these themes become lifelong preoccupations for Clarke, the ways that themes manifest in films about communities that she was outside of but entwined with, and the agency her mastery of editing gives her as a director to make films that no one else would, or could, make. This chapter, however, has scope for only one focus: the encounter with the unfinished that both dance and editing embody.

3. Dee Reynolds, *Rhythmic Subjects: Uses of Energy in the Dances of Mary Wigman, Martha Graham, and Merce Cunningham* (Hampshire, UK: Dance Books, 2007).

4. My professional dance career largely played out in New York, in the same kind of "downtown" and modern dance scenes that Clarke would have been a part of thirty years before me. But while she would have been mostly touring to university campuses, by the 1980s we were touring the Opera House stages of the world.

5. Shirley Clarke, cited in Angelos Koutsourakis, "Great Directors: Shirley Clarke," *Senses of Cinema* 65 (December 2012): n.p.

6. Shirley Clarke, cited in Mona Murphy, "Women in Film," *Hollywood Reporter* (3 January 1975).

7. Berg, "Interview with Shirley Clarke," 53.

8. Lev V. Kuleshov (1929), "Montage as the Foundation of Cinematography," in *Kuleshov on Film: Writings,* ed. Ronald Levaco (Los Angeles: University of California Press, 1974): 42–55, 52.

9. Footage may even have been directed by the editor to conform to a plan or an a priori idea, as is the case with Clarke's films (and my own). In this case, I contend that Clarke continues the work of directing through the editing process. See Karen Pearlman, "Editing and Directing 'The Cool World': Filmmaking as a Choreographic Art Form," *Textual Practice* 35.10 (2021): 1587–605.

10. See Karen Pearlman, *Cutting Rhythms, Intuitive Film Editing,* 2nd ed. (London: Focal Press; New York: Taylor & Francis, 2016).

11. Andrew Gurian, email to Wendy Clarke, 13 February 2021.

12. See Karen Pearlman, "After the Facts—These Edits Are My Thoughts," *[In]Transition* 6.4 2019): 1–7, http://mediacommons.org/intransition/after-facts.

13. See Karen Pearlman, John MacKay, and John Sutton, "Creative Editing: Svilova and Vertov's Distributed Cognition," *Apparatus* 6 (2018), https://doi.org/10.17892/app.2018.0006.122.

14. See Milestone Film's "Project Shirley" collection at https://milestone-films.com/collections/shirley-clarke.

15. For more on what I call "Singing the Rhythm," see Pearlman, *Cutting Rhythms,* 100–101.

16. Mark Doffman, "Making It Groove! Entrainment, Participation and Discrepancy in the 'Conversation' of a Jazz Trio," *Language & History* 52 (2009): 130–47, 132.

17. Tomie Hahn and J. Scott Jordan, "Anticipation and Embodied Knowledge: Observations of Enculturating Bodies," *Journal of Cognitive Education and Psychology* 13.2 (2014): 272–84, 272.

18. For more on my dance films, see "Woman with an Editing Bench," *Physical TV,* http://physicaltv.com.au/woman-with-an-editing-bench/; "After the

Facts," *Physical TV,* http://physicaltv.com.au/after-the-facts/; and "I want to make a film about women," *Physical TV,* http://physicaltv.com.au/i-want-to-make-a-film-about-women-2/.

19. Hahn and Jordan, "Anticipation and Embodied Knowledge," 275.

20. McArthur Henare Mingon and John Sutton, "Why Robots Can't Haka: Skilled Performance and Embodied Knowledge in the Māori Haka," *Synthese* 199 (December 2021): 1–34, 8.

21. See Karen Pearlman, "On Rhythm in Film Editing," in *The Palgrave Handbook of the Philosophy of Film and Motion Pictures,* ed. Noël Carroll, Laura Teresa Di Summa-Knoop, and Shawn Loht (Cham, Switzerland: Palgrave Macmillan, 2019): 143–64.

22. In dance theory it is generally understood that the energy or effort with which movement is performed roughly translates as the attitude and intention behind movement which informs the way it is done. See Irmgard Bartenieff, *Body Movement: Coping with the Environment,* ed. Dori Lewis (London: Gordon and Breach Science Publishers, 1980).

23. Berg, "Interview with Shirley Clarke," 53.

24. For images from this period of Clarke's creativity, see the digitized materials including tapes of the productions at the archives of the WCFTR, https://archive.org/details/wcftr?and%5B%5D=Tee+Pee. See also Beth Capper, "Ultimate Participation Video: Shirley Clarke's Tee Pee Video Space Troupe," *Art Journal* 72.1 (2013): 46–63.

25. Cited in *Videoball* (Antioch College), "Shirley Clarke: An Interview," *Radical Software* 4.2 (c. 1973): 25–27, 25, www.radicalsoftware.org/volume2nr4/pdf/VOLUME2NR4_art08.pdf.

26. *Videoball,* "Shirley Clarke: An Interview," 25.

27. Andrew Gurian, "Thoughts on Shirley Clarke and The TP Videospace Troupe," *MFJ* 42 (Fall 2004): 1–13, 1–2.

28. Lev V. Kuleshov (1921), "Proposal Addressed to the Photo-Kino Section of the Regional Centre of Political Education (Gubpolitiprosvet)," in "The Rediscovery of a Kuleshov Experiment: A Dossier," ed. Yuri Tsivian, with contributions from Ekaterina Khokhlova and introduction by Kristin Thompson, *Film History* 8.3 (1992): 366.

29. Kuleshov, "Montage as the Foundation of Cinematography," 52.

30. Bruce Bebb, "The Many Media of Shirley Clarke," *Journal of the University Film Association* 34.2 (1982): 3–8, 3.

31. Ana Hedberg Olenina, "Moto-Bio-Cine-Event: Constructions of Expressive Movement in Soviet Avant-Garde Film," in *The Oxford Handbook of Screendance Studies,* ed. Douglas Rosenberg (New York: Oxford University Press, 2016): 79–104, 87.

32. Berg, "Interview with Shirley Clarke," 53.

33. Olenina, "Moto-Bio-Cine-Event," 87.

34. It is clear from the eulogy that Clarke wrote for Deren that Clarke admired Deren, but it also feels as though there is much between the lines of that tribute. For more on their complex relationship, see Lauren Rabinovitz, *Points of Resistance: Women, Power and Politics in the New York Avant-Garde Cinema, 1943–71* (Champaign: University of Illinois Press, 2003).

CHAPTER 10

Shirkers and Its Afterlives

Six Epitaphs for an Incomplete Film

SOPHIA SIDDIQUE

ORIENTATION GUIDE

In the early 1990s, I applied for a spot in a 16mm filmmaking course at the Substation, "Singapore's first independent contemporary arts centre."[1] Established in 1990, the Substation was a beacon not only for aspiring artists but for the general Singapore public who could attend, for example, gallery openings, musical performances, and theater productions. Georges Cardona, the instructor for the course, interviewed me along with other applicants who had a passion for cinema. Upon acceptance, I and my fellow cinephiles and film compatriots began a journey that would exert a profound gravitational pull in my life.

Drawn to two particular women, Sandi Tan and Jasmine Ng Kin Kia, I felt seen and heard. As the class progressed, Sandi wanted to make an independent feature film based upon a screenplay she had written, titled "Shirkers." After much heated discussion, we, along with Georges, decided to shoot the film in the summer of 1992. Sandi was the screenwriter and lead actor, Jasmine was the assistant director and editor, Georges was the director, and I served as the film's producer. After we wrapped production, what should have been a seamless transition to postproduction transformed instead into a nightmare. Georges took possession of all the film and sound reels and eventually absconded with them. The film would never be completed.

Over many years, I and several other crew members tried to get the reels back from Georges without any success. I was left heartbroken and devastated. Georges's theft was so painful for me that after filming ended, I never spoke about the details of the production, not even to my closest friends in film school in the United States. For me, the film existed as, in Alix Beeston and Stefan Solomon's terms from this volume's introduction, a "dispersed collection of textual materials," always out of reach. What I call *Shirkers 1.0*—for reasons that will become apparent—would never coalesce into that critical mass, the revered object we know as a completed film.

Had it been completed, *Shirkers 1.0* would have been one of the few locally produced, independent, English-language features since the 1970s. In the early 1990s, feature filmmaking in Singapore was practically nonexistent, save for *Medium Rare* (1991). That film featured an international cast and centered on Adrian Lim, Singapore's notorious medium-turned-ritual killer. After the closure of two of Singapore's biggest film studios, Shaw Brothers' Malay Film Productions and Cathay-Keris, in 1967 and 1972 respectively, there was only intermittent independent filmmaking in the 1970s, followed by a fertile period of grassroots filmmaking in the form of short films in the 1980s. At the time of our production, in 1992, the state had barely begun to build an ecosystem for funding Singaporean filmmakers: the Singapore Film Commission had not yet been established, and the National Arts Council was founded only a year earlier, in 1991, and existed only in a fledgling form.

In the immediate aftermath of Georges's theft and betrayal, I struggled with how to account for my labor and that of the cast and crew, which had effectively been erased. Could *Shirkers 1.0* "count" as a film if it had not been edited and released? And if it did not indeed "count," could I list a producer credit on my CV if I had not seen the film to completion? Even now, as I write almost thirty years after the making of *Shirkers 1.0*, I grapple with the vagaries of my sensuous memories surrounding the production of the film. I chafe against the hegemonic hold that completion exerts on Singapore film historiography, which privileges male authorship and the finished feature-length film. In particular, I question how the narratives of Singapore film historiography reckon with—or, more to the point, do *not* reckon with—fissures, gaps, and erasures, including the spectral (non)presence of *Shirkers 1.0*.

I also sit with my vulnerability as a subject for the documentary film that debuted at the Sundance Film Festival in Park City, Utah, in 2018 as *Shirkers*—in my terms, *Shirkers 2.0*. This film represents Sandi's personal meditation on the loss of our film and, at once, a celebration of her creative redemption. I use the present tense of "sit" because *Shirkers*

2.0 continues to be viewed via Netflix, which acquired the distribution rights to the film. Evocative precisely because of the vestiges of *Shirkers 1.0* lurking within it, *Shirkers 2.0* foregrounds the aesthetic potentialities of incompletion and its advantages for understanding the creative process. *Shirkers 2.0* hinges on the story of the reemergence of the film reels (but not, importantly, the sound reels) of *Shirkers 1.0*, following the death of Georges in 2007. This is a contested and complex story that I choose not to revisit here, for some stories are not mine to tell. What I will say is that many years after the loss of the film, Jasmine, Sandi, and I found ourselves able to reopen its crypt and to begin taking stock of its remains. Eventually Sandi took on the project of reanimating and revivifying the film materials, as well as interviewing me and other crew members. *Shirkers 2.0* was the result.

When I attended the premiere of the film at Sundance in 2018, I had not yet seen a single cut of the film. The postscreening question-and-answer session represented the first time that we three—Sandi, Jasmine, and I—had shared the same physical space in over twenty years. I do not exaggerate when I say that my encounter with the film at Sundance precipitated a crisis in subjectivity. I saw my younger self, grumpy and sassy, holding a slate during outtakes while filming *Shirkers 1.0*. I also saw a much older version of myself on screen as a documentary subject being interviewed by Sandi in 2015. I felt as if I had entered a wormhole and hurtled through space-time.

My sense of dislocation was a jarring and poignant reminder that I had, for the most part, forgotten that young woman of grit and gumption. Although I had previously taught a course on documentary history and theory, nothing had prepared me for the degree of vulnerability I felt when seeing myself on screen amid an audience of strangers. I gazed furtively between my representation on-screen and the audience, both as a documentary subject wondering what members of the audience thought about me and as a scholar who understood the power and ethics of editing to shape perception. Dislocation, erasure, loss, and melancholia are feelings or haunting intensities that I experience whenever I think of *Shirkers 1.0*. I inhabit such subject positions as producer, scholar, teacher, documentary subject, and biracial Singaporean cis woman because of *Shirkers 1.0*. One would think that thirty years is enough time to sit with the ghost of *Shirkers 1.0* and to hear what it wished to communicate. But I would be wrong about that.

In what follows, I share a map with you, reader, that I cocreate with *Shirkers 1.0*'s spectral presence. A conventional map comprised of concrete longitudes and latitudes with finite coordinates will not suffice. Such a map cannot locate a film that does not quite exist. Nor can this map account for the myriad subject positions I inhabit or my ambivalent and painful relationship with *Shirkers 1.0*. As a spectral traveling companion, *Shirkers 1.0* calls for a map with coordinates that exist in an occult space-time. I grasp "occult" in all of its polyvalent meanings: as a noun or adjective relating to "magic, alchemy, astrology, theosophy and other practical arts of a serious or mysterious nature," and as a verb meaning to "cut off from view by interposing something."[2] In their introduction to this volume, Beeston and Solomon write: "The cajoling ghosts of incomplete films are, in a sense, only ever elsewhere, unmoored—or suspended—in space as well as in time. This leads us to ask: *when* is the missing movie or unfinished film? Is it past, or present, or future—or somehow all of these at once?" *Occult space-time* provides one path among many to navigate this vexed condition: cajoling ghosts of incomplete films (occult), an elsewhere (space) and elsewhen (time) that locates the missing movie or unfinished film.

I turn toward Gilles Deleuze and Félix Guattari, as well as Giuliana Bruno, as key traveling companions along my journey, for they illuminate my path with their respective meditations on mapping fissures, gaps, disjunctures, and loss. Like mine, Deleuze and Guattari's rhizomatic map does not celebrate completion or localizable units but rather "is open and connectable in all of its dimensions; it is detachable, reversible, susceptible to constant modification."[3] Such a map gives shape and texture to my complex and variegated experiences of loss and return. And Giuliana Bruno, in her engagement with the lost work of Italian filmmaker, Elvira Notari, like me confronts a "ruined and fragmentary map," one dotted with "textual absences and voids." Bruno embraces these "lacunae" and traverses through them as "overlapping textual journeys in a series of 'inferential walks' through novels, paintings, photographs, and architectural sites."[4]

Unlike Bruno's map, however, my map does not offer a vision of "analytic detail with a panoramic vision."[5] Instead, it is populated with several Sophias in states of becoming: Sophia as documentary subject, as teacher, as scholar, as producer. As these becoming-Sophias—Sophias-in-process, to borrow the terms we adopt in this section of *Incomplete*—traverse dimensions of space-time with their (my, our) spectral companion, we produce a map with dimensions of occult space-time I call epitaphs. In an occult space-time, what lurks within epitaphs refuses to remain buried; these are the sites in which I adapt

Bruno's practice of "critical necrophilia," an approach that recognizes "the multiple pleasures and deaths inscribed in the inquisitive gaze of analysis—a gaze that moves in and dissects a body of work."[6]

Indeed, references to murder and the afterlife abound in *Shirkers 1.0*, where a woman named S, the central protagonist, must find and kill other people to bring to the afterlife with her. Whether the killing spree is only a dream remains uncertain. Meanwhile, in *Shirkers 2.0*, Georges's haunting presence lingers; and, as Sandi expresses in the 2018 film, the vestigial fragments of *Shirkers 1.0* start to send her "distress signals," as if such fragments vibrate with the pulse of an otherworldly life. I also experience the haunting presence of these fragments, especially the place held by my production notebook in my sensuous memory. I locate each of these hauntings in occult space-time, which also, in the context of Singapore film historiography, reveals what presence and completion occlude—namely their constitutive counterparts of absence and incompletion. At once, occult space-time structures my writing process, as I use the tools of divination (tarot and oracle cards) for inspiration and guidance.

"[T]he fabric of the rhizome," Deleuze and Guattari write, "is the conjunction, 'and . . . and . . . and . . . '"[7] I use the conjunction "and" to suggest ongoingness, such that these epitaphs can be read in any order you wish, though I offer them in one order, shaped through association and exchange, and I also provide this preamble as an orientation guide. As you explore our map, I invite you to chart your own path through these epitaphs and generate your own "circles of convergence," in Deleuze and Guattari's phrase.[8]

and

EPITAPH: SENSUOUS MEMORY
Sophia-Documentary Subject:

"You gave me this notebook when you arrived. So I have, I have not seen this for twenty-three years. And this is my notebook. So, I'm analyzing and breaking down the script for, like symbolism and metaphor and allusions. This notebook contains the kernel for my profession, unbeknownst to me. 'Scene Seven, interior, S's house, afternoon. The toys would be physical manifestations of her personality. They must reflect HER'—in all caps. 'Is she seeking immortality through her dreams?' See, even then I was digging, right, for subtext."

Sophia-Scholar:

My spiral production notebook from *Shirkers 1.0* is many things to me: a time capsule; a gestating seed for the film scholar I had yet to become; a revenant from my past; an evanescent tether to my nineteen-year-old self. Even the plastic sheath that holds its well-worn pages serves as a reliquary. I reacquaint myself with the handwriting of my youth. I see that my penmanship sometimes struggles to obey the confines of the page. On occasion, my upstart pen pushes past those lined, ruled boundaries to chart an alternative path across the page.

Sandi gave my notebook back to me during my interview with her in 2015, and when I am finally alone with it, I smell its pages and trace its perforations. What wafts through me is grief and longing. Grief is unruly; it refuses to contort itself to fit into a seamless chronology of healing. I feel this grief now, even as I write this sentence. I sit with my younger self who looks at me, mutely, with reproach. She longs to bind herself to me as I long to invite her back into myself, for I have exiled her for so long. I had forgotten her—my creative fire. (Is she seeking immortality through her dreams?)

During the premiere of *Shirkers 2.0* in 2018, faced with the lingering fragments of *Shirkers 1.0*, I find myself jolted by a scene that does not, for some reason, appear in my production notebook. This scene features young ballerinas in fuchsia posing amid a topiary in the Singapore Botanic Gardens in 1992. The scene's abrasive absence in my production notebook continued to vex me. That saturated fuchsia was ethereal, the lush warm green of the topiary felt otherworldly. The ballerina scene was my "radioactive fossil"—one of many, it turns out. As Laura Marks writes, "when a fossil is 'radioactive' that is because it hints that the past it represents is not over, it beckons the viewer to excavate the past, even at his or her peril."[9] She continues,

> When an image is all that remains of a memory, when it cannot be "assigned a present" by an act of remembering but simply stares up at one where it has been unearthed, then that image is a fossil of what has been forgotten. It is possible, though as Deleuze warned, dangerous, to examine these images and learn the histories they have witnessed.[10]

It is indeed dangerous for me to examine and engage with this radioactive fossil, for it propels my neurodivergence to the surface. I am an aphantasic and therefore have no mind's eye. I do not think in images nor can I visualize images in my head.[11] Neither the penetrating, warm glow of fuchsia nor the verdant green of the topiary were seared into my mind, which is a deep, continuous well of inky blackness. Aphantasics possess poor autobiographical memories because of this inherent inability to visually encode memories. My sense memories are olfactory (so fleeting) and kinesthetic and *still* the memories of filming the ballerina scene elude me. As hard as I commune with this spectral fragment in *Shirkers* 2.0, it will never transform into a recollection-image.[12] Yet its radioactivity continues to burn.

and

EPITAPH: SPECULATIVE HISTORIOGRAPHY
Sophia-Documentary Subject:

"You know, *Shirkers* is like the ghost in-between the lines of books written on Singapore film history, and for me, *Shirkers* has this very palpable absence. And I have this voice going, 'No, no, no, *Shirkers* needs to be there.'"

Sophia-Scholar:

I see myself wistful on-screen, tantalized by the what-ifs and feeling the tension between my positions as both documentary participant and film scholar who writes on Singapore film history. When Beeston and Solomon ask, in the introduction, "*when* is the missing movie or unfinished film?," their question raises other related ones about how Singapore film historiography is written. What counts as a film that merits a presence, a time and place, within this historiography? How does Singapore film historiography answer to or accommodate an unfinished film, one that was neither completed nor distributed? As scholars, critics, curators, and spectators, what we privilege or give visibility to decides the films that count and are counted in film history.

As scholars, we practice alchemy and fabulation. We transform facts into a narrative that presents itself as a truth or reality; and we perform acts of fabulation that heed the seductive desire or lure to fill gaps and fissures with a cohesive form. Or, to put it another way, we, like the taxidermist, revivify the past. Zekiye Antakyalıoğlu emphasizes historiography's intimate connections to taxidermy when she writes,

> History is about something that never did happen in the way in which it comes to be represented. . . . The events that happened in the past are stuffed by the archival research, second hand information, other texts and other points of view, and represented by the historian in a way much similar to what a taxidermist does. He exhibits the past with new stuff, and it works, because the dead cannot speak.[13]

But what if the dead can speak? What other absences populate, punctuate, and puncture that veneer of smooth chronology and completion?

The completed feature film and the revival narrative of Singapore cinema in the 1990s dominate the national film historiography.[14] This narrative has four stages: beginning with the end of the studio era, specifically the closures of Shaw Brothers' Malay Film Productions in 1967 and Cathay-Keris in 1972, it acknowledges a smattering of independent filmmaking in the 1970s, before lamenting the dearth of filmmaking activity in the 1980s—which is answered, finally, by a revival in the 1990s. Scholars such as Gerald Sim have offered counternarratives; for Sim, arguing against such a disjuncture between the two historical moments, we might center instead on the primacy of a spatial orientation that serves as a connective tissue between the colonial and the postcolonial.[15]

In my own work I have sought to challenge the notion of the paucity of filmmaking in Singapore in the 1980s, specifically by redefining the term "film industry" and adopting a more fluid understanding of production that includes non-studio or non-institutional modes of filmmaking. "Production," as I define the term, encompasses three spheres of filmmaking: institutional (studio), independent, and grassroots. These spheres of filmmaking are dynamic as they fluctuate in content and form across various socio-cultural-political-economic moments and decades. The studios Cathay-Keris and Shaw Brothers' Malay Film Productions were at their height during the 1950s and early 1960s, and in the late 1990s and 2000s Raintree Pictures (Mediacorp) emerged as a new studio presence; yet a more expansive vision of the nation's film industries—and its products—allows us to see the 1980s as a vibrant decade of grassroots filmmaking, centered on the short film form. In fact, I argue that the short film form, more than the completed feature film, shapes Singapore's national cinema, since more short films are produced in Singapore than feature films.[16]

My revised narrative of Singapore film history emphasizes the tension between synchrony and diachrony, along with the importance of process over product. Yet when I was confronted with the revivification or revival of vestiges of *Shirkers 1.0* within *Shirkers 2.0*, I realized the extent to which I remained under the seductive allure of the completed film. The film's incompletion is generative, then, in that it calls into doubt and questions my assumptions about Singapore film history. A speculative microhistoriography of *Shirkers*—such as the one I write now, my map of becoming-Sophias in occult space-time—is an intervention into Singapore film historiography that acknowledges the instability and porosity of historical narratives, as well as the absences that constitute them. As Allyson Nadia Field argues with respect to nonextant films from the silent era: "Absence is defined by the object it regrets; it is marked by the location, position, positing, and emplacement (both in time and space) of the missing piece. It is just as temporally and spatially situated as is presence."[17]

and

EPITAPH: AUTHORSHIP AND LABOR
Sophia-Documentary Subject:
"Give us the materials so that we can finish the film."

Sophia-Producer:
What did being a producer mean to a soon-to-be twenty-year-old woman? I hustled for funding; I acted, as my mother told Sandi in her interview for *Shirkers 2.0*, as a glorified "gopher"; I handled production logistics; and I was even a crowd wrangler, at one point faking a seizure to draw a crowd of people for a particular scene. We had no money for extras nor did we secure permits to shoot on location. We carried heavy equipment, worked long hours in the hot, humid, tropical environment. We did what was necessary, fueled by a collective and shared desire to make *a* film, *this* film. This desire problematizes auteurist notions of authorship—indeed, it disaggregates authorship from auteurism. As Jane Gaines has written: "The desire to make movies may just represent the desire to make movies."[18]

Ours was a form of guerrilla filmmaking, making the most of what little we had. I remember shooting at a location without air-conditioning. The scene: a young family shares in the communal delight of ice cream. Only the *whoop-swoosh* of a fan punctuated the thick air; it was not enough to offer respite from the afternoon heat and the long, sweaty hours of filming. Our production team faced an intriguing dilemma. How could we arrest the vagaries of time that spared no ice cream its solid form? In a long line of creative and innovative solutions, our team transformed mashed potatoes into ice cream. An ice cream scoop ensured the integrity of its shape. With the addition of food coloring and an ersatz whipped cream of tissues dipped in milk, we held onto the cool textures of strawberry, vanilla, and chocolate, which lingered, impossibly, on the tips of our warm tongues.

Later, after the arduous shoot was finished, tensions that had simmered throughout the production peaked. When Georges took possession of the film and sound reels, leaving Singapore with the fruits of our difficult yet exhilarating labor, he assumed sole ownership—and authorship—of *Shirkers 1.0*, even though the effort had been fully collaborative and several members of the crew, myself included, donated money to move the production forward. I thought we were investing in the production company as shareholders and board members with stakes in the ownership of the film. Unbeknown to me, I was not of legal age to sit on the board of directors of any company in Singapore. I learned a painful lesson: that authorship did not mean a shared, collective desire for filmmaking but was instead, legally and practically, a property of gender (male) and age (twenty-one or above).

Over the years I and other members of the crew renewed our efforts to get the film and sound reels from Georges. Finishing the film was of paramount importance because of the collective labor of our cast and crew. We even told Georges that we would complete the postproduction, including editing, and still give him the credit of director. This did not suit Georges, and he refused to hand over the reels. I had to accept what his version of "'paternal' authorship" ensured: that the individual and collective labor of our wonderful cast and crew, prominently young women, would not be formally recognized nor validated.[19] After all, the cast and production credits only appear at the end of a completed film.

Sophia-Teacher:

As a teacher, I encourage my students to stay and witness the end credits of any film they see. End credits, I point out, are not just endless lists of names, for in the structure of scrolling, each name represents both specificity (individual names) and communal labor (corporate identity), for filmmaking is a collective enterprise. Observing the end credits is therefore an ethical practice and one that demystifies the realities of film production. As Gaines argues, "Credit means recovery of the lost and languishing and reconstitution of the historical record."[20]

Sandi chose to revivify the original *Shirkers 1.0* credits by including them at the end of *Shirkers 2.0*, and the sight of the names was bittersweet for me. Though finally present, the credits of *Shirkers 1.0* were still incomplete. What haunted me the most were the credits to crew and cast members now deceased—a tangible reminder of the unlikely, decades-long journey of *Shirkers* to the screen, which meant that we were no longer all alive to witness, together, the strange beauty of what we had shot. The credits were thus as much an epitaph as anything else.

and

EPITAPH: THE AFTERLIVES OF FAN LABOR
Sophia-Documentary Subject:

"It's strange because it doesn't exist as a film, and yet it does. Right? It exists here for me [pointing to my chest] and it exists here [pointing to my head]. And so what you're doing is, is not bringing *Shirkers* back to life but giving it an afterlife and back to us."

Sophia-Scholar:

After the premiere of *Shirkers 2.0* in 2018, I started following the official *Shirkers* Instagram account (@shirkersfilm). Through this account I stumbled across the hashtag #Shirkers, where I discovered an outpouring of *Shirkers*philia. The posts by fans of the film expressed a deep and intense love not only for *Shirkers 2.0* but for the spectral traces of *Shirkers 1.0* it contained or gestured toward. Some posts featured more-or-less faithful reproductions of still images from the film or the documents that constellate around it, while others transformed those remnants and fragments of *Shirkers 1.0* into stunning works of art.

At the heart of *Shirkers*philia is creative labor that is embodied and artisanal, practices that were very much in tune with our labor in *Shirkers 1.0* and Sandi's in *Shirkers 2.0*. Sketches, short-form animation, drawings, paintings, and models are but some examples of the diverse artifacts that populate what I think of as a *Shirkers*cosmos, created in, and as, the afterlives of *Shirkers 1.0*. Fans cocreate and curate the generative and creative possibilities of incompletion; there is no completed ur-text that demands fidelity, and much like our map of becoming-Sophias, as well as Sandi's 2018 film, these fans participate in authoring a *Shirkers*cosmos with the spectral presence of the original film project.

For example, @yshenq and @chickentattoo contend with the mesmerizing image of ballerinas and a topiary. @yshenq constructs a detailed, hand-drawn diorama of objects from *Shirkers 1.0*'s spectral fragments, rendering the white pins and the bright red chairs from the bowling alley scene, the signature vibrant red of the phone booth, and the deep green hues of the topiary deer. These objects may have been in the background of *Shirkers 1.0*, but in this artwork they assume a position of prominence. We enter into the occult space-time of the film's production as textures are evoked through the depiction of the pebbled stone wall and the green- and white-striped awning. @yshenq's illustration thus transforms into a haunted diorama. It extracts elements from *Shirkers 1.0* from the narrative unfolding of *Shirkers 2.0* and offers its own spectral narrative of collision, juxtaposition, and association.

Meanwhile, @chickentattoo's rendition of the ballerinas pulses with an otherworldly glow. On a lush green ground three ballerinas appear in shades of fuchsia and light pink; the topiary deer are adorned with what look like pink stars. What I find most poignant and compelling about @yshenq and @chickentattoo's different representations of this scene is how they are shaped by the artists' tastes and feelings. The actual scene in *Shirkers 1.0* contains not three ballerinas but four, and instead of four deer, the scene features five deer. The scene's saturated color-corrected palette, shot on celluloid and refracted through golden, tropical light, opens a space to revel in "subjective sensory time."[21] Hence rather than merely repeating the scene, these fan artworks express and expand the sensuous logic of the film's alluring color palette, and suggest how the occult space-time of the *Shirkers*cosmos opens the film to an infinite array of afterlives.

and

EPITAPH: FRAGRANT STORIES

Sophia-Documentary Subject:

"It's strange because it doesn't exist as a film, and yet it does. Right? It exists here for me [pointing to my chest] and it exists here [pointing to my head]. And so what you're doing is, is not bringing *Shirkers* back to life but giving it an afterlife and back to us."

Sophia-Scholar:

I traveled to Singapore in April–May 2021 during the COVID-19 pandemic to be with my mother, who suffers from a debilitating neurodegenerative disease. I had not been to Singapore since 2019 because of COVID-related travel restrictions. When I arrived, I could only visit my mother at her nursing home for one hour a day, according to government health protocols. During one visit, as I looked at her frozen body, I remembered her interview in *Shirkers 2.0*. I knew Sandi had interviewed her for the film, but I had not seen my mother's cameo until the premiere at Sundance in 2018. She looked vital then, and her robust intellect and wry sense of humor were in full swing. Sitting next to her in the nursing home, I remember my bemusement at the screening when she bestowed the noun "gopher" upon my labor.

In-between nursing home visits, *Shirkers* would not leave me be. Like a ghost that refused to depart, it beckoned me to return to the Botanic Gardens (established 1859), where we had filmed ballerinas in fuchsia cavorting amid the topiary. I could not find the topiary during this visit, but I did discover the Ginger Garden (launched in 2003). The intoxicating scents of "over 550 species, varieties and horticultural cultivars of the plants of the ginger order (Zingiberales)" including "Native Gingers of Singapore" moved me to multisensory delights with their aromatic complexity.[22] In my "fragrant stories" the rhizome is aromatic, taking the material and literal form of ginger and inextricably linked to my taste and olfactory memories of Singapore.[23] I am sipping my favorite *teh halia*, "ginger tea," at Adam Road Food Centre. I am relishing home-cooked Indian food. I am visiting the Ginger Garden with my cousin. I can still resurrect those delicate, sweet-pungent scents through memory if I want to, though their fragrance fills me with melancholy.

While I was in Singapore, *Shirkers 1.0*, ever the cajoling ghost, moved me to give an informal talk to students and interested faculty at the LaSalle College of the Arts with the title "Returning to Singapore and *Shirkers*: Reflections on Incomplete Journeys." In between visits to my mother's nursing home, I sorted through boxes of my youthful possessions. Like an archaeologist sifting through long-lost artifacts, I found a *Shirkers* script (though not the shooting script). As I leafed through it, turning over the musty pages, I could not find any mention of that ballerina scene. No matter how much I tried, I could not recollect the production context for that scene nor did any sense memories pour forth. But I chose not to reach out to Sandi or Jasmine for clarity, and instead to rest within my own mind, my incomplete memories, and the losses of the past and the present.

and

EPITAPH: DIVINATION
Sophia-Documentary Subject:
"There was a piece of my spirit that died."

Sophia-Crone, Sophia-Healer:
I use tarot and oracle decks to help me bring what is intuitive, unconscious, and sometimes painful to the surface. In this epitaph of divination, I tap into material and symbolic expressions through my tarot and oracle readings; alchemy happens when these creative nudges transform into usable prose. Such readings, like the unfinished film, embody multiplicities of meanings where fixed interpretations hold no place. Rather, my movement through a reading enacts a creative exploration of how each card generates, to return to Deleuze and Guattari, "circles of convergence" between my inner perceptual world and my external reality.[24]

In devising my map of becoming-Sophias, I consulted two decks: the Archetypes deck, designed by Kim Krans, and the Shadowscapes Tarot, designed by Stephanie Pui-Mun Law.[25] The Archetypes deck is structured according to four archetypal energies known as The Selves, The Tools, The Places, and The Initiations; the Shadowscapes Tarot beckoned me with its colorful, lush, and intoxicating illustrations.[26] In the week of 21 June 2021, I asked of the Archetypes deck: What archetypal energies should I draw upon, cultivate, or even exorcise to inform my writing? I drew the Crone and the Healer. I began my journey with *Shirkers 1.0* just before I turned twenty; I was most certainly considered a maiden within the archetypal journey of maiden-mother-crone. In 2021, I write at the age of forty-nine as a crone-in-training. The Crone asks that I respect my creative labor. She demands that I reclaim my voice and center my lived experiences. The Crone reminds me to honor the generative possibilities and intuitive wisdom of the divine feminine.

The Healer, meanwhile, gently asks me to see the gifts that incompletion may bestow—not as a form of failure but instead as a robust space of possibilities, of "all manner of 'becomings.'"[27] The Healer reminds me that though a piece of my spirit had died with the loss of *Shirkers*

1.0, a grief I feel anew with *Shirkers 2.0*, the 2018 film—along with the fan labor it generated—offered me an opportunity to reconnect with my nineteen-year-old self and to rekindle the creative fire that burned inside of her. I could rediscover my early passion for filmmaking—which may allow me to connect to my passionate, impatient, and tenacious film students in newly visceral and authentic ways.

On 22 July 2021, I asked of the Shadowscapes Tarot deck: What energies does *Shirkers 1.0* bring to my writing process? I drew the Death Card, the thirteenth Major Arcana card of the seventy-eight-card Tarot deck. The Major Arcana "is an experiential journey comprising symbolic lessons that the soul must learn in the school of life during the process of what Jung dubbed individuation of the Self."[28] How this description resonates with becoming-Sophias! In the Shadowscapes Tarot, Death is not a harbinger of loss or even of literal death. At its heart lies purification, breathed into it by the fire of the Phoenix. The card celebrates threshold moments that lead from endings to beginnings and back again. The Death card can be foreboding for it is so often misunderstood, and never more so, perhaps, than by Cléo in Agnès Varda's masterpiece, *Cléo from 5 to 7* (*Cléo de 5 à 7*, 1962). In the beginning of the film, Cléo receives a tarot reading. The card that most surprises her and fills her with dread is the Death card. It is no accident that the promise of profound transformation should come in the only sequence Varda shoots in color; the rest of the film is in black and white.

Death card energies vibrate through *Shirkers*. *Shirkers 2.0* is, as I've suggested, a kind of haunted house, populated with the ghosts, seen and unseen, of Georges Cardona and other crew members now lost to us. And *Shirkers 1.0* is a cycle of beginnings and endings, moving from screenplay to disembodied 16mm film and sound reels to new life in *Shirkers 2.0*, in the fan labor, in this map—and, yes, in me. Guided by the Crone, the Healer, and the Death energies, perhaps this writing will offer pathways by which I might move from the fraught and painful experience of making and losing *Shirkers* to a new experience of hope and pleasure at the film's vibrant, incomplete and incompletable afterlives.

During the various question-and-answer discussions I've done in connection with *Shirkers 2.0*, someone has invariably asked: Will *Shirkers* as it was originally shot exist as a finished film? To which I respond, in no uncertain terms, that *Shirkers 1.0* will never exist as a finished film. Although the film reels were returned to Sandi, and incorporated into *Shirkers 2.0*, the sound reels will be forever missing, and with them the unresurrectable soundscapes of us and of Singapore in 1992. Perhaps *Shirkers* could be released as an edited film with a new score, or maybe *Shirkers* reels could be uploaded where fans and anyone interested can reedit scenes to their heart's content. Becoming-Sophias is but one shoot of the rhizome; the lines of flight, all manner of becomings, remain open and boundless.²⁹

and

NOTES

I wish to thank Jasmine Ng Kin Kia, Sandi Tan, and all the cast and crew of *Shirkers 1.0* and *Shirkers 2.0*, without whom this reflection would not have been possible. I owe a debt of gratitude to my writing group members—Jeffrey Schneider, Susan Hiner, Silke von der Emde, and Eva Woods Peiró—for their constructive and careful feedback on numerous drafts of this work. Most importantly, I dedicate this writing to my mother, Dr. Sharon Siddique.

1. "Singapore's First Independent Contemporary Arts Centre," *The Substation*, www.substation.org/about.
2. *Oxford English Dictionary*, s.v. "occult," https://www-oed-com.simsrad.net.ocs.mq.edu.au/view/Entry/130166; "occult, v.," https://www-oed-com.simsrad.net.ocs.mq.edu.au/view/Entry/130167.
3. Gilles Deleuze and Félix Guattari, *A Thousand Plateaus: Capitalism and Schizophrenia*, trans. Brian Massumi (Minneapolis: University of Minnesota Press, 1987), 12.
4. Giuliana Bruno, *Streetwalking on a Ruined Map: Cultural Theory and the City Films of Elvira Notari* (Princeton, NJ: Princeton University Press, 1993), 3.
5. Bruno, *Streetwalking on a Ruined Map*, 3
6. Bruno, *Streetwalking on a Ruined Map*, 239, 237.
7. Deleuze and Guattari, *Thousand Plateaus*, 25.
8. Deleuze and Guattari, *Thousand Plateaus*, 22.
9. Laura U. Marks, *The Skin of the Film: Intercultural Cinema, Embodiment, and the Senses* (Durham, NC: Duke University Press, 2000), 81.
10. Marks, *Skin of the Film*, 84–85.
11. See the materials collected by the Aphantasia Network, https://aphantasia.com.
12. Gilles Deleuze, *Cinema 2: The Time-Image*, trans. Hugh Tomlinson and Robert Galeta (Minneapolis: University of Minnesota Press, 1997), 46.
13. Zekiye Antakyalıoğlu, "Peter Ackroyd's Chatterton: History as Taxidermy," Çankaya Üniversitesi Fen-Edebiyat Fakültesi, *Journal of Arts and Sciences* Sayı 12 (Aralık 2009): 19–30, 29.
14. See Jan Uhde and Yvonne Ng Uhde, *Latent Images: Film in Singapore* (Singapore: National University of Singapore Press, 2009); and Edna Lim, *Celluloid Singapore: Cinema, Performance and the National* (Edinburgh: Edinburgh University Press, 2019).

15. See Gerald Sim, *Postcolonial Hangups in Southeast Asian Cinema: Poetics of Space, Sound, and Stability* (Amsterdam: Amsterdam University Press, 2020).

16. See Sophia Siddique Harvey, "Nomadic Trajectories: Mapping Short Film Production in Singapore," *Inter-Asia Cultural Studies* 8.2 (2007): 262–76.

17. Allyson Nadia Field, *Uplift Cinema: The Emergence of African American Film and the Possibility of Black Modernity* (Durham, NC: Duke University Press, 2015), 25.

18. Jane M. Gaines, "Of Cabbages and Authors," in *A Feminist Reader in Early Cinema*, ed. Jennifer M. Bean and Diane Negra (London: Duke University Press, 2002), 110.

19. Bruno, *Streetwalking on a Ruined Map*, 234.

20. Gaines, "Of Cabbages and Authors," 110.

21. Jocelyn Szczepaniak-Gillece, "The Hues of Memory, the Shades of Experience: Color and Time in *Syndromes and a Century*," in *Color and the Moving Image: History, Theory, Aesthetics, Archive,* ed. Simon Brown, Sarah Street, and Liz Watkins (New York: Routledge, 2013), 104–13, 112.

22. "A Guide to Ginger Garden at Singapore Botanic Gardens," National Parks Singapore, www.nparks.gov.sg/-/media/sbg/documents/ginger-garden-trail-guide.pdf?la=en&hash=37158CC981E1CAB2D7FF1C06E50E47CC4BB818F0.

23. Laura U. Marks, *Touch: Sensuous Theory and Multisensory Media* (Minneapolis: University of Minnesota Press, 2002), 126.

24. Deleuze and Guattari, *Thousand Plateaus*, 22.

25. See Kim Krans, *The Wild Unknown Archetypes Deck and Guidebook* (New York: HarperOne, 2019); and Stephanie Pui-Mun Law and Barbara Moore, *Shadowscapes Tarot and Companion* (Woodbury, MN: Llewellyn Publications, 2010).

26. Margy Thomas, founder of ScholarShape, introduced me to the idea of using tarot and oracle decks for scholarly and creative writing. She refers to the guiding questions I ask of the decks as "cosmic writing prompts." See https://network-1333123.mn.co/courses/5307289/content.

27. Deleuze and Guattari, *Thousand Plateaus*, 21.

28. Inna Semetsky, "Words, Things, Signs: Semiosis and the Memories of the Future," *Synthesis Philosophica* 39.1 (2005): 193–209, 202.

29. Deleuze and Guattari, *Thousand Plateaus*, 9.

PART FOUR

Posthumous Returns

CHAPTER 11

Kathleen Collins . . . Posthumously

ALIX BEESTON

In a lecture to film students at Howard University in 1984, recorded on video by an audience member, the writer and filmmaker Kathleen Collins described her desire to push back against two opposing but parallel tendencies she observed in US film and literature: to romanticize or demonize Black people as "saints" or "sinners." "Neither one has anything to do with reality," she declared, her rising voice and rapidly moving arms conveying the strength of her conviction. "Both are traps to dehumanize you. Both refuse to accept the fact that you live, breathe, and die out of an internal psyche, which is extremely private, extremely idiosyncratic." Collins went on to identify her 1982 dramatic feature *Losing Ground* as an instantiation of this principle. "The premise of the movie," she explained, "is that no one ultimately is going to mythologize my life. No one is going to refuse me the right to explore my experiences of life as normal experiences . . . as human experiences."[1]

Collins's drive to demythologize the lives and experiences of Black people, and particularly Black women, defines her work across diverse mediums and genres, which encompassed two films, numerous short stories and plays, at least one unfinished novel, and at least eight original screenplays.[2] During her lifetime she was known primarily as a playwright, but few of her plays moved beyond the workshop stage. Her two completed films were scarcely shown at their release, and only a handful of her fictional works were published. When Collins died of cancer in 1988, at the young age of forty-six, only a small group of artists, collaborators, and critics knew the full extent of her work.

In recent years, however, that has begun to change. In 2015, *Losing Ground* was remastered and released on the festival circuit and to widespread critical acclaim.³ The following year, in 2016, a collection of Collins's short stories was published as *Whatever Happened to Interracial Love?*, with blurbs from Zadie Smith and Miranda July.⁴ Then, in 2019, a second volume from Collins's archive was published: a miscellany of fiction, letters, plays, and screenplays titled *Notes from a Black Woman's Diary*.⁵ This newly available body of work, as well as Collins's recently accessioned papers in the Schomburg Center for Research in Black Culture at the New York Public Library, has been secured largely through the efforts of her daughter, Nina Lorez Collins.

In studying Kathleen Collins's film work and writing over the past few years, I've often returned to a description of her directorial practices made by the art historian Alvia Wardlaw during a 2020 discussion of *Losing Ground*. Wardlaw, who played a bit part in the film, said that watching Collins on the set—working closely with the actors, making decisions moment by moment, and arguing passionately with her cinematographer Ronald K. Gray—was like seeing "creativity in motion."⁶ Yet if the object lesson of Collins's archive is her extraordinary vitality and productivity, which find a corollary in the richly drawn Black women characters that populate many of her stories, plays, scripts, and films, that lesson is laced with pathos. For it is Collins's absence that is made paradoxically present in the repository of textual materials that survived her death. Because of her relative obscurity during her lifetime and her early death, most of Collins's viewers and readers receive her work out of time, in a gesture of posthumous return.⁷ Her films and writings are cast as textual remains disinterred from the 1960s, 1970s, and 1980s—the time in which they were conceived but not, for the most part, viewed or read.

I said that Collins is *survived* by or in her archive, and this phrasing aligns with the logic of (re)surfacing that (re)animates the dissemination and reception of her work since the mid-2010s. The notion of Collins as doubly lost—in her historical neglect, including the difficulty she had in getting her plays and screenplays produced or her writings published, and in the tragedy of her death—has functioned in this period as the key subtext to her work, modulating its reception in a minor key. In this, the posthumous Collins offers an important case study in the determining and overdetermining frame of "recovery" in the contemporary global markets for women's film, literature, and art. The publicity materials and cultural commentary related to Collins's work have positioned her as a forgotten artist undergoing a much-delayed recovery.[8] Though there is truth in this framing, it also reflects the dominance of certain narrative tropes used to conceptualize the historical functions and fortunes of art by women, perhaps especially women of color, in contemporary culture.

In the context of popular feminist discourse—at a moment of "heightened awareness of the gendered obstacles women face in their creative and professional lives," as Joanna Scutts writes—it's as if virtually every woman artist and author in history is now available to us as a discovery: she who once was lost is now found by a culture that claims itself redemptive, even heroic, in the gesture.[9] The contemporary emplacement of women artists comes to assume, or require, a previous displacement; remembrance serves as a function of neglect rather than (only) its redress. As the art historian Kristen Frederickson points out, the "recovery" of women artists within feminist scholarship and popular cultures "is desirable, a shift from oblivion to recognition, yet the term implies prior disease as well."[10] A recovered artist's work is afforded value and freighted with melancholy—or it is freighted with melancholy to be afforded value.

My concern in this chapter is not to assess the appropriateness of the recovery framework with respect to Collins but rather to explore its effects on the dissemination and reception of her work, particularly as that work is marked by various forms of incompletion. Writing of African American literature after its heyday of canon-formation from the 1970s through the 1990s (which is also a formative period for the feminist canon, and the period during which Collins was working), Kinohi Nishikawa observes that those who discover "lost" works in the archives of Black writers today are forced to "play the hoary game of recognition—that is, to address the significance of whatever they find in the archive to a satellite of predetermined, canon-conserving interests."[11] For Nishikawa, recovery work in this vein is highly instrumentalized, acting to authorize rather than to challenge our assumptions about the past. As it "substitutes an ideology of textual presence ('Look what I found!') for an assessment of archival absence ('Why is this here at all?')," this archival practice obscures the discovered work's place in history: the conditions through which it got made as well as those through which it got lost.[12]

In Collins's case, an emphasis on recovery simultaneously overplays her lostness and underplays the capaciousness and reach of her work—

in its abundance and variety as well as in its political and aesthetic aims. In the first instance, Collins was an active member of the Black film and theater scene in New York and a popular educator at City College, and though her films weren't widely distributed until 2015, in the intervening years they were viewed in libraries by students, fans, and scholars of Black independent film, discussed in journals such as *Black Film Review*, and taught and studied by Black film scholars and teachers from precious 16mm prints procured from the DC-based Mypheduh Films, operated by the Ethiopian filmmaker Haile Gerima.[13] It's crucial to acknowledge that Collins wasn't neglected by or unknown to everyone and, in turn, that it's often specifically for white programmers, audiences, and scholars (including myself) that her work constitutes a discovery.

In the second instance, the imperatives of recovery work by audiences and scholars are pitched at a slant to Collins's project of representation. As Hayley O'Malley has shown, Collins's work across mediums is shaped by the question of how one can "explore the collective identity of black women while also accounting for the particularized experiences of individual subjects."[14] These ends are served, O'Malley suggests, by the autobiographical basis of Collins's work. However, in its posthumous circulation, Collins's work is shot through with a memorializing impulse that converts the traces of her experiences into fleeting, tantalizing glimpses of a woman lost and (un)found. Against Collins's efforts to draw from the well of her life to demythologize herself and her subjects, many members of her audience after her death—what I'm calling her posthumous audience—are bound precisely to mythologize Collins in her absence, or at the least to reduce her to her characters, compensating for her loss by multiplying her ghosts.

In engaging the limitations of recovery in this chapter, I offer the first scholarly analysis of Collins's "A Summer Diary," a screenplay revised to its extant form in the early 1980s. Never produced by Collins, "A Summer Diary" is the only screenplay apart from the script of *Losing Ground* published in *Notes from a Black Woman's Diary*. Its logic of inclusion in the 2019 volume reflects and reproduces the circulation of Collins's unfinished film work under the sign of its posthumousness. Locating "A Summer Diary" in Collins's oeuvre, and drawing on archival research and oral histories, this chapter sketches out alternative and more pragmatic means for approaching Collins's film work, including in its essential, but not uncomplicated or straightforward, relation to her lived experience. I seek to clear space beyond the associations of deficiency, lack, or failure that cling to the posthumous Collins—as well as to the screenplay as a form, in its status as precursory to the film proper—by conceptualizing "A Summer Diary" from *within* the archive of Collins's creative practice.

That archive evinces her iterative labor across numerous projects in various states of (in)completion. It demonstrates the fruitfulness of her lifelong practice of creative work and collaboration, which drives toward ideas and ideals of completion but which doesn't, I suggest, ultimately depend on them. The generative or propagative qualities of Collins's work can be seen to allegorize those of the screenplay as a textual form: a conditional, functional object that is also a radically open-ended one, a site of resonant possibility—much like the unfinished film as it is theorized across *Incomplete*. Indeed, the screenplay's status as potentially completable in one form or many is indicated directly in the fact that, after the publication of *Notes from a Black Woman's Diary*, Issa Rae Productions optioned the script, with Nina Collins attached as a producer and the novelist Angela Flournoy as screenwriter.

In making this argument, I don't mean to deny the valences of loss, abortiveness, and dislocation that inhere in Collins's life and work, nor the grief that encircles her memory. Her posthumous return, real if unevenly experienced, hinges on and is structured by the devoted and strategic labor—conservationist, editorial, promotional, and more beside—of her daughter, Nina, who was only a teenager when her mother died. I also don't mean to ignore how Collins's experiences of disappointment and frustration as a filmmaker relate to a more diffuse, heterogeneous phenomenon—namely the marginal and obscured place of Black women in US film history, especially in terms of the privileged genre of the feature film. The vexed progress of Collins's incomplete film projects seems to foreshadow the fates of several Black women directors whose careers coincided with or followed hers, including Ayoka Chenzira, Julie Dash, Zeinabu irene Davis, and Darnell Martin, several of whom Collins actively mentored. After the mini-boom in Black-led films in the late 1980s and early 1990s, many Black filmmakers found themselves consigned to what's known colloquially as "Director's Jail," essentially a kind of exile from the major studios that prevented them from making further feature films. Even so, I believe that Collins's unfinished films, as much as her finished ones, should be understood first and foremost as an expression of creativity in motion, to return to Wardlaw's phrase. For this reason, this chapter adapts one of Collins's writerly idiosyncrasies—her penchant for ellipses—into a theory not for the regrettable, unbridgeable chasm between her and us but instead for the vital rhythms and continuities of her work-in-process.[15]

. . .

The covers of Collins's posthumous publications, *Notes from a Black Woman's Diary* and *Whatever Happened to Interracial Love?*, carry works by the multimedia artist Lorna Simpson (see, for example, figure 11.1).[16] The images are drawn from an ongoing series, begun in 2010, in which Simpson repurposes found materials from midcentury Black women's magazines such as *Ebony* and *Jet* into collage and watercolor works on paper. Most of these images feature the faces and upper bodies of Black women cut from advertisements, their hair rendered as vibrant masses of paint. Simpson combines without collapsing effects of control and spontaneity; her works turn on the contrast between the precise, contained placement of the figures and the energy and movement conveyed by the watercolors—the latter also interacting with the flatness of the magazine materials. With its saturated, gemlike colors, Simpson's paint has a just-set quality that holds in suspense its moment of creation: a cloud billowing to sky or the sky itself cracked to storm.

Simpson's works reinterpret the charged "medium" of Black women's hair, in Kobena Mercer's terms, which has served historically as "the most visible stigmata of blackness, second only to skin."[17] Black women's hair is a "field of relations" between flesh and representation in which Blackness and femininity are contested.[18] The poet and essayist Elizabeth Alexander provides the introductions to both Collins's *Whatever Happened to Interracial Love?* and a 2018 volume of Simpson's collages. In the latter, Alexander describes how Simpson depicts "Black women's heads of hair [as] galaxies unto themselves, solar systems, moonscapes, volcanic interiors. The hair she paints has a mind of its own. It is sinuous and cloudy and fully alive."[19] Figuring Black women's hair as an ecstatic overflow, Simpson's images manifest the complexity of Black women's interior lives. As they are incorporated in the design of *Notes from a Black Woman's Diary* and *Whatever Happened to Interracial Love?*, they illustrate Collins's major theme, which is, as Collins says in the Howard lecture, the private and idiosyncratic psyches of Black women.

Not only this, but the curving, feathering paint also opaquely traces the creative labor that defines the two books. Or perhaps I should say it *washes* or *glosses* that labor. After all, the blots and trails of black paint in "Back of Yellow Dress," the 2013 work that graces *Notes from a*

FIGURE 11.1 Cover of the first edition of *Notes from a Black Woman's Diary* (Ecco/HarperCollins, 2019), featuring Lorna Simpson, "Back of Yellow Dress," from the *Ebony* series (2013). Image courtesy of Ecco/HarperCollins.

Black Woman's Diary, resemble the spilled ink of the writer's pen, such that the paint seems to encode Collins's writerly and directorial labor—and, secondarily, the editorial labor of her daughter Nina Collins. In fact, Simpson's multiyear collage series is an extended act of memory and return, the terms of which resonate with Nina's project in constructing *Whatever Happened to Interracial Love?* and *Notes from a Black Woman's Diary.* Simpson has explained that her collage series emerged from her discovery of a stash of old *Ebony* magazines that belonged to her grandmother, and that in working with these materials, which recall her grandmother's experience, she feels herself taken back to her childhood.[20] Nina describes her work sorting, preserving, and disseminating her mother's papers in a similar way. "In those first weeks after we buried her," Nina wrote of her mother in 2016, "I filled an old steamer trunk with every scrap of paper I could find among my mother's things." The heavy trunk went with her through several moves until, in 2006, she found herself amid a difficult divorce that seemed to shadow and repeat the breakdown of her parents' relationship when she was a child. It was then that Nina decided to open Kathleen's papers. "In order to find a path out of the mess I'd made," Nina realized, "I needed to wrestle with the history that had shaped me."[21]

Nina's narration of this process affiliates her with Simpson: one woman's stash of magazines is another woman's paper-stuffed trunk. Indeed, in an interview in June 2021, Nina informed me that she and Simpson are long-term friends, having once attended the same high school—though it was not Nina but rather the publisher's design team that initially suggested Simpson's work for the covers.[22] The connection between the two women, implicit in the design of the books, might be seen to identify Simpson—whose career in conceptual photography began in the final few years of Collins's life—as another of Kathleen Collins's daughters, establishing between them a relationship of succession and exchange that simulates the mother–daughter relationship from which the book materializes. As the tragedy of Collins's death yields to legacy, brokered belatedly through posthumous publication, *Notes from a Black Woman's Diary* alludes to an interartistic tradition in which Collins is located—the continuation of which heightens, rather than minimizes, an appreciation of her untimely loss. It also plays to a generational or genealogical model of African American women's writing and art. With Simpson as her surrogate and sister, Nina searches for her mother's garden, looking for Kathleen much as Alice Walker once looked for Zora Neale Hurston—posing as Hurston's niece, seeking Hurston's unmarked grave in an overgrown, snake-infested cemetery.[23] (As it happens, a one-act play included in *Notes from a Black Woman's Diary*, "Begin the Beguine," pays tribute to Hurston as "a real vagabond for ... dreams.")[24]

In keeping with this daughter's quest, *Notes from a Black Woman's Diary* maintains its proximity to Collins's unpublished writing and ephemera, the scraps of paper that fill Nina's suitcase. As John Bryant writes in his thesis on the fluidity of all texts, the absence of the author is apparent in draft manuscripts not as "an undifferentiated blank" but as "layerings of absence," traceable in the vacillations and competitions of its revisions.[25] A pristine version of the handwritten and typescript manuscripts from which it is derived, *Notes* is nevertheless aligned to these asperous, irregular surfaces. Named after not one but two genres associated with contingency, extemporaneity, and dailiness—these are *notes* from a Black woman's *diary*—the book presents Collins's writings as a continuum of abbreviated, allusive textual forms, with selections from the letters and diaries inserted between sections comprising fictional works. Nina Collins confirmed to me her desire for *Notes from a Black Woman's Diary* to serve as a "loose compilation" of materials—one that would help to give a balanced sense of Collins's heterogeneous body of work.[26]

In my view, the selection, admixture, and framing of these materials registers in particular the centrality of Collins's lived experience to her creative work. A stronger way of putting this would be to say that *Notes from a Black Woman's Diary,* in preserving the connotations of the notebook or diary, effectively transmutes Collin's creative work into a form of "private" utterance. Of course, as scholars have suggested, the diary as a genre straddles private and public discourse; the act of writing a diary almost always holds an audience in prospect, whether in the present or the future—and all the more when the author is a professional writer, for whom, as Lynn Bloom argues, "there are no private writings."[27] Still, to read someone's diary—or, equally, someone's draft materials—without their knowledge is to scrutinize "something that was not intended for your eyes," as Carolyn Steedman writes of the experience of reading in the archive.[28] From either direction—posited as a series of diary entries or as a series of provisional notes—*Notes from a Black Woman's Diary* produces illicit practices of reading, elegiac and sensual in their effects.

Certainly for Collins the boundary between life and art was porous. However, as *Notes from a Black Woman's Diary* promises—or affects— access to its absent author, it arguably underemphasizes the degree of fictive artfulness in the writings it collects. Collins seems to signal her awareness of the communicative force, the *un*privacy, of her writing in "The Reading," one of the plays published in the volume, when a character states: "One never talks out loud without wishing for an audience."[29] In making this point—a metatextual point about the author herself rather than about the character she narrates—I am giving in precisely to the temptation of *Notes,* namely to receive it as ventriloquy, a voice thrown by Collins not merely across a room but across the decades, addressing us as the audience she (mostly) didn't have in life.

Formed in pursuit of Collins, *Notes from a Black Woman's Diary* privileges just these kinds of texts: texts that seem to refer in an immediate way to, and hence to offer a momentary connection with, Collins's life; or else texts that seem to uncannily presage, and hence amplify the tragedy of, her death.

This structure is especially evident in the book's incorporation of materials ostensibly from Collins's diary. In an early section that bears the same name as the larger volume, a series of dated entries tend toward pithy, aphoristic statements about the fleetingness of life and the certainty of loss. Dated 12 December 1971: "It is our disappointments that mold us the most." Dated 23 January 1972: "The extremism, the tenacity in me. I will hold on. I *will* to hold on. Until all the cards have been played."[30] Dated 24 February: "A woman's life is a terrible thing." And 18 March: "Whatever we have to live through we have to live through until its time is up."[31] Although this section integrates reflexive passages in which Collins expands on particular entries, no contextual information is given to indicate how it was composed. In that absence, the entries read as though they've been directly lifted from the pages of Collins's diary.[32] Their sense of spontaneity and ingenuousness is even more striking for how the content of Collins's prose corresponds to the air of fatality that surrounds her after her death.

But in truth, this section was published—in a more tightly edited form—as an article titled "Notes From a Diary" in the September 1976 issue of the Black women's magazine *Essence*.[33] And the version in *Essence* is far more equivocal than *Notes from a Black Woman's Diary* about the nonfictional status of Collins's writing. Across a double-page spread, the material is laid out as if on a writing table, placed in columns alongside a fountain pen and an open-faced notebook scrawled with handwriting (figure 11.2). This carefully crafted and dramatically lit visual design, in concert with the clear typographical distinction between Collins's metacommentary of the practice of keeping a diary and the entries themselves, strongly implies that she is adopting the diary form as a literary conceit (if not only as a conceit). In comparison to this version, the ending of the diary section in *Notes from a Black Woman's Diary,* in which Collins describes herself meeting "a dead end, when things get muddy and my mind races overboard into a fog," hits a far more mournful note—tethered, as it is, to Collins's life and loss.[34]

Presented in the 2019 volume as an "authentic" and eerily prescient record of Collins's thoughts and experiences, this section of prose pressurizes our reading of the screenplay "A Summer Diary," which appears

FIGURE 11.2 Page spread from Kathleen Collins, "Notes From a Diary," *Essence* (1 September 1976). Reproduced from the Women's Magazine Archive and used by permission of the Estate of Kathleen Collins.

in the final section of *Notes from a Black Woman's Diary* alongside the script of *Losing Ground*. One of Collins's most mature and well-developed screenplays, "A Summer Diary" follows two women, Caroline and Liliane, who decide to live together with their children at a country home for a summer in the wake of crises in their lives: the suicide of Liliane's husband, Giles, and the breakdown of Caroline's marriage to Rafael. It's unclear when this script was first written, though Nina Collins believes it was around 1974 or 1975.[35] Kathleen Collins's correspondence indicates that she was revising it in the early months of 1981, at the same time as she was finalizing the script for *Losing Ground*. She sent what she called the "just finished" script of "A Summer Diary" to her friend, the actress Carole Cole, on 9 April 1981, asking Cole to consider playing the lead role of Sara—the character later renamed to Caroline, presumably because the name Sara was used for *Losing Ground*'s protagonist. Collins seems to have intended to make "A Summer Diary" after *Losing Ground*, and in her letter to Cole she states that she and the producer Cheryl Hill were seeking to raise money for its production.[36]

By the time she was working on *Losing Ground* and "A Summer Diary" interchangeably in 1981, Collins was drawing on over a decade of screenwriting experience, and the latter script reflects her regular practice of repurposing and reimagining motifs, plots, dialogue, and characters across projects. Indeed, both *Losing Ground* and "A Summer Diary" overtly thematize the imbricated relations of Collins's different projects. Whereas *Losing Ground* includes the conceit of a film-within-a-film, in which the Black intellectual Sara performs in a student's film, "A Summer Diary" features the rehearsals and staging of a theater performance that is an abridged version of "Portrait of Katherine," a musical play Collins devised with the composer Michael Minard in the late 1970s. At once, the character of Caroline, a set designer, serves as a reincarnation of a woman named Lillie from Collins's first screenplay, "Women, Sisters, and Friends" (1971). When Caroline makes an intricate stage piece for the theater production from broken shards of painted glass, she essentially repeats the actions of Lillie in the mysterious final scene of the earlier screenplay. "Women, Sisters, and Friends" was itself expanded and revised as a different screenplay in 1975, "The Story of Three Colored Ladies"—and the linkages and reverberations only continue.

Drawing together various strands from many years of work, and representing a relatively complete shooting script, "A Summer Diary" is an intuitive choice for inclusion in *Notes from a Black Woman's Diary*. Equally, however, its focus on grieving and loss interacts with the other materials in the volume, notably the diary sections, in further clarifying an intimate relation between Collins and her fictional characters. In *Losing Ground* we see Sara teaching a college class and writing an academic paper on the philosophical question of ecstasy; in "A Summer Diary," Caroline (née Sara) likewise serves as a substitute for Collins, through her creative practice in the theater as well as her own acts of writing. But what Caroline writes is the diary of the screenplay's title. At intervals we cut to her as she sits at her desk late at night, working through her separation from her husband. Near the screenplay's midpoint, the directions call for a close-up of her hands as she writes of her friend Liliane: "In some perverse way I envy her Giles's death . . . the relief of it . . . if it is over between us, what a clean thing death would be . . . freeing . . . rather than all the shoddy stuff that comes with separation and divorce . . . "[37]

Caroline's diary entries, notated in the script as a series of fragmentary phrases, are to be delivered in voiceover. In fact, Caroline's voice is often heard off-screen. In the early scenes she offers context in voiceover to explain her and Liliane's circumstances; across the script, Collins's camera cues call for shots from Caroline's point-of-view: the camera is to hold, for instance, on a mid-close-up of Liliane as the two women talk, such that Caroline's voice comes from off-camera; and several times we hear but do not see her as she tends to a child in another room or makes a phone call down the hall. Aligned in these ways with the functions of a narrator, Caroline is situated with Collins behind the camera (and "behind" the script). The diary is, then, a kind of screenplay—and the screenplay is a kind of diary.

These modes of writing are most fully conflated in a conversation between Caroline and Liliane that occurs immediately before the scene in which Caroline admits to her envy of her friend. Realizing that Caroline is "still hoping" that her marriage might be salvaged, Liliane remarks, "I was just thinking . . . death marks the end of living in the future, there's nothing left to hope for . . . "[38] The reader of *Notes from a Black Woman's Diary* receives these words as an echo from the diary section of the book, in which a single-line entry reads: "Death marks the end of living in the future." This entry is glossed in one of Collins's reflexive asides, which locates the genesis of the phrase in a conversation with "a very close friend whose husband committed suicide":

> When she tried to explain to me what was the hardest thing for her to face, she came to see that it was the absence of any future possibilities. With separation, divorce, or a long absence, there is still hope that the future will bring a reconciliation or a return. But death marks the end of living in the future. And this, for her, was almost unbearable.[39]

Even accounting for the literary uses of the diary form in this earlier section, it's obvious that aspects of the narrative and dialogue of "A Summer Diary" emerge out of Collins's friendship with this woman. In an informal document giving a record of the editing process of *Notes from a Black Woman's Diary*, included with Collins's papers at the Schomburg Center, Nina Collins recalls a time in the early 1970s when her parents' marriage was falling apart and the family, without Nina's father, went to live with her mother's "best friend Bluette [Lambelet Dammond], recently widowed by her younger lover Hank, who shot himself in the head and left her with three kids."[40]

There's therefore no doubt that the screenplay is inspired by experiences in Collins's life. Yet given how tightly Collins's life and work are welded together in the framing and construction of *Notes*—the screenplay as a kind of diary, the book itself as a kind of memorial—moments such as this raise the specter not of Bluette's lover Hank but rather of Collins herself: she whose posthumous recovery will never surpass her death's finality, its curtailing of the future in which we read her work.

Notes from a Black Woman's Diary, in other words, repeatedly lifts us into metatextual meditations on the circumstances of the work's delayed publication and posthumous reception. The issue is not merely that the fictive worlds—and the carefully individuated, if serially rendered, women characters—depicted in "A Summer Diary" and the other writings are eclipsed by the figure of Collins. It is the way that this eclipsing figure is drawn: as a writer bound for, and portending, death; as a woman who turns away from us, like the woman in Simpson's "Back of Yellow Dress." On the cover of *Notes*, the orientation of the woman in yellow concisely illustrates Collins's poignant inaccessibility to her posthumous audience. Even as her work is seen to deliver her (back) to us, she remains apart from us. Turned away, her face unseen, she is inscrutable, departicularized, and somehow unreal. And to this extent she is, as Collins might say, mythological.

As I suggested earlier, Simpson's collages symbolize Collins's writerly and directorial labor as well as her daughter's editorial and reconstructive work. In "A Summer Diary," Caroline takes on the same double duty. When her father dies toward the end of the screenplay, Caroline stands in for Nina, and all those Collins left behind at her death, as she phrases her father's death as an act of retreat and refusal: "Why now Daddy . . . why did you walk away from me now . . . "[41] In earlier scenes Caroline dreams of her mother, who died when she was a teenager; the night before her father's death, we enter with her into a dream in which he digs a hole in his garden, placing in it a photograph of Caroline's mother and filling it with flowers. The midshot of disembodied hands turning over the ground is repeated almost verbatim a couple of scenes later, only now Caroline takes her father's place: "An urn is placed in the hole, then covered over. The hands begin to plant flowers on top and around it . . . "[42]

Because of Caroline's role in focalizing and structuring the film's narrative—especially through her diary writing, linked with Collins's own writing—the effect of this duplicated action is to afford Caroline a strange sense of agency in relation to the events of the screenplay. It's as if Caroline's dream doesn't simply predict the future, the unfolding scenes, but somehow determines it. It's as if she designs the future like a set. This radical expansion of Caroline's creative work in the theater is, again, commensurate with the work of the screenwriter, Kathleen Collins, who also lays out spaces and scenes—and with the work of her editor, Nina Collins, who does the same.

. . .

How then might we, those of us who constitute Kathleen Collins's posthumous audience, avoid mythologizing her in the aftermath of her death? How might we better account for the historical conditions and affordances of her (in)complete work, acknowledging its interface with her life—the fact of its mixed, personal–professional dimensions, from inspiration to production—but also wresting it from the shroud of its posthumousness? In searching out less overdetermined and more pragmatic means of engaging Collins and her work here, I want to contemplate one of what Nina Collins refers to as her mother's "stylistic quirks," specifically her frequent use of ellipses, which Nina preserves in *Notes from a Black Woman's Diary*.[43]

In "A Summer Diary," ellipses are put to work in variable ways, all of which subtend the screenplay's structure of brief vignettes, shuttling between domestic scenes, dream sequences, and immersive episodes at rehearsals for the play nested in the film. They signal the pauses that give dialogue its tempo, like musical notation, but they also register absent information, as when we hear only Caroline's side of a phone conversation, or mark transitions between scenes and locations, becoming aligned with the filmic cut and its abbreviations of place and time.[44] Referring to something (or someone) missing, something that isn't there, the *dot dot dots* that puncture the pages might be seen to track the distance between the screenplay and the complete film to which it does not (yet) correlate—or between Collins and her posthumous audience. But a typographic sign of deferral and disconnection might just as well be formulated as one of duration and ongoingness: the ellipsis as a figure of life's—and art's—continuity, its flow of moments and encounters. After all, the ellipsis is a "dotological" form, in Jennifer DeVere Brody's terms, which enacts "repetition and difference"—a description that is especially apposite in Collins's case, as one project cedes to another via her adaptive and collaborative labor.[45]

In "A Summer Diary," we see Caroline working intensively over the backdrop for the theater production, "crying, sweating, as if driven by some strong, internal need," as the script's directions explain. Breaking off pieces of colored glass and gluing them on a board, she likens the design in voiceover to "a personal collage I was pulling out of my stomach."[46]

The symbolism is overt, reflecting Caroline's psychological distress and her lack of clarity about herself or her future. But what's operative in the screenplay is less the brittleness and fragmentation of the glass than its metamorphosis into a dazzling, vivid work of art, the achievement of which is crucial to Caroline's arc, which follows her efforts "to make sense of loss and change" and "to come to grips with herself." I'm quoting from the synopsis Collins affixed to her shooting script, not reproduced in *Notes from a Black Woman's Diary*, in which she also invites a comparison between her film work and Caroline's art when she explains how "the mosaic of the film widens" through events in the script.[47] In the refracted light of a stained-glass collage, the ellipsis is a sign of how things or people come together, how they cohere or connect, at least as much as how they fall apart or disperse. Hence the ellipsis needn't be a gesture reaching—plaintive, wistful—to a future that cannot meet it; it gives the shape of a beat, a cadence of creativity in motion, keeping the time of the present before it becomes the past, the screenplay before it becomes unproduced, unfinished.

So let me posit anew the questions with which I began this section. How might we inhabit the ellipses of "A Summer Diary," reading them in line with its drama of psychological and material transformation—and in line with Collins's lifelong efforts to show, as she wrote in the screenplay's synopsis, "that Black women have a multi-layered life whose psychological and emotional fabric reaches far beneath the external condition of race"?[48] How might we inhabit the ellipsis that *is* "A Summer Diary," the screenplay being a text that opens itself to other texts—speculatively and, in the case of Collins's iterative practice, quite literally?

One way to inhabit these ellipses is to approach the screenplay as an industrial and relational document poured over in table readings, scribbled on by a range of creative agents, and discussed in letters, planning meetings, and funding bids. By situating the screenplay in relation to other extant archival materials and oral histories, we can reconstruct the working relationships that produced it, including Collins's relationships with actors, which were central to her screenwriting and directorial practice (figure 11.3). In recent interviews Seret Scott, who played Sara in *Losing Ground,* has testified to the bond of personal understanding and creative reciprocity that developed between her and Collins after they met in late 1969 or early 1970 at the Westbeth artists' house in New York City. In a 2015 conversation with Amy Heller and Dennis Doros, Scott recalled how Collins would write a new script or

FIGURE 11.3 Louis Draper, Kathleen Collins working with Seret Scott and Duane Jones on the set of *Losing Ground* (1981). Image courtesy of Milestone Films and the Estate of Kathleen Collins.

play and then have Scott read it for her, sitting around the kitchen table.[49] When I interviewed her in May 2021, Scott described to me Collins's habit of writing "for" people she knew; rarely did she devise a significant role without someone in mind to perform it, such that her relationships were in a practical sense the ground of her fiction.[50] At once, Collins was highly responsive to the interpretative instincts of actors. As an actress, Scott always found Collins's writing challenging, and in retrospect she believes that Collins cultivated in her a generative, improvisatory "confusion." She recalled: "I wasn't saying the words, the dialogue, the lines with a certainty about anything—I was always exploring it."[51]

Scott told me that during the shooting of *Losing Ground,* Collins often didn't offer much by way of upfront, verbal direction for a given scene, and sometimes after a take she would let Scott know that her performance hadn't aligned with what she had imagined for the character. "She would say something like, 'Sara is angrier than that, but when I heard you just now, I think we're not going to go there yet so it will be more explosive later on.'" Such moments probably reflected Collins's relative inexperience as a filmmaker, and if she'd been able to continue making films her style of direction would have developed in difficult-to-predict ways. Nevertheless, she proved herself willing to learn from and with the actors and to calibrate her vision for the work based on their performances. Scott took this lesson to heart in later years when she transitioned to working as a theater director, learning how to recognize that an actor has, in her words, "made the next step with that character," giving them space to determine a role's trajectory and trusting in collaboration as a formative process.[52]

For her part, Collins found in Scott "*my* actress," as she put it in a beautiful letter marking the end of production on *Losing Ground* in August 1981. She told Scott:

> You're right that in many ways I wrote this script for you, as a friend. But the performance you gave *back*—perhaps in part as *your* gift to me—is of such a fine and subtle quality that [. . .] it transcended friendship and placed us squarely in the professional arena as actress to director, director to actress. That is a lovely feeling, perhaps the loveliest of the whole movie, for it inspires a deep wish to do another movie with you and explore a new character with you, and something tells me that the spirits that guide both yours and my rather complex existence have that in mind for us. And that the next time, the "opposition" will be less fierce or at least "different."[53]

It seems likely that when Collins wrote of her desire to work with Scott on another film, she was hoping that that film would be "A Summer Diary." Collins's correspondence during this period with another friend, Carole Cole, indicates that she was reserving for Scott the part of Vera, the wife of the director of Caroline's theater production, while she had Cole pegged to play the role of Caroline. The letters between Collins and Cole cast "A Summer Diary" as an event that catalyzed constructive, flexible, and exploratory work, even if it didn't eventuate as a feature film. It appears that Collins shared several incarnations of the script with Cole in the early 1980s. In a letter Cole wrote to Collins in February 1983 or perhaps 1984, queries about Collins's family life appear alongside detailed notes on the script, including about the relative merits of earlier and newer drafts and about casting decisions (she suggested her sister, the singer Natalie Cole, for one of the parts in the musical play in the film). The letter demonstrates Carole Cole's significant personal investment in the project as well as the high regard in which she holds her friend. "Thanks for being *so* alive!" she wrote in a postscript—repeating back to Collins a turn of phrase that is itself repeated in *Losing Ground,* when Sara is praised by her students for being "so alive" and "lively."[54]

Inextricable from their shared creative labor, Collins's relationships of mutuality and affirmation with Scott and Cole, among others, cast her in a new guise. Collins was no stranger to pain and rejection, and she was unafraid of allowing such experiences to inform her writing and films. Moreover, in many cases—including "A Summer Diary"— her iterative mode of working responded to professional setbacks. The repurposing of scenes and songs from the play "Portrait of Katherine" for the play-within-the-film in "A Summer Diary" came about in the wake of the play's failure to be produced, which was, according to another of Collins's close collaborators, the musician Michael Minard, a source of deep frustration and embarrassment for Collins. As Minard told me in a June 2021 interview, this makes "A Summer Diary" a perfect example of her ability, in his wonderful phrase, "to turn lemons into lemon chiffon cake."[55] Thus Collins's creative practice, however much it was forged in disappointment or difficulty, wasn't dominated by the connotations of failure and loss we may be tempted to import to her today. Instead, her working practices demonstrated her resilience and adaptability: her alchemic transformation of lemons as of broken shards of glass.

This new guise is also a new orientation. Collins isn't to be conjured merely as a composite of her characters, a figure withdrawing from her posthumous audience in layered shadows, but rather as a filmmaker and writer in productive relation with others, working side by side. Instead of turning away from us, she turns toward her collaborators, and they turn toward her, in the tensile unfolding of her historical moment. "A Summer Diary" emerges as an important site of this passionate creative activity, existing not in a paucity of materials—the absent, complete feature film—but in material abundance: the various versions of the screenplay; letters, ephemera, and oral histories related to this work; and materials from the other film, theater, and literary projects that it developed out of and alongside over many years.

"A Summer Diary" is, for instance, the actions of Lillie in Collins's first screenplay, "Women, Sisters, and Friends," a character who not only makes a glass collage while "sweating feverishly" but who also tends to speak to herself as if "she were having a conversation with someone," much as in a voiceover.[56] "A Summer Diary" is also the gorgeous studio recordings of the songs Michael Minard composed for the play "Portrait of Katherine," made in connection with the workshopping of the play at the Public Theater in New York City in 1978, in which the R&B singer Jenny Burton performs Katherine's show-stopping ballads "It Might Be" and "Mr. J."[57] Had "A Summer Diary" been produced by Collins, Katherine would have morphed into Marie, the lead character in the theater production whose songs touch Caroline deeply and express her pain. As I listen to Burton's rich alto dipping and soaring above moody synths, I hear the lyrics printed in the screenplay come alive, Collins's stage directions enacted, and I come to dwell, momentarily, in the (in)complete film: "Marie onstage, singing her heart out . . . "[58]

And "A Summer Diary"—conceived in tandem with *Losing Ground*, set to include Collins's favorite actress—is also Seret Scott's masterful performance in that completed feature. Like Burton's renditions of Katherine's songs, which were to become Marie's songs and finally Caroline's songs, Scott's performance in *Losing Ground* plays out a woman's ennui and inner turmoil delicately but surely: in the tempests that gather in her eyes; in her tight smiles and slightly jutting chin; in the way she repeatedly throws up her lithe, muscular arms in a gesture of frustration and release; and in her nervous energy, cut by sudden bursts of uninhibited laughter.

At the climax of *Losing Ground*, we see Sara performing in the student's film, which is a reinterpretation of the ballad of Frankie and Johnny, an African American folk song based on a historical incident in which a woman killed her husband after she discovered he was having an affair.[59] Across the film the camera often shows Sara from a measured distance, or else in profile, notably in the scenes when she's working on her research and writing; here, however, the camera holds on her in a steady midshot. Like that of "A Summer Diary," the ending of *Losing Ground* is ambiguous, but it's clear that Sara—as much as Caroline—has been altered by the film's events, arriving at a point of awareness, reckoning, and change. With gun in hand, her hair loose and whipping in the wind ("sinuous and cloudy and fully alive"), Sara's acting is infused with her deeply felt anger at her husband's infidelity and indifference. Though she is powerfully absorbed in the performance, the director still cues her movements from off-screen: "Take your time . . . and when it feels right, blow him away."

With this knowing reference to Collins's directorial labor—and her working relationship with Scott—the gun goes off, and we cut, finally, to Sara's anguished face in close-up (figure 11.4). Sara is, as I said earlier, a surrogate for Collins, and as she almost (but not quite) looks directly into the camera, it's almost (but not quite) as if Collins herself

FIGURE 11.4 In the final scene of Kathleen Collins's *Losing Ground* (1982), Sara (Seret Scott) performs the role of Frankie in the student's film. Frame enlargement courtesy of Milestone Films.

looks at us. Yet if in this moment we think we can see Collins's face rather than her turned back, hers is an act of self-disclosure made, as ever, through levels of fictive artfulness—just as Sara's psychological reality is rendered most forcefully in the staging of the tale of Frankie and Johnny. In any case, the final shot of *Losing Ground* holds in suspense—in ellipsis—the feature film that was meant to follow it but didn't: the performance Scott would have given alongside Cole; the work Collins would have done with these actresses and her other collaborators; the meanings the completed "A Summer Diary" would have had for us as viewers, fans, and scholars; and the meanings it still may have, in the hands of Issa Rae and her production team or some other filmmakers. In the instant before the screen turns to black, *Losing Ground* broaches a film uncompleted but not exactly unmade . . .

NOTES

This chapter could not have been written without the expert assistance of archivists at the Schomburg Center for Research in Black Culture at the New York

Public Library, especially Bridgett Pride, who provided me with access to digitized materials throughout the COVID-19 pandemic; nor without the generosity of Nina Collins, Seret Scott, Michael Minard, Amy Heller, and Dennis Doros, each of whom spoke with me at length about Collins's life and work. In addition, Hayley O'Malley, Samantha N. Sheppard, Karen Redrobe, Katherine Fusco, Pardis Dabashi, Stefan Solomon, and my colleagues at the Modern and Contemporary Workshop at Cardiff University gave helpful feedback on early drafts.

1. Milestone Films have made available the video recording of the lecture, https://vimeo.com/203379245. The text of the lecture is reproduced in Kathleen Collins, "I Refuse to Create Mythological Characters," ed. Stoffel Debuysere, *Sabzian* (2 June 2021), www.sabzian.be/text/i-refuse-to-create-mythological-characters.

2. I focus on Collins's screenwriting in this chapter. Seven of the screenplays are held in the Kathleen Collins Papers in the Schomburg Center for Research in Black Culture at the New York Public Library (Sc MG 938, hereafter "Collins Papers"): "Women, Sisters, and Friends" (1971; Box 10, Folder 4), "Lila" (1974; Box 10, Folder 5), "The Story of Three Colored Ladies" (1975; Box 10, Folder 6), "Losing Ground" (1980; Box 8, Folder 8), "A Summer Diary" (1982; Box 8, Folder 7), "But Then She's Madame Flor" (1986; Box 10, Folder 7), and "Conversations with Julie" (1988; Box 10, Folders 8–9). Collins also wrote "Only the Sky is Free" in 1985, a screenplay based on the life of Bessie Coleman, the first Black woman aviator, which is held in the Camille Billops and James V. Hatch Papers at the Stuart A. Rose Manuscript, Archives, and Rare Book Library, Emory University (MC 927, Box 7, Folder 9). Hayley O'Malley discusses this last script in "Art on Her Mind: The Making of Kathleen Collins's Cinema of Interiority," *Black Camera: An International Film Journal* 10.2 (2019): 80–103, 80–81, as does L. H. Stallings (alongside "Women, Sisters, and Friends" and "But Then She's Madame Flor") in *The Afterlives of Kathleen Collins: A Black Woman Filmmaker's Search for New Life* (Bloomington: Indiana University Press, 2021), 53–88.

3. The restoration and DVD release of *Losing Ground,* alongside Collins's earlier short film *The Cruz Brothers and Miss Malloy,* was undertaken in 2015 by Nina Lorez Collins in collaboration with Amy Heller and Dennis Doros at Milestone Film and Video, based on an original negative courtesy of the Yale Film Study Center Archive. Further references to *Losing Ground* refer to this DVD. In 2022 the Yale Film Archive received funding from the Film Foundation for a major new restoration of *Losing Ground*: a new 4K digital master from the original 16mm film elements, a new 35mm film negative, and a restored 35mm optical soundtrack.

4. Kathleen Collins, *Whatever Happened to Interracial Love?,* ed. Nina Lorez Collins (New York: Ecco/HarperCollins; London: Granta Books, 2016).

5. Kathleen Collins, *Notes from a Black Woman's Diary: Selected Works of Kathleen Collins,* ed. Nina Lorez Collins (New York: Ecco/HarperCollins, 2019).

6. See "Kathleen Collins's Film *Losing Ground*: A Conversation with Alvia J. Wardlaw, Ronald K. Gray, and Marian Luntz," virtual event hosted by the Museum of Fine Arts, Houston, August 2020, https://vimeo.com/446483487/fc4b238009.

7. I echo here Stallings, who writes that Collins was "out of time and place" in a different sense, "because she made films that questioned notions of realism and forms of humanism" (*Afterlives of Kathleen Collins*, 5). Whereas Stallings innovates a queer rendition of Collins's "afterlives," I deploy the frame of *posthumousness* and *recovery* due to my interest in the publication and reception history of Collins's work since the mid-2010s.

8. The back cover of *Whatever Happened* bears a blurb by Zadie Smith that reads: "To be this good and yet to be ignored is shameful, but her recovery is a great piece of luck, for us." A prominent example of the recovery discourse is Richard Brody, "Lost and Found," *New Yorker* (30 January 2015), www.newyorker.com/magazine/2015/02/09/lost-found. Danielle A. Jackson gives a critical reflection of Collins's recovery in "A Quest That's Just Begun," *Lapham's Quarterly* (9 September 2019), www.laphamsquarterly.org/roundtable/quest-thats-just-begun.

9. Joanna Scutts, "How We Find—and Lose—Women Writers," *Literary Hub* (13 May 2019), https://lithub.com/joanna-scutts-on-how-we-find-and-lose-women-writers/. The film programmer Daniella Shreir describes this state of affairs in terms of a "fetishism of the unfindable, of the 'forgotten'" in an interview with Caitlin Quinlan, "Transforming Limitation," *MAP* 61 (April 2021), https://mapmagazine.co.uk/transforming-limitation. For an earlier critique of the "lost-and-found" paradigm in feminist film history, see Jane M. Gaines, "Film History and the Two Presents of Feminist Film Theory," *Cinema Journal* 14.1 (2004): 113–19.

10. Kristen Frederickson, "Introduction: Histories, Silences, Stories," in *Singular Women: Writing the Artist*, ed. Frederickson and Sarah E. Webb (Los Angeles: University of California Press, 2003), 1–19, 3.

11. Kinohi Nishikawa, "The Archive on Its Own: Black Politics, Independent Publishing, and 'The Negotiations,'" *MELUS* 40.3 (2015): 176–201, 176.

12. Nishikawa, "Archive on Its Own," 177.

13. These claims are supported by the scholarly essays that discuss *Losing Ground* prior to its 2015 rerelease (notably L. H. Stallings, "'Redemptive Softness': Interiority, Intellect, and Black Women's Ecstasy in Kathleen Collins's *Losing Ground*," *Black Camera* 2.2 [2011]: 47–62), as well as the following evidence. In a letter to Collins dated 1 October 1982, the actress Carole Cole describes her experience viewing *Losing Ground* in the screening room of the Louis B. Mayer Library, Los Angeles, where the projectionist stated that "this was about the third time he [had] screened it" (Collins Papers, Box 3, Folder 2). In addition, in the commentary track to *Losing Ground*, Terri Francis describes how she taught the film from a 16mm print, after she was introduced to it as a graduate student by Jacqueline Najuma Stewart.

14. O'Malley, "Art on Her Mind," 85.

15. My citations of Collins retain her ellipses. Where I need to signal an excision I make in quoting from her writing, I use a bracketed ellipsis.

16. Lorna Simpson's work appears on the hardback and paperback copies of the first US and UK editions of these books. Granta's 2018 UK paperback of *Whatever Happened* features a black-and-white photograph of a young Black woman by Raphael Albert.

17. Kobena Mercer, "Black Hair/Style Politics," in *Welcome to the Jungle: New Positions in Black Cultural Studies* (New York: Routledge, 1994), 97–130, 100, 102.

18. Mercer, "Black Hair/Style Politics," 128.

19. Elizabeth Alexander, "Introduction: Of the Black and Boisterous Hair," in *Lorna Simpson Collages,* by Lorna Simpson (San Francisco, CA: Chronicle Books, 2018), n.p.

20. Joseph Akel and Lorna Simpson, "A Photographic Memory: In the Studio with Lorna Simpson," *The Paris Review* (15 October 2015), www.theparisreview.org/blog/2015/10/15/a-photographic-memory-in-the-studio-with-lorna-simpson/.

21. Nina Lorez Collins, "How Kathleen Collins's Daughter Kept Her Late Mother's Career Alive," *Vogue* (5 September 2016), www.vogue.com/article/kathleen-collins-filmmaker-career-daughter-nina-lorez-collins.

22. Nina Lorez Collins, interview with Alix Beeston, 2 June 2021.

23. See Alice Walker, "Looking for Zora," in *In Search of Our Mothers' Gardens: Womanist Prose* (Orlando, FL: Harcourt, 1983), 93–118.

24. Collins, *Notes from a Black Woman's Diary,* 177.

25. John Bryant, *The Fluid Text: A Theory of Revision and Editing for Book and Screen* (Ann Arbor: University of Michigan Press, 2002), 12.

26. Nina Collins, interview with Beeston.

27. Lynn Z. Bloom, "'I Write for Myself and Strangers': Private Diaries as Public Documents," in *Inscribing the Daily: Critical Essays on Women's Diaries,* ed. Suzanne L. Bunkers and Cynthia A. Huff (Amherst: University of Massachusetts Press, 1996), 23–37, 24.

28. Carolyn Steedman, *Dust* (Manchester, UK: Manchester University Press, 2001), 150.

29. Collins, *Notes from a Black Woman's Diary,* 159.

30. Collins, *Notes from a Black Woman's Diary,* 44, 46.

31. Collins, *Notes from a Black Woman's Diary,* 47.

32. Farah Jasmine Griffin makes a similar point about the lack of contextualization given to the materials in *Notes from a Black Woman's Diary* in "Remaking the Everyday: The Interior Worlds of Kathleen Collins's Fiction and Film," *The Nation* (15 July 2019), www.thenation.com/article/archive/kathleen-collins-book-review/.

33. See Kathleen Collins, "Notes From a Diary," *Essence* (1 September 1976): 48–49, 124–25. My thanks to Hayley O'Malley for drawing my attention to this publication.

34. Collins, *Notes from a Black Woman's Diary,* 54.

35. Nina Collins, interview with Beeston. Seret Scott had in her possession an undated, different version of the screenplay, which I believe represents an earlier draft; it is held in the Kathleen Collins Scripts Collection at the Schomburg Center (Sc MG 948), Box 1, Folder 4.

36. Kathleen Collins, letter to Carole Cole, 9 April 1981, in Collins Papers, Box 3, Folder 2.

37. Collins, *Notes from a Black Woman's Diary,* 264.

38. Collins, *Notes from a Black Woman's Diary,* 263.

39. Collins, *Notes from a Black Woman's Diary*, 43.

40. Nina Lorez Collins, typescript of writing for *Notes from a Black Woman's Diary* (2007), in Collins Papers, Box 11, Folder 4.

41. Collins, *Notes from a Black Woman's Diary*, 322.

42. Collins, *Notes from a Black Woman's Diary*, 319.

43. Nina Lorez Collins, "Editor's Note," in Collins, *Notes from a Black Woman's Diary*, xii.

44. The notion of the editorial cut as an ellipsis is supported by Collins's pedagogical practice, which stressed how film could be used as a (punctuated) language. As Collins explained in a 1982 interview with Phyllis R. Klotman at Indiana University, included as a special feature in *Losing Ground*: "In almost every class I teach I start them with a basic vocabulary. Just as if you were learning English, you have to learn where to place a comma and a parentheses and where to put a paragraph."

45. Jennifer DeVere Brody, *Punctuation: Art, Politics, and Play* (Durham, NC: Duke University Press, 2008), 65.

46. Collins, *Notes from a Black Woman's Diary*, 280.

47. Collins, "Summer Diary," 2.

48. Collins, "Summer Diary," 3.

49. Seret Scott, interview with Amy Heller and Dennis Doros, 2015, in *Losing Ground*.

50. Seret Scott, interview with Alix Beeston, 24 May 2021.

51. Scott, interview with Heller and Doros.

52. Scott, interview with Beeston.

53. Kathleen Collins, letter to Seret Scott, 3 August 1981, Collins Papers, Box 3, Folder 9.

54. Carole Cole, letter to Kathleen Collins, 27 February 1983 or 1984 (postmark partially illegible), Collins Papers, Box 3, Folder 2.

55. Michael Minard, interview with Alix Beeston, 1 June 2021. The events in question occurred in New York City in 1978. As Minard recalls, after "Portrait of Katherine" was workshopped at the Public Theater (under the alternative title "Almost Music"), Collins was led to believe there was support to stage the play at this venue from Joseph Papp and Gail Merrifield Papp. Collins also understood that Lynne Meadow wanted to stage it at Manhattan Theater Club. In each case, this support was retracted or disavowed.

56. Collins, "Women, Sisters, and Friends," 53, 5.

57. Minard, interview with Beeston. Minard kindly provided me with access to the recordings, which, at the time of writing, were in the process of being accessioned as part of the Collins Papers.

58. Collins, *Notes from a Black Woman's Diary*, 272.

59. See Cecil Brown, "Frankie and Albert/Johnny," in *Encyclopedia of African American Popular Culture*, ed. Jessie Carney Smith (Santa Barbara, CA: Greenwood, 2011), 542–46.

CHAPTER 12

The Fierce, Unfinishable, Feminist Legacies of Helen Hill

KAREN REDROBE

REFRAMING HELEN HILL

Helen Hill (1970–2007) was a white experimental animator/filmmaker and social justice activist from Columbia, South Carolina. Her filmmaking gained national attention after an intruder entered her New Orleans home and murdered her on 4 January 2007. The intruder also shot Hill's husband, Paul Gailiunas, several times as he protected the couple's son, Francis Pop, but both Gailiunas and Francis Pop survived. Hill's was one of a spate of murders in the city that included the shooting of the twenty-five-year-old drummer of the Hot 9 brass band, Dinerral Shavers, on 28 December 2006.[1] These two fatal shootings, along with many others, remain unsolved.

Hill began making animated films as a fifth-grade public school student at a moment when, in the wake of desegregation's implementation, the majority of white students began attending "Segregation Academies," and segregation became an underlying concern of Hill's final project.[2] After graduating from Harvard University in 1992, Hill relocated to New Orleans with her classmate Gailiunas. She completed a master of fine arts at CalArts in 1995 and moved to Nova Scotia as Gailiunas finished his medical degree. There, she made films and taught animation before returning to Mid-City, New Orleans, in 2001. While Gailiunas founded an affordable health-care clinic, Hill taught animation through the New Orleans Video Access Center and cofounded the

New Orleans Film Collective.³ The couple was involved in a variety of community activist projects, including Food Not Bombs, sometimes attending protests against racist and gentrifying local government policies, and the meetings of an antiracism group, "Eracism."⁴ They participated fully in the creative landscape of New Orleans: in Mardi Gras and Halloween, punk anarchism, and a DIY culture that Dan Streible describes as "rooted in anti-corporate grassroots practice."⁵

Historian Tiya Miles, who participated in a feminist collective with Hill and was one of her roommates at Harvard, suggests that Hill's mode of being resonated with the opening line of one of Hill's poems, "It is as though . . . ," for she was always experimenting with self-presentation through dressing up.⁶ Hill was a dedicated thrifter and trash-picker, and on Mardi Gras morning of 2001, she discovered a fairytale–like pile of more than a hundred discarded handmade dresses. She took them home to wash and repair. As a filmmaker who prized the handmade, collage, and vibrant colors, Hill felt a kinship with the maker and decided to make the dressmaker the subject of her most ambitious project, which would ultimately be released as *The Florestine Collection*. By talking to neighbors who lived near the trash pile, Hill learned that the dressmaker was Ms. Florestine Kinchen, also known as "Sister Kinchen," an African American deaconess who had recently passed away on 12 February 2001, at the age of ninety-five, shortly before Mardi Gras.⁷

Although Hill often completed films within a year or less, *The Florestine Collection* was unusual in that she began it in 2001 and worked on it over the next six years through a series of life-changing events, including childbirth, a year's displacement from her New Orleans home to Columbia, South Carolina, after Hurricane Katrina, and a return to New Orleans in August 2006. In 2004 she received a Rockefeller Foundation fellowship to support the project. The grant application provides some sense of how Hill thought about the dresses: "I washed the dresses and tried them on. They fit. They not only fit, but in a very particular way that I prefer: loose on top and cut just above the knees. And they were quirky and lovely, just my style."⁸ But Hill's film was only one part of a much more elaborate community-based project that set the dresses in motion in a variety of ways: "Besides entering the film in festivals, I hope the film will begin a community project. I love the dresses and I wear them, but I do not need all 100. I plan to display all the dresses at the New Orleans premiere screening and give many of them away." She continued,

> The Dress Project would be a small grant to encourage people to create their own unique wardrobe. Four people would be chosen from anonymous applications. Each person would receive a small grant (one hundred dollars) to help cover costs. Each member of The Dress Project would design and make 4 everyday outfits and one holiday outfit.... This project would honor Ms. Kinchen and bring back the lost art of hand sewn dresses. People would be chosen based on a unique vision and a desire to design their own everyday clothes, regardless of sewing ability. The group would be encouraged to help each other out, in a sewing bee atmosphere.[9]

Handmade zines would also tell the story of the dresses, to "inspire dress clubs in other cities."[10]

This project had set out to explore interracial dynamics between women across generations, media, and class via attention to objects both discarded and found. But the film and its paracinematic offshoots acquired new dimensions after the breaking of the levees on 29 August 2005 caused approximately fifteen hundred deaths and rendered millions homeless, with the city's Black population disproportionately affected as a result of many factors, including environmental racism.[11] Watching these events on television in Columbia catalyzed in Hill a deepening commitment to include the interracial and spatial dynamics of New Orleans in the "Florestine Project," a term I use to differentiate Hill's expansive work-in-progress from the film that was ultimately released under the title *The Florestine Collection*. The grant's emphasis on project completion spurred Hill on in spite of the flood having destroyed or damaged much of her work as well as Florestine's dresses, which she recovered, cleaned, and repaired a second time. One of several "postKatrina *Florestine Collection*" scripts begins: "But I still had a grant and with it, an obligation to make my finish an animated film."[12]

Over the objections of her family, Hill insisted upon returning to New Orleans on the one-year anniversary of Katrina, wanting to participate in the city's rebuilding and develop the community-based work that the Florestine Project was becoming. Hill's murder terminated her six-year-long attempt to find ethical ways to learn about, animate, and uplift Florestine's interior life and creative practice, and to do so in comparison with these aspects of Hill's own life and in dialogue with both Florestine's community and the interracial history of the city. Although the exceptional conditions of Hill's death have led to exceptional critical framings of her work, situating Hill and this project more firmly within film history and the history of New Orleans clarifies the evolving nature of *The Florestine Collection*. This chapter seeks to establish the multiple traditions in which Hill was working and to understand some of the ways they interacted with each other.

Daphne Brooks describes New Orleans as a place where codes of belonging, of the local and the foreign, have historically intersected with racial codes in complex and changing ways that shaped the city's creative and performative dynamics.[13] Brooks explores how New Orleans's risky performances that crossed lines of race and gender, at times overlapping with the "racial misogyny" of minstrelsy, nevertheless created a unique "polyvalence" of cultural categories at the very moment when these categories were being fixed and helped to generate the city's "fleeting opportunities for self-defining agency."[14] Hill was fascinated by New Orleans's performance cultures and the Florestine Project, in particular, was a site-specific endeavor. She explicitly reflected in script drafts on her sense of being "at home in" but not *from* New Orleans and of feeling "in exile" from the city after Katrina.

Here I build on the work of Anne Major, who has astutely highlighted how Hill's murder produced a discourse of rosy, romantic, and beatific sweetness derived from the colors, hearts, and humor permeating Hill's films at the expense of other important critical conversations.[15] For example, Streible, while acknowledging the influence of the American avant-garde, argues that the qualities John Canemaker describes as "angelic sensuality, sensitivity, and fun" also set Hill apart from that movement's tendencies toward "conflict, internecine grudges, denunciation, and darkness" and put her in a category of her own.[16] Though offered in the spirit of eulogy, this affectionate language of exception is also gendered, playing to the feminized discourse of the "pretty image" that Katherine Groo discusses in chapter 3 in relation to early film colorists, who were mostly women, and it inhibits Hill's work from taking its rightful place in film history. Sweetness, color, love, and craft are undeniably strong elements of Hill's films, but this chapter emphasizes how these elements interact with her other filmmaking influences, including Lotte Reiniger, New American Cinema, Third Cinema, and experimental feminist filmmaking. Immersion in Hill's archive and attention to her unfinished—and potentially unfinishable—film project reveal a community-based feminist filmmaker grappling with a series of complicated issues, including the histories carried by material objects; her own emplacement as a white woman in histories of racial injustice; and the role of animation in engaging these issues. This shift of frame amplifies, I hope, the rigorous and determined ways Hill used poetry, experimental filmmaking, and animation, however playfully, as infinite tools for cultivating communities that work to reimagine and repair the world in continuous, contestable, and unfolding ways.

THE FLORESTINE COLLECTION: FINISHED OR UNFINISHED?

The Florestine Collection both is and is not a finished film. By one account it was finished posthumously by Gailiunas using the materials that were in process at the time of Hill's death, combining Hill's plans for the film with Gailiunas's elegiac explanation of why he, and not Hill, completed the work. Gailiunas was meticulous in his efforts to keep Florestine in view and to give proper credit to those members of her community who had assisted Hill in her research efforts. But the film inevitably, given the circumstances, becomes primarily a work of mourning for Hill, even as Gailiunas sustains a sense of another incomplete film haunting the one he completed. As I discussed the film's completion with Hill's wide circle of family and friends, it emerged that the film component of the Florestine Project was incomplete at the time of Hill's murder in part because Hill had been experiencing a "block" on the film and had rethought it more than once.[17] Over several months, as Gailiunas and Hill's mother, Becky Lewis, made different parts of Hill's paper and audio archive gradually available to me, my sense of "the film" has kept evolving throughout the writing process.

According to IMDb, the film was completed in 2011, but already in 2008 an announcement for an exhibition of Florestine's dresses at the McKissick Museum in Columbia, South Carolina, had promised "a premiere viewing of the finished film in conjunction with the exhibition."[18] The finish line for this film, then, is a moving target, for complex and generative reasons. An opening title describes the work as "A film by Helen Hill completed by Paul Gailiunas." Yet in the final minutes Gailiunas states: "And that is how the story must end: an incomplete film and an incomplete life." Gailiunas's production notes confirm both his and others' ambivalence about how to deal with the entwined issues of authorship and endings. A working draft of the script from 14 September 2007 ponders the issue of authorship and toys with the possibility of "A Film by Helen and Paul."[19] Elsewhere, after a screening for friends, Gailiunas notes, "Randall: Maybe contextualize earlier (at the beginning) so that people understand that film is finishing Helen's film (maybe in titles)," and later adds, "(A film started by Helen Hill Completed by Paul Gailiunas?)."[20] Gailiunas wonders in the same notebook on 18 June 2009: "Do I need to say it is 'incomplete' as I wrote? Film feels complete."

Hill's post-Katrina scribbles confirm that she was fully reimagining her film: "Get going." "Rewrite script and storyboard/index cards." "Draw draw draw ink paint." For me, studying *The Florestine Collection* neither as the finished film that it ended up being nor as a projection of the work it would have been, but instead as the overlapping, messy fragments of an interrupted work-in-progress that increasingly deemphasized the final work in favor of building relationships with the people involved, has meant disrupting scholarly business as usual. It has involved moving my attention from a finished film to an uncatalogued archive and still-developing conversations; finding a method for writing about a film that hovers in a confusing grammatical space; and holding on to what that grammar might reveal while attempting to get a sense of the order of things as Hill's work changed and developed over time. It has meant writing in relation to an evolving object of study (the films, the dresses, the Dress Project, and the posthumous exhibition), and to an evolving cast of both "filmmakers" (Helen, Paul, friends and family, and Florestine's community) and "missing" people (Florestine, the filmmakers who shot the film's found footage and the people in it, the family members who didn't respond to Hill's invitations, and Hill herself).

The shifts and conversations that have defined this project have left me with questions I am still pondering: Who has the right to throw things away or take up discarded objects? What is the difference between a person's refusal to participate in historical research and the resistance given to knowledge by a material object discarded for unknown reasons? What kinds of making and thinking do missing people and found objects provoke? For whom is this work when it is written or made?[21] Gailiunas's ending directly addresses these issues when he knots together the technical skills of the animator, the needlewoman, and the doctor through the language of stitching, leaving love for the broad community created by the film in the place of the irreparable: "Now I want to resurrect her, to mend her wounds, to take care of her, but I can't. So instead I have taken the frayed and flooded pieces that remain of the Florestine Collection and I have stitched them together with love, for you, for her."

The temporal location of my object of study is close-to-but-not what linguists describe as the *past irrealis,* associated with counterfactual historiographic modes, where temporal pastness and speculative realities encounter each other and can be confused.[22] Janine Marchessault rightly suggests that *The Florestine Collection* resists the concept of "Katrina time," which binds New Orleans inescapably to social collapse, through its emphasis on Hill and Gailiunas's persistent investment in collective being. I agree with this assessment, not least because the very idea of "collection" is etymologically rooted in the act of bringing together.[23] But Marchessault also sees *The Florestine Collection* as "profoundly place bound" in contrast to the "anywhere" and "fantasmatic escape and reverie" of Hill's earlier film, *Mouseholes* (1999), in which animation seems to resurrect Hill's deceased grandfather, Poppy, as an animated mouse. Here, I would depart from Marchessault's reading. Hill had included *Mouseholes* as a work sample with her Rockefeller grant application, noting, "The tone and mood of *Mouseholes* is most similar (of my films) to the mood I imagine for *the Florestine Collection*. Both tell a personal story."[24] Activating a variety of media formats, Hill was beginning to explore across multiple times and spaces the relation among lived personal experience, local and transnational histories, the continuously provisional project of living in community, and experimental film.

As is clear from Alix Beeston's discussion of Kathleen Collins's unproduced screenplays in chapter 11, the unfinished film's archive raises the question of how fairly to account for work a filmmaker has not released into the world and that is spread across a variety of provisional and nondefinitive plans in the form of scripts, notes, letters, shot material, storyboards, sketches, unedited audio recordings, plans for collaboration, and so on.[25] This issue becomes particularly charged in the neoliberal academic landscape described by Imani Perry, where a scholar's professional success can be linked to taking strictly positive or negative positions on complicated objects or issues, leading to oversimplification of complicated questions.[26] The dresses that Hill found, took home, cleaned, twice repaired, and animated are what Perry calls "vexy things," hovering between recovered histories and appropriated objects and therefore demanding "nuanced deliberation."[27]

Unfinished works are useful because the uncertainty surrounding them suspends hasty critical judgments and creates more patient spaces for sifting through nonlinear material and engaging in thought and dialogue. "Incomplete" scholarly projects like the ones in this book also respond to Lisa Cartwright's call to pay more attention to the making of a film when trying to understand "what media work offers in the way of emotional satisfaction."[28] And perhaps attending to unfinished films might also enrich how scholars approach finished films and humanistic work more generally. Hill's archive suggests a filmmaking philosophy, expressed more in practice than in words, that rejects the territorialization of film and challenges scholars to reflect on how film history is shaped by the prioritization of completed objects, and who or what gets lost in the process.

UNFINISHING AS FEMINIST, DECOLONIZING METHOD

Unfinishing is an essential quality of Hill's late work, drawing critical attention to the imagined duration of a filmmaker's relationship with the subjects she films. It had also always been part of her ongoing film activism. Hill's day-to-day anticapitalist work involved enabling the community-rooted cultivation of individual creativity, often through an informal collective process of viewing and discussing unfinished films. She clearly understood film-finishing in a deliberately provocative way, closely bound up with the feminist art and practice of making clothes, sharing food, and chatting.[29] In a hand-drawn flyer from 1999, made shortly before she moved from Nova Scotia to New Orleans and republished in her collectively authored handbook for DIY filmmakers, *Recipes for Disaster* (2005), Hill announces: "all ladies film bee! For chemically driven handicrafters (includes free tea) . . . like a sewing bee, you see" (figure 12.1).[30]

A description of the first session, held in Halifax, Canada, in March 2000, explains: "You buy and shoot one cartridge of black and white film TRI-X super-8 film. . . . A subject of clothes (fashion, sewing, knitting, fabric, accessories) would help us with the program description, but your own inspired themes are more important so feel free to film anything." A more general description follows:

> Each person will shoot one roll of film, then bring it to my house where we will handprocess it in the bathtub. Then, on a Sunday afternoon, we will all be together for the film bee, for tea, cookies, biscuits, cucumber sandwiches, chit chat and to finish our films, by painting colours onto them, scratching away on them, and bleaching out the parts we don't want. We'll keep screening them to check our progress. For example, you could bleach away a shot and then draw little yellow stars on the clear leader. The idea is to finish the film by manipulating it rather than by editing it.[31]

This event—which recalls Miranda July's efforts in the mid-1990s in Portland, Oregon, discussed by Alix Beeston and Stefan Solomon in the introduction, to generate in women "a thirst for the unmade that is also a thirst for making"—demonstrates Hill's long-standing interest in the relation between sewing and filmmaking, and her sense that sewing provided a preexisting model for her project of building creative feminist communities. Though *The Florestine Collection* foregrounds particular

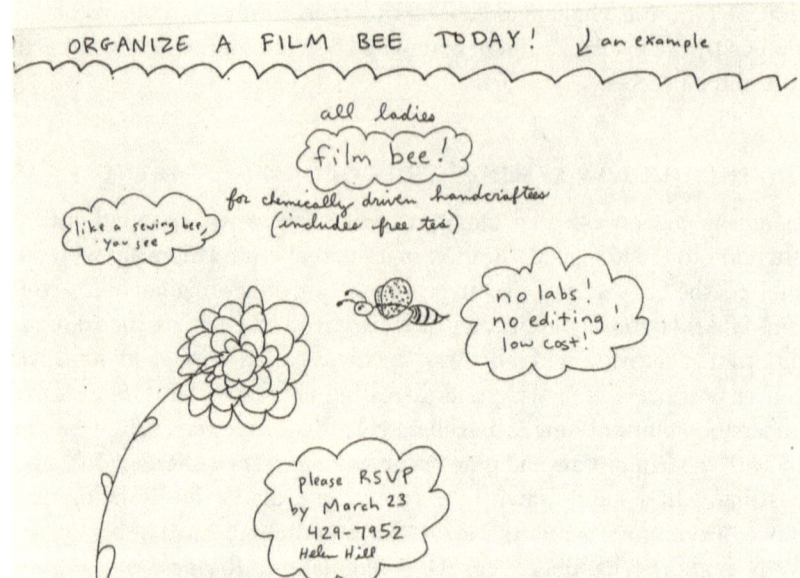

A film bee! Instructions

The 2000 Splice This! Super-8 Film Festival in Toronto will be held June 23-25. They have asked me to put together a show of brand new Halifax films. I decided to ask y'all to be part of a ladies film bee theme program. Each person will shoot one roll of film, then bring it to my house where we will handprocess it in the bathtub. Then, on a Sunday afternoon, we will all be together for the film bee, for tea, cookies, biscuits, cucumber sandwiches, chit chat and to finish our films, by painting colours onto them, scratching away on them, and bleaching out the parts we don't want. We'll keep screening them to check our progress. For example, you could bleach away a shot and then draw little yellow stars on the clear leader. The idea is to finish the film by manipulating it rather than by editing it. There will be inks, markers, scratching tools, and bleach for everyone to share.

How it works
MARCH
You buy and shoot one cartridge of black and white film TRI-X super-8 film (at Reid Sweet, Carshand-Mosher or for $17.55 at the NSCAD bookstore). Call me if you need to borrow my easy-to-use super-8 camera.
A subject theme of clothes (fashion, sewing, knitting, fabric, accessories) would help us with the program description, but your own inspired themes are more important, so feel free to film anything.

APRIL 13 OR 14 OR 15
You come to my house for one hour on one of these days and we'll handprocess your film together. We'll all chip in some money for the chemicals and art supplies (less than $20 each).

SUNDAY, APRIL 16 noon to four
The Film Bee!!!

MAY
All the films will be mailed to the festival along with your two sentence description of your film. Because this is a requested show, your film has already been accepted into the festival! Congratulations!

FIGURE 12.1 Helen Hill, hand-drawn flyer from 1999, republished in *Recipes for Disaster*, 2nd edition (2005), www.filmlabs.org/docs/recipes_for_disaster_hill.pdf. All images in this chapter are found in the Helen Hill Archive at the home of Becky and Kevin Lewis, Columbia, South Carolina, and are reproduced with permission from Becky Lewis.

parallels between a seamstress and a filmmaker, including her own practice of making movable puppet joints with a needle and thread, this flier situates those parallels within a larger feminist experimental tradition that is simultaneously creative and destructive, and includes recursive filmmakers like Peggy Ahwesh and Leslie Thornton, and films such as Annabel Nicolson's *Reel Time* (1973), in which Nicolson runs a film strip loop through her sewing machine and projector until it breaks.[32]

Reel Time claims filmmaking as belonging to the sphere of women's work while also highlighting the potential violence of feminized labor. Prefiguring Hill, Nicolson refuses the often-unrecognized, feminized, and skill-intensive labor of stitching images into commodified completion, ending her work instead by shredding it.[33] Furthermore, as Tiya Miles makes clear, sewing not only unites women but also divides them along lines of race and class through infrastructures of servitude and enslavement within racial capitalism. Hill participates in this feminist tradition of radically questioning without wholly discarding the shared, complicated feminized experiences out of which collective futures might be built. As Hill wrestled with the value of film finishing and commodifiable products through a language of crafting, she simultaneously reflected on the differing reasons why people hand-make clothes.[34]

The film bee's description juxtaposes Hill's colorful animation and the stark black-and-white palette of hand-processed live-action film. Filmmaker and Hill's former student Heather Harkins explains that Hill was attracted to black-and-white Super 8 both because she could easily hand-process it at home, and because it allowed her to experiment with extreme contrasts through variable exposures.[35] Hill's black cut-out silhouettes function, among other things, as an aesthetic bridge between animated and live-action worlds. Working across a variety of forms, Hill prioritizes being together in real time for continuous screenings of incomplete work, as well as bleaching, scratching, and painting—actions likely to reopen, remake, or undo images that may have seemed "done," both chemically and conceptually.

Elsewhere in Hill's archive, these same "finishing" techniques are advertised as part of the interminable and unforeseeable afterlife possessed by all films, establishing a deliberately open timeline for film objects that makes room for at-times violent transformations and renders all films potentially unfinished. A "Welcome Back To School" flyer made by Hill advertising Nova Scotia College of Art and Design's "experimental animation show" features a fragment of a found film strip (figure 12.2).[36] Its first frame announces: "LET THIS HAPPEN TO

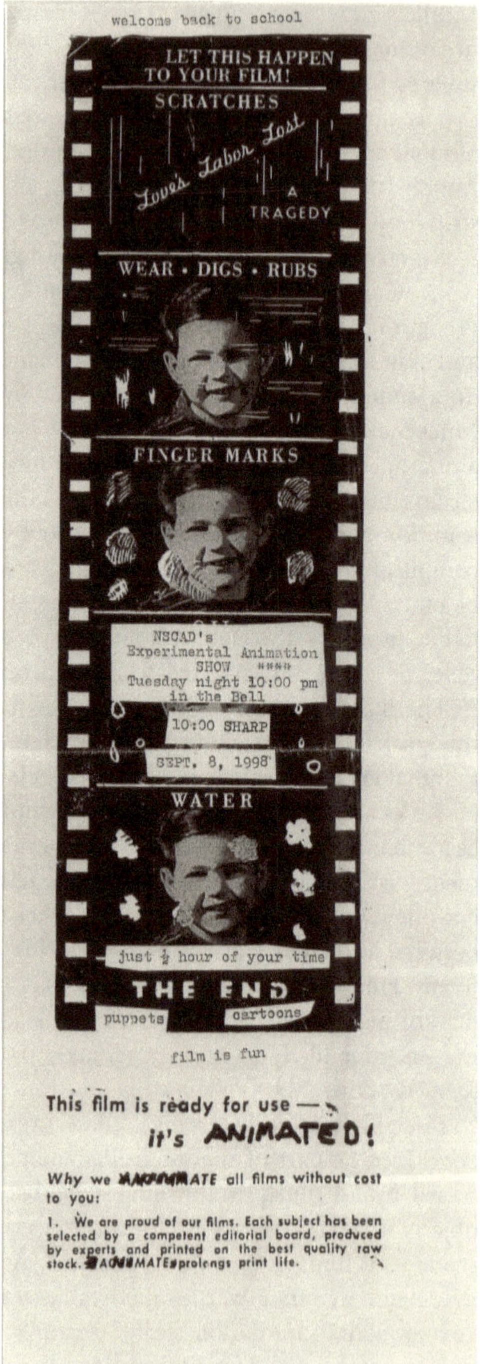

FIGURE 12.2 Helen Hill, "Welcome Back to School" flyer, Nova Scotia College of Art and Design, n.d. Photograph by Becky Lewis.

YOUR FILM!" Film finishing appears as a potentially passive and continuous affair involving submission to the actions of others, including the act of spectatorship. Subsequent frames feature a boy's face overlaid with words such as "SCRATCHES," "WEAR," "DIGS," "RUBS," and "FINGER MARKS," and with the interventions these words describe.

Though clearly traumatized by the damage the flood inflicted on her work, Hill recognized that her family had survived when many others had not. She possessed perspectives on the unforeseen life of images that allowed her to make something of the flood's chemical and indexical inscription of itself on her films.[37] This shaped the Florestine Project's trajectory, which registered not only Hill's own point of view as she filmed her community but also, however abstractly, the water itself that, through structures of environmental racism, had killed, displaced, dispossessed, and traumatized massive numbers of people of color.

After Katrina, Hill's notes use arrows to highlight the words "community" and "unfinished projects." One scrap includes a "What I miss" list: "the kids coming by," "home movies," and "undone projects."[38] These connections resonate strongly with Fernando Solanas and Octavio Getino's embrace of "unfinished" and "unordered" works and their rejection of the "fully rounded film."[39] Like Hill, they call people to show movies in homes to small groups, to despecialize film knowledge through demystified "basic instruction" and to reject films that are "born and die on the screen."[40] They too imagine films as "unfolding" acts, a "detonator or pretext" for activity beyond the film, performing both "destruction and construction."[41] There is, of course, a limit to this comparison. Hill was a committed pacifist, and, although Lewis describes her daughter as having been "fierce," Hill's playful animated films are far from "violent works made with the camera in one hand and a rock in the other."[42] Yet in both cases, experimental filmmaking is unafraid of, and indeed "implies failure," a practice where "the possibility of introducing variations, additions, and changes is unlimited."[43]

Hill had studied Third Cinema in Spring 1994 as a CalArts MFA student, when she took animator and queer activist Margery Brown's "Politics of Culture: Feminist and Third World Animation Theory."[44] Particularly important to Hill was Brown's statement: "People often approach animation with fewer prejudices and with an expectation of being entertained, so it can be an effective medium for social statements."[45] Hill filed the syllabus and notes from this class, often recirculating the course's ideas in conjunction with her production practice. Hill's teaching notes state: "Everyone got in a circle and we passed

FIGURE 12.3 Helen Hill, "Cut Out Puppets" teaching handout illustrating how to sew loose limb joints (n.d.). Photograph by Susan Lenz.

around a needle, spool of thread, watercolor paper, loose limbs and clear tape.... Everybody sewed together a loose limbs hinge to take home.... I went through the handout, explained about storyboards and explained Marge Brown's idea that animation is good for making political statements" (figures 12.3 and 12.4).[46]

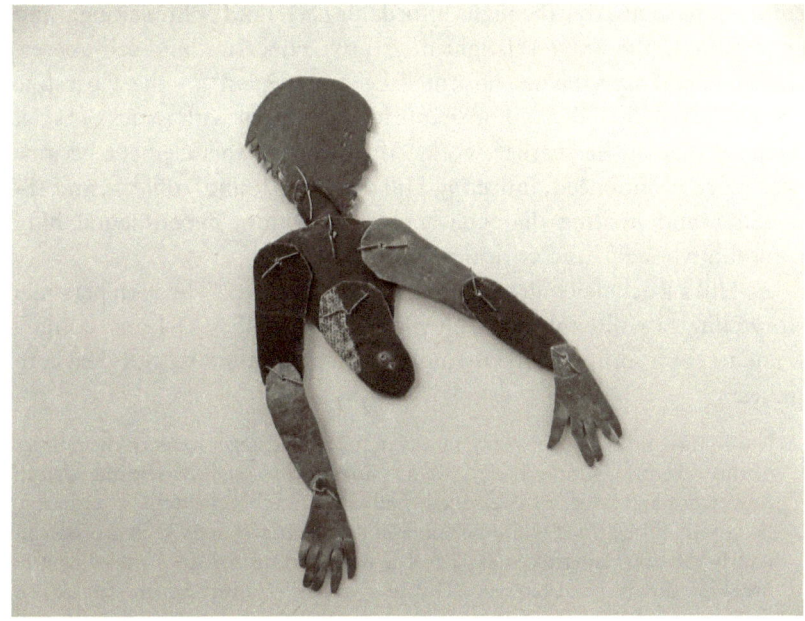

FIGURE 12.4 Helen Hill, cut-out lead puppet (n.d.). Photograph by Susan Lenz.

In her Rockefeller grant application in 2004, Hill displays clarity about her timeline and confidence about finishing films in general and the filmic component of the Florestine Project in particular: "This project is certainly feasible as I have made over a dozen films and understand the process of filmmaking from start to finish. With the financial help and encouragement of a Film and Video Fellowship, I believe I could finish the film within a year."[47] Although this emphasis on finishing may have been strategic at the time of writing, the grant's expectation of completion motivated Hill in the wake of Katrina. Yet new script fragments register the extraordinarily traumatic impact of the hurricane on Hill's family, community, and work-in-progress, which combined with the ordinary challenges of being a new mother. These experiences shifted her priorities toward aspects of the film that had always been more relational and unfolding than teleological.

REFRAMING THE FLORESTINE PROJECT

Hill's peace activism had focused on alleviating hunger; building interracial community in her home; supporting media access and DIY culture, particularly through affordable celluloid filmmaking; and championing the universal right to creative education and self-expression in life. These themes informed her initial plan for the Florestine Project, which included a more explicit engagement with issues of racial inequity than in her earlier work. After Katrina this element became ever more pronounced, inflecting Hill's use of "found" objects and silhouettes and inviting dialogue across animation, experimental film, community media, and critical race studies.

As Hill's Rockefeller grant application explained: "Through personal storytelling, I will explore the themes of race in New Orleans, coming home to the South, and the dwindling of handcrafted work." She continues:

> [Gailiunas and I] are both community activists and eager to learn the politics of this eccentric, southern city. We are surprised to see how seldom African Americans and white people mix socially, even within the activist and artistic communities. As a white person and a community activist in a predominantly African American city, I feel it is important for me to take part in breaking down racial barriers. This film will be one way for me to address these issues. I hope it will inspire dialogue during the process as well as at screenings of the finished film.[48]

Hill had planned to compare Florestine's habit of piecing together "parts of skirts or shirts to make the dresses" to another "find" that occurred during that same Mardi Gras: "a grocery cart full of found films. . . . Many were beautiful home movies, forever lost to families."[49] An elaborate storyboard that Hill gifted her mother shows Hill moving from segment 12, "Found film of small acrobatic girl. Found home movie clips," to segment 13, "Silhouette animation of dresses hanging on line" (figure 12.5).

Yet this storyboard—presumably before Katrina because it makes no reference to the Hurricane, but after February 2005 because it incorporates material that postdates Hill's meeting with Florestine's church community—contains elements that become increasingly important to Hill's post-Katrina plans and complicate the relation between Hill's two discoveries. New Orleans's culture of cross-racial performance appears in segments 3 and 4 through "Silhouette animation of Skull Gangs and other Mardi Gras traditions" and "hands catching Mardi Gras parade throws," including a thrown Zulu coconut. The city's racial segregation and colonial history is visually registered in segment 10, "Maps of New Orleans (returning home to the South)," which features a black-and-white animated globe pasted over a map of the city; and an early script fragment reinforces Hill's awareness of these issues as she narrates a Canadian visitor's surprise at the "kitschy remnants" of slavery to be found in the city's tourist zones.[50] With the exception of segment 22, Hill planned to dedicate the remainder of the film (segments 14–30) to a multidimensional celebration of Florestine's creative life, imagination, and spirit. She was working with no fewer than five aesthetic forms, each form functioning both independently and in relation to the other dimensions of the planned film.

Though the second half of the storyboard does not use found footage, it includes Super 8 documentary footage that Hill had shot and developed. In addition to her early use of footage of Florestine's house and her nephew Dwight Carter in segment 5, Hill planned to include footage of Florestine's grave in segments 25 and 26. Bridging documentary and animated components, Hill planned to add a "scratched-on glimpse of a spirit" and a "scratched-on-film flower" to the hand-processed graveyard shots. Thus she invited viewers to travel between the indexical and drawn traces of Florestine's world, and between the distinct technical skills of Florestine and Hill, both by dissolving the scratched flowers into live-action collage shots of the actual dress fabric and through the analogy she establishes between "found" dresses and films.

In sequences 17 and 18, Hill employed abstract drawn animation to represent Florestine's interior dream space: "Florestine Kinchen falls into a dream of falling flowers" and "Falling flowers fall into dress patterns." Even before Katrina, and in tension with her own analogical paradigm, Hill was working to distinguish Florestine's motivations for fabric reuse from those of Hill's DIY community, as shown in a flood-damaged page where she notes: "reason for DIY ◊ Ms. F.K's reason."[51] Katrina forcefully underscored the political importance of this differentiation. One post-Katrina *Florestine* script fragment begins with reflections on the freedom to move with one's possessions as a racial privilege, giving the emerging film a quite different tone:

> For two long weeks, we watched New Orleans on television. . . . As we watched the people of new oerleans [sic] chanting for help and being called refugees, Paul realized that the evacuation was the ultimate white flight. Many people with the ability left with all their resources, leaving New Orleans to fend for itself. A few days after the hurricane, many of the people left behind tried to walk out of New Orleans, into Jefferson or across the river to Algiers. They were blocked by police, who explained that they didn't want another Superdrome/ a Superdrome problem in Algiers.[52]

Helen Hill   STORYBOARD for The Florestine Collection

1. Rotoscoped drawings of dresses on line. zoom into the one dress filled with color, for title background

2. TITLE: The Florestine Collection Animation: letters appear bit by bit as though being sewn (or perhaps titles to be sewn onto cloth)

3. Silhouette animation of Skull Gangs and other older Mardi Gras traditions

7. Footage of a dress in water, being washed by hand in bucket

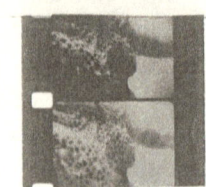
8. Dress being washed dissolves into person in dress, swimming underwater

9. Footage of dresses hanging on cloth line, dissolves into cutout paper silhouette dresses on line

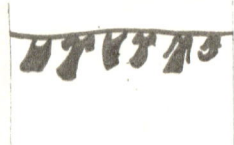
13. Silhouette animation of dresses hanging on line.

14. Silhouette background of Florestine Kinchen's house, at night.

15. Silhouette animation of Florestine Kinchen, sewing her dresses. Flowers seen through window.

19. Patterns dissolve into patterns of cloth used in Florestine Kinchen's dresses.

20. Collage of close-up shots of dress patterns.

21. Drawn animation of dress outlines patterns of dresses change inside outline

25. Footage of Florestine Kinchen's graveyard, with a scratched-on-film glimpse of a spirit.

26. Close-up of Florestine Kinchen's grave marker (it reads **KINCHEN**). Scratched-on-film flower appears.

27. Scratched flower dissolves into flower pattern on dress.

FIGURE 12.5A–E Helen Hill, *The Florestine Collection* storyboard. Gift from Helen Hill to Becky and Kevin Lewis. Photographs by Susan Lenz.

ette animation of hands
Mardi Gras parade throws

5. Footage of Florestine Kinchen's house where the dresses were found

6. Silhouette animation of finding the dresses in the dress pile.

aps of New Orleans
ning home to the South)

11. Finding a home in New Orleans, Footage of small New Orleans house

12. FOUND FILM of small acrobatic girl, Found home movie clips

lose-up of the flowers through window.

17. Florestine Kinchen falls into a dream of falling flowers.

18. Falling flowers form into dress patterns.

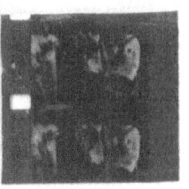
Footage of friends of filmmaker, odeling their own hand made clothes, a local craft fair.

23. Drawn animation of hands: sewing, handprocessing films, doing other handcrafts.

24. Filmmaker meeting with older members of Florestine Kinchen's church. Dress pattern flowers float by window.

ls of the dresses are shown (sleeves).

29. More details of the dress (loops of thread instead of buttonholes).

30. Silhouette animation of Florestine Kinchen in her house.

This new version of the script also contains Hill's notes on an 11 January 2006 episode of NPR's *All Things Considered* in which John Burnett discusses the uneven impact of Katrina on historically Black universities and the displacement of long-standing Black communities by white people after the storm: "deeply African-American city, Xavier Dillard, oldest Black neighborhood, highest proportion of native born Blacks in any Southern city . . . after Katrina, not welcome back, 2/3 Black before the storm, now mostly white." On the other side of this paper, Hill scribbled: "New Orleans was drowning before Katrina . . . corrupt police department, public housing system, public school system." She was determined to go back to the city and her notes suggest a film becoming much more explicitly engaged with racism and the infrastructure of inequality.

Though this evolution could easily have moved the film in the direction of documentary realism, these issues instead seem to have moved Hill more deeply into the abstraction that marks segments 19, 20, 27, 28, and 29, which feature collage shots of the pattern combinations in Florestine's found dresses, as well as close-up montages of her designs' distinctive features, such as loops of thread instead of buttonholes and decorative sleeve and hem edges. After Katrina, Hill developed this element during a California-based residency, suggesting that it continued to matter within the more explicitly political framework of the evolving script. She produced images that Gailiunas describes as "Very nice moving dress collage—faster and faster with chaos."[53] Though this footage documents the beauty and color of Florestine's dresses, it simultaneously disrupts viewers' access to them as consumable, sentimental objects, holding at a distance what Miles calls "the contemporary market in Black heritage items."[54]

Hill did not readily identify with the documentary film community, although she engaged with it in March 2006 when she and her damaged films participated in the Orphan Film Symposium in Columbia, South Carolina. Within that community there is a well-developed dialogue about the history and ethics of incorporating found films, including home movies, into new works.[55] Whereas amateur material can, as Jacqueline Stewart has shown, supplement absences in film archives that reflect racial biases in archiving decisions, it also raises complex issues about authorship, privacy, and the relationship between public and private histories, especially when the provenance of the objects is unclear.[56] Hill's film-in-progress put these questions about film into dialogue with the dresses that she had come upon and taken. Though found movies may seem clearly to differ from Florestine's dresses because of film's indexical qualities, the clarity of this difference is complicated by what Jaimie Baron describes as the "noise" that unprovenanced found movies convey. The distinction is further blurred by Miles's discussion of clothes-making as a form of self-expression and assertion in situations where other forms of communication and being are blocked; and by her claim that another person's things have the potential—albeit not guaranteed—to generate empathy and "social glue" and to operate "in the service of compassion and communal life."[57]

Hill's comparison of found films and dresses activates questions of how items of clothing communicate across time, and who does or does not have the right to throw things away privately—a legal and ethical question that has some connection to the dead's rights to privacy, explored by Katherine Fusco in chapter 13. Since 1988, unless a state and city pass local ordinances to the contrary, the curb has legally been designated as a space where the right to privacy disappears and trash left there is declared to be "public domain." As the Supreme Court put it when defending "warrantless trash searches": "It is common knowledge that plastic garbage bags left along a public street are readily accessible to animals, children, scavengers, snoops, and other members of the public."[58] Historically, Miles reminds us, trash is an equity issue: "Compared to other groups with a stability afforded by earnings, wealth, or racial privilege, Black people's possessions were more likely to wind up in dump pits and rag bins as families lost elder members, moved on, or were pushed out during the height of Jim Crow segregation and racially motivated violence"—something that is equally relevant today.[59]

When considering the status of objects within the context of animation, it is important to note Miles's observation that discarded "moveables," including possessions like dresses, can contain traces of the personhood of people who have lived in the shadow of an institution—slavery—that treated people like objects.[60] "In the U.S. South," Miles suggests, "dress 'became a language' in which enslavers and enslaved were fluent"; and such objects have the potential to "speak" in a way that allows historians to "backstitch a path" to the owners.[61] Writing about a sack decorated with embroidered text written/sewn by an enslaved woman but found by a white woman at a flea market, Miles states:

> Saving this sack so that it could arrive at a point where we can together reflect on its meanings has required an all-hands-on-deck ethos despite the complications of racial politics. The sack still carries a burden of layered power relations, but it also contains within its preservation history a model

for repurposing that past and for regenerating relationships as we engage in work of shared purpose across racial and regional lines.[62]

Florestine's dresses "speak" of a life lived at a later moment in history than that of the sack, one that began in 1906 and ended in 2001. Although the racialized histories of trash as well as of appropriation provide important backdrops for grappling with the complexity of "found" materials, especially across racial lines, Miles pointed out to me in conversation that there are many things that remain to be determined about Florestine's dresses: not simply why they were thrown away, but even *if* they were thrown away. For it remains an open possibility, especially given that Hill found them on Mardi Gras morning, that the dresses were both discarded and a kind of gift to the people of the city on a day of dressing up, a fitting way to honor the life of a recently deceased dressmaker who had partly defined herself, like Hill, through her clothes, most notably on religious feast days.[63] There is an incomplete, dispersed, and ongoing story of the dresses Hill found—some were distributed to friends after Hill's death, a couple are in the McKissick Museum, some Hill lost in the flood, and some are carefully folded in the home of Hill's mother, awaiting archival decisions—as well as uncertainty about whether the dresses Hill found represented the totality of Florestine's collection. Perhaps other people had already helped themselves to some of Florestine's dresses before she arrived; perhaps some still remain in the possession of Florestine's family. These gaps in knowledge are part of the unfinished legacy of Florestine's sewing, Hill's film about it, and indeed this chapter about the film.

In the wake of Katrina, Hill planned for Gailiunas to map the narrative's key locations, to give increased attention to the spatial politics of the city and her film. She had also begun to explore the temporal complexities of her animated objects, including Florestine's dresses, twice salvaged by Hill, and the flood-drenched remnants of Hill's own creative life. In a page of notes on the topic of "What Was Learned," Hill muses: "how strange houses are ◊ time capsules, frozen time / After the flood, nature healed while the insides festered away." Her notes return to this theme of preserved time: "How strange and fragile houses are / There was shelter and now these time capsules," and then a document titled "New Script," full of crossed-out and reworked sentences, contemplates how such a concept might open the film:

> ~~I lived in New Orleans before the hurricane.~~
> It seems a long time ago, before the hurricane, when I used to say to Paul,

~~Imagine if everyone left New Orl~~
I think if all the people left New Orleans for a week, nature would take over. No problem. It'd be easy. It's already trying, it's already half done.

Silhouette in a car.

Time lapse.. too tall sunflowers and paper houses.[64]

Such speculative, temporally unconventional thinking, where past, present, and future exist in imaginative connection with each other, aligns with Hill's animation pedagogy. For example, in the "Absolutely Required Animation Survey" that she always assigned at the end of her courses, she asks students: "If you had to change places with one of the animators who[se] work we saw, which one would you choose and why?"[65]

Hill's answer would almost certainly have been Lotte Reiniger (1899–1981), who inspired Hill's use of cut-out silhouette animation, including in this film, where she planned to use silhouettes to depict Mardi Gras, her own discovery of the dresses, Florestine sewing and cooking in her home, and Hill's interviews with Florestine's congregation. Reiniger's role in avant-garde film history has been underestimated because of critical biases against narrative animation, work for children, and women's filmmaking, and of an oversimplified view of her use of what Katherine Rochester describes as "oriental ornament."[66]

This is how Hill explains her decision to use silhouettes in her Rockefeller application for the Florestine Project: "Pioneered by the German animator Lotte Reiniger, this style of animation involves the movement of hinged paper cutouts, cut from black paper and lit from behind. I feel this delicate, old-fashioned style would be appropriate. Also the absence of details seems appropriate since I never met Ms. Kinchen."[67] Though Hill invokes Reiniger, the filmmakers' approaches are distinct. While Reiniger saw silhouettes as "a true and unquestionable likeness of the sitter" representing with "complete accuracy" the portrait's subject, Hill emphasizes her silhouettes' absence of detail to underscore that she did not know Florestine, thereby distancing herself from the history of racializing and stereotyping operations enacted through drawn outlines that Kara Walker has so rigorously and persistently engaged.[68]

Hill's use of abstraction in her puppets interacts with the way the labor and art of the puppet animator positions her in relation to those she animates. Reiniger describes the puppeteers of Chinese shadow theater as "players" because they do so much more than manipulate their puppets. Of the animation of animals, she advises: "You must not copy a naturalistic movement, but must feel the movement within yourself, for when you will have to animate an animal, you will have to be that animal, moving as it does."[69] This idea of the animator becoming or enacting (two different things) the animated subject preempts how Hill's most influential animation teacher at Harvard, Suzan Pitt, understood the relationship between animator and subject: "One thing that many people don't understand about animation is the way the animators ... the artists who create the motion for a given character are really the actors."[70] Hill's Florestine project raises the question of how this paradigm works when the character is a Black woman, the animator a white woman, and the context New Orleans, with its long history of cross-racial performance.

Hill described herself as "a romance activist," and while the proliferation of hearts in her animated work is partly responsible for the rosy version of Hill that I hope to revise, her work undoubtedly invites viewers to move between hearts and history, love and sentiment.[71] Writing about the transmission of love across generations of enslaved African American women through material objects, Miles states boldly: "We forget that love is revolutionary. The word, cute and overused in American culture, can feel at times like a stuffed animal devoid of spirit. . . . But love does carry profound meanings."[72] Lauren Berlant suggests that the word *love* "is the enemy of memory," a feeling that can, when channeled through what they call "institutions of intimacy," organize "life and the memory of life" in ways that frequently disappoint or fail. As Berlant shows in their study of American melodrama and sentimentality, there will always be excesses and displacements within these sites of failure, landscapes of feeling inextricably bound up with issues of race, power, and history.[73] And yet these excesses, these "smoldering remains" of sentimentality, can also function, they suggest, as "a resource, an unfinished event," "archives of tactics for being undefeated," places from which to imagine how "to become not-something" and "to unlearn a way of being."[74]

Hill's unfinished project of animating the silhouette form and the handmade, multipatterned dresses of Florestine Kinchen—patterns that, depending on context, might invoke West African clothing design, jazz rhythm, an anticapitalist culture of the homemade, poverty, or the patchwork clothing that is a hallmark of the American minstrel show—emerges as a film-in-progress being constructed out of the "smoldering remains" of American sentiment.[75] Like the patterns of Kinchen's dresses, the silhouette is laden with cross-racial histories. This makes it a polyvocal medium speaking at once of white middle-class women from the South, physiognomy's techniques, the pioneering work of Moses Williams, Sojourner Truth's control of her own image, and Kara Walker's fearless engagement of the violence of interracial "love" and stereotype.[76]

But in addition to attending to the diverse meanings of the dresses and the silhouette form, the Florestine Project became increasingly engaged with the spoken words—and silences—of Florestine's community. Dialogue with Florestine's community had always been a part of the project, as the 2004 Rockefeller application makes clear: "I hope to include some recordings of Florestine Kinchen's family and friends. The Reverend of her church is arranging a meeting of some of its older members to tell me about Florestine Kinchen."[77] Though the film Gailiunas finished includes only snippets of the recordings that Hill made on 13 February 2005 at the Second Free Baptist Mission Church, the tape made that day did survive the hurricane.[78] The original recording reveals much about Kinchen and her circle—about the things she said and liked to do, about how she moved and related to others. It also reflects some aspects of how Kinchen's community regarded Hill's project, how Hill's conversations with church members shaped Hill's subsequent plans for the film's development, and how openly Hill shared with the church community her concerns about the project, her questions about Florestine, and her aspirations for the film.[79] Though it is impossible to know how, or even whether, Hill would have finished the film had she lived, these recordings help to fill out a picture of Florestine Kinchen while also giving some sense of the direction in which Hill's project was moving and a sense of the voices she hoped to amplify more.

Miles suggests that historians need "to learn the language absences speak" in order to resist "the default in which historical gaps feed contemporary forgetfulness."[80] And for this reason, as I conclude this chapter, I turn to the voices of Florestine's community, to the memories as well as refusals that they shared. Leonie Mims notes that Florestine was usually late for church; Frank Moran describes how, when the choir sang, she did "her famous Kinchen step." Lorraine Payton reports that Florestine loved to cook and sew quilts as well as dresses, although her eyesight had been failing late in her life. She never accepted a ride home, sometimes saying, "I'm old but I'm not cold!" Vera M. Dyer remembers that Florestine carried a cloth pouch of chewing tobacco "like the baseball players do . . . and she would put it in her jaw"! Beverly Ray, Pastor Warren Ray's wife, reports that "she got sick all of a sudden and then she died. Before that, she never missed a Sunday." Mrs. Ray adds that Florestine's death came as a real shock. With Reverend Ray's brother and choir member Ronald Ray, Hill discusses the possibility of returning to the church for a choir rehearsal, perhaps to record either Florestine's favorite songs or the songs sung at her funeral. Lori Adams gives her explicit approval for Hill's project, stating, "I think it's wonderful that you're doing a story because she was beautiful and she had such an infectious smile.... I'm glad you're doing this and I'd like to be able to see it when you've finished."

Florestine's nephew, Dwight Carter, describes how his aunt was known by her family as "Aunt Ticy," that she was one of seventeen children, and that her son, Kinchen, had preceded her in death. Carter offers to take Hill and Gailiunas to the house that Florestine had lived in, and that visit is documented in flood-damaged footage included in the finished film. In many of the conversations, Hill expresses her concern to connect with living family members, and when she finally meets Carter, she exclaims, "I'm so glad to meet you because I wanted to make sure it was ok with the family." A few moments later, Hill adds, "I'd love to meet any living relatives. I wonder if I should get your phone number . . . that would be great if I could interview your mother or [Florestine's] grandchildren if I could." Carter's silence in response to her questions about further family meetings, which contrasts with his openness to showing Hill and Gailiunas Florestine's home, suggests that not everyone was as glad to talk about Florestine or to Hill as those who appear on the tape are.

I want to end by lifting up the unknown stories carried by the silences of those who chose not to stay after or attend the service, who refused Hill's invitations to talk, who she did not know to invite, or who had already passed away. In those silences lie other stories, perhaps some too difficult to tell, or simply not for viewers of Hill's film, about Florestine, her dresses, and the worlds we continuously make and undo.

NOTES

This chapter relied upon the deep generosity of Paul Gailiunas, Becky and Kevin Lewis, and Jake Hill. I extend my gratitude to them. I also thank Alix Beeston, Kittee Berns, George Blood, Shira Brisman, Paul Cobb, Iggy Cortez, Susan Courtney, Dejáy Duckett, Courtney Egan, Ian Fleishman, Katherine Fusco, Haden Guest, Heather Harkins, Darlene Jackson, Mark Johnson, Eugene Lew, Louis Massiah, Tiya Miles, Amy Sloper, Stefan Solomon, Katie Trainor, and Lynn Robertson.

1. Adam Nossiter, "Just Days into the Year, Killings Toll Hits 8 in New Orleans," *New York Times*, 6 January 2007, www.nytimes.com/2007/01/06/us/06orleans.html.

2. See Vernon Burton and Reece Lewie, "The Palmetto Revolution: School Desegregation in South Carolina," in *With All Deliberate Speed: Implementing*

Brown v. Board of Education, ed. Brian J. Dougherity and Charles C. Bolton (Fayetteville: University of Arkansas Press, 2008), 59–91.

3. Dan Streible, "Media Artists, Local Activists, and Outsider Archivists: The Case of Helen Hill," in *Old and New Media after Katrina*, ed. Diane Negra (New York: Palgrave Macmillan, 2010), 149–74, 154.

4. See "Founding Erace," www.eracismneworleans.org/about-1. This name troubled Gailiunas, he told me during a Zoom interview of 13 June 2021, because it suggests racism can just disappear.

5. Streible, "Media Artists, Local Activists, and Outsider Archivists," 166.

6. Karen Redrobe, conversation with Tiya Miles, 29 September 2021. Miles's book, *All That She Carried: The Journey of Ashley's Sack, A Black Family Keepsake* (New York: Random House, 2021), has been invaluable to this project.

7. Hill usually refers to "Ms. Kinchen," but as Ms. Kinchen's son was called "Kinchen," I will use Florestine's first name to avoid confusion.

8. Helen Hill, "Artist's Statement," Rockefeller grant application draft, Becky Lewis Archive, Columbia, South Carolina. Hill's archival materials are currently spread over three locations. Most of her films are held at the Harvard Film Archive (HFA), but they are also easily accessible through the Vimeo site that Gailiunas established, https://vimeo.com/helenhill. Most of Hill's papers, as well as many of Florestine's dresses and some films, are held at the Lewis family home in Columbia, South Carolina (Becky Lewis Archive, hereafter "BLA"). Some of this material has been organized by Heather Harkins. Plans are currently under way to transfer this material to the HFA. Most of the Florestine Collection papers as well as some other audiovisual and paper materials are currently at Paul Gailiunas's home in California (Paul Gailiunas Archive, hereafter PGA).

9. Hill, "Artist's Statement," PGA.

10. Hill, "Artist's Statement," PGA.

11. See "Aftermath of Katrina: A Time of Environmental Racism," www.arcgis.com/apps/Cascade/index.html?appid=2106693b39454f0eb0abc5c2ddf9ce40.

12. Helen Hill, "postKatrina Florestine Collection Script," n.d., 1, PGA.

13. Daphne A. Brooks, *Bodies in Dissent: Spectacular Performances of Race and Freedom, 1850–1910* (Durham, NC: Duke University Press, 2006), 131–206, 137. For a discussion of American animation's entwinement with blackface minstrelsy, see Nicholas Sammond, *Birth of an Industry: Blackface Minstrelsy and the Rise of American Animation* (Durham, NC: Duke University Press, 2015).

14. Brooks, *Bodies in Dissent*, 203, 142.

15. Anne Major, "Sweet Magic: The Preservation of Helen Hill's Cinema," *The Moving Image* 19.1 (2019): 15–40, 35–36.

16. Streible, "Media Artists, Local Activists, and Outsider Archivists," 163–64 and 167–68.

17. Gailiunas, interview with Redrobe.

18. See "The Dresses of Florestine Kinchen," *Under the Dome: Telling the Story of Southern Life. McKissick Museum Newsletter* (Spring 2008): 2, https://scholarcommons.sc.edu/cgi/viewcontent.cgi?article=1006&context=dome. Following a conversation with Jason Shaiman and Lynn Robertson, Gailiunas writes,

"I expressed my concern about sensitivity to family and race issues and allowing me to contact Rev. Ray first. Avoiding artspeak—they are in agreement" (Gailiunas production notebook, 20 December 2007, PGA). These concerns suggest an attempt to avoid the problems that (Kiowa) artist and curator Teri Greeves, speaking in an Indigenous context, suggests occur when the clothing of formerly colonized people is exhibited in the absence of community dialogue. See Greeves's comments in "Decolonizing Art: A Conversation about Indigenous Arts and Exhibitions with Teri Greeves and Dr. Jill Alhlberg Yohe," Villanova University, 18 March 2021, www.youtube.com/watch?v=hjd7vlpuFoA. Anna C. Chave addresses similar issues with the Gee's Bend Quilts in "Dis/Cover/ing the Quilts of Gee's Bend, Alabama," *Journal of Modern Craft* 1.2 (2008): 221–54.

19. Script draft, 14 September 2007, 1, PGA.

20. Gailiunas, notebook, 29 February 2009, PGA.

21. I am grateful to Miles for helping me articulate and think about these questions.

22. On the relationship between pastness and reality in this mood, including such examples as "John was to have gone on a trip to Italy," see Paul Larreya, "Irrealis, Past Time Reference and Modality," in *Modality in Contemporary English*, ed. Roberta Facchinetti, Frank Palmer, and Manfred Krug (Berlin: De Gruyter, 2003), 21–46, 31.

23. Janine Marchessault, "Some Recipes for Disaster in the Films of Deidre Logue and Helen Hill," in *Process Cinema: Handmade Films in the Digital Age*, ed. Scott MacKenzie and Janine Marchessault (Montreal: McGill-Queen's University Press, 2019), 353–68.

24. See Helen Hill, Sample Work Forms 1–3, 2004, Rockefeller Grant Application, PGA.

25. Marchessault, drawing on Monika Kin Gagnon, notes that the posthumous film is "always generous and expansive"; see Marchessault, "Some Recipes for Disaster," 366, and Monika Kin Gagnon, "Unfinished Films and Posthumous Cinema: Charles Gagnon's *R69* and Joyce Wieland's *Wendy and Joyce*," in *Cinephemera: Archives, Ephemeral Cinema, and New Screen Histories in Canada*, ed. Gerda Cammaer and Zoë Druick (Montreal: McGill-Queen's University Press, 2014), 137–58.

26. See Imani Perry, *Vexy Things: On Gender and Liberation* (Durham, NC: Duke University Press, 2018), 98–128.

27. Perry, *Vexy Things,* 109. Perry is not alone in this call. See, for example, Miles, *All That She Carried*, 40; Eric Lott, *Black Mirror: The Cultural Contradictions of American Racism* (Cambridge, MA: Belknap Press, 2017), 48; and Daphne A. Brooks, "'Ain't Got No, I Got Life': #OscarsSoWhite & the Problem of Women Musicians on Film," *Los Angeles Review of Books* (28 February 2016), https://lareviewofbooks.org/article/aint-got-no-i-got-life-oscarssowhite-the-problem-of-women-musicians-film/.

28. Lisa Cartwright, "The Hands of the Animator: Rotoscopic Projection, Condensation, and Repetition Automatism in the Fleischer Apparatus," *Body and Society* 18.1 (2012): 47–78. See also Hannah Frank, *Frame by Frame: A Materialist Aesthetics of Animated Cartoons* (Oakland: University of California Press, 2019).

29. Gailiunas confirmed that while Hill did finish films, she considered each film as something from which to learn as part of a larger, continuous experiment.

30. On Hill's "film bees," see also Marchessault, "Some Recipes for Disaster," 364 and 368, n. 12.

31. Helen Hill, *Recipes for Disaster*, 2nd ed. (2005), 92, www.filmlabs.org/docs/recipes_for_disaster_hill.pdf.

32. For a description of this work, see Lucy Reynolds, "Reel Time" (1973), *Lux Online*, www.luxonline.org.uk/histories/1970-1979/reel_time.html.

33. See Su Friedrich's collaborative website, *Edited By*, http://womenfilmeditors.princeton.edu. See also "editors" in the *Women Film Pioneers Project*, initiated by Jane Gaines, https://wfpp.columbia.edu/pioneers/?sort=occupation. Hill regularly taught the work of experimental female filmmakers from the UK.

34. See Miles, "Rose's Inventory," in *All That She Carried*, 127–63.

35. Heather Harkins, interview with Karen Redrobe, 18 June 2021. Harkins received the inaugural Helen Hill Animated Award in 2007 in support of her ongoing project, "She's a Lady Animator."

36. Box 1, n.d., BLA. Although Hill's name is not on the flier, Gailiunas confirmed that Hill made the poster via email to Karen Redrobe, 29 September 2021.

37. Marchessault points out that the second edition of *Recipes for Disaster* "was explicitly connected to the damage wrought to films and media by the floods, putrefaction, and mould." Marchessault, "Some Recipes for Disaster," 364.

38. Helen Hill, n.d., PGA.

39. Fernando Solanas and Octavio Getino, "Toward a Third Cinema," *TRICONTINENTAL* 14 (October 1969): 107–32, 131, 125.

40. Solanas and Getino, "Toward a Third Cinema," 122, 120.

41. Solanas and Getino, "Toward a Third Cinema," 130, 123.

42. Becky Lewis, conversation with Karen Redrobe, 16 June 2021; Solanas and Getino, "Toward a Third Cinema," 131.

43. Solanas and Getino, "Toward a Third Cinema," 125, 128, 131.

44. See Margery Beth Brown, Obituary, *The Olympian* (13 July 2006), www.legacy.com/us/obituaries/theolympian/name/margery-brown-obituary?pid=100123964.

45. Heather Harkins, email to Karen Redrobe, 11 July 2021.

46. Helen Hill, Handwritten notes for "Class 3," Box 2, "Helen Hill Teaching," BLA.

47. Hill, Rockefeller Project Narrative, 3, BLA.

48. Hill, "Project narrative," Rockefeller grant application, PGA (*FK* materials).

49. Hill, "Project narrative," Rockefeller grant application draft, BLA.

50. Helen Hill, flood-damaged script page labeled "4," n.d., PGA.

51. Helen Hill, fragment, n.d., PGA.

52. Helen Hill, fragment, n.d., PGA.

53. See Gailiunas notebook, "Master from USC (Helen's CSSA Trip)," 28 July 2008, PGA.

54. Miles, *All That She Carried*, 37–40.

55. See Jaimie Baron, *The Archive Effect: Found Footage and the Audiovisual Experience of History* (New York: Routledge, 2014), and *Reuse, Misuse, Abuse: The Ethics of Audiovisual Appropriation in the Digital Age* (New Brunswick, NJ: Rutgers University Press, 2020).

56. Jacqueline Najuma Stewart, "South Side Home Movie Archive Project," https://sshmp.uchicago.edu/2019/05/01/may-1-sshmp-launches-digital-archive/.

57. Miles, *All That She Carried*, 266.

58. See *California v. Greenwood*, 486 U.S. 35 (1988), Opinions, 486 U.S. 39–44, https://supreme.justia.com/cases/federal/us/486/35/.

59. Miles, *All That She Carried*, 266. Gailiunas notes that Kinchen's family confirmed the dresses had been discarded. Zoom conversation with author, 10 July 2022.

60. Miles, *All That She Carried*, 189.

61. Miles, *All That She Carried*, 132, 228.

62. Miles, *All That She Carried*, 40.

63. Church member Vera M. Dyer told Hill that Florestine would especially dress up and even make her own shoes on "Ethnic Sundays." Cassette recording of conversations with members of the Second Free Baptist Mission Church, 13 February 2005.

64. Helen Hill, "New Script," PGA. This plan also preempts the post-Katrina images of houses frozen in time and overgrown by nature in Kimberly Rivers-Roberts's *Fear No Gumbo (stop stealing our sh*t)* (2016).

65. Helen Hill, Box 1, n.d., BLA. Hill taught at a variety of venues, including the Nova Scotia College of Art and Design (now NSCAD University), the Atlantic Filmmakers Cooperative (AFCOOP), the New Orleans Video Access Center (NOVAC), the New Orleans Film Collective, the New Orleans Center for Creative Arts, and the California State Summer School for the Arts. Her teaching evaluations (Box 2, "Helen Hill Teaching," BLA) show that she was beloved by her students.

66. Katherine Rochester, "Silhouette Films, Weimar Cinema, and Ornaments from the Orient," in *Lotte Reiniger, the Silhouette Artist*, ed. Rada Bieberstein (Marburg: Schüren Verlag, forthcoming). See also Rochester's *Lotte Reiniger and the Animated Ornament in Experimental Film, 1919–1937* (PhD dissertation, Bryn Mawr College, 2018).

67. Hill, Rockefeller Project Narrative, 2, PGA.

68. Lotte Reiniger, *Shadow Puppets, Shadow Theatres and Shadow Films* (Boston: Publishers PLAYS, Inc., 1970), 13. Kara Walker's "Song of the South" was shown at REDCAT, CalArts between 3 September and 23 October 2005. This work builds on Walker's earlier "Fibbergibbet and Mumbo Jumbo" (2004), https://fabricworkshopandmuseum.org/artist/kara-walker/. "Song of the South" opened just a few days after Hurricane Katrina and was explicitly linked to it by Walker, www.redcat.org/exhibition/kara-e-walker. Walker also claims Reiniger as a primary influence. See also Major, "Sweet Magic," 25.

69. Reiniger, *Shadow Puppets*, 16, 101–102.

70. Suzan Pitt, in *Suzan Pitt: The Persistence of Vision*, dir. Blue Kraning and Laura Kraning (2006).

71. Becky Lewis, email to Karen Redrobe, 9 July 2021.
72. Miles, *All That She Carried*, 3.
73. Lauren Berlant, *The Female Complaint: The Unfinished Business of Sentimentality in American Culture* (Durham, NC: Duke University Press, 2008), 169.
74. Berlant, *Female Complaint*, 273.
75. See also Fred Moten, *In the Break: The Aesthetics of the Black Radical Tradition* (Minneapolis: University of Minnesota Press, 2003), 25–84.
76. Hill's list of things to do post-Katrina includes the note "Silhouette book," suggesting increased engagement with the silhouette's history. For this, see Gwendolyn DuBois Shaw in "Moses Williams, Cutter of Profiles: Silhouettes and African American Identity in the Early Republic," in *Portraits of a People: Picturing African Americans in the Nineteenth Century* (Andover, MA: Addison Gallery of American Art, 2006), 45–53; Gwendolyn DuBois Shaw, *Seeing the Unspeakable: The Art of Kara Walker* (Durham, NC: Duke University Press, 2004); Philippe Vergne, "The Black Saint Is the Sinner Lady," in *Kara Walker: My Complement, My Enemy, My Oppressor, My Love* (Minneapolis, MN: Walker Art Center, 2007), 7–26; and Darcy Grimaldo Grigsby, *Enduring Truths: Sojourner's Shadows and Substance* (Chicago: University of Chicago Press, 2015), 85–102.
77. Hill, Rockefeller Project Narrative, 2, PGA.
78. In 2008, Gailiunas reached out to the church's pastor, Reverend Warren Ray. Katrina had displaced many church members, but with Ray's help, Gailiunas received signed Personal Release Agreements from the majority of the people Hill interviewed for the film, and those names appear in the credits of the film he finished. The agreements are held in the PGA.
79. Helen Hill, Interviews with Members of the Second Free Mission Baptist Church, 13 February 2005, audio-cassette, PGA.
80. Miles, *All That She Carried*, 89.

CHAPTER 13

Girls Who Can't Say No

Celebrity Resurrections and the Consent of the Dead

KATHERINE FUSCO

In *Regarding the Pain of Others,* Susan Sontag writes: "Memory is, achingly, the only relation we can have with the dead."[1] If only this were true. Increasingly, digital technologies ensure that we can have a variety of quite lucrative and creative relationships with our celebrity dead, as in the case of *Virtual 2Pac*'s resurrection of Tupac Shakur at the Coachella music festival in 2012, the creation of a CGI Marilyn Monroe by the forces behind the 1997 film *Spice World,* Peter Cushing's appearance in *Rogue One: A Star Wars Story,* Carrie Fisher's posthumous performance in *Star Wars: The Rise of Skywalker,* James Dean's casting in the now-shelved Vietnam War film *Finding Jack,* and celebrity chef Anthony Bourdain's beyond-the-grave voiceover narration in Morgan Neville's 2021 documentary *Roadrunner.*

Although still a relatively new media phenomenon, deepfakes have begun to garner scholarly recognition, with a recently published issue of *Convergence* exploring the many ethical, artistic, and legal ramifications of deepfake facial replacements. As the editors of the issue state, deepfakes raise "questions about the very nature of the star body, performance, [and] film meaning."[2] Stunning technologies aside, the matter of what can and cannot be done with dead celebrities is not a new question. Case law in the United States indicates as much, with laws on the books reflecting the local provenance of celebrities, such as Minnesota's "PRINCE" (Personal Rights in Names Can Endure) Act and Tennessee's Personal Rights Protection Act, popularly known as "Elvis's Law."

The United States legal system is structured such that there are a multiplicity of star afterlives across the nation, with individuals living on differently from one location to another. The Right of Publicity, sometimes called "personality rights," prevents the unauthorized use of one's likeness for commercial purposes. Falling under state law, only about half of the states recognize such a right, either under this name or under the umbrella of a Right to Privacy ("Publicity").[3] The case of Marilyn Monroe is a particularly tragic and famous one in this regard. One of the reasons Monroe's case is complicated is that California, where she lived and worked for much of her life—and, indeed, died—grants a posthumous right to publicity, whereas New York state, where Monroe was a resident at the time of her death, has until recently limited the right to one's lifetime. At Monroe's death in 1962, her estate was split between her acting coach Lee Strasberg and her psychiatrist Marianne Kris. Since then, a number of lawsuits between her estate, controlled by Anna Strasberg, and others who wish to profit from her image have sought to either recategorize the actress as a Californian or retain her residency as a New Yorker at the time of death, a decision of great financial consequence.[4]

The discrepancy across states is interesting and even controversial in the case of Anna Strasberg, who was not Lee's wife at the time of Monroe's passing; but I'm less interested in Monroe's things, or even the appearance of Monroe *on* things, than in the treatment of Monroe and other celebrities like her as a category of performer made possible by an incomplete career: a living-dead thing that continues to labor, even after death. Pertaining to the questions of this book, the deepfake performer disarticulates any *necessary* relationship between unfinished celebrity careers and unfinished films. An actor's passing need not generate recastings or rewrites; the film can be completed in her absence, and new film performances can be imagined.

Somewhat overlapping the right to publicity is the broader and frequently contested right to privacy, which has been subject to much legal and philosophical debate. Most well known in the United States for its use in *Roe v. Wade,* the right to privacy is taken up in constitutional and tort law as well as in wider discussions of natural rights. Whereas some privacy theorists known as "reductionists" argue that privacy issues primarily entail matters more properly belonging to other rights, such as property, others contend that there is a "coherence" to the matters that fall under the rubric of privacy. Among those who subscribe to a doctrine of coherence, theorists argue that identifiable matters of access and self-efficacy are at stake in questions of privacy. Adam Moore, for instance, suggests that controlling who has access to one's person and information is fundamental to the notion of privacy; for Judith DeCrew, further, this control is necessary for building interpersonal relationships and for self-expression.[5] These latter two uses are of obvious and central importance to an actor.

The historical origin of privacy law in the United States chimes with the present. The right to privacy emerged at an earlier moment of technological transformation, during which recordings were seen as an invasive supplement to the textual representations typically managed under libel and slander law. In 1890, with widespread newspaper adoption of photography, Samuel Warren and Louis Brandeis published their essay "The Right to Privacy," in which they recognized a "right to be let alone" and posited the idea of "the right to one's personality."[6] More than a century later, new technologies for producing CGI and deepfake performances raise questions for philosophers and jurists about whether or not the rights granted the living should be extended to the dead.

In this chapter I argue that feminist film studies should also have something to say about such matters. Feminist film theory has long taken up the motif of the disappearing and reappearing woman, with scholars including Lucy Fischer, Karen Redrobe, Mary Desjardins, Maggie Hennefeld, Alix Beeston, and Genevieve Yue exploring images, material practices, and industry patterns of the woman who comes in and out of view.[7] Desjardins's account of aging actresses' transitions from Hollywood to television offers an especially helpful framework for understanding the stakes of our particular media moment. As she argues, "the loss and resurrection of the gendered star across multiple temporalities and media ... point[s] to metaphysical states (the emergence into and disappearance out of subjectivity and being that is shared by all subjects) and to the cyclical material practices of the female star in her relation to commodity exchange."[8]

The digitally and algorithmically resurrected star offers a heightened example of Desjardins's claims. This chapter proposes that resurrections of celebrities for posthumous second acts raise issues of rights and consent not just for the actress's estate, but for the deceased performer herself, a matter of no small significance in the wake of #MeToo. (As well, the fact that the famously blonde star is the visible instance of this ethical tangle echoes the problem of #MeToo's focus on white celebrities.) To evidence this claim, I analyze the way filmmakers and cinematographers discuss the fabrication of dead celebrity performers and turn to the place where the problematic nature of posthumous resurrections is clearest: the realm of deepfake pornography. As I argue, the specter of consent haunts the words of those engaged in resurrecting dead celebrities. One of the questions I posit is whether the difference between a CGI Monroe in an upcoming biopic and an algorithmically generated Monroe in a deepfake gangbang is a difference of degree rather than of kind. Although I discuss other figures, Monroe offers a particularly helpful test case for, as theorists such as Sarah Churchwell, Jacqueline Rose, Griselda Pollock, and Wendy Lesser have established, the cultural obsession with a posthumous Monroe will always reflect back to us our thinking about the relations among art, death, and gender.[9]

WHAT INTERESTS HAVE THE DEAD?

An ugly anecdote illustrates the obvious about our celebrity dead. There are many things that a dead star cannot do. For example, Marilyn Monroe does not have the ability to grant or refuse companionship in her final resting place. In 1992, Hugh Hefner bought a plot in Westwood Village Memorial Park Cemetery next to Monroe, so that he might spend eternity sleeping with the famous blonde. When Hefner discussed his plans with Jay Leno, the TV host joked that for the price, Hefner should be buried on top of the actress.[10] Because this story is about Hugh Hefner, Marilyn Monroe, and a desire that sounds very much like necrophilia, it's easy to see it as a cautionary tale not about property but about consent.

As CGI and especially deepfakes improve, the ethical questions raised by our uses of dead celebrities reach a level such that we might turn from the questions of property asked in the legal realm to the questions of posthumous intentions and consent more commonly explored in the field of bioethics. One thread in bioethics centers on a basic question: Can the dead be injured? For example, in *Death, Posthumous Harm, and Bioethics,* philosopher James Stacey Taylor argues, following from Epicurus, that it is impossible to harm the dead because "a person's well-being will depend solely on the pleasures or pains that she experiences."[11] Taylor extends this argumentation from the realm of organ donation to posthumous reproductive procedures as well as the dead's right to privacy, arguing that a posthumous violation of a woman's body "would have no effect on her antemortem ability to exercise her autonomy."[12] In contrast, T. M. Wilkinson has argued for the existence of posthumous interests and privacy, arguing that a number of such interests survive postmortem, and some new interests, such as in bodily integrity and the treatment of remains, may emerge.[13]

Of course, one might object that Taylor and Wilkinson are debating the treatment of actual, material bodies and that what *Virtual 2Pac* and deepfake Monroe represent is something else altogether. However, the desire—particularly where Monroe is concerned—*to see more, to have more* access, brings up many of the same issues as those raised around postmortem privacy in, say, discussions of public autopsies. Several years ago, a textual dissection of Monroe's body could be found on the website for Abbott & Hast Mortuary, Inc., in Los Angeles, which was still trading on the publicity the mortuary earned when they managed Monroe's funeral. The article rehearsed the role founder Allan Abbott played in the three days of preparing the body, working alongside Monroe's regular hairdresser and makeup artist. In the website's text Monroe's famous image is again re-created, if somewhat tarnished:

> Before we started dressing her, the embalmer decided to use a surgical procedure to reduce the swelling in her neck, so he cut some hair away and made an incision on the back of her neck and sutured it up tight. As she was being prepared, one of the partners in the mortuary, Mary Hamrock, came into the embalming room. We had just dressed her in a chartreuse Pucci dress with a Florence, Italy, label in it.
>
> Mrs. Hamrock made the observation that in her opinion it didn't look like Marilyn Monroe because she was too flat-chested. The embalmer explained that the autopsy had rendered her physique in that condition. The family had actually brought into the mortuary a pair of breast enhancers that she had frequently worn, but they were too small to compensate for the effects of the post-mortem.
>
> Mrs. Hamrock removed the falsies from the dress, discarded them and proceeded to form her own version out of cotton from the prep-room shelf. When she finished, she took a few steps back and declared, "Now that looks like Marilyn Monroe!"[14]

There is much worth saying about this strange recounting: the way the Pucci dress detail resonates as a celebrity magazine item; the one-to-one association of Monroe and her breasts; the discussion of Monroe's "breast enhancers" as a second-stage dissection of the body. It is also worth considering how the declaration "Now that looks like Marilyn Monroe!" signifies. Mrs. Hamrock's use of the neuter demonstrative pronoun points to the corpse as the *that* which is not Monroe but has been made to resemble her. Rather than being a case of Monroe failing and then succeeding to look like herself, the story speaks to the creation of a new entity: an impersonation of sorts. The Abbott & Hast episode identifies more than the uncanniness of open-casket funerals in which the embalmed corpse is rouged-up to echo life; it also uncovers the way death allows the star image to become newly abstracted—a kind of empty container flexible enough to be occupied by other bodies, whether fleshy or virtual.[15]

The postmortem discussion of Monroe's appearance, the opening of the cadaver: each slice offers a new view after death. This is a form of access particular to death that the deceased may have an interest in retaining as private and that, if not consented to, constitutes a posthumous violation. The mortuary encounter also recalls Monroe's inquest photographs, which have troubled many. Discussing the Monroe morgue photographs, Griselda Pollock coins the term "unguarded intimacy," supposing, "I could argue that any circulation of this image in effect stole an image of her death from its derelict, unguarded subject," before going on to complicate this notion by questioning who the subject of death might be.[16] The CGI and deepfakes I discuss in the remainder of this chapter similarly raise the question of who gets to be death's subject, but with an important difference. Whereas the mortuary newsletter and the autopsy photographs are gruesome instances of nonconsensual intimacy with the dead, the CGI and deepfake performance might similarly constitute a violation of the deceased star's right to privacy—including her rights to control her relationships and her self-expression—but with a sanitizing erasure of the particulars that feel too historically specific in the case of the celebrity corpse.

OF DOGS AND DEEPFAKES

A recent phenomenon in which Marilyn Monroe figures prominently makes the issue of posthumous consent clear: deepfake pornography. For example, on the website adultdeepfakes.com, one finds a page with a short bio of Monroe, a photo of her in the dress from *The Seven Year Itch* (1955), and links for "Marilyn Monroe's New Videos." On 9 March 2021 the featured video was "Marilyn Monroe Deepfake (Gangbang)."[17] Another site, sexcelebrity.net, likewise has a page devoted to the dead actress, featuring a deepfake Monroe in a number of scenarios, including a Nazi-themed film.[18] The public outcry over deepfake pornography has understandably focused on harm to the living, and the pages contain numerous celebrities such as Jessica Alba, Beyoncé, and Scarlett Johansson, as well as politicians such as Tulsi Gabbard and Kamala Harris. In addition, the legal community has been concerned about the rise of deepfake revenge porn for all citizens, celebrity or not, and states have begun passing legislation against nonconsensual deepfake pornography.[19]

However, as is pointed out in a recent roundtable discussion among Shaka McGlotten, Susanna Paasonen, and John Paul Stadler, the ontologically slippery status of deepfakes makes this legislation difficult: "the laws we have . . . largely fail to protect against such a unique phenomenon, which could be argued to be a kind of parody and, in regard to the question of harm, is troubled by the actual 'unreality' of the media produced, or its mixed ontology."[20] Instead, as Mathilde Pavis has argued, writing in the context of UK laws regulating deepfakes, an expansion of performer's rights to cover *imitations* might address the problem of nonconsensual deepfake performances.[21] However, as new video creations, deepfakes are largely protected by the First Amendment in the United States, making this an unlikely solution in the American system.

The deepfake's status as a tricky blend of "real" elements with fictional situations is both not new to porn, which is always concerned with "faking it" and the documentary value of the money shot, *and* may well be one of the pleasures of the form. For, as Stadler observes, viewers of deepfake pornography are savvier than legislators give them credit for and indeed may be taking new pleasures from the deepfake genre. "These pleasures," he says, "can range from technical mastery (especially for those making the deepfakes) to imaginary visual control over the bodies depicted: yet other kinds of intensities can certainly emerge as well."[22] In other words, the pleasure of the deepfake is not in thinking one is surreptitiously viewing the "real," but in knowingly encountering the unreal in a heavily synthesized situation. This is part of the boringness of the Monroe deepfake. Not just because she means sex, but, as Wendy Lesser has argued, because "exploitation was the essence of Marilyn Monroe—in its positive sense, as 'full use,' as well as in its negative sense."[23] Deepfake pornography makes Monroe useable again. Deepfake Monroe is therefore perfect not because she offers a previously unseen view of the actress, but because she opens the actress to exploitation *again*. After all, it's hard to imagine a viewer foolish enough to imagine Monroe made a color porno with Nazis. The pleasure here is in the counterfactual possibility: not *what if she did?* but *what if she could?*[24]

The *what if* mood of the deepfake is equally spectacular in the resurrections of other stars, but the public pushback against one kind of deepfake over and above certain others perhaps reveals more about attitudes toward sex than about the ethics of privacy. The deepfake also appears in what might be called the memory industry, with the rise of applications producing "deep nostalgia." Deep nostalgia technology users resurrect deceased loved ones to deliver ghostly messages. The most well-known example is Kanye West's 2020 gift to then-wife Kim Kardashian of a resurrection of her deceased father, attorney Robert Kardashian. Surviving family members may find this opportunity to interact again with the deceased moving. And while it is unlikely that Robert Kardashian would have objected to visiting with his daughter and likely that he would object to appearing in a porno, we do not, in fact, know this. Perhaps Kardashian hated Kanye and loved adult entertainment. In either case, we cannot know, and the senior Kardashian cannot consent to being made to interact and perform in this new manner. In contrast, we *do* know that some people want this sort of afterlife and have begun self-archiving in anticipation of their deaths.[25] Despite the possibility of short-circuiting consent and rights to privacy with any deepfake, legislation thus far has focused on deepfake pornography and intentional damage to political candidates.[26] Ghostly interactions with one's deceased loved ones does not rise to legislative interest.

However, technologists have warned about the dangers of the spread of these technologies. For example, in the *Washington Post* in March 2021, technology columnist Geoffrey Fowler offered a cautionary op-ed about the deep nostalgia trend, explaining that he had created two deliberately over-the-top and ridiculous deepfakes of American icons: George Washington and Marilyn Monroe. One of these figures he created to sing disco, the other to blow a kiss. (No points for guessing which is which.) Despite this cheeky use of Washington and Monroe, Fowler is concerned about the effects of sites such as myheritage.com, which offer deep nostalgia videos. Even in this "softer" form, deepfakes raise ethical issues, as is indicated by a quotation in the article from Ben-Zion Benkhin, the CEO of lip-synching deepfake app Wombo: "Deepfakes play with identity and agency because you can take over someone else—you can make them do something that they've never done before."[27]

Whereas deepfake pornography and deep nostalgia may serve idiosyncratic personal desires, my argument is not about fans, about whom interesting things might be said relative to questions of melancholy, mourning, and posthumous resurrection. Instead, the issue of consent seems most important in the relationship between the star and her performance as labor. A brief moment from Laura Mulvey's *Death 24x a Second* helpfully delineates the stakes. Mulvey reflects on two posthumous manipulations of Monroe by fans: Andy Warhol's *Marilyns,* made in 1967, and Mulvey's own editing of the "Two Little Girls from Little Rock" sequence from *Gentlemen Prefer Blondes* (1953). Describing a moment from *Blondes* that caught her off-guard, Mulvey's engagement with Monroe clarifies the difference between the specificity of individual fan desires and the generic quality of commercial ones:

> In this particular fragment, played to the camera, she pulls up her shoulder strap in a performance of an almost sluttish disorder of dress that is completely at odds with the mechanical precision of this and each gesture. Even though the gesture was so self-consciously produced, it has, for me, something of Barthes's *punctum,* and I found myself returning over and over again to these few seconds of film.[28]

Mulvey continues, speaking of herself, Warhol, and all "possessive fans": "The fetishistic spectator, driven by a desire to stop, to hold and repeat these iconic images, especially as perfected in highly stylized cinema, can suddenly, unexpectedly, encounter the index."[29] The deepfake Monroe, in contrast, offers no such relation to the index, no *punctum,* none of the messiness of the real. Describing the cinematic index's relation to death, Mulvey writes: "To see the star on the screen in the retrospectives that follow his or her death is also to see the cinema's uncertain relationship to life and death. Just as the cinema animates its still frames, so it brings back to life, in perfect fossil form, anyone it has ever recorded, from great star to fleeting extra."[30] But the deepfake resurrection is no fossil; its treatment of the dead celebrity is more *Jurassic Park* than natural history museum. In this way the resurrected celebrity gives us something very like André Bazin's "supreme cinematic perversion," not just the *re-morts* of cinema's indexical reproduction of death, but "the projection of an execution backward like those comic newsreels."[31]

Unlike film as index of death, with a dead celebrity and a new film, the actor seems always to be giving a performance she's never provided before. The possibility that deepfake pornography is different only in degree but not in kind from the resurrections coming out of mainstream studios and big media companies such as the Digital Domain Group surfaces, I argue, in a certain anxiousness of directors and other film practitioners involved in films featuring dead celebrities. I'll offer here three brief examples drawn from interviews discussing the posthumous resurrections of Carrie Fisher, James Dean, and Marilyn Monroe. Carrie Fisher's appearance as Leia in *The Rise of Skywalker* is the most straightforward because it involves the use of scenes she shot for *The Force Awakens* that were unused by the earlier film. Even here, though, one of *The Rise of Skywalker*'s screenwriters, Chris Terrio, registers the problems of interpreting the deceased's intentions when he notes: "We didn't use any on-camera lines that she didn't say. It was important to us that every time Leia says a line, it was really a line that Carrie said and that the way we created the scene around her, her acting intention was relatively intact."[32]

In Fisher's case, consent is extrapolated from her work in life and justifies her resurrection. The discourse around contemporary resurrections of long-dead stars is more vexed and reveals a wariness around the question of consent. In a series of *Hollywood Reporter* interviews in October 2021, Anton Ernst, the codirector of *Finding Jack*—a film about US soldiers and their dogs in Vietnam—discusses and defends the choice to cast a deepfake James Dean. In the initial interview Ernst speaks strangely about the actor, stating of the casting: "We searched high and low for the perfect character to portray the role of Rogan, which has some extreme complex character arcs, and after months of research, we decided on James Dean."[33] Apparently, Elvis had also been in the running. Of recent resurrections the casting of Dean has created the strongest outcry. I suspect there are two reasons behind this. First, because the use of Carrie Fisher, Paul Walker, and Peter Cushing took place in the context of either films begun but not completed or franchises with which they had been strongly associated, it was easy to presume the actors' consent. For example, referring to Bruce Lee's bizarre but generally accepted "completion" of *Game of Death,* Lisa Bode notes, "performance completions generally have been better received than those that are seen as a repurposing of the dead actor's image . . . completions are framed as salvaging the last precious frames of a lost actor's creativity."[34] This is not the case for Dean, however, whose career consists predominantly of three stand-alone films with relatively closed narrative worlds: *Rebel Without a Cause, East of Eden,* and *Giant.* It cannot be plausibly argued that the actor's oeuvre includes dog-based war films. Second, Dean is an actor, not an actress.

With Dean's casting in *Finding Jack*, we have an actor both unaffiliated with the new film and a male star. This combination seems to have disturbed other stars in a way that deepfake Marilyn (and CGI Marilyn, as I discuss below) apparently has not. But a resurrected white male performer in an entirely new film role is a novel phenomenon, and other white actors responded with outrage to the casting news. Chris Evans tweeted sarcastically, "I'm sure he'd be thrilled," before continuing, "This is awful. Maybe we can get a computer to paint us a new Picasso. Or write a couple new John Lennon tunes. The complete lack of understanding here is shameful."[35] Despite his impassioned protests and accusation that *Finding Jack*'s makers and the Dean estate "lack understanding," Evans's complaint is muddled, perhaps reflecting anxiety about the fate of the star in the face of an endless army of digital ghosts who might work for free.[36] It is not simply the case that a computer is making another *Guernica* or "Imagine"; rather, both the performer and the performance—that is, the artist and the artwork—are being posthumously created. Another critic of the trend, the late Robin Williams's daughter Zelda Williams, captures what is at stake more accurately in her tweet: "Publicity stunt or not, this is puppeteering the dead for their 'clout' alone and it sets such an awful precedent for the future of performance."[37] Her description of the phenomenon as puppetry captures the problem of consent at stake in a celebrity body set to unwitting and unwilling motion.

Following the deepfake Dean backlash, Ernst attempted to delineate appropriate from inappropriate resurrections: "Anyone that is brought back to life—you have to respect them. . . . I think the line should be . . . you must always honor the deceased's wishes and try to act in a way that is honorable and full of dignity."[38] In addition to suggesting norms around the dead, Ernst's language of "honor" and "respect" are also terms of sexual propriety—a resonance suggestive of the resurrection's challenge to ideas of consent. For the long-dead celebrity who cannot consent, it seems, the project of deriving permission is an interpretive one, with the director imagining counterfactually what Dean *may* have wished. Of course, it would be hard to say how Dean, who died in 1955, might have felt about being cast in a pet-forward Vietnam War film. Or about the Vietnam War at all.

It's a truth universally acknowledged that every new medium is in want of its pornography. We might also say that every new medium wants its Marilyn. For the 2017 film *Blade Runner 2049*, the actress and Monroe impersonator Suzie Kennedy appears briefly playing a holographic Monroe of the future in a nightclub. In 2018, in a moment of life imitating art imitating life, Kennedy was scanned and digitized at Pinewood Studios in England to create a CGI Marilyn for an upcoming film about the actress. In an article for *The Sun,* producer Kim Fuller had two things to say, which are worth juxtaposing: "As she's digital, you can do anything. You have a lot of license dramatically," *and* "She was a massive glamour star and was exploited. If she was around today, there would be a lot of 'Me Too.'"[39] Fuller's statements lack irony and also perhaps an awareness that "she's digital" refers to Kennedy as much as Monroe. It's a bonus for him that a glamorous and exploited star can be exploited once again.

While the directors and screenwriters working with Fisher and Dean have emphasized intent and legacy, Monroe's posthumous career inspires very little of this discourse. As Lesser points out, this too is part of Monroe's meaning: "Everybody professes to be inside her, to know her true wishes and to be carrying them out. Nobody can leave her alone. She is there to be used, to be entered into."[40] Whereas the consternation over Dean seems to be over presuming his wishes, Monroe is a star whose wishes must always be managed or interpreted by those who know better. Indeed, the concerns named by Jamie Salter of Authentic Brands Group (ABG) are entirely profit-based, with no charade of consent necessary. In 2011, ABG purchased rights to Monroe's image from her estate (led by Strasberg) for close to fifty million US dollars. Describing his intentions, Salter initially sounds like the directors discussed above, emphasizing better, more dignified, more lucrative uses of Brand Monroe. For example, he indicates his desire to move away from cheap souvenir items, noting, "I mean, a Hallmark card, I'm perfectly fine with. But a shot glass? I don't think that's good for her image."[41] Instead, Salter speaks in the *Toronto Star* of planning to partner Monroe with higher-end companies, focusing on the type of marketing represented by a recent commercial for Dior J'Adore Eau De Parfum, which also features CGI Grace Kelly and Marlene Dietrich alongside Charlize Theron, who resurrects these icons in a different manner, through her physical embodiment of the type.

It's not until Salter begins discussing future film roles for Monroe that his language turns explicitly to the opportunities afforded by a performer whose wishes might be ignored. After all, it is easy enough to imagine the perfume ad might align with Monroe's preferences (quips about Chanel no. 5 be damned!) and that most celebrities would prefer selling watches to shot glasses. When he turns to discussing Monroe *as performer*, Salter shows his hand: "I don't know if it's a 007 movie or if it's action or it's drama but she's going to be an actress that the director chooses, no different than Kate Hudson or Meryl Streep." While he initially claims that it will be "no different" to cast Monroe, he quickly reveals the appealing difference between actresses living and dead. Living actresses, Salter knows, are a hassle. In contrast, "[Dead] celebrities don't talk back. . . . They don't go out on the town. They are ready to film every day."[42] While from Salter's perspective the posthumous star is a real performer, she is, importantly, not an agential one. The resurrected celebrity performer has no rights in Salter's fantasy of the celebrity who doesn't "talk back": the ideal actress is a girl who "can't say no."

The status of the actor as laborer is one with a vexed history, as scholars such as Danae Clark have documented.[43] The deepfake performer adds a new layer to this history of the actor as laborer, recalling the racialized fantasy of zombie labor and larger problems of a rights discourse embedded in exclusion of certain groups from the category of the human. For just as the early #MeToo movement focused on the exploitation of white actresses, so too does a focus on resurrected white stars risk occluding Hollywood's exploitation and objectification of Black actresses, both in Monroe's lifetime and our own. As Jennifer González and others have noted, the nonconsensual display of Black women's bodies for white audiences has a long history in US and European regimes of viewing and control; González writes: "The visual discourse of race involves a conceptual and categorical slippage between the body as object and the body as subject."[44]

In his aforementioned discussion of deepfake pornography's similarity to video games, John Paul Stadler argues that the deepfake's appeal depends crucially on its ability to offer control: "What deepfakes do is turn porn spectatorship into something more like a video game that we control and manipulate. They alter the reception practices and socialization practices of pornography into something else than what we've seen before."[45] The appeal Stadler locates appears clear in the pornography websites, which advertise their deepfake nature to viewers, and also in the case of producers seeking bodies without preferences. In the case of Monroe's resurrection, we might consider the significance of resurrecting the ultimate sexy (blonde) actress in the #MeToo era. As these discussions indicate, casting Monroe now (as opposed to in her lifetime) includes capturing some of the tragedy of Monroe. However, at the same time that the complexity of Monroe's life and stardom is evoked, the resurrection belies a fantasy of consequence-free exploitation. At a time when laborers, people of color, and actresses in particular are demanding more rights and more dignity in the workplace, the deepfake (white) actress becomes the perfect laborer.[46]

Of course, this perfection requires a death. Genevieve Yue's recent *Girl Head* helpfully elucidates the violence required by technological and aesthetic spectacle for women throughout film history. As she explains, the woman's body "is converted into material for and incorporated into the film production process.... The motif of the vanishing woman that attends these nonrepresentational disappearances is more than analogy, but a sign of the production processes."[47] And while the image of Monroe presented by her posthumous resurrections is more onscreen than Yue's examples, the necessity of a corpse to produce the spectacle is very much in line with the type of violence in the production process Yue describes. Describing how the China Girl was used to calibrate film color, Yue points to the way one woman's vanishing body allows others to materialize. In the case of Monroe, one body—the living, talking, difficult actress—must be disappeared in order for the deepfake to make its debut. Writing of a stunning absence in art historians' rendering of the Medusa myth, Yue draws attention to the violence of such processes: "None mention her discarded body ... figuring it [instead] as a necessary material substrate that is ultimately negated."[48]

Yue's language helpfully reminds us why Monroe's resurrection is so overdetermined, so very boring. For as scholars on Monroe have noted, and as is obvious from her filmography and its surrounding star discourse, Monroe has always been both "the body" *and* "the girl" or "the woman." Indeed, as Lesser argues: "She is a being who, despite the fact that the emphasis is on her body, is in constant danger of becoming disembodied, invisible, nonexistent. Of her performance in *The Misfits*, her last (completed) movie, Norman Mailer says: 'She seems to possess no clear outline on screen. She is not so much a woman as a mood, a cloud of drifting senses in the form of Marilyn Monroe.'"[49] Freed from the body, deepfake Monroe gives an ultimate performance of woman as uncomplicated, ageless fantasy—a mist—uncontaminated by historicity.[50]

INCOMPLETION AND NOSTALGIA

That Monroe and Dean have been a focus for resurrections tells us something about the strange interaction between nostalgia and careers cut short. While the premature deaths of these actors give to their careers a sense of incompletion, the desire to cast these iconic 1950s stars reveals the remarkable incuriosity of a star nostalgia that treats stars as closed entities.[51] In her analysis of reflexive revisionist films such as *Forrest Gump* and *Pleasantville,* Sharon Willis notes the way in which "history becomes a special sort of screen for our fantasies," including fantasies of race and gender.[52]

This line of argument might be extended to the deceased midcentury star, who remains pleasurably artifactual. Monroe and Dean will always be *that* Monroe and Dean: the images adorning a kitschy diner, the cardboard cut-outs in a theater lobby. As dead stars, they need neither descend into camp versions of themselves, nor thematize their own fall from the cultural center in the manner Desjardins has documented, managing the aging process through a shift to television programs featuring, often, gothic portrayals of older women.[53] Rather than develop tacky scents of their own for the television shopping channel QVC, they instead promote expensive perfume as glamor icons of the past. And, at once, they can neither develop unfortunate political positions nor make disturbing accusations about one or another director or media mogul. In this regard, the unfinished star career allows for a sealed vision of a star's meaning.

As I have argued elsewhere, the resurrection of Black celebrities such as Tupac Shakur reveals a desire to control Black performers and performances.[54] A similar phenomenon takes place in the case of an actress such as Monroe—one who can be made appealingly pliable. For Monroe simultaneously embodied ease *and* difficulty. As Richard Dyer discusses, Monroe symbolized the *Playboy* philosophy. Dyer quotes Norman Mailer as exemplifying this view of Monroe: "sex might be difficult and dangerous with others, but ice cream with her."[55] Monroe's most pornographic shoot is also one of her earliest and, in December 1953, it launched the *Life Magazine* of pornography—*Playboy*. However, Hefner's magazine of nudie pics that no one need feel ashamed to look at previewed the issues of consent and compensation that continue to characterize Monroe's posthumous stardom: as Dyer notes, the photo was taken by Tom Kelley years before.[56] When the images were reprinted, Hefner neither consulted nor paid Monroe.

But this is only half of the story. The rest of Monroe's story and her contemporary star persona have come to signify messy tragedy: the husbands, the pills, the hang-ups. As Daniel Herwitz argues, Monroe became iconic "mostly through her death"; he speculates that "had she gotten to the phone, her story would not have taken the turn it did, the melodrama would not have come to conclusion, the icon would not have properly formed before the public."[57] In our cultural imagination, Monroe is a player in a tragic morality tale of fame gone wrong, a narrative that more sympathetically supplements the tale of the neurotic pain-in-the-ass who prompted Tony Curtis's infamous description of *Some Like It Hot*'s love scene as "like kissing Hitler." The publication of Monroe's journals in 2010, under the title *Fragments*, supports this narrative, with entries bearing witness to her fear of hereditary mental illness and her terrible self-consciousness.[58] Until very recently, Monroe's star persona fed our contemporary sense not that there is no such thing as consequence-free sex, but that there is no such thing as consequence-free celebrity.

But perhaps the most apt characterizations of Monroe are captured in what Lesser admits to being a rather brutal description of her as "the empty hole" and in Churchwell's description of her as a vehicle for cliché, two accounts that explain the actress's ability to embody the dual poles of difficulty and ease.[59] As Churchwell argues of the many Monroe biographies, "Marilyn's lives promise the truth, but they more often recycle formula, telling us what we already think we know, satisfying our expectations."[60] The promise of the hassle-free, guilt-free (for the spectator) Monroe put forward by Salter thus represents a rejection of one set of meanings and a efficacious return to a particularly strong fantasy—a fantasy not unlike that promised by *The Seven Year Itch,* in which Monroe played "The Girl," a character defined by and desirable for her almost total lack of complicating details. Her character's profession as photographer's model involves supplying the material for others' representational desires. The image mentioned in the film as her greatest success is a winkingly-titled photograph called "Texture." Deepfake Monroe promises a return to this lack of complexity, the possibility of returning to an earlier ideal of sexual norms with an actress who can't "talk back" and might again act as pure material.

CONCLUSION: LOVEABLE OBJECTS

In Henry Hathaway's *Niagara* (1953), the only film in which Monroe's character dies, the plot abandons her Rose Loomis for an exciting third-act adventure involving the titular falls, her murderer husband George Loomis (Joseph Cotten), and the everywoman witness to the Loomis's unhappy marriage, Polly Cutler (Jean Peters). But before this unfolds, George returns briefly to the scene of his crime.

The murder itself is heavily aestheticized, taking on a more expressionistic visual style than the rest of the film, including several insert shots of the still bells of the tower, graphic cast shadows, and an extreme high-angle shot on the violent action of the scene. From this high angle, above the bells, we see Rose collapse on the floor and George flee the tower. After George leaves, the film cuts in to a shot that isolates Rose's

FIGURE 13.1 Rose Loomis (Marilyn Monroe) as object in Henry Hathaway's *Niagara* (1953).

corpse from the contextualizing detail of the scene. The angle on the action, the shot scale, and the strong shadows contribute to an image of Rose suspended on a horizontal theater screen, picked out against the blankness of the industrial floor (figure 13.1). Rose's death, her stilling and horizontal orientation, allow for Rose to appear as film material. As Jacqueline Rose argues, this is a culmination of a trajectory the film has set for Rose/Monroe; she notes: "I counted no less than five earlier images where she is lying prone—whether asleep or fainted—splayed out, to all intents and purposes already dead."[61]

But compared to the dimensionality of Rose's earlier pink satin dress, the black dress is notable for being oddly dull, absorbing light and adding to the flatness of the image. Once the film aestheticizes Rose's corpse as decorative object—or, in Jacqueline Rose's terms, aestheticizes Monroe as corpse a final time—it leaves her, cutting to the outside of the tower before tilting down and tracking in to reveal the locked door that has trapped George in the tower with his murdered wife's corpse. Realizing that he's momentarily stuck, George goes back up the tower stairs, where he first encounters not Rose but rather an object that captures her essence: a jeweled lipstick case.[62] He turns it in his hands and opens it, revealing the pinkish-red lipstick Rose has been wearing throughout the film. A small divot is missing from the lipstick bullet, a deeply human imperfection that recalls Rose's intimate physical contact with the cosmetic. The loving attention to this second beautiful object triggers action toward the now-inanimate woman. Rolling the tube between his hands, George looks upward to the top of the tower, where Rose's body remains. George ascends the stairs and goes to her, taking on a tender posture as he sits on one hip, gazing down at her form.

Of all the scenes featuring the married couple, this one is the most caring and intimate in its staging. Live, Rose was a pest, a source of woes, and torture to George. "I loved you Rose. You know that," he tells her. But it's her death, the quiet form, that brings out this tenderness. Fixed in place as image, Rose performs as the receptacle for George's affection that she couldn't in life. It's easy to love the dead.

NOTES

1. Susan Sontag, *Regarding the Pain of Others* (New York: Picador, 2003), 115.
2. Lisa Bode, Dominic Lees, and Dan Golding, "The Digital Face and Deepfakes on Screen," *Convergence* 27.4 (2021): 849–54, 850.
3. "Publicity," Legal Information Institute, Cornell Law School, www.law.cornell.edu/wex/publicity#:~:text=The%20right%20of%20publicity%20prevents,recognizable%20aspects%20of%20one's%20persona.&text=Under%20the%20Restatement's%20formulation%2C%20the,of%20one's%20name%20or%20likeness.
4. Nathan Koppel, "A Battle Erupts over the Right to Market Marilyn Monroe," *Wall Street Journal* (10 April 2006), www.wsj.com/articles/SB114463306707721479.
5. See Adam Moore, *Privacy, Security and Accountability: Ethics, Law and Policy* (London: Rowman & Littlefield International Ltd, 2006); and Judith DeCrew, "Privacy," *Stanford Encyclopedia of Philosophy* (Spring 2018), ed. Edward N. Zalta, https://plato.stanford.edu/archives/spr2018/entries/privacy/.
6. Samuel D. Warren and Louis D. Brandeis, "The Right to Privacy," *Harvard Law Review* 4.5 (1890): 193–220.
7. See Lucy Fischer, "The Lady Vanishes: Women, Magic, and the Movies," *Film Quarterly* 33.1 (1979): 30–40; Karen Redrobe (Beckman), *Vanishing Women: Magic, Film, and Feminism* (Durham, NC: Duke University Press, 2003); Genevieve Yue, *Girl Head: Feminism and Film Materiality* (New York: Fordham University Press, 2021); Maggie Hennefeld, *Specters of Slapstick and Silent Film Comediennes* (New York: Columbia University Press, 2018); Alix Beeston, *In and Out of Sight: Modernist Writing and the Photographic Unseen* (New York: Oxford University Press, 2018); and Mary Desjardins, *Recycled Stars: Female Film Stardom in the Era of Television and Video* (Durham, NC: Duke University Press, 2015).

8. Desjardins, *Recycled Stars*, 3.

9. See Sarah Churchwell, *The Many Lives of Marilyn Monroe* (New York: Picador, 2004); Jacqueline Rose, "Respect," in *Women in Dark Times* (London: Bloomsbury, 2014): 100–138; Wendy Lesser, "The Disembodied Body of Marilyn Monroe," in *His Better Half: Men Looking at Women through Art* (Cambridge, MA: Harvard University Press, 1991), 193–224; and Griselda Pollock, "The Missing Wit(h)ness: Monroe, Fascinance and the *Unguarded Intimacy* of Being Dead," *Journal of Visual Art Practice* 16.3 (2017): 265–96.

10. Bill Zehme, "Interview: Hugh M. Hefner," *Playboy Magazine* 47.1 (January 2000): 63–80, 240–45, 242.

11. James Stacey Taylor, *Death, Posthumous Harm, and Bioethics* (New York: Routledge, 2012), 39.

12. Taylor, *Death, Posthumous Harm, and Bioethics*, 144.

13. T. M. Wilkinson, "Consent and the Use of the Bodies of the Dead," *Journal of Medicine and Philosophy* 37.5 (2012): 445–63; and Wilkinson, "Last Rights: The Ethics of Research on the Dead," *Journal of Applied Philosophy* 19.1 (2002): 31–41.

14. "Marilyn Monroe's Funeral," Abbot and Hast Publications, www.abbottandhast.com/mmfuneral.html, accessed 22 March 2012.

15. See, for example, the infamous Lindsay Lohan *Playboy* shoot, which Melissa Hardie has discussed in relationship to discourses of the index and the real, analyzing the nostalgic choice to shoot on film and unpacking various claims that Lohan looked more like the "real" Monroe than Monroe did. Melissa Hardie, "The Closet Remediated: Inside Lindsay Lohan," *Australian Humanities Review* 48 (May 2010), http://australianhumanitiesreview.org/2010/05/01/the-closet-remediated-inside-lindsay-lohan/.

16. Pollock, "Missing Wit(h)ness," 268, 270.

17. See "Marilyn Monroe," https://adultdeepfakes.com/celebrities/marilyn-monroe/.

18. See "Marilyn Monroe," https://sexcelebrity.net/actor/marilyn-monroe/, and "Deepfake of Marilyn Monroe Will Surrender in All Poses to the German Fascist," https://sexcelebrity.net/deepfake-of-marilyn-monroe-will-surrender-in-all-poses-to-the-german-fascist/.

19. Karen Hao, "Deepfake Porn Is Ruining Women's Lives. Now the Law May Finally Ban It," *MIT Technology Review* (12 February 2021), www.technologyreview.com/2021/02/12/1018222/deepfake-revenge-porn-coming-ban/.

20. Shaka McGlotten, Susanna Paasonen, and John Paul Stadler, "The Deep Realness of Deepfake Pornography: A Conversation," in *Deep Mediations: Thinking Space in Cinema and Digital Cultures,* ed. Karen Redrobe and Dan Scheible (Minneapolis: University of Minnesota Press, 2020), 351–60, 354.

21. Mathilde Pavis, "Rebalancing Our Regulatory Response to Deepfakes with Performers' Rights," *Convergence* 27.4 (2021): 974–98, 975.

22. McGlotten, Paasonen, and Stadler, "Deep Realness of Deepfake Pornography," 358.

23. Lesser, "Disembodied Body of Marilyn Monroe," 194.

24. Christopher Holliday has also described the world of deepfake in terms of the conditional mood, writing of recastings of iconic film performances:

"The variant levels of digital manipulation increasingly available in relation to facial content have led to Deepfakes videos being deployed in imagining a possible world of Hollywood film history predicated on a premise of the hypothetical, conditional or 'what if?'" Christopher Holliday, "Rewriting the Stars: Surface Tensions and Gender Troubles in the Online Media Production of Digital Deepfakes," *Convergence* 27.4 (2021): 899–918, 908.

25. Elaine Kasket, *All the Ghosts in the Machine: Illusions of Immortality in the Digital Age* (London: Robinson, 2019), 220.

26. "First Federal Legislation on Deepfakes Signed into Law," *JD Supra* (24 December 2019), www.jdsupra.com/legalnews/first-federal-legislation-on-deepfakes-42346/.

27. Geoffrey A. Fowler, "Anyone with an iPhone Can Now Make Deepfakes. We Aren't Ready for What Happens Next," *Washington Post* (25 March 2021), www.washingtonpost.com/technology/2021/03/25/deepfake-video-apps/.

28. Laura Mulvey, *Death 24x a Second: Stillness and the Moving Image* (Chicago: University of Chicago Press, 2006), 172.

29. Mulvey, *Death 24x a Second*, 173.

30. Mulvey, *Death 24x a Second*, 18.

31. André Bazin, "Death Every Afternoon," in *Rites of Realism: Essays on Corporeal Cinema*, trans. Mark A. Cohen, ed. Ivone Margulies (Durham, NC: Duke University Press, 2003), 27–31, 31.

32. Zack Sharf, "'Star Wars: The Rise of Skywalker' Left Unused Carrie Fisher Footage on the Cutting Room Floor," *IndieWire* (24 December 2019), www.indiewire.com/2019/12/star-wars-rise-of-skywalker-cut-unused-carrie-fisher-footage-1202199234/.

33. Alex Ritman, "James Dean Reborn in CGI for Vietnam War Action-Drama (Exclusive)," *Hollywood Reporter* (6 November 2019), www.hollywoodreporter.com/news/afm-james-dean-reborn-cgi-vietnam-war-action-drama-1252703.

34. Lisa Bode, "No Longer Themselves? Framing Digitally Enabled Posthumous 'Performance," *Cinema Journal* 49.4 (2010): 46–70, 50–51.

35. Lisa Respers France, "Chris Evans and Others Sound Off against CGI Casting of James Dean," *CNN* (7 November 2019), www.cnn.com/2019/11/07/entertainment/james-dean-cgi-casting-trnd/index.html.

36. Thanks to Stefan Solomon for this formulation.

37. France, "Chris Evans and Others Sound Off."

38. Sharareh Drury, "Director of New James Dean Movie Speaks Out over Backlash to Star's 'Casting,'" *Hollywood Reporter* (7 November 2019), www.hollywoodreporter.com/news/director-new-james-dean-movie-speaks-backlash-stars-casting-1253232.

39. Lauren Probert, "Modern Day Itch: Marilyn Monroe Is Being Brought Back To Life with Latest Technology Using a 'Digital Double,'" *The Sun* (31 March 2018), https://www.thesun.co.uk/tech/5942168/marilyn-monroe-digital-double-technology/.

40. Lesser, "Disembodied Body of Marilyn Monroe," 195.

41. "Toronto Businessman Plans to Make Marilyn Monroe a Digital Movie Star," *Toronto Star* (31 January 2011), www.thestar.com/entertainment

/movies/2011/01/31/toronto_businessman_plans_to_make_marilyn_monroe_a_digital_movie_star.html.

42. James McMahon, "Hello, Norma Jean ... Could CGI Help Marilyn Monroe Star in a New Film?" *The Guardian* (4 February 2011), www.theguardian.com/film/filmblog/2011/feb/04/marilyn-monroe-cgi-star-film.

43. See Danae Clark, *Negotiating Hollywood: The Cultural Politics of Actors' Labor* (Minneapolis: University of Minnesota Press, 1995).

44. Jennifer González, *Subject to Display: Reframing Race in Contemporary Installation Art* (Cambridge, MA: MIT Press, 2008), 5.

45. McGlotten, Paasonen, and Stadler, "Deep Realness of Deepfake Pornography," 352.

46. As Will Scheibel and Steven Cohan have shown, the issue of labor and its erasure is also at stake in Monroe. In his writing on Monroe's early years at 20th Century Fox, Scheibel unpacks the way Monroe's performances thematized the experience of her image's construction, thereby "destabiliz[ing] the media's efforts to regulate her sexual identity in the public sphere." In contrast, the deepfake Monroe is very much the construction, with very little room for the kind of nuance Scheibel documents. And, as Cohan argues, recent biopics have a habit of erasing Monroe's labor, including efforts to assert herself on set, instead emphasizing the actress as a figure of glamorous and tragic eroticism. The deepfake Monroe represents the culmination of such fantasies. Will Scheibel, "Marilyn Monroe, 'Sex Symbol': Film Performance, Gender Politics and 1950s Hollywood Celebrity," *Celebrity Studies* 4.1 (2013): 4–13, 5; and Stevan Cohan, "'This Industry Lives on Gossip and Scandal': Female Star Narratives and the Marilyn Monroe Biopic," *Celebrity Studies* 8.4 (2017): 527–43, 535–36.

47. Yue, *Girl Head*, 15.

48. Yue, *Girl Head*, 18.

49. Lesser, "Disembodied Body of Marilyn Monroe," 195.

50. Similarly, in *Over Her Dead Body*, Elisabeth Bronfen writes of Samuel Richardson's *Clarissa*: "Embalming her corpse would be an exquisite form of control over the mobility that enabled Clarissa to continually elude [Lovelace's] grasp. For if the process of decomposition can be prevented, then death is the perfect moment when Clarissa's body can be completely and indefinitely at his disposal." Elisabeth Bronfen, *Over Her Dead Body: Death, Femininity, and the Aesthetic* (Manchester, UK: Manchester University Press, 1992), 95.

51. This nostalgia is somewhat different from that Dan Golding describes as taking place in the deepfake de-agings of "legacy" films such as those in the *Star Wars* franchise in which an actor's image may become as iconic as that of Darth Vader's mask. As I've discussed, the deepfakes used to continue a star's affiliation with a series have been met with far less controversy, although I'd also suggest that the issue of consent is still at play in posthumous performances in the legacy film. Dan Golding, "The Memory of Perfection: Digital Faces and Nostalgic Franchise Cinema," *Convergence* 27.4 (2021): 855–67, 857.

52. Sharon Willis, *The Poitier Effect: Racial Melodrama and Fantasies of Reconciliation* (Minneapolis: University of Minnesota Press, 2015), 73.

53. Desjardins, *Recycled Stars*, 73.

54. Katherine Fusco, "Voices from beyond the Grave: Virtual Tupac's Live Performance at Coachella," *Camera Obscura* 30.2 (2015): 29–53.

55. Cited in Richard Dyer, *Heavenly Bodies: Film Stars and Society* (New York: Routledge, 2004), 39.

56. Dyer, *Heavenly Bodies*, 25.

57. Daniel Herwitz, *The Star as Icon: Celebrity in the Age of Mass Consumption*.(New York: Columbia University Press, 2008), 15–16.

58. See Marilyn Monroe, *Fragments: Poems, Intimate Notes, Letters*, ed. Bernard Comment and Stanley Buchthal (New York: Farrar, Straus and Giroux, 2010).

59. Lesser, "Disembodied Body of Marilyn Monroe," 205.

60. Churchwell, *Many Lives of Marilyn Monroe*, 5.

61. Rose, "Respect," 124.

62. Writing of this same moment, Rebecca Burditt has suggested that the lipstick stops the narrative to "become a spectacle in itself, compelling audiences to pause—like potential consumers before an advertising spread—in admiration of its desire-inducing splendor." Rebecca Burditt, "Death and Lipstick: Commercial Moments in *Niagara*," *Journal of American Culture* 44.2 (2021): 99–115, 99.

The Ruined Map, Relinked

A Postscript

GIULIANA BRUNO

Relation relinks (relays), relates. . . .
The relinked (relayed), the related, cannot be combined conclusively.
—Édouard Glissant

There are stories, books, works of art, and life events that are positively unfinished. Their fluid state constitutes an opportunity for a scholar. Artistic materials that are incomplete invite her to activate her interpretive capacities with receptive creativity and explore imaginative ways to relay and relink them. One needs to engage closely with the objects of analysis to see how they exist in the larger universe of things that circulate in cultural life. This requires an inventively material historiographical approach as well as a philosophical imagination. When handling the materiality of unfinished matters, a sense of aperture and opening ensues. Speculative and relational, this material research process can access diverse fields to craft transdisciplinary passageways and junctures, compositing views and at times even blending realia and fabulation. But there is a particular openness and movement in this form of receptive relatedness that I want to foreground here, which is "projective" in nature. A special vitality is engaged in the act of working with the incomplete, because the process releases potential energies intrinsic in a project that is ongoing or unfinished. And this form of projection can also be a propelling, resonating force, pushing the scholar to constantly move forward in her own project, in response to objects that do not wish to remain static.

This projective cultural energy is a by-product of what such a method can do but also of what it does not wish to do. An unfinished, relational way of thinking resists centralized or totalizing visions in favor of side perception, neighboring moves, peripheral detours, and attunement to the off-screen space.[1] This errant research mode that leans toward the edge of unactualized matters cannot be concluded or even conclusive. In precluding closure as well as enclosure, it affirms the potential force of virtuality and resists exhausting possibilities. The unfinished is an open, porous, virtual matrix—a flux of becoming. The generative process released from incomplete objects can thus generate a processual analytic method, open to potential, resonant, receptive relationality.[2] And because this undone is also an undoing, it cannot be done with.

It is no wonder, then, that I find myself facing the unfinished again, thirty years after the publication of my book *Streetwalking on a Ruined Map: Cultural Theory and the City Films of Elvira Notari*.[3] I eagerly responded to Alix Beeston and Stefan Solomon's invitation to write this postscript because I felt an "elective affinity" with their project and the scholarly approach of the book's contributors to the feminist possibilities of the unfinished film. This opportunity to reflect on my book's methodological implications led me to think especially about the kind of relational explorations they continue to generate. And so I embarked on a meditation into the porous, combinatory weave of elements that constitutes my unfinished, "becoming" process of inquiry. My move through adjacent but diverse materials, which aims to stimulate creative contiguous proximities, is sustained by an endless desire for a poetic aesthetics of relationality. The incomplete, here, is a potential form of receptive transfer, a relational current: the resonant energy of a transmission turning into material transformation (see figure 14.1). As I hope to relate and transmit here, my continually unfinished search seeks intimate forms of connection that can, indeed, "relink, relay, relate."

FLASHBACK TO FAST FORWARD: A POTENTIAL UNFINISHED

To frame my unfinished story, and to begin to articulate this relational research process, let me first provide some context for the self-reflexive analysis. Traveling back to the future, it is good to see that a collective book on the feminist implications of the incomplete can be welcomed and eagerly published today. There was more resistance in 1990 to accepting a transdisciplinary manuscript shaped by unfinished histories and conceptual meditations on lacunae. There was even clear opposition to this research method, and especially to my treating a woman's nonextant work and the process of cultural memory in terms of the undone.

FIGURE 14.1 Exhibition view, *Carta Bianca: Capodimonte Imaginaire*, curated by Giuliana Bruno, Museo e Real Bosco di Capodimonte, Naples, Italy, 12 December 2017–9 December 2018. Installation view: metal grid modeled on display in museum storage rooms, with ruined canvases and art objects by unknown artists. Photograph by Luciano Romano.

As mentioned by Beeston and Solomon in this book's introduction, *Streetwalking on a Ruined Map* emphasized the undone in reconstructing the forgotten, pioneering work of Elvira Coda Notari (1875–1946), Italy's first and most prolific film director as well as a screenwriter of original subjects and literary adaptations, producer, distributor, and film company owner. Between 1906 and 1930, Notari made more than sixty feature films, over one hundred actualities, and numerous shorts commissioned by immigrants in North and South America to document their places of origin. Fascist censorship and the transition to sound forced her film studio, named Dora Film after her daughter, to cease production. And the majority of this woman's prolific film production did not survive: only three feature films and a few fragments are extant.

At a time when there was no internet, no search engines or websites, and no eBay or digitization of films or documents, the search for the dispersed materials on two continents had been an adventurous one that involved lots of "streetwalking," from the winding streets of Naples to the straight avenues of New York. Many stories accumulated as, working both with and against given notions of the archive, I traveled to anywhere that might provide a remnant, perusing all kinds of sites and unearthing many personal, domestic collections. Various strategies had to be invented just to open the doors to customary research sites, such as Italian archives of film or state records, libraries, and cinematheques, for they did not function as places of circulation but rather as strict, enclosed sites of preservation. Most of the time I enjoyed turning them into less structured enclosures, but there were always obstacles. And it was not always comfortable perusing dilapidated Neapolitan warehouses that might once have been film production houses or visiting gritty Italian American social clubs in New York's Little Italy. Finally, this search that mined diverse disciplinary territories and turned up only marginal ephemera and societal clues resulted in a specific cultural cartography: a manuscript that ended up emphasizing the nonextant, theorizing the lacunae of "the ruined map" that was the production of a pioneering woman filmmaker.

Yet the editor of a distinguished publishing house challenged the core of my feminist method: Why did I insist on the loss of this work? Did I really wish to convey a sense of history as lacunar? Yes, I responded, it was important to concentrate on the nonextant and position it within a larger cultural and textual terrain. The exposure of Notari's lost filmic objects by means of other objects was a way of making the reader materially feel both their presence and absence. The act of treating absence not as an accidental or incidental factor but as a marker, a place in itself, generated by specific conditions, would make it a presence in its own right. And this exposure could account for the persistence of cultural memory and the female voice as well as their erasure. Moreover, if this interdisciplinary, processual approach to the undone became a place of inquiry, even a position, it might undo traditional methods of historiographical analysis and more conventional theories of authorship. "That is seriously committed to the incomplete," the editor retorted disapprovingly. "Why not simply write on the films that remain?" In conclusion, it was suggested that I consign my manuscript to the trashcan. Forget "the ruined map." Write a different book: three straightforward chapters of textual analysis, one for each of the extant films. This kind of book the editor would publish. As a young assistant professor at Harvard University, where, at the time, prospects for tenure were dismal, especially for women, I knew the risk of refusing this offer. But I was aware of the loss involved in accepting it. And so I declined, veering

FIGURE 14.2 Front and back dust jacket for Giuliana Bruno, *Streetwalking on a Ruined Map: Cultural Theory and the City Films of Elvira Notari* (Princeton, NJ: Princeton University Press, 1993). Cover design by Pierluigi Bruno.

off a well-traveled scholarly road in favor of an intellectual journey of discovery that affirmed the importance of the undone.

Luckily there is a happy ending to this story, for my manuscript found a more adventurous publisher, and the book won major awards on both continents (figure 14.2). Most important, the method has appeared to be transmissible and generative of further research, in the sense that unfinished feminist strategies can generate transmissions that are both fluid passages and residual continuance. One of my greatest pleasures is that my ruined map could even translate into creative work, inspiring, for example, an artist such as Renée Green to make *Some Chance Operations* (1999). In this film, as Beeston and Solomon recount, my scholarly research process is embodied, and even fictionalized, in the character of Clara, the Italian researcher who travels in search of Notari's traces. If one sets in motion a relational practice that stimulates disparate linkages to connect and creates diverse nexuses that bond, this process generates a spiral of unfinished contaminations. In this way a feminist practice of relationality can even turn into a collective modality. But this only happened sometime later, so let us take a step back to discuss the methodological process that took us to this place.

INCOMPLETE MARGINS: AN OPEN, GENERATIVE METHODOLOGY OF MARGINALITY

In facing a ruined map that was missing all its major parts, different but related forms of marginality emerged. As a woman, Notari could not legally own her own production company. Her husband, Nicola, often got the credits; the Fascist regime censored her; and, finally, she was unrecognized for her pioneering work and altogether expunged from history. Marginalized, and finally lost, were her unusual representations of real locations, consistent use of vernacular registers, emphasis on urban popular culture, and strikingly realistic portraits of the conditions of women and underprivileged communities.

I was thus confronted with a specific kind of incompletion: a landscape of the margins and of marginalized social spaces. But the missing parts and the loss had to be positively transformed. A methodological shift had to occur for this locus of lacunae to become a generative site of production and analysis of discourses. Combining extensive archival research with a strong theoretical drive, I strove to turn the undone into a way of undoing more traditional approaches. As I went beyond the scope of textual analysis of the extant films, I questioned another strategy common in feminist scholarship at the time: the auteurist principle. I resisted the impulse to write a single authorial study or monograph of Notari and instead widened the authorial perspective to include the discursive agents that emerged in a search on the margins, which intended to picture a contextual and paratextual panorama.

In trying out a "marginal" way to navigate the material, I realized that a feminist reading based on the unfinished could positively acknowledge the fact that the very archive of film history is undone—a fact with which the contributors of this book also engage. The unfinished—a constellation that is never comprehensive or coherent but always open-ended and in progress—is the result of movement, transmission, and dissemination. The complex cultural apparatus that accompanies a film's creation and circulation creates gaps and voids, pauses and lulls, interruptions and intervals, hiatuses and interludes, breaks and breaches. But these cracks and lacunae are also apertures and openings. They can provide access into the multiple layers of the experience of film as well as markers of its existence.

In order to create this geography of openness, one had to work with the empty space that is the margin. Specifically, the process of traversing a territory punctuated by physically lost or even unrealized materials had to engage what had been pushed to the margins, and in various forms of circulation. And thus the focus on the unfinished—the ruined map—became a gesture of recovery of practices marginalized within both film history and scholarship. I called these "minor" practices, in reference to Michel Foucault's focus on *savoirs mineurs* in his *Archaeology of Knowledge,* which inspired my way of constructing a nonlinear cultural genealogy.[4] Traversing a landscape of loss consisting of "suppressed knowledge," I focused on the archival detritus and the discarded documents of the paratextual, treating the remains and the fragments, working on the margins to expose the process of marginalization. To mine the minor is indeed a tangible way to feel the historical margins, to sense and expose history itself as an archaeological site of knowledge. Treating the incomplete as a minor practice enables an actual haptic encounter with history's own blanks, limits, and edges. In the process one can not only see a terrain spread out in layers, composed of geological strata, but feel locatedness in a territory, and sense the tensility of an unfinished motion.

CULTURAL ARCHAEOLOGY BEFORE MEDIA ARCHAEOLOGY

In sensing these systemic movements, my exploratory, geographical, even geological approach to visual culture emerged, as did its processual modality. Mapping a genealogy that was a cultural archaeology, I adopted a processual method that tried to expose itself. Whereas filmmakers were used to laying bare the process of making, and experimented with it, film and art historians did not engage with this mode as frequently at the time, often preferring to hide their practice. To make the processual method of excavation and analysis apparent, exposing the ruined map, was to make its wounds tangible and to turn the lacerations into passages. This work on the margins led to constructing a more complex mapping of women's roles, beyond the monographic focus on individual authorship, for it created an aperture onto different narratives and interpretations of women's history that expanded their agency. A feminist reformulation of film with less focus on singularity and plenitude aimed to transform received notions by using the gaps as junctures for reimagining even its own terrain, both by paying attention to materialist histories and pushing interdisciplinary strategies of reading across different mediums as well as media.

This could clear the passage toward what today we call a feminist media history. But how to actually accomplish this? My strategy was to illuminate the historic contribution of Notari's lacunar production by mining and exposing the cultural terrain in which she operated, with its different agential elements, which were subjects but also cultural operations. I thus embarked on a series of "inferential walks" through various other artistic mediums and technical media. The process of streetwalking through literature, photography, art history, urban studies, and the history of medicine as well as film history was aimed at expanding the horizon of feminist film scholarship to comprise not only a wider cultural territory but also the larger social impact of women's work. While exposing the cultural and social fabric of which Notari's films were a part, I did not shy away from unraveling the complexity at stake in this enterprise. As Laura Mulvey nicely put it in her blurb for *Streetwalking on a Ruined Map*, the book is "an intellectual tapestry, but one that is prepared to unravel its own surface."

Unraveling, after all, is also an undoing. In order to undo centralized perspectives by weaving an intellectual tapestry at the margins of texts, one had to keep looking sideways, both laterally and across. This adjacent or off-screen gaze revealed, for example, how central and influential women's popular literature of the late nineteenth and early twentieth centuries was, and how its construction passed into the filmic realm, as a foundation for Notari's narratives. Art history, too, was embedded in her filmic iconography and visual style of narration. It shaded her eye, for her tragic way of picturing stories recalled, and even filmically restaged, the representation of the martyrdom of female saints that is so present in Italian art. Notari's consistent way of shooting on location intersected with renditions of landscapes and streetscapes by local artists, who had a particular penchant for drawing *en plein air*. Photographic realism was also part of this visual tapestry that emphasized the fabric of material space, localized urban culture, and metropolitan texture. Last but not least, the history of science and medicine enabled me to navigate Notari's construction of the female body itself as wounded.

If I had to choose one crystallizing example, it was uncovering the illustrated program notes for the lost film *'E scugnizze (Female Urchins,* 1917), which presents underprivileged women driven to madness by class and societal strictures. Before my eyes was the image of a *popolana* (a woman of the people), whose unclaimed cadaver had been given away to medical science for experimentation. We see Maria laid bare on the anatomical table, about to be "operated" upon by a doctor—the very lover who had abandoned her, driving her to insanity and death. There were many composite elements of laceration "bared" in this remnant of the kind of visual "operation" that is an anatomy lesson. And ultimately, this operational fragment served to expose the anatomy itself of my feminist analysis. It became a site for reflecting upon the very fragmentation of film language, and for theorizing it as embodied, even a theater of the body. In particular, the cut exposed here showed me that the techniques of "cutting" that are exhibited in film theaters bear a trace of their origin in the spectacle of the anatomical theater. Translated and represented in the history of art, this theatricality prefigured the very birth of spectatorship.

Although theorization was a more prominent discourse in gender studies at the time, it was the interlacing of historiography that enabled me to push these boundaries in *Streetwalking on a Ruined Map*. To weave a cultural tapestry, in fact, I had to resist the established separation, or even a clear-cut juxtaposition, of the two fields. Looking backward but fast-forwarding to the contemporary, there are affinities between this interlinked perspective and current views of media archaeology.[5] Here was the beginning of the combinatory, media-genealogical approach later fully fleshed out in my *Atlas of Emotion: Journeys in Art, Architecture, and Film*.[6] This cultural cartography, as media theorist Jussi Parikka noted, prefigured "some of the infrastructures of theory and method of contemporary contexts," including the field of media archaeology.[7] Although the latter methodology is at times more linearly constructed than a tapestry, both books nonetheless share with contemporary media archaeology even more than the incorporation of history by a theorist. They share the desire to embrace wide-ranging historically attuned methods and eclectic archival research to reflect on the theoretical and philosophical implications of these approaches. In *Streetwalking on a Ruined Map*, the gesture of investigating a variety of sources to document a suppressed, neglected, or forgotten history became a way to map a media-cultural condition, and to see it shaped by unnoticed continuities as well as ruptures.

Continuing even beyond those "inferential walks" to traverse the terrain of disciplines generally considered separate has led me to where I am now in my research, always looking for means through which new methods and languages can be invented to bridge the chasm between unfamiliar epistemological spheres. This is a process of unlearning as much as one of learning—a systematic undoing while navigating the undone. I practice a form of media-cultural archaeology as a traveling method that, driven by curiosity for the unfinished, prefers wandering through territories rather than arriving at destinations. This is itself an unfinished process, threading through a composite, layered landscape in which the humanities and the arts are not isolated. In this sense, shaping a process of streetwalking introduced transdisciplinary methodologies and topics that I continue to revisit throughout my work, in particular a "kinetic analytic" that emphasizes an embodied and mobilized approach to visual and spatial cultures. In *Streetwalking on a Ruined Map,* specifically, this takes the form of a female psychogeography oriented around a *flâneuse* roaming through and with a ruined map: a landscape of lacunae and incompleteness, a panorama of sites in motion that explores modernity's moving architectures.

This is because the unfinished is ultimately a terrain of movement. One might even claim that a processual motion is the actual material condition of film. The unfinished speaks of the resistance of the moving image to be contained, of its inherent drive to escape completion with its characteristic constant material mobility, fragile mode of existence, and unstable sites of distribution and circulation. While emphasizing the boundless movement of the moving image, however, one can also locate it in a specific cultural form of transit as well as mediatic context. For film not only moves, it is a modern site of movement: an agent of modernity's motion. As I argued in *Streetwalking on a Ruined Map,* modernity itself is not a stable paradigm but a culture in transition and in transit. In this sense, the book insisted on shaping a genealogic relation of cinema to sites of modernity such as arcades and the railway. Not simply techniques of modern vision or observation, these are apparatuses of cultural mobility: processes of unfinished spatial construction and cultural mobilization. Looking at the reception of sites of transport such as trains, films, or *passages* shows how the motion of visual media drives the reconfiguration of space, in its continual transformations. And so in paying attention to this unfinished cultural transport, including mobile forms of circulation and mediums of communication, a site of mixture can begin to take shape: the crossroads between film and media studies, mobility studies, and material culture studies.

MATERIALITY AND MATERIALIST HISTORIES OF VISUAL CULTURE

Traversing adjacent terrains to create new crossroads can result in this kind of cross-pollination only if one puts the different materials in close touch and in contact with one another. A materialist, unfinished method of analysis largely depends on expanding the range and relational treatment of research materials to test their capacity to interweave a composite panorama of spatio-visual cultural life. In *Streetwalking on a Ruined Map*, I created networks of visual communication through the use of physical objects, linking material traces of the nonextant and treating all archival materials in their specific materiality while connecting together their visual or written forms. Like the materials discussed throughout *Incomplete,* these networks of material objects extended from film fragments to photographs that portrayed the filmmakers, the studio, or the locations as well stills from the films. They also included screenplays and lengthy film program notes, which were distributed at movie theaters, as was the custom for stage theaters or opera houses, providing extensive plot summaries as well as pictures from the films. Critical writings in journals were especially crucial to understanding the experience of film culture and the reception of the work of this pioneering woman filmmaker. And I did not shy away from the commercial aspect of the media network as I researched publicity documents such as flyers and posters or advertisements in newspapers and journals and also considered many industrial documents.

Particularly important and sensitive were the censorship visas, which provided access to crucial information about the existence of film culture and its circulation under a dictatorship. Research on the unfinished revealed how Notari inventively circumvented the censors, sending her films to North and South America before they could be shown in mutilated form in Italy or risk not being shown at all. While Notari herself never traveled overseas, her act of creating Dora Film of America, with a distribution office in New York, made her films not only move paradigms but entirely shake them. In crossing an ocean, her now-lost moving images provided an imaginary binding for Italian immigrants, and not simply because the theater was a site of sociability. The displaced immigrants, whose lives bore the wounds of separation from their native land and cultural milieu, found in her cinema a public *piazza* from which to negotiate an unfinished, culturally hybrid identity.

In unearthing, analyzing, and relinking this wealth of materials—a presence that correlated and even expressed the absence of the films—I tried to restore the intricate weave of Notari's nonextant production rather than resurrect her or her work from oblivion. It is worth elaborating methodologically on the substantial difference between these two positions. It lies in the fundamental treatment of the material archive, and in the choice of relaying and relinking it. My form of restoration consisted in a relational work of montage. As an associative process of relaying and compositing incomplete materials, this assemblage did not aim to remanufacture Notari's textual loss, invoking an authorial original form, but rather was intent on leaving the cuts, the wounds, and the stitches exposed. Like any self-reflexive work of montage that a filmmaker might produce, my editing of materials would even try to expose disparities and gaps in its own analytic assemblage, in a process that tried to make the film work visible while maintaining the invisibility of the nonextant.

I was inspired to restore Notari's production in this way by considering actual techniques of art restoration. At different times in history, there had been dissimilar if not opposite strategies for the restoration of incomplete artworks. Sometimes restorers of these damaged works would leave the missing parts alone and expose them as empty spaces or blanks. At other times they would instead fill in every gap entirely, seamlessly reconstructing the areas of the works that had been harmed, wounded, or plain lost. But as I approached my own ruined map, I realized that the perspective had changed in ways that both defied these two opposing positions and combined them. A third, hybrid way was found to reconfigure the methodological matter of restoration while restoring a material loss.

This third way to restore was an eye opener, as I noted in the introduction to *Streetwalking on a Ruined Map*. I became fascinated by the movement of (in)visibility that I saw at work in the contemporary preservation of paintings, and especially of frescoes. Viewed from afar, the overall restored picture might appear to have been seamlessly reconstructed to its integral condition. And yet, if one moved from that position and looked up close, the sites of absence became evident. One could see the reconstructed parts because they had a different texture, which felt like a screened surface. As the observer moved into the picture, a surface encounter occurred. The weave of layered surfaces revealed the fabric of their artistic fabrication. Furthermore, as the reconstructed work came to the surface in this moving process, the restorer's work of intervention became palpable. Even the actual handiwork of the invisible analyst-restorer might end up being felt.

This methodological and material shift that transformed the way in which preservationists work on art objects offered a resonant way to approach my own work of restoration. The method was particularly appropriate to a filmic nonextant because it seemed not only kinetic but utterly cinematic. It is in fact based on an action of movement and an act of screening. At work in this art historical process of restoration is a dynamic that clearly evokes passing from a long take to a close-up, tracking or zooming in from afar into a detail. And this movement built into the picture both implies and requires a mobile observer who would in turn "screen" these moving images. In this processual motion, the hand that restores turns a painterly canvas into the kind of tapestry that is screen fabric.

This process of fabricating a "superficial" textural weave stayed with me as I interwove layers of screened surfaces in *Surface: Matters of Aesthetics, Materiality, and Media*.[8] In taking a material approach to visual texts that is fundamentally textural, I continued here the process of crafting that had produced *Streetwalking on a Ruined Map,* which now turned texture into trace and even stain. This process made me fully recognize how the unfinished has real substance. It not only has layers and tissues but contains strata that are sediments and deposits. It reveals the patterns of history, in the form of a coating, a "film," or a stain. The unfinished can really *wear* its own history, inscribed as an imprint onto its own textural surface, which always leaves behind a trace.

This kind of material surfacing—an energy wave that traverses a weave of diverse materials to expose their interconnected fabric—characterizes my work of analytic intervention on textu(r)al objects. This is the case even when a work is extant, because I am always interested in telling the history and the story of an object in its unfinished form. This means exposing the material, even technical condition of a work's existence in the movement of its cultural operations, wading through the layers of surface manifestation of art objects. Relaying and relating such conditions together, in their particularity, distinction, diversion, and variance, I aim to establish a dynamic processual method, keen on undoing itself while exposing how the becoming configurations of "cultural techniques" can reveal the undone.[9]

UNFINISHED HANDIWORK: HAPTICITY AND FILM MANUFACTURE

In approaching material culture techniques of the unfinished, even beyond restoration, in *Streetwalking on a Ruined Map* I emphasized practices of hapticity and materiality, including the labor of handiwork. Early silent cinema was in fact a filmic culture of "manufacture." In the face of films that are now globally more than 80 percent nonextant, the Italian locution *manifattura cinematografica* speaks clearly of this, as well as for the loss. As per its medieval Latin root, a film manufacture is a handmade enterprise, even a homemade cultural practice—that is, a

FIGURE 14.3 A woman's work: Manufacturing silent films in Naples. Collection of Giuliana Bruno.

form traditionally inhabited by the female worker. It was largely women who worked in the assembly room of the film production houses and also hand-tinted the films. An underpaid job, this required patience, attention, and care, and was repetitive—all characteristics of female housework. Unlike the public role of working on a set, assembling a film could be done inside: editing reproduced the invisibility as well as the modalities and time expenditures of women's work. While most women in the early assembly room remained simply the bricklayers of film production, Elvira Notari was among the few who moved from working at coloring films to establishing her own film company.

I wanted to make visible this invisible aspect of the unfinished history of women's labor. And so I was especially thrilled to find pictures of women working in Neapolitan film production houses, for they eloquently documented the nature of early film-manufacturing processes (see, for example, figure 14.3). The few extant images that emerged from the research led me to see clearly that, in both form of labor and spatial location, assembling films resembles sewing. The places portrayed are like sweatshops: the site is inhabited only by females, attending to work and cleaning prints in large spaces, working alone at their machines and yet all crowded in the same space. These women were working in film just as they were working at their sewing machines in the sweatshops.

Like a dressmaker, the woman editor cuts and puts together pieces of film text(ure) with a haptic process that relies on hands and tools. There are tears and incisions to be made, gaps and ellipses to negotiate, holes to stitch, cuts to turn into joinings. In other words, editing exposes the very haptic process of the unfinished that we have been unraveling here. In some way, as I also remarked in *Streetwalking on a Ruined Map,* the analytic material process of editing is akin to the anatomy lesson—a "cutting" into the material body of film. And so, understood in this way, an unfinished process that relays and relinks can both expose lacerations and suture wounds.

When theoretically unfolding the labor of the incomplete in this relational way, the force of its sartorial process thus emerges. In my book *Surface* the unfinished language of film itself became theorized as such a cultural technique: an actual material form of tailoring. After all, even if not constructed from strips of celluloid, film is still stitched together in strands of digital formations, woven into patterns, designed and assembled, even if virtually, like a customized garment. So when those invisible women editors labored on folds of film, in production houses that resembled fashion houses, they not only made intimately visible but *authored* this sartorial process we call filmmaking. As they cut and stitched together materials, reinventing the very process of clothing construction, they developed a new language of the unfinished, out of the mode and model of tailoring.

FEMINIST CLOSE ENCOUNTERS: PROCESSUAL THEORY AND RELATIONALITY

This material exploration of the labor of manufacturing silent film culture in Naples exposed the fact that the unfinished is not simply close to my scholarly sensibility but is intimately connected to my own ruined map. *Streetwalking on a Ruined Map* was a personal journey—a close, even intimate "voyage to Italy." As I tried in my imagination to move, provoke, and listen to "silent" voices, and to feel the resistance that silenced them, I could not silence what emerged from my own voice. Through Notari's eyes and location shooting, I was able to rediscover Naples, my Italian city of origin, which I had left as a young woman to live in New York. Incomplete, then, was a specific journey: a story of separation and reconnection. The unfinished here was the movement of migration. And it took a real work of joining to transform its cuts and wounds into connective threads, turning the ruined map into a generative processual journey.

To locate oneself personally in a scholarly journey of discovery one needs to stay open to the possibility of intimate encounters. Different forms of intimacy were in fact generated in the process of navigating the ruined map. My sense that the unfinished generates close encounters was driven home, quite literally, in Renée Green's *Some Chance Operations*. Passing from the book into film, the unfinished resurfaced as Clara, the Italian researcher, travels through Naples with Renée in search of the locations of Notari's production that had been reconstructed in *Streetwalking on a Ruined Map*. This fictionalization of my research process in the film exposed the double layers of my unfinished journey through Naples, all the while creating yet another close encounter and imaginary collaboration between a scholar and an artist-filmmaker. It reinforced the sense that a feminist approach to the unfinished has real potentiality, especially when generating a processual method of knowledge exchange in the formation of an archive.

This can occur if a material archive is truly conceived as unfinished, which means not forced into fixed schemes of memorization or preservation. Stories like that of Notari, and my search for her, can be revisited with new elements incorporated; and this can change the form—the territory—of the ever-growing archive. The intimate, collaborative formation of a feminist archive can thus resist the all-encompassing, enclosed structure of an exhaustive encyclopedia. It can be more like an atlas. It can function as a geographic territory, open to shifts in shape and constant transformation. This unfinished atlas-archive does not strive to give definite form to the knowledge it presents but acknowledges environmental moves and territorial shifts. Such research work is boundless and yet bound: a space of constant motion and emotion.

Affects, and their forms of transmission, are in fact major constituent agents in a process of research that declares itself unfinished. Finally, I can see clearly why this method is so close to my heart: it is because, as a strategy of intimate encounters, open to creating passage, it generates resonance and relationality. The feminist unfinished is a collaborative, creative method that produces hybrid forms of contact. Its process of assemblage creates complex encounters between different objects and live matters as well as between subjects. It encourages collaboration not only methodologically and texturally but also at other more personal levels. Here, connections that are forms of contact generate sympathy, the elective affinity of interpersonal connectivity with animate worlds.

Adopting such a processual approach to the unfinished is thus a feminist way of continuing to produce forms of relation in a cultural environment. This specific relational aspect drove me to write about projective environments in *Atmospheres of Projection: Environmentality in Art and Screen Media*.[10] The effort to conceptually address "the projective imagination" with forms of "atmospheric thinking" turned into yet another way to pursue unfinished relational strategies as forms of becoming. At a very basic level this involved exploring forms of contact established in and through ambient conditions to which we are exposed and with which we interact, and seeing how this affects and even changes both. This contact often takes the form of a psychic projection—that is, a transmission of affects, an energy that can be felt passing through the atmosphere and harnessed in an ambiance.

In this vein, the unfinished can itself function as such an environment. This is a project that enables projection. It is a true relational space, where encounters between subjects and with objects are not passive influences but can reconfigure both. This is because, as occurs with any projective environment, this research modality also engages awareness of a process of introjection and incorporation. A morphing of materials that merges or even blends matters together is not fusional; it encounters resistance, and in this movement of matters the process of becoming does become transformative. Moreover, an environment of projection can also project. It is a sign of possibilities, an actual generative process. In this sense the relational aspect of an unfinished process is also a work in progress. And thus I continue to work on how this incomplete work may construct places of intermixing and generate the transmission of cultural energies.

At the time of this writing, during a pandemic and the deprivation of contact it entails, it seems particularly relevant to understand unfinished strategies as such precious sites of connection and to actively promote this form of vital exchange. Pursuing this line of thinking, I am especially interested in what Édouard Glissant calls "new zones of relational community," and in the kind of geocultural entities that are "aggregates formed through encounters and kinships."[11] In this relational sense an unfinished method can continue to undo dominant systems by exploring not only the objects of relation but also its own forms of relationality. And this can be done only if one accepts that relation both *is* and *makes* movement. Or rather, if one understands it as a particular kind of movement, which Glissant calls an "errantry": a motion akin to an experience of exile.

In writing this self-reflexive text, this latter aspect has assumed even more significance in relation to the incompletion of *Streetwalking on a Ruined Map*. Sensing the scars, the real weave of loss inscribed in my own personal experience as well as in the ruined map that was my terrain of inquiry, I can better grasp now why, thirty years ago, I embraced errantry as a fundamentally migratory mode. And I can see why I keep pursuing an endless erring through various terrains, trying to stitch and tie together unfinished relations. It is because now, more than ever, I want to reclaim the kind of unfinished form of relation that is an intimate projection—a poetics of relation that, as Glissant writes, "relinks (relays), relates."[12]

NEW MATERIAL RELATIONS: THE UNFINISHED AS CURATORIAL STRATEGY

Relink, relate again, feel the energy of relay. In this spirit I offer a final set of reflections on the unfinished as a relational, material, processual modality of research. For quite some time I had been considering that this processual way of thinking, with its creative, relational assemblage of materials, might be akin to a curatorial strategy. When writing about the few extant instruments from the scientific laboratory led by the psychologist Hugo Münsterberg at Harvard University, the curatorial modality took clear shape as an approach to the incomplete.[13] In the end I even described an imaginary art exhibition that would activate, energize these instruments that had a role in producing one of the first books of film theory but now lay still and scattered in an archive.[14] If only one could tune in to the internal motion of these now stilled objects, one could reanimate them in the form of an art exhibition. In this sense the archival research on the incomplete not only showed me that it was akin to the act of curating but also made me recognize that this work shares an elemental, alchemic process with curation. The process of creative theorizing in this interpretive alchemic way can itself constitute an imaginary form of exhibition.

Some years later, a thrilling yet challenging opportunity arose to transpose this approach to the incomplete into actual curatorship. When invited to curate a section of an art show at the Museo e Real Bosco di Capodimonte in Naples, I eagerly accepted in order to put my scholarly curatorial mode into practice. The process of actualizing this became another way to relink, relay, and relate. Returning to Naples in 2017, and relinking pieces of the ruined map, I devised a strategy for the exhibition *Carta Bianca: Capodimonte Imaginaire* that was much related to, and expanded on, the curatorial form of cultural mapping I had begun to forge with *Streetwalking on a Ruined Map*.[15] "Carte blanche" was given to curate a space freely, in the context of an exhibition that sought the participating curators' personal and creative interpretations of the museum's massive, majestic collection. Given my scholarly inclination, I overlooked masterpieces usually put on exhibition and rather asked to be given access to the extensive storage rooms of the museum. Some residual institutional and bureaucratic resistance had to be appeased to open the doors to these safeguarded but imperfect archives, for which a complete database did not exist. In storage lay most of the museum's collection: 4,700 internal holdings.

The experiment of imagining an exhibition of the incomplete as it materializes in an art historical archive of this magnitude turned into both a personal and scholarly journey of discovery, through yet another kind of unfinished geography. Navigating this artistic terrain ended up even "suturing" that ruined map of separations that was, alas, my relation to the city of Naples. Reconnecting to the world of my grandfather, who had been an architect and a painter there, I imagined an exhibition about my city of origin to highlight its haptic representational history and especially its Baroque "taste." Bringing to light works conserved in storage, I looked for still lifes, with their everyday objects, including food and pottery. The city's venerable history of decorative arts, especially as embodied in the eighteenth-century ceramics of Capodimonte, was of particular interest, but it was still marginalized as "minor" art. And so I mined the minor again, searching for remnants of porcelain pieces, plates and vases that might have been the models for the still lifes, where memory is always memento mori. I exhibited both paintings and vessels together, showing the real, physical objects as if they could have emerged from their representation on the canvas. The stored ceramics came alive as they haptically materialized for observers, in an exhibition that connected the laboratory of an alchemist to kitchen work.[16]

Acting as an archaeologist careful in the handling of minor works, for *Carta Bianca* I explored the storage facilities of the museum as if they were geological deposits, or layers of time. It is no surprise that navigating sideways and veering off well-traveled roads, I looked offscreen for artworks worn down by the ages, ruined, partly lost. The storage rooms revealed numerous pieces never completed or that had lost their completed appearance. I even found a storage facility entirely devoted to the incomplete, filled with an accumulation of unfinished artworks, many unattributed. They were so damaged that preservationists could not even restore them. The museum did not seem to know what to do with these derelict canvases other than pile them away.

These canvases had an erratic, weathered, unstable existence that attracted me. Here was a marine landscape with a melancholic, undulating appearance. Surfacing out of the worn canvas, barely visible, was a house with a sea view looking out onto calm waters, from which a sailing boat emerged in a flow of liquidity. In this unfinished, fluid seascape, both home and vessel appeared to be floating away in memory, onto a sea of ruins. In another corner there was a still life by an unknown artist from the seventeenth century, faded in such an abstract way around the edges that it had taken on the future appearance of a work from the twentieth. The edges of figuration had melted into the off-screen space, and the threads of canvas had become materially visible and prominent. As a result, even the depicted fruits assumed a different contour. They popped out of this painting circumfused by a void of figures but a density of texturality. With figuration dissolving, atmosphere was all that emerged from these temporal scenarios.

Atmospheric, indeed, were my favorite forgotten, weathered artworks. This included a landscape by an unknown artist, which in time had simply become an ethereal landscape of light and a story of clouds. With half of the picture in a nonextant state, the "air" itself of the painting had become the work's protagonist. Separated from the trunk that had faded, the leaves of a tree rustled in the wind as the sky appeared to turn from luminous to dark. Light filtered cinematically through particles of air, through the thickness of clouds, and one could feel its "projective" capacity. An atmosphere of projection was exposed in this painting, dense with what I call "environmentality."

These undone canvases—environments dense with meteorological affects—were neither static nor still. They even appeared to be moody. Their unstable state enhanced the motion of an emotion, and even projected the mood for love. A decayed painting by an unknown artist revealed an amorous embrace so interwoven with the physical, textural state of the exposed canvas that it had become part of its fabrication. The color, too, had morphed to such an extent that the worn-out skin of the canvas melted with the lovers' intertwined flesh in this ruined map of love. A work had been so materially processed by time that it had become *materico* in its entirely undone state. This painting was simply marked "Fragmentary Scene by Unknown."

Weathered, scratched, stained, wounded, decayed, or even disintegrated, these unattributed, unstable paintings wore the atmospheric mark of time on their surfaces with extreme elegance. No matter what resistance or critique I would encounter, this collection of "superficial" canvases—whose fabric weaves exposed the processual fabrications of history—had to become an exhibition of the unfinished process. But how could this be done effectively? The texture of these forgotten canvases would have to be featured along with dusty and empty frames. But to really communicate the force of the ruined objects, I would have to come up with an inventive way of exhibiting them. While exposing their physicality, I had to expose a method or, rather, design that could reinvent their status as art objects. My new, atmospheric curatorial tapestry had to be, yet again, able to unravel its own surface.

A creative modality of installation, with a dynamic spatial construction, was key in the process of achieving this aim of featuring the undone. I decided to reconstruct in the exhibition space an archival modality to reflect the way artworks are deposited in museum storage spaces. Paintings are usually attached to the frames of large metal grids in these rooms. Disparate series of paintings are often strapped together randomly, or according to size alone, on these compact vertical panels that move on tracks. Taken together, these screenlike grids relate and relink disparate works of cultural memory, erratically packed and stored away.

I asked the museum to remanufacture one of these panels and put it on display, in an effort to relay the true erratic nature of the assemblages in the archives.[17] Functioning as if they were screens, these movable framed planes in fact host an accidental work of montage that enables incidental sequencing. This material form of relationality was enhanced by deploying not only these screens but a process of "screening" art. Because I had practiced a form of "errantry" in roaming about the museum's depositories, the exploratory journey resulted in a creative art historical erring that even allowed for potential errors. The exhibition design reinvented how objects erratically assembled in a museum storeroom create seemingly canonical errors that instead can be interpreted as surprising alliances. As not-on-view artworks were filmically exhibited, visibly exposed but as if still in their hidden spaces, a different kind of art historical archive emerged. The fortuitous placement and assemblage of art objects from different periods of history, genres, or authors—brought together by their state of ruin—triggered nontraditional art historical associations that became relays and relationships. In linking together traces of absence, an unfinished genealogy of art histories as well as an unconventional interpretation of artworks was brought to light.

A dialogic, relational way of reimagining an art space as unfinished can indeed relay a more inventive museology. Thus the undone was, yet again, put into action in the exhibition design of *Carta Bianca,* not only to undo more customary approaches to visual art but to push them forward. While the exhibition design engaged the vicissitudes of cultural memory, it looked toward the future of visual culture studies, showing that writing and curating can be brought together in productive relations. Joining two registers in a processual way, and intermixing them formally, can generate novel paradigms that might act to change fields of research.

Thinking in this future perfect was central to *Carta Bianca,* an exhibition that, following the lead of *Streetwalking on a Ruined Map,* and in line with the aims of *Incomplete,* did not wish to romanticize ruins of the past but harness their unfinished potential. Future possibilities were on display, even if this was not the actual object of that book or of this exhibition. Although there were no contemporary works of art shown in *Carta Bianca,* the selected works were arranged in a sequential screening in the space, *as if* this were an installation of contemporary art.[18] Curated as if relayed, these incomplete works of the past appeared to have resulted from the processual treatment of canvas made by contemporary artists interested in textile forms of design, working with weaves of surface and textural conditions to bring about atmospheres of materiality.

To enhance this sense that the incomplete relays a future perfect, and to emphasize the feeling of a contemporary art exhibition, the screen-like assemblage of unstable works on the framed panel was placed on a spectatorial itinerary that reinvented forms of screening in the museum site. The design of the exhibition was enlivened by white fabric panels that both separated and connected zones of display. These curtain-scrims functioned as actual translucent screens. They invited the visitor to follow a narrative trajectory that linked together the different stations, culminating in the exhibition of the large screen-panel of ruined works. The reception of the artworks unfolded in movement as viewers traversed white folds of fabric that effectively screened the space.

In the end, then, the *Carta Bianca* exhibition reinvented an actual cinematographic path through material art surfaces. In exposing its own process, it reaffirmed that a ruined map is itself a sartorial surface.

Such texture seeks intimate scholarly contact. As a work of the past that is tangibly thrust into the present, the unfinished map projects its potential to relink gaps of temporality and spatial intervals. To stay open to this material modality, to continue to relate to the unfinished, is a vital experience of binding and bonding for a scholar rapt by transformative processes. In the midst of the incomplete, one can feel the energy of a relay, its very points of contact—the projective currents of relationality.

CODA, WITH ELVIRA CODA NOTARI

The process of relating (relaying) keeps alive the act of relinking. Curating for the *Carta Bianca* art exhibition strongly relinked me to *Streetwalking on a Ruined Map,* even in uncanny ways. Let me indulge in relaying one last encounter with the undone process of undoing. To conclude the exhibition, I wanted to expose the idea that the design of the delicately woven ruined map, sited on the gridded archival screen, is a feminist, processual strategy of interpretation. Fond as I am of the unfinished, I do not like endings. (This postscript, you may have noticed, has several spiraling endings—much as the introduction to *Incomplete* has several beginnings). Because I much prefer experimenting with open works and processes, final closure had been difficult. Finally, I tried an erratic, cinematic move. Entering a storeroom, I randomly touched one of those panels on which paintings hung in stillness and slid it on its track to see what would emerge, and possibly move me.

And there she was, Francesco Guarino's *Saint Agatha* (c. 1640). Serendipity had put her again in my path. The undone is indeed never finished. And it can circle back to give meaning to a project and closure to a process. Twenty-five years earlier, I had suggested placing this exact painting on the cover of *Streetwalking on a Ruined Map.* So Agatha's portrait was joined in that design, just as it was in the book's interior, with a frame enlargement from Notari's *'A Santanotte* (1922), in which Nanninella, a stabbed *popolana,* exposes the scar on her breast.[19] This Agatha from the seventeenth century likewise displayed that she had been injured in resisting to comply with established rules. Here, however, the wound was suggested as an indexical trace. Blood seeps, as if screened, through a folded piece of white fabric that Agatha holds on her breast, as she looks defiantly out of the canvas. The way her lacerated skin is felt, emerging only through the fabric of the cloth, resonated strongly with the textural condition of the ruined canvases on display on the gridded archival screen at Capodimonte.

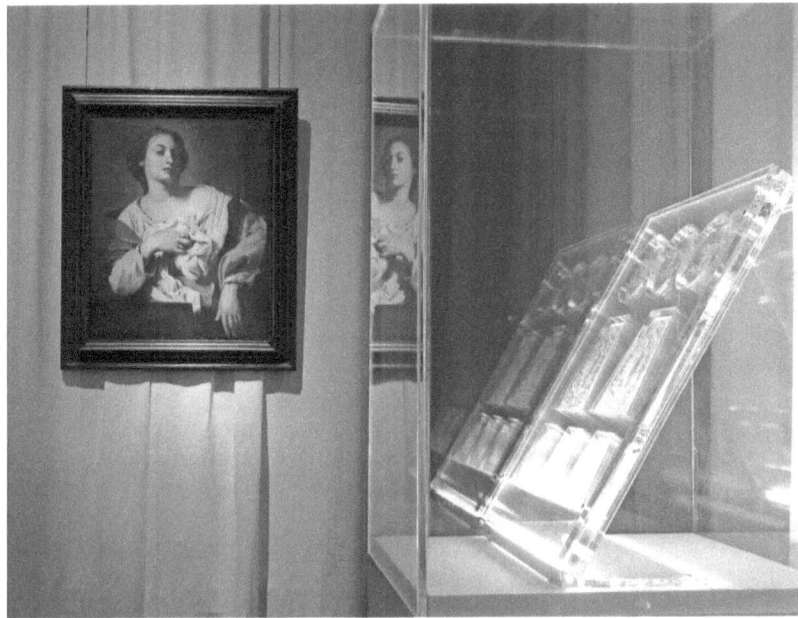

FIGURE 14.4 Francesco Guarino, *Saint Agatha*, c. 1640, oil on canvas, with rock crystals by Giovanni Bernardi (1494–22 May 1553). Installation view, *Carta Bianca*. Photograph by Luciano Romano.

Agatha, by herself, was the image that closed the trajectory of the *Carta Bianca* exhibition, and it was luminously placed in a reflective, projective light (figure 14.4). On the cover of the 1992 book she had been turned around, her oblique gaze redirected, as if wishing to look at Notari's Nanninella on the back of the jacket. In 2017, in a spiral of unfinished relations, both women had resurfaced for me, with their edgy way of looking sideways and off-screen. Their lateral gazes had met again, if only virtually, having become adjoined in my imagination in an imaginary exhibition. And thus their stories were relayed, relinked, reconnected.

NOTES

Epigraph: Édouard Glissant, *The Poetics of Relation*, trans. Betsy Wing (Ann Arbor: University of Michigan Press, 1997), 173.

1. My first venture into the unfinished began with a book I coedited with Maria Nadotti, *Off Screen: Women and Film in Italy* (New York: Routledge, 1988).

2. This processual way of thinking is inspired by the philosophy of Alfred North Whitehead, and especially his book *Process and Reality: An Essay in Cosmology*, ed. David Ray Griffin and Donald W. Sherburne (New York: Macmillan, 1978).

3. Giuliana Bruno, *Streetwalking on a Ruined Map: Cultural Theory and the City Films of Elvira Notari* (Princeton, NJ: Princeton University Press, 1993).

4. Michel Foucault, *The Archaeology of Knowledge*, trans. A.M. Sheridan Smith (New York: Pantheon Books, 1972).

5. For an introduction to this field of study, see Erkki Huhtamo and Jussi Parikka, eds., *Media Archaeology: Approaches, Applications, and Implications* (Los Angeles: University of California Press, 2011).

6. Giuliana Bruno, *Atlas of Emotion: Journeys in Art, Architecture, and Film* (New York: Verso, 2002).

7. Jussi Parikka, "Review of *Atlas of Emotion: Journeys in Art, Architecture, and Film*," *Leonardo* (September 2018), https://leonardo.info/review/2018/09/review-of-atlas-of-emotion-journeys-in-art-architecture-and-film.

8. Giuliana Bruno, *Surface: Matters of Aesthetics, Materiality, and Media* (Chicago: University of Chicago Press, 2014).

9. For an introduction to this notion, see Bernhard Siegert, *Cultural Techniques: Grids, Filters, Doors, and Other Articulations of the Real*, trans. Geoffrey Winthrop-Young (New York: Fordham University Press, 2015).

10. Giuliana Bruno, *Atmospheres of Projection: Environmentality in Art and Screen Media* (Chicago: University of Chicago Press, 2022).

11. Glissant, *Poetics of Relation*, 142.

12. Glissant, *Poetics of Relation*, 173.

13. Giuliana Bruno, "Film, Aesthetics, Science: Hugo Münsterberg's Laboratory of Moving Images," *Grey Room* 36 (Summer 2009): 88–113.

14. See Hugo Münsterberg (1916), *The Photoplay: A Psychological Study and Other Writings*, ed. Allan Langdale (New York: Routledge, 2002).

15. The *Carta Bianca* exhibition was initiated by Sylvain Bellenger, director of the Museo e Real Bosco di Capodimonte, and Andrea Viliani, former director of the Madre Museum in Naples. I was invited, along with nine others from diverse fields of knowledge, art, and music, to reinterpret in personal ways the wonderful collection of Capodimonte. Each of the guests—Laura Bossi Régnier, Gianfranco D'Amato, Marc Fumaroli, Riccardo Muti, Mariella Pandolfi, Giulio Paolini, Paolo Pejrone, Vittorio Sgarbi, Francesco Vezzoli, and myself—was given a space in the museum to curate individually with complete carte blanche. The exhibition was on view for nearly a year, from 12 December 2017 to 9 December 2018.

16. The domestic display of the exhibition had a personal subtext that relinked me to family history, for the showroom of precious porcelains and crystals my father operated on the floor beneath our house was my childhood playground. Even the ruined paintings and the tragic, final image I would choose for the exhibition, discussed at the end of this postscript, brought to mind memories of my mother, who sensitized me to the meaning of lacerations.

17. I had first asked the museum to move the large metal grids on tracks out of storage into the exhibition space, but the floor of the ancient building could

not bear the weight. I am grateful to the architect Lucio Turchetta, who superbly interpreted my vision for the design of the exhibition, including the white scrim-partitions.

18. The ruined works of the past themselves asked for this design that enhanced contemporaneity. Taken in their materiality as aesthetic objects, these paintings of the past could in fact have been produced in recent times. One could think them the work of an artist associated with *arte povera* or following the "matterism" of Alberto Burri or practicing a postminimalist approach to art. It was as if the fabric of the canvas had been treated by a modern or contemporary painter who had intently worked on its material fiber to expose its materiality.

19. Princeton University Press gracefully accepted the suggestion. My brother, the visual designer Pierluigi Bruno, designed the book's cover.

About the Contributors

PEGGY AHWESH is a Brooklyn, New York–based media artist whose work has traversed a variety of technologies and styles in an inquiry into feminism, cultural identity, and genre. Her work has been featured in Whitney Biennial Exhibitions (1991, 1995, and 2002) and is held in the film collection of the Museum of Modern Art. *Vision Machines,* a survey of work, was presented at Spike Island in 2021 and Kunsthall Stavanger in 2022. Ahwesh is Professor Emeritus of Film and Electronic Arts at Bard College, where she taught video production, history of technology, and archival media practices. She also taught in the Bard Prison Initiative and al-Quds Bard College, West Bank, Palestine.

ALIX BEESTON is Senior Lecturer in English at Cardiff University, Wales, where she teaches and researches twentieth- and twenty-first-century literature, film, and photography. She is the author of *In and Out of Sight: Modernist Writing and the Photographic Unseen* (Oxford University Press, 2018, paperback 2023) and the coeditor of the Visualities forum at *Modernism/modernity* Print Plus. Alix is currently at work on a critical-creative account of women in photography, under contract with MIT Press. Her essays appear in *PMLA, Signs, Modernism/modernity, Arizona Quarterly,* the *Edinburgh Companion to Modernism and Technology,* and elsewhere.

GIULIANA BRUNO is Emmet Blakeney Gleason Professor of Visual and Environmental Studies at Harvard University. Internationally known for her interdisciplinary research on visual arts, architecture, and media, she is the author of several award-winning books, including *Streetwalking on a Ruined Map: Cultural Theory and the City Films of Elvira Notari* (Princeton University Press, 1993), winner of the Society for Cinema and Media Studies book award; *Atlas of Emotion: Journeys in Art, Architecture, and Film* (Verso, 2002), winner of the Kraszna-Krausz prize for best Moving Image Book; *Public Intimacy:*

Architecture and the Visual Arts (MIT Press, 2007); *Surface: Matters of Aesthetics, Materiality, and Media* (University of Chicago Press, 2014); and *Atmospheres of Projection: Environmentality in Art and Screen Media* (University of Chicago Press, 2022).

KATHERINE FUSCO is Associate Professor of English at the University of Nevada, Reno, where she has previously served as the Director of the interdisciplinary Core Humanities program and developed the popular Cinema and Media Studies minor. Katherine's scholarship focuses on American literature and film studies. She has written two academic books, *Silent Film and U.S. Naturalist Literature* (Routledge, 2016) and, with Nicole Seymour, *Kelly Reichardt* (University of Illinois Press, 2017), and more than a dozen articles, some of which have won the most prestigious awards in her field. She has also written about motherhood and popular culture for public-facing outlets such as *Avidly, The Atlantic,* and *Harper's Bazaar.*

JANE M. GAINES is Professor of Film at Columbia University and Professor Emerita of Literature and English at Duke University. She received the Society for Cinema and Media Studies Distinguished Career Award in 2018 and an honorary doctorate from Stockholm University in 2022. She is author of three award-winning books: *Contested Culture: The Image, the Voice and the Law* (University of North Carolina Press, 1991), *Fire and Desire: Mixed Race Movies in the Silent Era* (University of Chicago Press, 2001), and *Pink-Slipped: What Happened to Women in the Silent Film Industries?* (University of Illinois Press, 2018). Her articles on intellectual property and piracies, documentary theory and radicalism, feminism and film, early cinema, and critical race theory have appeared in *Cinema Journal, Screen, Critical Inquiry, Cultural Studies, Framework, Camera Obscura,* and *Women and Performance.*

LEO GOLDSMITH is Visiting Assistant Professor of Culture and Media at Eugene Lang College, the New School. He is a coauthor of Robert Stam's *Keywords in Subversive Film/Media Aesthetics* (Wiley, 2015) and the author of a forthcoming book on the filmmaker Peter Watkins (Verso). His critical writing appears in *4Columns, Screen Slate,* and *The Brooklyn Rail,* where he was film editor from 2011 to 2018. He has curated film series and exhibitions at the Museum of the Moving Image, the Ann Arbor Film Festival, and Contemporary Art Centre (Vilnius, Lithuania), and is a programming adviser for the New York Film Festival.

KATHERINE GROO is Associate Professor in Film and Media Studies at Lafayette College. Her essays have appeared in *Journal of Cinema and Media Studies, Framework, Discourse,* and *Frames,* as well as numerous edited collections. She is the author of *Bad Film Histories: Ethnography and the Early Archive* (University of Minnesota Press, 2019) and coeditor of *New Silent Cinema* (Routledge/AFI, 2015). She is also the recipient of the Alexander von Humboldt Experienced Research Fellowship. Her current book project, *Images at the End of the World: Historicity and Mourning in the Twenty-First Century,* examines the referentiality and artifactuality of contemporary visual media.

MAGGIE HENNEFELD is Associate Professor of Cultural Studies and Comparative Literature and McKnight Presidential Fellow at the University of Minnesota, Twin Cities. She is the author of *Specters of Slapstick and Silent*

Film Comediennes (Columbia University Press, 2018), coeditor of *Unwatchable* (Rutgers University Press, 2019) and *Abjection Incorporated: Mediating the Politics of Pleasure and Violence* (Duke University Press, 2020), coeditor of the journal *Cultural Critique* (University of Minnesota Press), and cocurator of a four-disc DVD/Blu-ray set, *Cinema's First Nasty Women* (Kino Lorber, 2022). She is currently writing a second monograph about the history of women who allegedly died from laughing too hard.

KAREN PEARLMAN writes, directs, and edits screen productions. She researches creative practice, cognition, and feminist film histories. Collected by major film archives around the world, her trilogy of films about historical women editors—*Woman with an Editing Bench* (2016), *After the Facts* (2018), and *I want to make a film about women* (2020)—has won thirty competitive national and international awards including three for best editing, three for best directing, and six for best documentary. Pearlman is the author of the widely used textbook on editing, *Cutting Rhythms* (Focal Press, 2015), now in its second edition and with translations into Chinese, Korean, Arabic, and Turkish. She teaches screen production and practice at Macquarie University in Sydney.

ELIZABETH RAMÍREZ-SOTO is Assistant Professor in the School of Cinema at San Francisco State University. Her research focuses on feminist film history, transnational film and media practices, and documentary. She is the author of *(Un)veiling Bodies: A Trajectory of Chilean Post-Dictatorship Documentary* (Modern Humanities Research Association, Legenda, 2019) and the coeditor of *Nomadías: El cine de Marilú Mallet, Valeria Sarmiento y Angelina Vázquez* (Metales Pesados, 2016). Her work has appeared in such collections as *Feminist Worldmaking and the Moving Image* (MIT Press, 2022) and journals including *Quarterly Review of Film and Video, Journal of Latin American Cultural Studies,* and *Rethinking History.* Elizabeth is also founder and coordinator of the Latin American Women's Audiovisual Research Network (RAMA).

KAREN REDROBE is the Elliot and Roslyn Jaffe Professor of Cinema and Modern Media at the University of Pennsylvania and a board member of Scribe Video Center. She is the author of *Vanishing Women: Magic, Film, and Feminism* (Duke University Press, 2003) and *Crash: Cinema and the Politics of Speed and Stasis* (Duke University Press, 2010), and she is currently completing *Undead: Animation and the Contemporary Art of War.* She is the editor of *Animating Film Theory* (Duke University Press, 2014) and the coeditor of *Still Moving: Between Cinema and Photography* (Duke University Press, 2008), *On Writing with Photography* (University of Minnesota Press, 2013), and *Deep Mediations: Thinking Space in Cinema and Digital Cultures* (University of Minnesota Press, 2021).

MATHILDE ROUXEL holds a PhD in film history, specializing in Arab cinema. She is a postdoctoral researcher at the New Sorbonne University and co-artistic director of the Aflam festival in Marseilles. She was Jocelyne Saab's personal assistant for the last six years of the filmmaker's life, and when Saab passed away in 2019, Rouxel cofounded the Association of Friends of Jocelyne Saab, which she now directs. Rouxel is the author of *Jocelyne Saab, la mémoire indomptée* (Dar An-Nahar, Beirut, 2015) and the coeditor, with Stefanie Van de

Peer, of *ReFocus: The Films of Jocelyne Saab* (Edinburgh University Press, 2021).

ISABEL SEGUÍ is a Lecturer in Film and Leverhulme Early Career Fellow at the University of Aberdeen, Scotland. She obtained a PhD at the University of St. Andrews. She is the founder and a member of the steering committee of the Latin American Women's Audiovisual Research Network. Her work, in English and Spanish, has been published in journals and edited collections in Europe and the Americas and awarded by the British Association for Film, Television, and Screen Studies. She is coeditor of the special issue of the journal *SSLAC*, "Documents for a Feminist History of Latin American Cinema."

SOPHIA SIDDIQUE holds a PhD from the University of Southern California's School of Cinematic Arts. She is an Associate Professor in the Department of Film at Vassar College. Her areas of research include Singapore cinema, Asian horror, cinema and the senses, the short film form, film phenomenology, and global science-fiction cinema.

STEFAN SOLOMON is Senior Lecturer in Media Studies at Macquarie University. He is the author of *William Faulkner in Hollywood: Screenwriting for the Studios* (University of Georgia Press, 2017) and the editor of *Tropicália and Beyond: Dialogues in Brazilian Film History* (Archive Books, 2017). He is also the coeditor of *William Faulkner in the Media Ecology* (Louisiana State University Press, 2015) and *The Moving Form of Film: Historicising the Medium through Other Media* (Oxford University Press, 2023).

Index

absence: archival, 18, 247, 288; and Collins, 246–47, 252–54, 257; and feminist recovery, 28; fetishization of, 29; and Hill, 291, 293; and Léontine, 72; and Méliès, 95; as presence, 20, 332; and Notari, 8, 229, 325, 332–33, 343; and Singaporean film historiography, 230–34; and women of Popular Unity government, 125, 131. *See also* trace

abstraction: in Ahwesh, 174; in Brakhage, 193; in Hill, 285, 288, 291

activism: archival, 66; feminist, 32n28, 127; and Hill, 270–71, 277, 283–84, 292; in Latin America, 117, 123n7, 132, 143; queer, 281; and Fusako Shigenobu, 149, 160

actualities, 7, 75–76, 86, 324

aesthetics: of appropriation, 170; and color, 90–91; Kantian, 91; of knowledge, 185; of open-endedness, 15; of relationality, 32

affect: despair, 176, 185; grief, 231, 240, 249; hope, 3, 7, 12, 39–40, 43, 64, 66, 78–81, 114, 119, 121, 143, 240, 257; melancholy, 7, 96–97, 178, 238, 247, 307. *See also* catastrophic optimism

affect theory, 84n56

agency: in Clarke, 224n2; in Collins, 258; and deepfakes, 307; of marginalized filmmakers, 7, 14, 52, 328; and New Orleans performance, 273; in Palacios, 118; of spectators, 20; women's, 23, 52, 328

Ahwesh, Peggy, 27, 169–86, 194, 213, 279, 349; *Beirut Outtakes*, 170, 175–76; *Bethlehem*, 178; *The Blackest Sea*, 170; *Border Control*, 174; *City Thermogram*, 173–74; *The Color of Love*, 170, 179, 180; *The Falling Sky*, 170; *Lessons of War*, 170; *Lies and Excess*, 176–77; *Nocturne*, 170; *The Scary Movie*, 172–73; *She Puppet*, 170, 181–82; *The Star Eaters*, 176–77; *The Third Body*, 170; *Verily! the blackest sea, the falling sky*, 174, 183–86; *Warm Objects*, 174

Alexander, Elizabeth, 250

Alleg, Henri: *The Question*, 44

Alter, Nora M., 9

Amad, Paula, 25

amateur filmmaking, 179, 200, 288–89. *See also* found footage

Andréani, Henri: *Moïse sauvé des eaux*, 93

animation, 29, 162, 183–84, 236, 270, 273, 279–94

anonymity, 26, 41, 43, 70, 87, 92–93, 97–100, 145n23, 178, 272

Antakyalıoğlu, Zekiye, 232–33

Antonioni, Michelangelo: *L'Avventura*, 8–9

Archer, Sandy, 132

archive: detritus of, 16, 328; gaps in, 9–12, 25, 79, 177, 183, 188, 227, 229, 232, 290, 293, 327–28, 333, 336, 344;

353

archive (continued)
    gendered politics of, 25; restoration of, 88, 333; transnational imaginary, 126, 129
archive studies, 16
Aristotle, 91
Armatage, Kay, 66
Arnheim, Rudolf, 92
attachment, 62, 64, 72, 74, 78, 81, 96
auteurism, 14–15, 43, 100; critique of, 13–15, 44, 170, 234
avant-garde, the, 169–70, 190, 192–94, 200, 208n14, 223, 273, 291. See also filmmaking: experimental; New American Cinema

Balázs, Béla, 92
Baldwin, Craig: *Tribulation 99*, 172
Balsom, Erika, 185
Barakat, Henri, 149, 156, 158, 166n16
Barea, María, 26, 107–9, 114–24; *Hijas de la Violencia*, 115; *Mujeres de El Planeta*, 114, 118; *Porque quería estudiar*, 115; *Rocío y los pollitos*, 107–8, 114–22, 124n21. See also Warmi Film and Video Collective
Baron, Jaimie, 289
Barthes, Roland, 11, 95–97, 308
Bataille, Georges, 176, 180–81
Batchelor, David, 91–92
Bazin, André, 72, 95, 308
Bean, Jennifer, 66, 72, 84n56
Beard, Thomas, 191, 196
Bebb, Bruce, 221–22
Beeston, Alix, 29, 213, 227, 229, 232, 276, 277, 302, 323–26, 349
Benamou, Catherine L., 32n26
Benjamin, Walter, 31n15, 77, 173, 185, 186n9
Benning, Sadie: Pixelvision diaries, 200–201
Berlant, Lauren, 63–64, 67, 71, 72, 78, 81, 292
Bertini, Francesca, 50
Biehl, João, 23
bioethics, 303
Biograph Company, 50, 60n33
Black independent film, 248. See also individual filmmakers
Blanchot, Maurice, 176
Bloom, Lynn, 253
Bode, Lisa, 309
Bosetti, Roméo: *Zoe's Magic Umbrella*, 67, 83n46

Brakhage, Stan, 193; *Songs*, 193
Brandeis, Louis, 302
Braune, Sean, 20, 34n56
Bryant, John, 33n40, 252–53
Brenez, Nicole, 180
British Film Institute (BFI), 77, 87–88
Brody, Jennifer DeVere, 259
Brooks, Daphne, 273
Bronfen, Elisabeth, 320n50
Brown, Jayna, 79
Brown, Margery, 281–82
Brown, Wendy, 78
Bruno, Giuliana, 8–9, 17–19, 22, 30, 66, 129, 229–30, 322–47, 349–50
Burditt, Rebecca, 312n62
Burgin, Victor, 21
Burton, Jenny, 264

Cadava, Eduardo, 17
Campt, Tina, 24, 35n72
Cardona, Georges: "Shirkers," 28, 226–28, 235, 240
Cartwright, Lisa, 276
case law, 29, 300–301, 303, 305
catastrophic optimism, 64, 71–72, 77–78
Cathay-Keris, 227, 233
Cavell, Stanley, 21
celebrity, 300–315; resurrections of, 29, 302–3, 306, 308–10, 313
censorship, 8, 15, 26, 44, 152, 203, 211, 324, 327, 332
Certeau, Michel de, 18
Chenzira, Ayoka, 249
Chiarini, Alessandra, 20
Child, Abigail: *Is This What You Were Born For?*, 193
Chilean cinema, 26, 125–43, 145n23, 146n32, 201
Chile Films, 133–35, 145n25
Chomón, Segundo de: *Les Dés magiques*, 93, 103n34
Churchwell, Sarah, 303, 315
chromophobia, 91–93
circulation, 12, 15, 19, 75, 179, 189–90, 200, 206, 248, 305, 325–28, 331–32
civil war: American, 57; Lebanese, 147–48, 150, 152–53, 161–64, 175; Spanish, 129, 141
Clark, Danae, 312
Clarke, Shirley, 28, 211–25: *Brussels Loops*, 215–16; *The Connection*, 211; *A Dance in the Sun*, 212–13, 217, 223; *In Paris Parks*, 218–19, 222; kinetic films, 211, 213, 218–19; *Ornette*, 219; *Portrait of*

Jason, 211; *Skyscraper*, 219; TP Videospace Troupe, 219–20
Clarke, Wendy, 215, 219
closure, 19, 79, 189, 205–6, 207n5, 344; refusal of, 15, 22, 196, 323; and seriality, 189
Clouzot, Henri-Georges: *L'Enfer*, 13
Cohan, Steven, 320n46
Cole, Carole, 255, 262–63, 265, 267n13
collage, 171, 250–51, 259–60, 263, 271, 285, 288. *See also* montage; pastiche
Collins, Kathleen: intertextuality in the work of, 257–58; *Losing Ground*, 245–46, 248, 255–56, 260–65, 266n3, 267n13, 269n44; mythologizing of, 248; *Notes from a Black Woman's Diary*, 246, 248–60; "Portrait of Katherine," 256, 263, 269nn55,57; reception of, 29, 246–47, 258, 267n7; "The Story of Three Colored Ladies," 256; "A Summer Diary," 29, 248–49, 254–65; surrogates for, 252, 264; *Whatever Happened to Interracial Love?*, 246, 250–51; "Women, Sisters, and Friends," 256, 263. *See also Losing Ground* (Collins); *Notes from a Black Woman's Diary* (Collins)
Collins, Nina, 246, 249, 251–53, 255, 257–59, 266n3
color processes, 85, 88–93; feminized discourse of, 92
Combès, Isabelle, 113
comedy, 65, 68, 70–72, 74
computer-generated imagery (CGI), 29, 170, 174, 300, 302–5, 309–11. *See also* deepfakes
Conner, Bruce, 175–76, 178; *A MOVIE*, 175
Conrad, Tony, 170
consent, 29–30, 302–5, 307, 309–11, 314, 320n51
contingency, 7, 9, 15, 17, 23, 97–98, 100, 189, 200, 253
copyright law, 29, 60n33
Coppola, Eleanor, 204
Corry, Frances, 6
counterfactuality, 23–24, 41, 49, 275, 306. *See also* speculation
cultural archaeology, 328–31
Cunard, Grace, 50
Cushing, Peter, 300, 309

Dagher, Assia, 147, 149, 155–59, 164, 166n16

Dall'Asta, Monica, 12, 20, 22, 24, 61n63
dance, 28, 158, 211–23, 224nn2,4; theory, 225n22
dance film, 211, 218, 222
Daney, Serge, 150
Dash, Julie, 249
Davide Turconi Collection Database, 26, 85–103
Davis, Zeinabu irene, 249
Dean, James, 300, 308–11, 313–14
death: of the avant-garde, 170; celebrity, 303, 305, 308–9, 312, 314; in Collins, 254, 256–59; and dancing, 212; drive, 69, 78; Tarot card, 240
de Beauvoir, Simone, 131
decay, 86, 175–76, 180, 205
DeCrew, Judith, 302
Decroux, Etienne, 222
deepfakes, 29, 300–315, 318n24, 320nn46,51
Dekuyper, Eric, 43
de la Vega, José, 135
Deleuze, Gilles, 229–31, 239. *See also* Guattari, Félix
Deren, Maya, 15, 21, 27, 169, 171, 177, 218, 223, 225n34; *A Study in Choreography for Camera*, 223; *The Witch's Cradle*, 171, 177
desire: and absence, 6; authorial, 22; collective, 234–35; for color, 90; and racialized control, 314; of Hershman Leeson, 205; and Léontine, 67, 72–73; scopophilic, 304; for unfinished film, 143
Desjardins, Mary, 302, 314
diary film, 190, 200; tension in, 200
digital technologies, 11, 31n17, 87, 184, 300, 302, 308, 319n24, 336
distribution, 11, 71, 75, 96, 115, 133–34, 228, 331
DIY culture, 271, 277, 283–85
Doane, Mary Ann, 72, 96, 191, 206n1
documentary film, 28, 43, 45, 110, 114–15, 121, 130–31, 133, 136, 140–43, 149–54, 157, 161, 164, 170, 184, 191, 193, 201, 204, 215, 218, 227–41, 285, 288, 300, 306
Doffman, Mark, 217
Dora Film, 8, 18, 324, 332
Duchamp, Marcel, 179; *Fountain*, 179
Dufrêne, François, 180
Duhamel, Sarah, 65, 75
Dulac, Germaine, 66
Dyer, Richard, 314

356 | Index

early cinema, 25, 66, 85–100, 188, 335
Edison Company, 47–50, 60n33
editing, 28, 35n60, 50, 171, 178, 190, 196–97, 200, 203–4, 211–23, 224n2, 228, 235, 257, 277, 308, 333–36; as kinaesthetic process, 211–23
Eldridge, David, 13–14, 35n70
Elsaesser, Thomas, 35n61
embodiment, 23, 26, 97, 214–15, 218–19, 222, 236, 311, 314, 326, 330–31, 340. *See also* dance
entrainment, 217–19
ethics, 228, 288, 303, 307
exile cinema, 126

failure, 3, 12–13, 15, 20, 23, 27, 29, 31n23, 61n63, 78, 81, 153, 159, 189–91, 239, 249, 263, 281, 292
fandom, 236–37, 241, 307–8
Farge, Arlette, 129
Farocki, Harun, 181
Fassbinder, Rainer Werner, 43–44
Fellini, Federico: *The Journey of G. Mastorna*, 13
Fenwick, James, 13–14
feminism, 24, 51, 66, 125, 127–28, 131–32, 136; militant, 132, 136; and Popular Unity, 128, 131–32; and revolution, 128; Second Wave, 51, 127
feminist media historiography, 77
feminist media history, 328
Fenwick, James, 13–14
fetishism, 29, 32n28, 70, 267n9, 308
Feuillade, Louis: *Lagourdette, gentleman-burglar*, 68–69
Field, Allyson Nadia, 18–20, 34n50, 79, 234
Figueroa, Luis, 114
film: afterlives of, 28–29, 226–41; as communicative form, 7; company, 51–56, 62, 75, 335; digital, 11, 31n17, 35n72, 174, 184, 190–91, 197, 200, 336; lost, 19; materiality, 20, 87–88, 90, 97, 129, 322, 331–34, 343, 347n18; multiplicity of, 11, 44; oppositional, 26, 107; posthumous, 296n25; preservation, 64, 85–86, 88, 148, 164, 325, 337. *See also* documentary film; unfinished film; unmade film
film history: Arabic, 159; feminist, 328; gaps in, 25; women's, 11, 17
filmmaking: amateur, 19, 179, 200, 288; experimental, 15, 26–29, 160, 164, 169–70, 189–94, 200, 206, 207n7, 209n39, 216, 270, 273, 276, 279, 281,

284; guerrilla, 234; oppositional, 26, 107; serial, 190; and sewing, 272, 277, 279, 290, 335–36
Fischer, Lucy, 302
Fisher, Carrie, 308–9, 311
Fletcher, Alicia, 86–87, 103n35
"Florestine Project, The" (Hill), 29, 271–74, 283–84, 291–93; and Hurricane Katrina, 29, 271–73, 275, 284–85
Flueckiger, Barbara, 89–90, 101n9
Foster, Kieran, 13–14
Foucault, Michel, 328
found footage, 20, 27, 170, 172, 178, 180, 183, 190–91, 275, 285
Fowler, Catherine, 21–22, 25n61
Fowler, Geoffrey, 307
Fox, Broderick, 210n47
fragmentary, the, 8–9, 15–17, 19–20, 25–26, 43, 62, 66, 71, 77, 80, 85–88, 93, 96, 99, 126, 129, 156, 169–71, 201, 221–22, 229–31, 236–37, 256, 275, 218, 315, 324, 328, 332, 342
Frampton, Hollis: *Hapax Legomena*, 193
Frank, Hannah, 88–89
Frieder Film Company, 53–54

Gagnon, Monika Kin, 15
Gailiunas, Paul, 29, 270, 274, 284, 288, 290, 293–94, 295n18, 297nn29,36, 299n78
Gaines, Jane, 12, 14–15, 22, 24, 99–100, 234, 236
Gallagher, Catherine, 41
Gallo, Rubén, 71
Galt, Rosalind, 92
Gangitano, Lia, 169
García Espinosa, Julio, 111, 171
Gardner, Helen, 50
Gaumont Films, 67–69, 73, 80
Gauntier, Gene, 50
Genet, Jean, 44
genetic criticism, 16
genre, 81, 118, 172–73, 189, 200, 253, 306
Gerima, Haile, 248
Getino, Octavio, 281
Giunta, Andrea, 127
Glissant, Édouard, 322, 338–39
Golding, Dan, 320n51
González, Jennifer, 312
Gorfinkel, Elena, 19, 170
Graham, María, 138
Graham, Martha, 212
Gramsci, Antonio, 120
Grant, Catherine, 14

Green, Renée: *Some Chance Operations*, 7–10, 15–18, 21, 25, 213, 326
Griffith, David Wark, 57, 66; *Birth of a Nation*, 57
Grosz, Elizabeth, 24
Guarino, Francesco: *Saint Agatha*, 344–45
Guattari, Félix, 229–30, 239
Gunning, Tom, 89–91
Gurian, Andrew, 214, 219–20
Guy-Blaché, Alice: *Matrimony's Speed Limit*, 60n33, 66

Hahn, Tomie, 217–18
Halleck, DeeDee, 219
Hamad, Hannah, 32n28
Hamama, Faten, 149, 155–58, 164
hapticity, 90, 328, 334, 336
Hansen, Miriam, 85n56
Hartman, Saidiya, 18, 24, 79
Hayakawa, Sessue, 45
Hediger, Vinzenz, 11
Héléna, André, 44
Hennefeld, Maggie, 302
Hershman Leeson, Lynn, 27, 188, 190, 197, 199–206, 210n47, 213; *The Electronic Diaries*, 27, 190, 199–206
Herwitz, Daniel, 314
Hill, Helen, 29, 270–94, 297n29, 297n33, 298n65, 299n78; *The Florestine Collection*, 29, 271–72, 274–77; "The Florestine Project," 272–74, 281, 284–84, 291–93; *Mouseholes*, 276; *Recipes for Disaster*, 277–78. See also "Florestine Project, The" (Hill)
Hollywood, 4, 51, 53, 156, 302, 312, 319n24
Holmes, Helen, 50
Horak, Laura, 65
housework, 2, 335. See also labor
Houston, Drusilla Dunjee: *The Spirit of the South: The Maddened Mob*, 56–57
Hurricane Katrina, 29, 271–75, 281, 283–85, 288, 290, 299n78
Hurston, Zora Neale, 252
Huyghe, Pierre, 21

incompletion: as aesthetic and political strategy, 11, 15, 191, 339; and Black women directors, 249; feminist potential of, 13, 17, 27, 236; and film production, 12; as minor practice, 328; and multiplicity, 11; as process, 10, 15–16, 323, 338; and spectatorship, 12; vitality of, 322

Jacobs, Ken: *Perfect Film*, 177
James, David E., 200–201
Jameson, Fredric, 171
Jordan, J. Scott, 217–18
Joye, Josef-Alexis, 86–89, 99–100
July, Miranda, 4–7, 15–16, 19, 22, 24, 41, 51–52, 246, 277; *Big Miss Moviola*, 6–7, 15, 24, 36n76; *The Missing Movie Report*, 4–7, 16, 22

Kant, Immanuel, 91
Kardashian, Kim, 307
Kardashian, Robert, 307
Keathley, Christian, 21
Keller, Sarah, 15–16
Kinchen, Florestine, 271–72, 285, 291–94
Kirkwood, Julietta, 127, 137
Kostina, Anastasia, 35n60
Kubelka, Peter, 193
Kubrick, Stanley: *Napoleon*, 35
Kuchar, George: *Weather Diaries*, 209n39
Kuleshov, Lev, 221–23

labor: anonymous, 97; archival, 20, 26; and authorship, 234–36; collaborative, 15, 29, 235, 259; of colorists, 26, 85–100; conditions of, 7, 62; creative, 6, 11, 14, 151, 179, 236, 249–50, 263; curatorial, 77, 249; directorial, 20, 66, 227, 234, 250 51, 258, 264; domestic, 2, 68; editorial, 249, 251; fan, 240; feminist, 20; filmic, 22–23, 85–100; of handiwork, 334–36; and performance, 308, 312, 320n46; posthumous, 301, 312; of recovery, 80; scholarly, 24, 26; writerly, 251; women's, 11, 20, 24, 34–36; 86–100, 151, 279, 335. See also housework
Laemmle, Carl, 53
Leacock, Richard, 215
Lebanese cinema, 15, 27, 147–64
Le Bon, Gustave, 71
Lee, Bruce, 309
Lefebvre, Henri (poet), 42–44
left-wing politics, 132, 140, 165n7
Lejeune, Philippe, 199
Lemaître, Maurice, 180
Léon, Melina: *Song Without a Name*, 120
Léontine, 25, 40, 62–81; *Betty and Jane Go to the Theater*, 65; *Betty as Errand Girl*, 71; *Betty Is Still at Her Old Tricks*, 71; *Betty Pulls the Strings*, 65; *Betty Rolls Along*, 74; *Betty's Apprenticeship*, 74; *Betty's Boat*, 75; *Léontine and Rosalie*

Léontine (*continued*)
  Go to the Theater, 76; *Léontine Is Incorrigible*, 62; *Léontine Flies Away*, 63; *Léontine's Boat*, 62–63; *Léontine's Electric Battery*, 62–63, 78; *Léontine's Fireworks*, 62, 67–68, 78; *Léontine's Tomatoes*, 63, 67; *Rosalie Has Sleeping Sickness*, 67
Lesser, Wendy, 303, 306, 311, 313, 315
Lewinsky, Mariann, 64, 68
literary studies, 16
Llosa, Claudia: *Madeinusa*, 120; *The Milk of Sorrow*, 120
Locke, John, 91
Locke, Peter, 23
Losing Ground (Collins), 245–46, 248, 255–56, 260–65, 266n3, 267n13, 269n44; ending of, 264–65; performances in, 264
loss: archival, 131; certainty of, 254; and feminist historiography, 79; and incompletion, 27, 40; language of, 19; and mythology, 248; and recovery, 29, 333; and resurrection, 302; and retrospection, 21; scene of, 24
Lowe, Lisa, 24
Lyotard, Jean-François, 175

Madansky, Cynthia: *ESFIR*, 1–3, 15–16, 18, 21, 24, 35n60
Mahar, Karen, 45, 61n62
Mailer, Norman, 313–14
Major, Anne, 273
Malay Film Productions, 227, 233
Mallet, Marilú, 26, 125–40, 201; *Amuhuelai-mi*, 130; *Chère Amérique*, 141; *¿Dónde voy a encontrar otra Violeta?*, 130; *Journal inachevé*, 126, 141; *Tres por tres*, 26, 125–30, 133, 135–38, 143
Marchessault, Janine, 275–76
Margolis, Barbara, 132
Marks, Laura U., 231
Martin, Darnell, 249
Marx, Karl, 80
materialist history, 328, 331–34
materiality, 20, 322, 331–34, 323, 347n18; of film, 87–88, 90, 97, 129
Mayer, Louis B., 46–47, 59n26
Mayne, Judith, 14
Mazdon, Lucy, 13
McCutcheon, Wallace: *Personal*, 60
McGlotten, Shaka, 306
McMahan, Alison, 66

Mekas, Jonas, 200
Méliès, Georges, 94–95, 182; *L'Homme mouche*, 94–95
Melville, Jean-Pierre, 44
memory, 21, 35n61; in Ahwesh, 178, 183; in Bazin, 95; and Chilean cinema, 145; and Collins, 249, 251; in Hershman Leeson, 210; industry of, 307; and love, 292; in Notari, 30, 323, 325, 340–43; in Saab, 151, 153, 161; in *Shirkers*, 230–31, 238; in Sontag, 300
Mercer, Kobena, 250
#MeToo, 47, 302, 312
Micheaux, Oscar, 57, 79
Miles, Tiya, 271, 279, 288–90, 292–93
Minard, Michael, 256, 263
Mingon, McArthur Henare, 218
Minh-ha, Trinh T., 195
misogyny, 26, 194, 273
Monroe, Marilyn, 29–30, 300–301, 303–8, 310–16, 320n46; *Niagara*, 315–16; *The Seven Year Itch*, 305, 315; *Some Like It Hot*, 314–15. *See also* deepfakes
montage, 4, 160, 171, 185–86, 215, 218, 221, 288, 332–33, 342. *See also* collage; pastiche
Moore, Adam, 302
Morin, Edgar, 44
Mourier, Georges, 151
Müller, Jorge, 135–36, 141
Mulvey, Laura, 308, 329
Münsterberg, Hugo, 92
Muratova, Kira, 15
Mypheduh Films, 248

Nagrin, Daniel, 217
Nagy, Anton, 53
Nancy, Jean-Luc, 207n7
narrative: episodic, 190; rejection of, 86, 100, 177
Neely, Hugh, 47
Negra, Diane, 66
Nesbitt, Miriam, 47–50; *A Close Call*, 47, 49–50; *What Happened to Mary?*, 50
New American Cinema, 273
New Chilean Cinema, 141
New Latin American Cinema, 109, 123n4, 125
Ng Kin Kia, Jasmine, 226
Nicolson, Annabel: *Reel Time*, 279
Nishikawa, Kinohi, 247
Nishikawa, Tomonari, 180
North, Dan, 11, 14
Nostalgia, 78, 161–62, 307, 313, 320n51

Notari, Elvira Coda, 7–10, 16–17, 19, 22, 30, 66, 229, 323–29, 332–37, 344–45; *'A Santanotte*, 344; *'E scugnizze*, 329
Notes from a Black Woman's Diary (Collins), 246, 248–60; ellipses in, 249, 259–60; metatextuality of, 251–54
Novoa Donoso, Soledad, 127

O'Brien, Charles, 90
Olenina, Ana Hedberg, 222
Olsen, Tillie, 41
O'Malley, Hayley, 248
Ono, Yoko, 219
oral history, 16, 26, 29, 109–10, 128, 248, 263
outtakes, 16, 169, 175–77, 228
Oyarzún, Kemy, 125, 127

Paasonen, Susanna, 306
Paik, Nam June, 219
Palacios, Beatriz, 26, 107–13, 119–22, 123n6, 123n10; *La tierra sin mal*, 107–8, 110–13, 118–19, 121
palimpsest, 97, 100, 172
Papatakis, Nikos: *Les Abysses*, 44
paratexts, 8, 17, 205
Paredes, Eduardo, 134–35
Parikka, Jussi, 330
Pasolini, Pier Paolo, 20
pastiche, 170–71
Pathé Frères, 62, 67, 69–71, 73–74, 76–77, 79–80, 86, 89–90, 92–94, 98
Pavis, Mathilde, 306
Pearlman, Karen, 21, 28, 35n60; *Down Time Jaz*, 218; *I want to make a film about women*, 35n60, 218
Peckham, Linda, 195
Peggy and Fred in Hell (Thornton), 27, 190–201, 206, 208n26; gender difference in, 194–95; *High Heel Beloved*, 198; *Introduction to the So-Called Duck Factory*, 197–98; *Peggy and Fred: Folding*, 190–91; *Peggy and Fred in Kansas*, 197; prescience of, 196; *The Problem So Far*, 197; *The Prologue*, 191, 194
Peirce, Charles Sanders, 96
Pennebaker, D. A., 215
Perry, Imani, 276
Pessoa, Fernando, 171, 181
Phillips, David Graham: *Susan Lenox, Her Fall and Rise*, 47
photographic image, 95–96
Piaggio, Carlos, 135–36

Pitt, Suzan, 292
Pollock, Griselda, 303, 305
Popcorn, Faith, 209n29
Popular Unity, 26, 125–43
pornography, 305–8, 310, 312, 314. See also deepfakes
Porter, Edwin S.: *How the French Nobleman Found a Wife Through the New York Herald Personal Columns*, 49
postcolonial studies, 19, 233
Power, Margaret, 137
Prescott, Andrew, 128
presence: absent, 26, 72, 234, 332; fetishization of, 29, 32n28; spectral, 227–28, 230, 237
preservation, 64, 85–88, 148–50, 164, 289, 325, 333, 337, 341
privacy, 199, 253, 288–89, 307; right to, 301–5
production studies, 16
publicity, 18, 29, 47, 62, 69, 246, 304, 310, 332; right to, 301

queer studies, 18, 21, 31n23

race, 57, 260, 273, 279, 284, 292, 312–13; and chromophobia, 92
racial injustice, 29, 79, 109, 272–73, 281, 288
Ragona, Melissa, 200
Raintree Pictures, 233
reception, 11–12, 19, 21, 29–30, 74, 92, 135, 188–89, 193, 197, 206, 246–47, 312, 331–32, 343; posthumous, 258
recovery, 11–12, 28–29, 40, 62, 80, 215, 236, 246–48, 258, 267nn7–8, 328
Redrobe, Karen, 14, 302
refusal, 3, 11, 25–27, 75, 81, 100, 151, 180, 196, 258, 275, 293
Reiniger, Lotte, 273, 291
relationality, 71, 323, 326, 336–38, 342, 344
Renais, Alain, 44
resistance: to American avant-garde, 169–70, 194; to containment, 331, 338; Lebanese, 156; Movimiento de Izquierda Revolucionaria, 129; Palestinian, 150, 161, 165n7; Vietnamese, 154
revisionism, 15, 313
revolution: Chilean, 109, 111, 127–29, 131, 133, 135, 139–40; Palestinian, 150; proletarian, 2; and Saab, 154, 160–63
Reynolds, Dee, 212
Rhodes, John David, 170

Rich, B. Ruby, 123n4, 125
Roberts, John, 179–80
Robertson, Anne Charlotte: *Five-Year Diary*, 200
Rocha, Glauber, 140
Rochester, Katherine, 291
Rombes, Nicholas, 11
Romero, George A., 170
Rongen-Kaynakçi, Elif, 65, 67
Rose, Jacqueline, 65, 303, 316
Rosen, Jonathon, 90
Rosenbaum, Jonathan, 193
Rossellini, Roberto, 140
Rouch, Jean, 44
ruin, 170, 202
Ruiz, Raúl, 127, 132
Russell, Catherine, 197
Russell, Ken, 14

Saab, Jocelyne, 15, 27, 147–64, 165n3, 166n16, 175; "Assia Dagher," 147, 155–59, 164; *Beyrouth, jamais plus*, 152–53; *Beyrouth, ma ville*, 161; *Égypte, la cité des morts*, 155; "Faten Hamama's Honor," 149–50, 155–59; "Histoire de Fatehpur Sikri," 154; *Il était une fois Beyrouth: Histoire d'une star*, 135; *Imaginary Postcard*, 148, 163; "Joumana," 153–54; *Kiss Me Not on the Eyes*, 149, 155, 158; *La Dame de Saigon*, 154; *L'Arrière-quartier*, 152; *Le Bateau de l'exil*, 161; *Le Liban dans la tourmente*, 152; *Les Almées*, 155; *Les Enfants de la guerre*, 152; *Lettre de Beyrouth*, 163; *My Name Is Mei Shigenobu*, 149; *One Dollar a Day*, 148; "Portrait d'Hanoï ou Comment inventer la modernité," 154; "Shigenobu: Mother and Daughter," 149–50, 159–64; *Une vie suspendue*, 152, 155, 162
Salloum, Jayce, 175
Sanborn, Keith, 170
Sanjinés, Jorge, 107–8, 110–11, 119, 122n1, 123n5, 140
Sarmiento, Valeria, 26, 125–39, 144n13, 145n18; *Amelia Lopes O'Neil*, 139; *Elle*, 139; *El tango del viudo y su espejo deformante*, 127; *La femme au foyer*, 127; *La telenovela errante*, 127; *María Graham: Diario de mi residencia en Chile*, 138; *Notre mariage*, 139; *Qué hacer?*, 132; *Tres por tres*, 26, 125–30, 133, 135–38, 143; *Un sueño como de colores*, 130

Sartre, Jean-Paul, 44
Scheibel, Will, 320n46
Schneemann, Carolee: *Fuses*, 180
Scott, Seret, 260–61, 264–65
Scutts, Joanna, 247
Sedgwick, Eve Kosofsky, 78, 84n56
Segre, Dino: *Cocaine*, 43
Seguí, Isabel, 14
Sellier, Geneviève, 164
Serena, Gustavo, 50
seriality, 49, 68, 72, 188–93, 206, 207n11
Serrano, Nina, 132
Shakur, Tupac, 300, 314
Sharits, Paul, 193
Sheppard, Samantha N., 15
Shigenobu, Fusako, 149–50, 160–62
Shigenobu, Mei, 149, 160, 162, 164
Shipman, Nell, 59n27, 66
Shub, Ėsfir': "Women," 2–4, 16, 21, 24
silent-era film, 18, 25, 39–41, 45, 54, 65–68, 79, 86, 99, 158, 234, 334–36
silhouette form, 292–93
Sim, Gerald, 233
Simpson, Lorna, 250–52, 258; "Back of Yellow Dress," 251, 258
Singaporean cinema, 28, 155, 227–35, 238, 240
Sitney, P. Adams, 169–70, 193
slapstick, 65, 70, 72, 75, 77–79
Slide, Anthony, 47
Smith, Zadie, 246, 267n8
Sojourner Truth, 293
Solanas, Fernando, 281
Sontag, Susan, 300
spectacle, 62, 71, 77, 176, 185, 192, 313, 321, 330
spectatorship, 18, 29, 79, 96–97, 185, 281, 312, 330
spectrality, 28, 95, 227–30, 232, 236–37
speculation, 15, 18, 22, 25, 35, 41, 46, 56, 58, 183, 196, 260, 275, 291, 322; and historiography, 232–34; and history, 41. *See also* counterfactuality
Stadler, John Paul, 306, 312
Staiger, Janet, 14
Stallings, L. H., 267n7
Stamp, Shelley, 66
star studies, 16, 29
Steedman, Carolyn, 253
Stewart, Anita, 45–47, 56
Stewart, Jacqueline Najuma, 18, 288
Stiles, Kristine, 202
Streible, Dan, 271, 273
Sutton, John, 218

Tan, Sandi, 28, 226, 228, 231, 234, 236, 238; *Shirkers*, 28, 226, 228, 231, 234, 236, 238
Tavernier, Bertrand, 44
Taylor, James Stacey, 303–4
television, 44, 78, 148, 152–54, 159, 161, 188–89, 194–96, 220, 272, 285, 302, 314
theft, 179–80, 227
Third Cinema, 123n5, 273, 281
Thornton, Leslie, 27, 188–99, 206, 207nn7,11, 208n26, 209nn29,31, 213, 279; *Adynata*, 193; *Jennifer, Where Are You?*, 193; *Peggy and Fred in Hell*, 27, 190–201, 206, 208n26; *X-Tracts*, 193
Torlasco, Domietta, 24, 36n72
trace, 8, 15–17, 20, 22, 26, 65, 68, 86, 89, 91, 93, 96–98, 128, 163, 236, 248, 250, 285, 289, 326, 334, 344
Truffaut, François, 140
Turconi, Davide, 26, 85–100

Ukamau Film Group, 107–11, 121, 123n5
Universal Pictures, 52–53
unfinished film: collaborative labor of, 15, 23; as curatorial strategy, 339–44; desire for, 143; as feminist method, 12–14, 190, 277–83; materiality of, 16–17, 19–20, 28; potential of, 10, 24, 119, 249, 323; temporality of, 22, 229, 232; as transnational imaginary archive, 126; usefulness of, 267
unmade film, 3, 6–7, 16, 21–22

Valdivia, Juan Carlos: *Yvy Maraey*, 113
van Dyke, Willard, 215
Varda, Agnès: *Cléo from 5 to 7*, 240
Vázquez, Angelina, 26, 125–37, 141–43, 146n31, 201; *Crónica del salitre*, 130; *Fragmentos de un diario inacabado*, 201; *Presencia lejana*, 143; *Tres por tres*, 26, 125–30, 133, 135–38, 143
Vertov, Dziga, 173
video art, 6, 220
video games, 181–82, 312
Villar, Diego, 113
Virilio, Paul, 174
Vitti, Monica, 8
void, 9, 67, 70, 78, 151, 229, 327, 341

Walker, Alice, 252
Walker, Kara, 291, 293
Wardlaw, Alvia, 246
Warhol, Andy: *Marilyns*, 308; *Vinyl*, 208n26
Warmi Film and Video Collective, 115
Warren, Samuel, 302
Warrenton, Lule, 50–56; *Bartered Flesh*, 50, 52, 56; *Calling Lindy*, 53
Weber, Lois, 56, 66: *Shoes*, 56
Welles, Orson, 13; *It's All True*, 32n26, 43
West, Jennifer, 180
West, Kanye, 307
White, Patricia, 14
Wieland, Joyce, 15
Wilkinson, T. M., 303–4
Williams, Moses, 292–93
Williams, Tami, 66
Willis, Sharon, 313
Wollen, Peter, 192
Wreckers of the Limited Express, The (Lubin Manufacturing Company), 94
Wurgaft, Benjamin, 23

Yue, Genevieve, 28, 88, 302, 312–13
Yumibe, Joshua, 85–87, 90–91

zines, 20, 24, 36n76, 272
Zryd, Michael, 172
Zvokine, Eugénie, 15

Founded in 1893,
UNIVERSITY OF CALIFORNIA PRESS
publishes bold, progressive books and journals
on topics in the arts, humanities, social sciences,
and natural sciences—with a focus on social
justice issues—that inspire thought and action
among readers worldwide.

The UC PRESS FOUNDATION
raises funds to uphold the press's vital role
as an independent, nonprofit publisher, and
receives philanthropic support from a wide
range of individuals and institutions—and from
committed readers like you. To learn more, visit
ucpress.edu/supportus.

www.ingramcontent.com/pod-product-compliance
Lightning Source LLC
Chambersburg PA
CBHW030518230426
43665CB00010B/666